T0339805

NORMAN THOMAS

NORMAN THOMAS

The Great Dissenter

Raymond F. Gregory

Algora Publishing
New York

Library of Congress Cataloging-in-Publication Data —

Gregory, Raymond F., 1927-
    Norman Thomas : the great dissenter / Raymond F. Gregory.
       p. cm.
    Includes bibliographical references and index.
    ISBN 978-0-87586-621-5 (trade paper: alk. paper) — ISBN 978-0-87586-622-2 (case
laminate: alk. paper) — ISBN 978-0-87586-623-9 (ebook) 1. Thomas, Norman, 1884-1968.
2. Civil rights movements—United States—History—20th century. I. Title.

    HX84.T47G74 2008
    335.0092—dc22
    [B]
                        2008011591

For my grandchildren, Emma, Alanna, and George

TABLE OF CONTENTS

INTRODUCTION

Many Americans of the 1920s could not readily distinguish between "socialism and rheumatism,"[1] but that did not deter Norman Thomas from becoming a Socialist. As a member of the Socialist Party, he pursued the presidency six times, never garnering more than a fraction of the votes cast for the Democratic and Republican Party nominees. The Socialist Party never gained a firm foothold in American politics, and as a consequence membership in the Socialist Party was generally considered as reserved for political outcasts. In later years, during the McCarthy era, Socialists frequently were misidentified as Communists, and super patriots recklessly equated democratic socialism and the welfare state with communism, thus forcing Thomas repeatedly to deny any affiliation with the Communist Party.

As a pacifist, Thomas opposed America's involvement in both World Wars. Even after Pearl Harbor, it was only with great reluctance that he gave what he designated as "critical" support for the war effort. His positions in opposition to war never endeared him to the general public and his pacifist views were widely rejected. During both wars, and especially during the First World War, Thomas greatly displeased an overwhelming majority of the general public because of his steadfast support for religious and other conscientious objectors who refused to enter combat.

Others of his positions were equally unpopular. Despite the vilification the Communists rained down upon him, he contended that members of the Communists Party should be provided the same civil rights as other Americans. During World War II, he was one of a handful who publicly objected

---

[1] Thomas autobiography, 73.

to the internment of west coast Japanese-Americans. In that instance, even the American Civil Liberties Union at first rejected Thomas' position.

Despite the unpopularity of his positions, the public generally afforded him a forum for the presentation of his views. The rejection of his political positions did not lead to his personal condemnation and he nearly always commanded great respect. Even presidents listened to him. Presidents Warren Harding, Franklin D. Roosevelt, Harry Truman and Dwight Eisenhower corresponded and met with him from time to time. President Roosevelt addressed Thomas in his letters as "Dear Norman."[1] On one occasion President Truman, following a visit with Thomas, wrote to him stating that it had been "a pleasure to visit with you the other day and I appreciate it more than I can tell you."[2]

Expressions of respect for Thomas emerged from the most unusual sources. An organization known as the Circus Saints and Sinners honored Thomas in 1948 with a banquet at New York's Waldorf-Astoria Hotel. With more than 1200 club members in attendance, a former governor of New Jersey and president of the club introduced Thomas as "the man everyone loves and nobody votes for" and presented him with a diamond-studded soapbox.[3] One year later, on Thomas' 65th birthday, *The New York Times* editorialized that there were not many men in public life who commanded greater esteem. His "sincerity, eloquence, perseverance and faith have earned him an honored place in America's political annals."[4] The following year Thomas was honored at a testimonial dinner attended by more than 1000 guests, including James A. Farley, campaign manager for two of Roosevelt's presidential campaigns, Bernard Baruch, America's senior statesman, and many others who had opposed Thomas throughout his political career. On the occasion of Thomas' 70th birthday in 1954, *The New York Times* again heaped praise upon him, saying that America stood more firmly because he "has lived and striven among us for long, unselfish years."[5]

Thomas grew somewhat weary of these accolades, for he feared his reputation as a dissenting maverick was in jeopardy. He often responded to expressions of glowing praise with the story about the widow who, hearing her husband so grandly eulogized at his funeral, asked her little Jimmy to check to see if it really was his father that lay in the open coffin.[6]

But the praise continued unabated. On the celebration of his 80th birthday in 1964, *The Washington Post*, which years earlier had labeled Thomas

1 Franklin Roosevelt letter, dated 8/25/42, to Thomas.

2 Harry Truman letter, dated 8/30/50, to Thomas.

3 *The New York Times*, 10/27/48, 18.

4 Ibid., 11/20/49, E-8.

5 Ibid., 11/20/54, 16.

6 Murray B. Seidler, *Norman Thomas: Respectable Rebel* (Syracuse University Press, Syracuse, 1967), 242.

"America's Conscience," summed up what most of his countrymen felt about him: "There is hardly a cause involving compassion for the luckless or a decent respect for minority rights in which this great nonconformist has not played a part. He has fought hard, and always cleanly. And he will continue, we may be sure, to reproach his country for not being as good as it might and could. More power to his heart and tongue."[1]

One of Thomas' earliest biographers entitled his work *Norman Thomas: Respectable Rebel.*[2] The title was apt for other than the Communists who reviled him, the general public extended its honor, affection and respect to this notorious dissenter. But why? Why did people not react more negatively to Thomas' unpopular and dissenting positions? How did Thomas earn the public's honor, affection, and respect? Why was he considered "America's Conscience?"

Although Thomas' life and mine overlapped and we both lived in New York City, I never had the occasion to meet him. Once, however, we had a telephone conversation, and that conversation has led — at least indirectly — to the writing of this biography. If my memory serves me correctly, the conversation took place in 1963. At the time I was a young lawyer working for a mid-sized New York City law firm. Some of us in the firm had joined a group of lawyers from other law firms to raise funds to support the civil rights movement led by Martin Luther King, Jr. and the Southern Christian Leadership Conference. We decided to place our fund-raising efforts under the umbrella of a not-for-profit enterprise to be incorporated in New York, and Dr. King suggested that we call it the "Gandhi Society" in honor of the man who had introduced King to the philosophy of nonviolence.

It fell to me, as one of the youngest of these lawyers, to undertake the preliminary work in establishing a not-for-profit company. In New York, as in all states insofar as I know, a corporation cannot be lawfully registered if its name conflicts with a company already in existence. Before incorporating our not-for-profit fund raising organization, I had to determine whether we were free to use "Gandhi Society" as its name. I quickly learned that another not-for-profit company of that name was already registered in New York.

I had never heard of any enterprise operating under the name of the "Gandhi Society" and none of the city telephone directories listed a company of that name. In an attempt to gather more information about this entity, I asked the office of the New York Secretary of State to provide me with a copy of its certificate of incorporation, and upon receiving it I noticed that one of the persons who had signed the original papers of incorporation was Norman Thomas.

---

1 *The Washington Post*, 12/6/64, E-6.
2 Murray B. Seidler, *Norman Thomas: Respectable Rebel.*

Of course, I had heard of Norman Thomas. I was familiar with his several runs for president as a candidate of the Socialist Party, and he had often been in the news. I also knew he lived in the City, and when I checked the Manhattan telephone directory, I happily discovered that his number was listed. I immediately placed a call and an elderly male voice answered. After identifying myself, I inquired whether he was the Norman Thomas who had signed the certificate of incorporation for the Gandhi Society. He said that he was. I then proceeded to tell Mr. Thomas that I was calling him on behalf of Dr. King and my fellow lawyers and that we very much wanted to use the Gandhi name in our fund-raising efforts. He told me that he greatly admired Dr. King's work in gaining civil rights for African-Americans in the South and that he would be delighted to change the name of his enterprise, thus opening the door for us to designate our company as the Gandhi Society. I prepared the papers required to formally register our not-for-profit company and had them hand-delivered to Thomas' home. He promptly signed them and arranged for their delivery to my office.

In the weeks that followed, I thought a lot about my conversation with Mr. Thomas. I wondered why he had accepted, without questioning, my statement that I was acting on behalf of Dr. King? Certainly, he had never previously heard of me nor, in all likelihood, of my law firm. Was he so trustful of others as to accept the claims of a total stranger? In surrendering his rights to the corporate name, why had he not asked for any remuneration, or even reimbursement of the expenses he would incur in changing the name of his company? His behavior certainly was unlike that of any public figure I knew. Clearly, Thomas was marching to a different drummer.

Perhaps if I had been more familiar with Norman Thomas' long public career, his conduct would have appeared less unsettling. Thomas was a radical. He did not hesitate to attack any aspect of American economic or political institutions he believed unfair or unjust, thus provoking the complacent, and at times gaining a modicum of progress through the elimination of the causes of unfairness and injustice. When Thomas campaigned for the presidency in 1948, a *Washington Post* editorial approved his efforts to "subvert" unjust aspects of society, observing that his endeavors were rooted in "genuine Americanism — in a tested devotion to American political institutions and to the full freedom of conscience and expression which are the highest American ideals."[1]

Thomas' commitment, eloquence, candor, and intellectual honesty commanded attention and respect. While appealing to the good in men and women and expressing his total faith in democracy, he drew attention to his dissenting views. He communicated an innate dignity and sense of fairness

---

1 Murray B. Seidler, *Norman Thomas: Respectable Rebel.*

that greatly appealed to peoples of all walks of life. None could question his devotion to the public welfare. But perhaps the attribute that most endeared him to his fellow countrymen was his habit of leaping into any fray whenever he perceived the slightest potential for gaining justice or equality for the deprived and dispossessed.

When apprised of the deplorable living conditions endured by Arkansas sharecroppers and their families, Thomas placed his own life at risk to assist them in their fight against unscrupulous plantation owners. He walked picket lines in support of foreign-born, illiterate silk workers exploited by New Jersey mill owners. He worked to obtain financial support for striking West Virginia coal miners and North Carolina textile workers. He repeatedly spoke on behalf of civil rights for African-Americans and on several occasions testified at congressional hearings in support of civil liberties for all Americans.

For almost a half-century Thomas was uniquely looked upon as "the nation's conscience for social justice and social reform."[1] His craving for justice and equality defined his life. His life stands as the prototype for all those who persist in endeavoring to attain justice and equality for all Americans. As Martin Luther King, Jr. later wrote, "I can think of no man who has done more ... to inspire the vision of society free of injustice and exploitation.... The life of Norman Thomas has been one of deep commitment to the betterment of all humanity."[2]

Thomas did not believe that memory of his life would long endure.[3] What a shame if he were proven correct. The memory of this remarkable man should long live in American history. This is his story.

---

1 Alden Whitman, "Norman Thomas: The Great Reformer, Unsatisfied to the End," *The New York Times,* 12/22/68, E-2.

2 Martin Luther King, Jr., "The Bravest Man I Ever Met," Pageant, 6/65, 23.

3 Harry Fleischman, *Norman Thomas, A Biography: 1884–1968* (W.W. Norton, New York, 1969), 314.

CHAPTER 1. THE THOMAS AND MATTOON FAMILIES

Norman Thomas appeared destined for the ministry. With his father and both of his grandfathers Presbyterian ministers, who would have predicted otherwise? As a boy and later as a young man, Norman lived the rigid Calvinistic faith of his father and grandfathers and was greatly influenced by their courage, initiative, independence, integrity, and vital sense of social responsibility, all marks of character he would assimilate during his passage to adulthood. But contrary to all forecasts, Norman ultimately turned in another direction for his life's work.

His grandfathers' adult lives began on parallel courses but their career paths later diverged. In 1824, at the age of 12, Grandfather Thomas Thomas and his parents, siblings and several other Welsh families left their native Wales for the United States. After a short stay in lower Manhattan they settled in Bradford County in northern Pennsylvania.

Thomas Thomas' father died an early death. As the oldest child in the family, the young Thomas assumed responsibility for the care of his brothers and sisters and thus delayed his education and the realization of his plan to enter the ministry. It was not until he was 25 that he was sufficiently relieved of his family responsibilities to continue his education. He then set out for Lafayette College (then affiliated with the Presbyterian Church), and because the money in his pocket was next to nothing, he walked the entire one hundred and twenty miles to the campus. Over the next six years, he financed his tuition and room and board by working in various construction jobs — at one point, quarrying stone — and in custodial jobs at the college. At the age of 31, the oldest in his class, he graduated and then proceeded to enroll in the Princeton Theological Seminary. Two years later, after his ordination to the Presbyterian ministry, he returned to Bradford County, married Mary Evans, a local Welsh girl, and spent the remainder of his life preaching in nearby country churches.

Norman Thomas remembered his grandfather as "a man of few words, of simple devotion to a stern Calvinistic creed." When in later life an accident threatened him with a slow and agonizing death, "he simply thanked God that of His goodness He permitted him to die 'from the feet up rather than from the head down.'"[1] He found purpose and happiness in preaching in two or three small churches each Sunday and in administering to the faithful living in nearby farm communities.

While Grandfather Thomas led the life of a Presbyterian minister in the hill country of northern Pennsylvania, Grandfather Mattoon was living halfway around the world in Siam (now Thailand). Stephen Mattoon, born in northern New York, also worked his way through college — in his case Union College in Schenectady — and then, like Grandfather Thomas, attended Princeton Theological Seminary. Subsequent to his ordination, he married Mary Lowrie of Cambridge, New York, and in 1848 they departed for Siam as Presbyterian missionaries.

The Mattoons were favorites of the reigning Siamese king, Maha Mongkut. Stephen Mattoon translated the Bible into Siamese, acted as an interpreter for the king and assisted in the negotiation of treaties with the United States and England. While he was thus engaged, Mary Mattoon entered the forbidden areas of the palace — with the king's permission — to teach the women of the king's household. Later she urged the king to hire a full-time teacher to educate his children born of his many wives. The king hired Anna Leonowens, then residing in Singapore, to undertake the task. Some years later Leonowens wrote the story of her life as a teacher in the king's palace, and her account later formed the basis for *Anna and the King of Siam* and the Broadway musical production of *The King and I*. In her book, Leonowens highly praised the Mattoons' missionary efforts but also vividly portrayed the massive difficulties they confronted in trying to convert the king's Buddhist subjects to Christianity.[2]

On returning to the United States after living in Bangkok for twenty years, Stephen Mattoon served as a minister in a small town in northern New York but later moved his family south to Charlotte, North Carolina, where he was one of the founders and the first president of Biddle University (now John C. Smith University), a Presbyterian institution initially established for the education of Southern African-Americans. Norman relates in his autobiography that he once came across a graduate of Biddle who told him how much

---

1 Thomas autobiography, 16. Thomas' autobiography was not published. It is housed in the Main Branch of the New York City Public Library.

2 Anna Leonowens, *The English Governess at the Siamese Court* (James R. Osgood, Boston, 1873).

he had respected the Mattoons but also recalled that when Biddle students stepped out of line they inevitably were confronted by Mary Mattoon. "We would rather face any sort of discipline than have Mrs. Mattoon pray over us." That was the ultimate punishment. Norman gathered that his grandmother's missionary zeal may have accompanied a life of rigid puritanism.[1]

Norman's father, Welling Evan Thomas, one of Thomas Thomas' five children, followed the same path as his father, attending Lafayette College and Princeton Theological Seminary. He was ordained in 1878. Norman's mother, Emma Mattoon, led a far more exotic life. She was conceived while her parents were living in Siam; her mother returned to the United States to give birth to her and then immediately returned to Bangkok with her newborn daughter. When Emma was seven years old, she and her mother sailed for home, a trip that Emma would later describe in vivid detail for Norman and his brothers and sisters. While they were at sea for more than six months, the crew once threatened to mutiny, the ship caught fire, they sailed into the New York City harbor during a raging blizzard, and Emma nearly succumbed to pneumonia.[2]

Emma also related to her children stories about her early life in Charlotte, recalling that she was ostracized by youngsters in her neighborhood because her father, labeled by the locals as a "carpetbagger," taught "niggers" at the university. She later left North Carolina to attend Elmira College in New York where she met Welling Evan Thomas who at the time was in Elmira visiting his sister. In 1881, Welling Thomas and Emma Mattoon married, thus setting the stage for Norman's arrival.[3]

The newlyweds settled in Ohio, first in Ashley and a few years later in Marion, situated forty-nine miles north of Columbus and seventy-five miles south of Toledo. A small town with a population of seven thousand, it nonetheless was the site of a major manufacturer of excavating machinery, and local residents later boasted that Marion was the town that built the steam shovels that dug the Panama Canal. Here, on November 20, 1884, in the parsonage adjacent to the Presbyterian Church, Emma Thomas gave birth to a son whom she and her husband named "Norman."

The church and parsonage were brick structures surrounded by maple trees. Lacking plumbing and a furnace, the parsonage was heated in the winter months by burning hard coal in a base burner and soft coal in its several fireplaces. Drinking water was hand-pumped from a well and rain water was collected in a cistern for bathing and the laundry. Norman remembered the town as one having too many churches "for its own good," but it actually

---

1 Thomas autobiography, 20.
2 Ibid., 19-20.
3 Ibid., 20.

had far more saloons.[1] Visitors were steered to the cemetery as the town's chief place of beauty. The streets were not paved until Norman was nine years old.

Shortly after his birth, Norman's two-year-old sister died of diphtheria. Health problems seemed to run in the family. Norman, who weighed four pounds at birth, barely survived his first months. His earliest memories included having heard his mother's friends express the belief that he would not long survive. He remained sickly throughout his early childhood, later recalling that ordinary croup was for him a recurring terror and that winter and chronic colds went together.[2] For years his mother and father questioned whether he had a reasonable chance of reaching adulthood, and it was not until he was twelve that they realized that he indeed had a future.

Illness prevented Thomas from attending the local public grade school. All six-year-old children were required to attend morning and afternoon classes, and no exceptions were made for ill health. Thus his parents enrolled him in a small private school operated out of the home of one of his father's parishioners. Evelyn Gailey required Norman to attend only morning sessions and she allowed for his frequent absences. In two years time, despite his irregular attendance, Norman had learned enough from Miss Gailey to enter the public school's fourth grade.

Early in his life Norman became an avid reader, as his mother encouraged him to take up intellectual pursuits when his illnesses prohibited him from keeping up with the physical activities of children his age. His father had a sizable library, comprised mostly of theological works, but since he was fond of history, the collection also included a number of well-known historical texts and a few works of fiction as well. Norman read rapidly and indiscriminately, delving into Scott and Dickens and devouring Gibbons' *Decline and Fall of the Roman Empire*. Heretics and dissenters ranked high among his youthful heroes, perhaps forecasting his own role in life. If reading was his first love, music was a close second. He loved to sing and he learned to play the flute. Throughout his life, reading and music were his primary sources of relaxation and enjoyment.

In one respect, his parents' and Miss Gailey's approaches to education were sorely off the mark. Norman was naturally left-handed, but was forced to write with his right hand. His father persuaded him to throw right-handed and to participate in other physical activities as if he were naturally right-handed. Norman later commented, "I don't think the faulty process was even responsible for my socialism."[3]

---

1 Ibid., 3.
2 Ibid., 7.
3 Ibid., 10.

His intellectual pursuits may have led to a life style that militated against his overcoming persistent physical deficiencies. It was not until he was in his teens that he regularly participated in athletic and ordinary outdoor activities. But illness had taken its toll. He never achieved any degree of athletic proficiency in any sports activity and because he had grown too tall too fast, on occasion he appeared physically awkward. Still, he was able to put his height to advantage, playing a rudimentary form of basketball and engaging in the standing broad jump event in track and field.

As a teenager, he was involved in one other physical activity which, in light of a lifelong abhorrence of violence, appears somewhat incongruous. He took up boxing. He and a small group of friends formed the Tiger Athletic Club and met once a week to sharpen their pugilistic skills.[1]

Religion, in the form of an orthodox, Calvinistic Presbyterianism, was at the center of his boyhood home. As an orthodox Presbyterian, his father frowned on the playing of cards, dancing and theater-going. He even barred his children from playing marbles "for keeps." Drinking was immoral and smoking not much better. But as Thomas has written, the harshness of his parents' orthodoxy was obscured and mitigated, at least in part, by their basic daily acts of kindness and a total respect for others. His father, who believed in eternal damnation, would never say of anyone that he was damned.[2] He lived for family and for his ministry. He raised his children to believe in the fundamental rationality of life and its essential goodness, and most of all in the sure and certain progress of the human race.[3] Thomas inherited from his parents a vital sense of responsibility for one's fellow man, and the family life provided by his mother and father forged in him a deep-seated social consciousness.

As a college graduate, Emma Thomas was set apart from the women of her day. She was the dominant figure in the family, and her husband was content to have it so. She ruled over her children less by command than by appeals to loyalty and affection. Thomas later suspected that his mother's religious orthodoxy was far less questioning than his father's, that it was inspired by loyalty to her own tradition and that of her husband's, and perhaps even more by a fear where the questioning of established doctrine would lead.[4] She was a tall woman and her four sons in turn were tall (Norman grew to 6'3"), and she often joked in later life that she had "25 feet of sons."

By the standards of the day, the Thomas family lived fairly well. When a new church was constructed some years after Norman's birth, the family moved to a new dwelling adjacent to the railroad tracks that boasted indoor

---

1 Ibid., 11.
2 Ibid., 261.
3 Norman Thomas, *A Socialist's Faith* (W.W. Norton, New York, 1951), 9.
4 Thomas autobiography, 21.

plumbing but still lacked gas and electricity. In such demanding circum-stances, Welling and Emma Thomas raised six children, Norman the oldest, followed by brothers Ralph, Evan, and Arthur, and sisters Agnes and Emma.

As the oldest child, Norman was given responsibilities looking after his younger siblings, but he still found time to perform various odd jobs around the town to earn pocket money. One of those jobs involved the home delivery of the local newspaper, the *Marion Daily Star*. The paper, ostensibly managed by a very young Warren Harding, later to become the 29th president of the United States, was actually run by his wife while Harding, as Thomas re-called it, lounged around the office conversing with cronies and local towns persons.[1] Thomas was not overly impressed by the future president, as he was later unimpressed with sitting presidents at the time he was running for that office himself.

Many years later, while reviewing his early family life from the perspec-tive of a life lived as an inveterate dissenter and lifelong socialist, Thomas, in jest, commented about his childhood: "What a setup for the modern psycho-logically minded biographer.... A study in revolt born of reaction from Pres-byterian orthodoxy, and the Victorian brand of Puritanism in a Middletown setting! The only trouble is that isn't what happened."[2] Thomas certainly did not believe he was drawn to radicalism by reason of his relationship with his parents, nor is there any evidence to support such a theory.

Thomas loved, respected, and admired his parents, finding no reason to revolt against them. His father brought a strong Protestant tradition to the family, and although his acceptance of Calvinist theology was unquestioned, he was tolerant of other faiths. He spoke in cordial tones of the local Catholic priest and avoided the militant anti-Catholic organizations of the day. Anti-Semitism simply was nonexistent in his life. He was intelligent and studious, a preacher far above the average, and popular with his parishioners.

In 1932 — Thomas was 48 at the time — he wrote a volume he titled *As I See It*, wherein he described his early family life and the religious influence his mother and father brought to their children. They engendered "a sense of meaning, assurance and comfort in life which can be scarcely exaggerated. Evil there was, and suffering hard to understand. But overall was God who had His own in His care. His universe was man's home." Although his par-ents' lives may have been humble and obscure, they still could look forward to eternal life as subjects of God's care. Their conception of heaven was that of fulfillment of life on earth and an answer to questions for which they had no other answer.[3]

---

1 Harry Fleischman, *Norman Thomas, A Biography: 1884–1968* (W.W. Norton, New York, 1969), 28.
2 Thomas autobiography, 5.
3 Norman Thomas, *As I See It* (Macmillan, New York, 1932), 163.

At other times in his life he looked back from a more critical perspective. After he became involved in the Social Gospel movement in his seminary years, Thomas noted that his parents' ethical code and conscience had been inadequate since they focused on the goodness or badness of individual men and women rather than on the essential nature of the social system in which those men and women lived. This criticism was not wholly fair since his mother and father immersed themselves in community affairs and, unlike many of their contemporaries, gave serious thought to pressing world issues. Moreover, as previously noted, he owed his deep-seated social consciousness to his earlier family life.

In his senior high school year in 1901, Thomas was the president of his class of 43 students, and it was in connection with their graduation ceremony that he engaged in his first civil liberties struggle. The School Superintendent decreed that each of the senior students would make a short speech at the graduation exercises. The students, however, opposed this, preferring that a speaker be retained for the occasion. Under Thomas' leadership the class met and voted to invite an outside speaker. The Superintendent countered by rejecting their request and by banning further meetings of the students on school property, thus creating a holy cause for the students.

The Superintendent was not particularly well liked by the students, or for that matter, by their teachers. To the students, he appeared to be "a loud mouth bully" whose chief function was to discipline the boys the female teachers could not control. Thus the seniors looked forward to a fight and they vigorously pursued the matter. They assembled off the school grounds, campaigned for parental support, petitioned the Marion Board of Education, and argued before the Board members. In the end, they won a splendid victory — the Board retained a speaker for the occasion and the seniors were not required to make any speeches. Thus did Thomas begin his career as a dissenter and a defender of civil liberties.[1]

That summer the children and grandchildren of Grandfather Thomas held a reunion at the Pennsylvania home of the old preacher. This and previous reunions left a lasting impression upon Norman, and his deep love for his grandfather is reflected in a reminiscence that appears in his autobiography:

> I do not remember much that he said when he preached in Stevenville, but I do remember the little white church and its cabinet organ and its cheerful bell, the summers with the smell of the country coming in the windows while whole families from the countryside in uncomfortable best were led to look at life and its sorrows and joys with that mingling of humility and dignity which belonged of right to those chosen to be the children of God. With the years the benediction of peace and sure confidence settled about my grandfather's snow-white head. He . . . was "father" to a whole countryside.... However far his grandchildren have wandered . . . I do not think

---

1 Thomas autobiography, 11-12.

> we shall forget family prayers about his chair.... As we sat quietly around him, ... dimly at least we understood from him the sources of a light which gave meaning, yes and glory, to the humdrum task, and all the vicissitudes of the year, a light which bathed, in beauty greater than the sun's, the fields, the shining river, the wooded hills, the cottage and the cherished garden in which this Preacher of the Word lived out his days.[1]

Writing in his autobiography, Thomas also expressed love for his grandparents on the Mattoon side of the family, but they both died when he was quite young and thus his memories of them were not as defined as of those on the Thomas side of the family.

Later that summer, Norman's father moved his family to Lewisburg, Pennsylvania, where he succeeded to the leadership of the town's Presbyterian church. Lewisburg, beautifully located on the Susquehanna River, was laid out in a style somewhat unusual in the United States, with the houses built flush with the brick sidewalks that lined the streets and the lawns and gardens located to the rear of the houses. In contrast to Marion, Norman found the town attractive, and he expressed little nostalgia for the town of his early childhood.[2]

Had the family remained in Marion, Norman undoubtedly would have attended the College of Wooster, a small Presbyterian institution in northern Ohio. As it was, in the fall of 1901 he enrolled in Bucknell University, a Baptist school located in Lewisburg. That Bucknell was a Baptist rather than a Presbyterian institution was not deemed a sufficient reason for the family to strain itself financially to send Thomas elsewhere and, moreover, at that stage of his life, living at home offered greater benefits than living away from home. Bucknell was the logical choice for him to begin his college education.

Bucknell's one claim to fame in the early 20th century was that Christy Matthewson, the future great Hall-of-Fame pitcher for the New York Giants, had been a member of the class of 1902. Norman was not very enthusiastic about Bucknell, but that may have been because he was not yet ready for college life. He took advantage of the school's music department by resuming his flute lessons and for a time he also took up the cello. One of his regrets expressed in later life was that he had failed to continue with the cello.

Although he respected and was grateful for the efforts of some of his Bucknell professors, he felt that at that point in the school's history its standards were rather low, its extracurricular activities poor, and its cultural atmosphere all but nonexistent. But what disturbed him more than anything else was the degree of student cheating he witnessed. School administrators had neither initiated an honor system nor arranged for efficient proctoring, and thus cheating on examinations was widespread. This violated his acute

---

1 Ibid., 15-16.
2 Ibid., 22.

sense of fairness. Nevertheless he planned to continue his education at Bucknell, but at the end of his freshman year a generous (and financially well off) uncle offered him $400 a year if he were to transfer to Princeton. Thomas did not hesitate a moment, later referring to his uncle's offer as a "blessed miracle."[1] His parents gave their approval, recognizing that in the prior year he had matured to a point where he would be better served living away from home. Thus Princeton's doors were opened, offering Thomas opportunities and friendships that would shape the rest of his life.

His uncle's $400 annual offering covered only a portion of Thomas' tuition and living expenses, and he paid the rest through earnings from part-time jobs he held throughout his student days at Princeton. He tutored fellow students, wrote syllabi for less ambitious students, and worked at various summer jobs, once as a door-to-door aluminum-ware salesperson and another time as a chair factory laborer. Since his parents had five other children to educate, he very much wanted to limit — if not altogether eliminate — their monetary contribution to the payment of his expenses, and in this he succeeded.

On entering Princeton, he had the choice of attempting to qualify as a sophomore or starting over as a freshman. He opted to go forward rather than backward, which nearly proved a mistake. He struggled through the hot summer months in intense study and then took the entrance examinations for the sophomore courses to commence in the fall. After reviewing the test results the school authorities permitted him to enroll in the sophomore courses, but only upon specified conditions that his failure to fulfill would require reversion to freshman status. This forced upon him a period of total study, but by the end of his first term he had cleared the conditions and had attained a first group — equivalent to an "A" — in each of his sophomore courses. From that point to his graduation, he never received a grade other than a first group, a feat, according to Thomas, his children always held against him. Thomas insisted that he was not as brilliant as such a record would imply. "The average in some of these classes must have been low and grades don't prove much. Anyhow, I wasn't one who preferred a Phi Beta Kappa key to a varsity letter. I couldn't get the letter."[2]

No Princeton professor made a deeper impression on Thomas than Woodrow Wilson, who not long after was elected to the US presidency. Burdened with administrative duties after his elevation to the presidency of the university in 1902, Wilson continued to teach several courses in political science. Thomas signed up for every course of Wilson's that his schedule allowed. He particularly appreciated Wilson's ability to construct, step by step, an

1 Ibid., 25.
2 Ibid., 27.

argument whose logic appeared immune to attack. He supported Wilson's endeavors to raise the scholastic standing of the university, which had been known as "the best country club for boys in America." But he also identified flaws in Wilson, depicting him as "inclined to autocracy," one who "did not suffer fools gladly," and who viewed any opposition to his positions as "a sin against the Holy Ghost,"[1] faults that would later surface and undermine Wilson's post-World War I presidency. Some years later Thomas commented that Wilson, as an academic, "gave politics a rather narrow definition almost to the exclusion of economics. Had these things not been true he might have fared better at Versailles."[2]

Thomas joined three varsity debating teams, looking forward to developing his talents as a public speaker. On one occasion, after his team had defeated a Harvard team, he awoke the day following the debate with one eye swollen shut, apparently as a result of an encounter with poison ivy. Before escaping to the infirmary, Thomas was subjected to much kidding about how rough the Harvard debaters had been.[3]

Raymond B. Fosdick, later the president of the Rockefeller Foundation (1936 to 1948), was one of Thomas' closest friends at Princeton. As a fellow member of the debating teams, he often argued in opposition to Thomas. In his autobiography Fosdick recalls that Thomas was fundamentally more conservative than he on nearly all issues, and it never occurred to him at the time that Thomas' positions on anything would ever be further to the left than his. Strangely, in addition to his conservative stance on political issues, Thomas had little interest in economic matters. Fosdick felt that: "the impact of fresh ideas on the eager mind of Norman Thomas had to wait for a later period and for a more hospitable climate than the Princeton of our day."[4]

It was the custom each year at Princeton to conduct a debate on a subject related to French politics and to award to the winner of the debate a gold medal, said to have a value of one hundred and fifty dollars. In their senior year, Fosdick and Thomas were the only students to enter the contest, thus assuring that one of them would win the one hundred and fifty dollar prize. After the debate was over and the judges had conferred, one of them rose to speak: "Before announcing the name of the gentleman who has won the competition, the judges wish me to say that in their deliberate opinion it was the worst debate they ever listened to." The medal was then awarded to Fosdick, who rushed to a New York City goldsmith and found the medal was not made of gold and was worth not one hundred and fifty dollars but a mere

1 Ibid., 32.
2 Ibid.
3 Ibid., 27-28.
4 Raymond B. Fosdick, *Chronicle of a Generation: An Autobiography* (Harper, New York, 1958) 56.

seventy-five cents.[1] This was not, however, their only debating fiasco. When the Wright brothers made their historic first flight, Thomas and Fosdick agreed in debate that the feat had little if any practical significance.[2]

Debating was Thomas' most demanding college pastime, but not his only one. He joined both the choir and the glee club and still found time to play the flute in the orchestra. He took singing lessons, and these stood him well in later years, enabling him to manage his voice to endure long, continuous days of campaign speaking. Contrary to all expectations, one of Princeton's more prestigious social clubs selected him for membership. After he became a Socialist, his past selection for club membership provided him with the confidence that he had not been driven to the espousal of unpopular causes by an incapacity for social success.[3] As one of his biographers put it, "Thomas did not decide to remake the world because nobody would dance with him."[4]

In later years, Thomas was somewhat critical of the education he was afforded at Princeton. Although awarded high grades in such courses as the History of Philosophy, he left Princeton with little understanding of the subject. A course on socialism emphasized the reform of capitalism and the errors committed by the Socialists. Courses in English and American History added little to the knowledge he had already gained in high school.[5] But his Princeton years were among his happiest. Throughout his life — even when he was in his eighties — he remained a loyal and vocal fan of the Princeton football team.

Thomas was valedictorian of the Princeton Class of 1905, graduating *magna cum laude*. He was selected for membership in Phi Beta Kappa, received the highest honors in political science, and won first prize in history.

At the time of his graduation, his political beliefs were basically conservative, and although he considered himself to be progressive, he did not question his inherited Republicanism nor his faith in the superiority of capitalism. Along with the majority of his generation, he believed in the "fundamental rationality of life and its essential goodness," but most of all in a "sure and certain progress of the human race."[6] His political beliefs presented little if any evidence that once he left academia they would lead him to the life of dissent or to the advocacy of socialism, pacifism, and a host of other unpopular causes.

---

1 Harry Fleischman, *Norman Thomas, A Biography: 1884–1968*, 35-36. Thomas did not include this story in his autobiography. Apparently, he related it directly to Fleischman.

2 Ibid., 36.

3 Thomas autobiography, 28.

4 Murray B. Seidler, *Norman Thomas: Respectable Rebel* (Syracuse University Press, Syracuse, 1967), 10.

5 Harry Fleischman, *Norman Thomas: A Biography :1884-1968*, 38.

6 Norman Thomas, *A Socialist's Faith*, 9.

Chapter 2. Working in the Slum Areas of New York City

Thomas' parents did not pressure him to enter the ministry. He was well aware that they hoped he would elect the life of the clergy, but Thomas had serious doubts about following that path since he had not experienced a "mystical sense of call" to the religious way of life. These doubts were sufficient to deter him from moving directly from the Princeton campus to the seminary.

Even though he had concerns about entering the ministry, he still experienced a strong desire to perform some form of missionary work, if not as a member of the clergy, then as one trained in one of the other professions. His thoughts turned to the legal profession as a possible alternative to the clergy. At Princeton, politics had been one of his primary interests and he pondered whether a legal career was a course he might pursue as a step in the direction of the political arena. He had little concern about his ability to achieve excellence as a lawyer, but was hesitant to commit himself to a profession he did not then hold and in later life would never hold in high regard. As a provisional measure, he also considered teaching for a year or two. While in that state of uncertainty, his friend Tom Carter from Princeton introduced him to Rev. H. Roswell Bates of the Spring Street Presbyterian Church and Settlement House in New York City.

Carter had spent the previous year working with Bates and he encouraged Thomas to join them at the Spring Street church. The church was located in a poor, slum-ridden area of lower Manhattan, later revitalized as a section of Greenwich Village. Bates, while expressing conventional political and economic views, was passionately religious and genuinely concerned for the poor — distinctive qualities that provided him with great power as a preacher. His effectiveness, however, was often compromised by lifestyle eccentricities and neurotic responses to health problems, some real and others imagined

Bates recruited young college graduates with clerical ambitions to work at the church and the settlement house. With Carter's urging, Thomas accepted Bates's offer of a position paying a salary of $500 per year and a room in a rundown tenement adjacent to the church. Thomas thus began a period of more than ten years of ministry to the poor, while residing in poverty-stricken and disease-ridden areas of Manhattan. During the course of those years, he became acquainted with human misery, the extent and degree of which he could not have previously imagined, an experience that would shape and direct his life.

The Spring Street parish boasted a few relatively well-preserved old homes, but abominable slums covered most of the neighborhood. Cold water flats with small airless and overcrowded rooms infested with rats and roaches, served by unsanitary and reeking backyard toilets, were the common lot of the parish residents. Thomas later recalled in his autobiography the conditions he daily confronted in the Spring Street area:

> In my time big families often crowded into small rooms. I have visited some of these rooms, sitting gingerly on a broken wooden chair and watched cockroaches and worse vermin make irregular patterns on the grimy, broken plaster of the walls while I talked to a sick woman on a filthy bed around which dirty toddlers played.... Poverty was very great, strong liquor the chief escape, and much of the neighborhood was lost in a kind of sodden apathy to which drunken quarrels brought release.[1]

All kinds of misery were found within the dilapidated tenement buildings that dominated the neighborhood. A three-room apartment could be made to accommodate as many as a dozen or more people, from one or more families. Young children slept four and five to a bed and some adults slept in folding cots lodged temporarily in the kitchen. Hallways and stairways were filthy, airless and without light. Many tenements had no internal bathrooms, but in those that did, toilets were shared by as many as twenty-five people and cleaned by none of them, thus creating a situation depicted as "literally indescribable within the limits of printable English."[2]

On one Sunday evening, not long after he started working at the Settlement House, a frightened child came running into the building screaming, "Come quick; Papa is killing Mama!" Led by the child, Thomas ran through the neighborhood's narrow streets and up three flights of stairs to the top floor of a rundown tenement house, where a drunken longshoreman stood towering over his wife, brandishing an axe. Thomas confronted the man,

---

1 Thomas autobiography, 46.
2 Norman Thomas, *Human Exploitation in the United States* (Frederick A. Stokes, New York, 1934), 15-16, citing the editors of Fortune, *Housing in America* (Harcourt, Brace).

gradually calmed him down by talking to him quietly, and ultimately persuaded him to surrender the axe. The incident frightened Thomas to the core, and as he later said, "I still don't know just how I calmed him down enough to get the axe away."[1]

His life in Ohio, Pennsylvania, and the Princeton campus in New Jersey had done little to prepare him for the conditions he was then encountering. The poverty, degradation, disease and hopelessness he daily confronted extended far beyond anything he had ever witnessed and were far removed from and outside the scope of any economic or political theories he had been taught at Princeton, theories that could not account for these conditions. His sense of fairness was grossly offended. Why should these people be compelled to proceed through life living in such abysmal conditions? What could he do, if anything, to help these people?

City officials provided little or nothing in the way of assistance for the people living in the area. Medical care was nearly nonexistent. The Spring Street Settlement House had only one grossly overworked nurse who could attend only to the most desperate cases in the neighborhood. The City Health Department, controlled by corrupt politicians, failed to compel landlords to abide by the law, inadequate as the law was at the time, thus contributing to longstanding conditions of decay and degradation. The main concern of greedy landlords was the collection of rents and thus the tenement houses in the area, without care or upkeep, continued to deteriorate, falling deeper and deeper into states of total disrepair.[2]

Thomas was soon trying to do a little of everything appropriate to the work of the church and the settlement house. He visited families in trouble, formed and then conducted clubs for youngsters, sang in the choir, and talked long hours with individuals and groups of residents about their problems. He tried to raise the level of political awareness of local issues, but most of the residents thought the corrupt Tammany Hall was good enough for them.[3] He also on occasion worked with missionary groups who entered the area to conduct evangelical services. At one of these services, Thomas sat in the audience next to one of the downtrodden, a temporarily reformed alcoholic. The speaker, another reformed alcoholic, was boastfully reciting his wickedness from which God's grace had saved him. His companion leaned over to Thomas and said in a loud whisper, "Dat guy ain't seen nothin'. I was on de Bowery when it was a Bowery." In other words, he had lived on the Bowery when it was still a farm, before that part of the City had become notorious for its cheap bars and flop houses that catered to homeless derelicts.[4]

---

1 Thomas autobiography, 46.
2 Ibid., 45-46.
3 Ibid., 48
4 Ibid., 49. Thomas described him as an alcoholic, but "otherwise a very decent man."

Thomas must have questioned whether his companion could have survived that long as a drunkard.

Bates fell ill during the summer of 1906, leaving Thomas in charge of nearly all parish activities. Thomas gathered a group of college volunteers to assist him, one of whom was Charles Gilkey, later to become Dean of Theology at the University of Chicago and who remained one of Thomas' "prized" friends for life. Another of this group was Ted Savage, who had just graduated from Harvard.

Nothing in his autobiography suggests that Thomas believed he in any way succeeded in raising the level of existence of any of the people living in the Spring Street area. Working with individuals and small groups had not accomplished what he had hoped for, and this experience may very well have turned his thinking in the direction of broader-based endeavors to aid the poor. From this point in his life onward he moved in that direction.

As his one year commitment to the church and settlement house was nearing conclusion, Princeton offered him an instructorship in English, and he was sorely tempted to move on from this poverty-stricken area. At the time, Bates was still suffering the effects of a recent illness, Tom Carter was about to leave for the seminary, and Thomas had returned to considering the ministry, but putting his plans aside, he rejected the Princeton offer, postponed his entry into the seminary, and signed on for another year. He may not have succeeded during his first year in materially helping the Spring Street residents, but lack of success did not seem to discourage or deter him from renewing his commitment. He simply refused to allow his own plans for the future to interfere with or detract from his dedication to these people; the existing conditions of injustice and unfairness demanded his attention. As would prove to be central to his entire life, neither a halfway measure nor a watered-down, mediocre response was a course he found acceptable when standing in the presence of the poor, the downtrodden, and the oppressed.

By this time, Thomas had fully adapted to living in New York City. He still thought of himself as a small-town person, but the city had a fascination for him that developed slowly into acceptance and love. Years later he wrote in his autobiography that the city was "like a vice, first seen, then endured, then embraced. I can still remember my surprise one night returning to New York on a ferry to discover the affection I felt for the city of lights that lay ahead even though I knew something of the sordid ugliness their radiance concealed. Then for the first time I thought of the tumultuous city as home."[1]

As with Carter, Gilkey, and Savage, he developed lasting friendships with many others who passed through the Spring Street environs. One of

---

1 Ibid., 45.

these was Captain Paries who, along with other family members, owned two or three tugboats that worked the New York harbor. An elder in the church, Paries was well known along the waterfront for his friendliness, fairness and his staunch opposition to profanity and drunkenness. Thomas passed many a happy afternoon on one of Paries' tugboats in the waters surrounding Manhattan.[1]

Thomas tried another approach to raising the level of existence of the Spring Street residents. He turned to speaking at the settlement house to small groups. At first, he found speaking at outdoor evening meetings to larger gatherings of people to be excruciatingly painful. Prior to the first of these occasions, he spent the entire day hoping for a hurricane, an earthquake or the occurrence of any other calamity that would relieve him of the necessity of going ahead with his speech. But none occurred, and he made the speech.[2] Thus a career was born. As he discovered at Princeton that he excelled in debate, he found that speaking to large groups came naturally to him.

As his second year at Spring Street was nearing its end, he started planning for the seminary, but again fate intervened. Bates decided that a trip around the world would aid in the restoration of his health and he asked Carter and Savage to accompany him on the trip. Without telling Thomas, Bates contacted Thomas' uncle — the one who had financed his Princeton education — and asked him to provide the funds necessary to permit his nephew to join the group. Thomas was delighted when he received word he was to be included in the around-the-world trip.

They departed from Seattle at the end of July 1907, visiting Japan, Korea, China, the Philippines, Siam, Burma (Myanmar), India, and Egypt. Through Bates' friendships with missionaries, the group saw more of the Asiatic countries than most tourists. Thomas particularly enjoyed his stay in China as they traveled to distant provinces by mule and boat. He developed a greater appreciation for the Chinese people than for those of any other country he visited during the course of the trip.

In Shanghai, parts of which were then occupied by British, French and US military forces, he was horrified when he came across signs in the city's parks reading, "Dogs and Chinese not allowed." His revulsion was nearly as great as when in Calcutta he saw a British civilian strike an Indian streetcar conductor merely because his seat was dusty.[3] His observations of events of this kind would later develop into a consuming abhorrence of any form of colonialism.

---

1 Ibid., 49.
2 Ibid., 48.
3 Ibid., 51.

Thomas experienced his worst moments during the trip when he was caring for Bates. Physically, Bates was fairly well, although at times during the overland segments of their travels in China he had to be carried in a sedan chair. But he suffered recurring bouts of deep melancholia and at these times he would beg Thomas to watch him closely lest he commit suicide.[1]

Carter stayed behind in China to advance his studies while Bates and Savage moved onto Burma and Thomas to Bangkok, where he met some older residents who remembered his grandparents and his mother who had lived there until she was seven. Presbyterian missionaries then serving in the city showed him a church that had been constructed under the supervision of his grandfather, and he also met Ma Esther, who had been a governess for his mother and her sister. On the wall of her home — even after the passage of forty years — were pictures of his grandparents that had been painted from photographs. Ma Esther's joy in seeing Thomas was touching. She did not cease from telling him how much she had loved his grandparents and how she owed to them all the good things that had occurred in her life.[2]

The group of travelers then reconnected and traveled to Egypt. After a short stay, Bates and Savage departed for the United States. Thomas then toured Europe, returning to New York in March of 1908, thus concluding a nine-month journey.

On his return, Thomas found two intriguing offers awaiting him — an assistant's post at the First Presbyterian Church in Auburn, New York, and a similar position at Christ Church located in a tenement district on the west side of Manhattan. The Auburn church was led by a brilliant teacher of the Auburn Theological Seminary — Dr. Allen Macy Dulles (father of John Foster Dulles, Secretary of State under President Eisenhower, and Allen Dulles, Director of the C.I.A. from 1953 to 1961). Thomas gave serious consideration to the Auburn position, but when his good friend, Henry Sloane Coffin, who held posts at both the Spring Street Church and the Christ Church, urged him to accept the New York City position, Thomas agreed that this appeared to be the better choice for him.[3]

The assignment to the Auburn post would have required Thomas to pursue his seminary studies at the Auburn Theological Seminary, while the Christ Church position would allow him to enroll in the more liberal Union Theological Seminary. In deciding on Christ Church — and hence also on Union — Thomas clashed with his parents, who favored a seminary offering a more religiously orthodox course of studies. His mother, particularly, argued against Union, mostly on the ground that he should remain loyal to

---

1 Ibid.
2 W. A. Swanberg, *Norman Thomas: The Last Idealist* (Charles Scribner's Sons, New York, 1976), 20-21.
3 Thomas autobiography, 52.

his father's orthodox beliefs.[1] In selecting Union, Thomas undertook his first significant step in the direction of separating himself from the religious views of his parents.

The Christ Church parish was centered in a drab tenement section of the city bordering the garment district on one side and Hell's Kitchen on another. It was similar to, but not quite as poor nor as squalid as, the Spring Street parish. The activities of the church were financed in the main by the wealthy Fifth Avenue parishioners of the Brick Church located in the more fashionable east side of mid-Manhattan. As he preferred, Thomas again was working in a poverty-stricken area of the city. Fortunately his assistant's salary was sufficient to finance his courses at Union.

His work at Christ Church was memorable on several counts. It was here that he began a lifelong friendship with Sidney Lovett, a Yale student who worked at the church during the summer months. It was also while assigned to this church that he had his first experience with the political world, speaking on behalf of the Republican Party during the mayoralty campaign of 1909. And it was also at Christ Church that he would meet the woman who would become his wife.

Frances Violet Stewart, a volunteer worker at the Christ Church, organized the first class in New York City for the home treatment of tuberculosis. In addition to teaching elementary hygiene and basic home nursing care to tenement families, she also raised funds for the project and still found time to tend to patients as a visiting nurse.[2] It was not long before Thomas took note of her presence.

Violet was born of a family of wealth. Her grandfather, John Aikman Stewart, was one of the founders and later president and chairman of the board of trustees of the United States Trust Company. He had been Abraham Lincoln's assistant secretary of the treasury and trusted financial adviser during the Civil War. He dined with Lincoln at the White House a few days prior to the assassination.[3]

When Violet was only seven, her father, William A. W. Stewart, sailed from New York on his yawl bound for the Caribbean. He had suffered through a spell of poor health and felt the sea voyage might be restorative. On the day following his departure, the blizzard of '88 struck the eastern coast, and he was never heard from again.[4] His widowed wife dressed in mourning for the rest of her life.

Violet attended the Brearley School in New York, a private girls' school for the wealthy, and later studied nursing. At the time of her meeting Thom-

---

1 Ibid., 52.
2 Ibid., 53.
3 *The New York Times,* 12/18/26, 17.
4 *The New York Times,* 9/26/1888, 9.

as, she was 27 years old (three years older than Norman) and lived with her mother and sister; they were accustomed to a staff of servants and to frequent mention in the society columns of the city's newspapers. She was more than a head shorter than Norman's six foot, three inches, giving rise to the quip that he could talk to her eye-to-eye only from a sitting position or while on his knees.

According to Thomas, the manner of his engagement to Violet became a "family legend." His doctor had recommended that he undergo a minor operation. As it turned out, it was not minor at all, and he remained hospitalized for several days and faced a lengthy period of rehabilitation. Violet urged him to accept her mother's invitation to recuperate at their home. He mulled the matter over as he lay in his hospital bed, and then on the occasion of one of Violet's visits he made his decision. The rest of the story is best told in his own words:

> I was very much in love but I had never intended to propose from a sick bed. But alas for noble resolutions. I shamelessly took advantage of pity. I ... said that I wouldn't go unengaged to Mrs. Stewart's house.... Just after I had proposed, in marched a nurse to take my temperature pending which all conversation and action were held in suspense. It was, she said, "satisfactory," and went out. After which things far more important than temperature proceeded to my enormous lifelong satisfaction.[1]

"Compared with most of my children," Thomas later wrote in his autobiography, "I was a slow worker. I began at Christ Church in the spring of 1908 and didn't get married until September 1910."[2] They were married by his friend the Rev. Henry Sloane Coffin. Each loved the other dearly. Although they came from vastly different backgrounds, they shared a craving to assist the poor of the city. She shared his basic beliefs, was always loyal to him, and despite a chronic heart condition that tormented her, freely adjusted her life to his. They both were utterly fearless and shared a nimble wit and sense of humor.[3] Some years later, Thomas wrote that he was convinced there was no substitute for the kind of family life she made possible for him and their children.[4] After the marriage ceremony, Violet's name was not listed in the Social Register as "Mrs. Norman Thomas," and her name never appeared again.

They rented a small apartment in a West 42nd Street tenement, located just west of Times Square and a few blocks north of Christ Church. They persuaded the landlord to install a bathroom, and they spent a happy year in their basement and ground floor rooms. The location of the tenement, however, presented a problem they were unable to resolve. The building stood adjacent to the rectory of a Catholic church, and repentant drunkards mis-

---

1 Thomas autobiography, 55.
2 Ibid., 53.
3 W. A. Swanberg, *Norman Thomas: The Last Idealist*, 25.
4 Norman Thomas, *A Socialist's Faith* (Norton, New York, 1951), x.

takenly believing they were calling upon a priest in the rectory frequently arrived at their door late at night to "take the pledge."[1]

Thomas' entry into the Union Theological Seminary introduced him to the Social Gospel movement. This movement — prominent among major Protestant groups between 1870 and 1920 — marked a radical departure from traditional views of Protestant Christianity, tending to minimize the importance of metaphysics in favor of ethics, and viewing Christianity as the road to a just and equitable society on earth. One of the movement's founders was Walter Rauschenbusch, who would profoundly alter Thomas' religious, economic, and political views on human life.

Rauschenbusch, the son of a Lutheran missionary to German immigrants living in the United States, was ordained a Baptist minister in New York City, where in a Hell's Kitchen parish he first observed the social problems common to depressed city neighborhoods. He later joined the faculty of the Rochester Theological Seminary and following the publication of his book entitled *Christianity and the Social Crisis*,[2] he rapidly gained recognition as a major spokesperson for the Social Gospel movement in the United States. In advocating an equitable society, the movement was responding to rapid industrialization and urbanization, and it endeavored to secure social justice for the poor through labor reforms such as the abolition of child labor and the enactment of legislation providing for a living wage and a shorter work week. Those advancing the cause of the Social Gospel argued that the power of the business world must be set off and countered by the power of the workers. The Social Gospel movement continued to influence Protestantism in the decades that followed, especially in the shaping of the civil rights movement in the 1960s.

Rauschenbusch held that the purpose of all that Christ did, said and hoped for was the social redemption of human life. "His death was his greatest act of social service. His cross was the climax of world evil and the turning point of history toward a definite and permanent emancipation and redemption of the race."[3] The key to Rauschenbusch's theology lay in his concept of the Kingdom of God. For him, the Kingdom of God is not located in some place called heaven. It is recognized as the "immanence of God in human life and in the interconnected, interacting, independent nature of the entire hu-

---

1 Thomas autobiography, 58-59.

2 Walter Rauschenbusch, *Christianity and the Social Crisis* (Harper, New York, 1964, first published by Macmillan, New York, 1907; and reissued by Westminster/John Knox Press, Louisville, Kentucky, 1991. This work was again reissued, along with the commentaries of eight current religious thinkers, under the title *Christianity and the Social Crisis in the 21st Century, edited by Paul Raushenbush*, Harper One, New York, 2007).

3 Walter Rauschenbusch, *Christianizing the Social Order* (Macmillan, New York, 1919), 67, 68.

man species."[1] Relying upon Christ's proclamation in the Lord's Prayer that, "Thy will be done on earth as it is in heaven," he maintained that the Kingdom of God deals not only with the immortal souls of men and women, but with their bodies, their homes, their workplaces and it makes those who serve the fundamental necessities of human life veritable ministers of God.[2] Such an understanding of the Kingdom demanded a change in the role of the Church. While the chief purpose of the Christian Church in the past had been the salvation of souls, Rauschenbusch contended that societal needs required the Church to focus more on group rather than individual issues:

> Our business is to make over an antiquated and immoral economic system; to get rid of laws, customs, maxims, and philosophies inherited from an evil despotic past; to create just and brotherly relations between great groups and classes of society; and thus to lay a social foundation on which modern men individually can live and work in a fashion that will not outrage all the better elements in them. Our inherited Christian faith deals with individuals; our present task deals with society.[3]

Rauschenbusch insisted that moral principles must control and reshape the institutions of society. The Social Gospel thus conceived Christian doctrine in social terms. Christ's ethical teachings should be brought to bear upon solutions to societal problems. The Church, therefore, should take the side of the people and their demands for social justice. It should focus on the solution of problems that would lead to the betterment of society, on issues pertaining to poverty, unemployment, education, health care, and civil rights. For advocates of the Social Gospel, Christianizing the social order meant humanizing it in the highest sense.[4] "A mature social Christian comes closer to the likeness of Jesus Christ than any other type [of Christian]."[5]

Rauschenbusch condemned capitalism because it provided for ownership and control of industry by a limited group, while the mass of workers was without ownership or power over the system in which they labored. "A small group of great wealth and power is set over against a large group of propertyless men.... It is not Christian."[6] Socialism, on the other hand, fit comfortably into his concept of a Christianized social order. The Social Gospel, in his view, constituted the moral force underlying a Christian socialism.

Socialism, he wrote, should never be imposed upon the populace. It must be chosen voluntarily by the people; all social institutions should be fraternal and cooperative. Rauschenbusch's form of socialism, however, differed from Marxist socialism. Marxists were interested in the ends to be attained

---

1 Elizabeth Balanoff, "Norman Thomas: Socialism and the Social Gospel," *The Christian Century*, 1/30/85, 101-102.
2 Walter Rauschenbusch, *Christianizing the Social Order*, 99.
3 Ibid., 41-42.
4 Ibid., 36, 125.
5 Ibid., 111.
6 Ibid., 311, 312.

and focused less on the means to be used in achieving those ends, while Rauschenbusch's form of socialism placed greater emphasis on the means and less on the ends to be achieved.

Rauschenbusch's teachings profoundly affected Thomas.[1] Rauschenbusch confirmed religious and social positions Thomas already had adopted and led him to consider and later accept positions he might not have adhered to had he not read Rauschenbusch's works. Thomas himself stated that "insofar as any one man or any one book ... made me a socialist, it was probably Walter Rauschenbusch and his writings."[2] Thus by the time of his graduation from the seminary, Thomas was well on his way to accepting socialism as an appropriate substitute for capitalism.

Thomas was considered the brightest student enrolled in the Union Theological Seminary, and at his graduation he had the highest grades in his class. At the time of his ordination, he generally accepted the basic beliefs of Christianity, although he questioned the validity of some of them, such as the doctrine of the virgin birth and concept of hell that was then popular. His seminary training significantly broadened his intellectual life and provided a foundation for self-education that he pursued all of his life, reading voraciously and always remaining abreast of current scholarship.

Upon earning his divinity degree, Thomas had to select the path to follow as a Presbyterian minister. Should he continue to live with and help those at the bottom of society or should he change course and elect to minister to those of more fortunate circumstances? Working with the poor would require him in the future to live and raise his children in decrepit slum area conditions, while any other choice would undoubtedly raise the level of their daily existence.

While still attending the seminary, Thomas had experienced what it was like to minister to the wealthy and others living in better circumstances. When the pastor of the Brick Church — the Fifth Avenue church of the wealthy — died suddenly, his place was temporarily filled by a Princeton professor whose classes Thomas had attended. Since the professor intended to continue teaching at Princeton, he desperately needed an assistant at the church, and he offered the post to Thomas. Thomas doubted that the Brick Church would present him with the type of ministry he had in mind for his life work, but he also was aware that this was a prize appointment, one that could lead to the type of life that Violet had grown accustomed to as a child. Thomas accepted the position.

---

1 An element of anti-Catholicism runs throughout Rauschenbusch's writings. This aspect of Rauschenbusch's teachings had no influence on Thomas. He rejected anti-Catholicism and all other religious biases.

2 Dores Robinson Sharpe, *Walter Rauschenbusch* (Macmillan, New York, 1942), 414-415.

Thomas' popularity with the Brick Church parishioners grew rapidly, and by the time he completed his seminary studies he was in a position to secure a permanent appointment at the church, had he desired one. In fact, one of the pillars of the church, after listening to one of Thomas' sermons, addressed the search committee charged with hiring a new pastor and suggested that Thomas, although young and inexperienced, was a good candidate for the position.

Thomas was tempted. The pastorship of such a well-known and well-financed church offered security and prestige, and he could look forward to a good salary and association with the cultivated of the city. But Thomas lived with little regard for his own concerns or advantages, and ultimately he withdrew his name from consideration. He was seeking a more challenging position, and he found it in an area that had the highest homicide rate in New York City.

CHAPTER 3. PACIFISM AND SOCIALISM

Finishing first in his class at Union Theological Seminary, Thomas was awarded a traveling fellowship for advanced study. But anxious to begin his ministry without further delay, he declined the fellowship. Thomas could have elected to remain at the Brick Church. Indeed, due to his record at Union, he could have selected any open position he set his mind on having. Ultimately he decided upon the East Harlem Presbyterian Church, located in a desperately poor section of the city and which suffered every conceivable social problem. The church, old, rundown and with few active members, provided Thomas with the opportunity he had been seeking — working with destitute immigrants in one of the poorest sections of the city.

The decision to accept an appointment to the East Harlem church rather than to the Brick Church was a decision that had to have been made jointly by Norman and Violet. It was a decision that would exclude them from a life of privilege. Except for having been designated a beneficiary of a trust fund that provided her with an annual income of approximately $10,000, Violet at that time did not share directly in the wealth of the Stewart family. Although not an inconsiderable sum in those days, the trust fund income was far from sufficient to support her former lifestyle. The receipt of any other family monies was dependent upon being named in her grandfather's will and upon the beneficence of her mother, and although she was designated a beneficiary of the will and her mother was generous, Norman's and Violet's life style thereafter never approximated that lived by the other members of the Stewart family.

The Harlem of 1911 was not the Harlem of today. Its residents were primarily European immigrants, recently arrived from Italy and Hungary, living among a mixture of Slovaks, Swedes and Jews. Most of them spoke little or no English and were either unemployed or worked in low-paying jobs. Grossly overpopulated, with as many as five thousand persons crowded into a single block, it was a segment of the city that was particularly prone to violence, vice, and crime. Roaming street gangs were common. Extreme poverty was a way of life. Not unlike the Spring Street neighborhood, it was an area of the helpless and the hopeless.

Thomas moved his family — Violet and son Norman Jr., born in 1911 — to East 116th Street, between Second and Third Avenues, across the street from his assigned church. This was to be their home for the next seven years, during which four more children — Bill, Polly, Frances, and Becky — would join the family (Evan arrived later).

In addition to designating Thomas the pastor of the East Harlem Church, church officials also appointed him the chairman of the American Parish Among Immigrants in New York, a loose grouping of several other small Presbyterian churches and community centers located in the Harlem area. His administrative duties in both posts were daunting. As Thomas later described it, "I am always thinking of the next particular job on hand and my jobs seem to be many.... Much as I love the Parish and home mission work in New York in general I wish it did not load so many executive details upon me."[1]

His hectic pace, however, did not prevent him from serving on the local school board. He published a monthly paper for his various congregations and raised funds for a visiting nurse care program. With his friends, Sidney Lovett and Henry Sloane Coffin, he founded a summer camp in New Jersey for Harlem children. He organized a program to train college students to work in slum areas. He attempted to ease the crushing financial burdens of his parishioners by coaxing neighborhood merchants to exercise patience with defaulting debtors, by persuading landlords to defer evictions for nonpayments of rent, and by prevailing on doctors to reduce their fees or, on occasion, offer treatment without a fee. By helping parishioners to resolve their everyday human problems, Thomas — whether he was aware of it or not — was engaged in implementing the principles of the Social Gospel movement.

He firmly believed that education, along with decent wages and improved living conditions, provided the answer to antisocial behavior. He managed to obtain scholarships for young parishioners to the Mount Hermon School in northern Massachusetts. Steering his young parishioners away from lives of crime, however, was one of his endeavors that met with mixed success.

---

1 Thomas letter, dated 1/31/17, to Rev. Howard A. Walter.

Thomas liked to tell the story about one of his young charges who announced one Christmas day that he had come to believe in God. Questioned about his sudden conversion, he told how on Christmas eve he had held up a man at gunpoint, taking seven dollars from him. The man begged him to return the money else his wife and children would have no Christmas gifts. When he handed the money back, the man cried "God bless you," and hurried off. "And God did bless me," the young man affirmed, "I ... stuck up [another] guy for almost $100."[1]

Thomas experienced little success in organizing local workers to protest their working conditions. Local employers exploited the linguistic differences of their workers, playing Slovaks off against Hungarians and both groups against Italians, thus inhibiting any coordinated effort of the workers to organize to gain better wages and improved working conditions. Nonetheless, on one occasion a spontaneous strike broke out in one of the local factories. Thomas arranged a meeting between the strikers and an A.F.L. union organizer, hoping that the workers, with the assistance of the union, would organize the factory. The effort failed. The union organizer, who was reluctant to attend the meeting in the first instance, gave a perfunctory speech, and the workers left the meeting more discouraged than ever. "Well, that's done," the organizer remarked to Thomas, "My wife says she can tell what kind of wops I've been talking to by the smell of my clothes when I come home." Ultimately the workers drifted back to work, and the strike was defeated.[2] Thomas' disillusionment with both capital and labor steadily grew with other events of similar caste.

Compelled by an ever-expanding capacity for indignation — an indignation intensified by the injustice and unfairness he witnessed daily in East Harlem — Thomas turned to attempting to identify the underlying causes of the poverty, filth and degradation suffered by the people with whom he lived. Over time, he became convinced that the primary source of these conditions lay in the nation's economic system. Capitalism was the cause. He began to move toward and think more seriously about socialism.

The beginning of World War I in 1914 found Thomas moving still in another direction. Not yet a pacifist, either on religious or political grounds, he nevertheless rejected the views of his grandfathers and his father whom he described as "Old Testament Christians" who supported "good wars for holy purposes." He recalled one of his father's early sermons urging his parishioners to support President Grover Cleveland's ultimatum to Britain to stay out of Venezuela, even if it should come to war. His father also supported the war against Spain in 1898 and viewed America's armies as acting as the

---

1 The story is cited in many works including W. A. Swanberg, *Norman Thomas: The Last Idealist* (Charles Scribner's Sons, New York, 1976), 40-41.

2 Thomas autobiography, 63-64.

servants of the Lord in subduing the Philippines. But Thomas had long departed from such views. His horror of the prospect of America's entry into the European conflict in 1914 convinced him, even though his sympathies lay with the Allies, that the United States should remain strictly neutral.

As in other major decisions made during the course of his long life, Thomas did not experience a sudden, overnight conversion to pacifism. He later wrote in his autobiography, "In no major decision in my life can I remember a critical point or precise moment when my doubts were resolved. Mine was never any sudden vision on any road to Damascus."[1] But as the war proceeded, he was more and more persuaded that it was not a battle between light and darkness, as President Woodrow Wilson and others maintained, but a clash of rival imperialists and US financial ties were driving the country to support the Allied war effort. He later wrote:

> The causes of the war were not simple. British propaganda and the undeniable crimes of the Germans played their part, but we should not have got into war as active belligerents if our whole economy had not been increasingly tied to the service of the Allies, and if farmers and workers, as well as the House of Morgan, had not acquired an economic stake in Allied victory. Individual men with great sincerity fought for democracy, but the economic forces which President Wilson admitted . . . were responsible for the war, were also responsible for American entry into it.[2]

It was a combat between warring imperialists, and he failed to detect any "overwhelming margin of virtue on the Allied side," that would warrant sending Harlem's youth to fight and die in France.[3] He was wholly convinced that it was America's business to stay out of the war and use its enormous moral and economic strength to negotiate a peace agreement between the warring parties. As the war proceeded, he argued that President Woodrow Wilson had repeatedly missed opportunities to mediate a settlement of the dispute.[4] He condemned also the leadership of the Christian churches. "Could they not . . . assemble in some neutral country a conference of believers who at the very least would pray that God might no longer be grieved by the spectacle of men professing faith in the same Christ, using all possible means of destruction to kill one another?"[5]

Thomas' father died suddenly in November 1915. In the end, his father appeared to have affirmed his son's antiwar position. Family members discovered on his father's desk a copy of his last sermon which was read to his congregation on the Sunday following his death. His father questioned whether preparation for war was the surest preservative for peace. "Can it

---

1 Ibid., 67.
2 Norman Thomas, *We Have a Future* (Princeton University Press, Princeton, 1941)29-30.
3 Thomas autobiography, 66.
4 Norman Thomas, *We Have a Future*, 30.
5 Norman Thomas, "Conscience and the Church," *The Nation*, 8/23/17., 198.

be that this war in Europe is going to undo in great measure what centuries of Christian effort have accomplished?"[1]

That his own father — an Old Testament Christian — had turned against the war must have encouraged Thomas to pursue his examination of the proper role of the Church in the time of war. His opposition to the war was intensified when in the latter part of 1916 he associated himself with the Fellowship of Reconciliation, a group of Christian pacifists who perceived war as an affront to Christianity and who were totally opposed to the use of force in the resolution of international problems. In a letter to a college friend and fellow minister he set forth his reasons for joining the group:

> As you know, I have at last taken the step of joining the Fellowship of Reconciliation. I was a long while coming to it but finally became convinced that so far as I could see war and Christianity are incompatible; that you cannot conquer war by war; cast out Satan by Satan; or do the enormous evil of war that good may come. It seems to me that the validity of Christ's method of dealing with life's problems almost stands or falls with this test and that if we would honestly try His way, God would guide us to unimaginable solutions of our problems. I recognize that the great majority of our fellow Christians regard this as an extreme and unwarranted view but I cannot fail to record the faith that is in me. I write this with all appreciation of the noble motives which have led many men to war and support it in all generations.[2]

He also joined and later became a member of the executive committee of the American Union Against Militarism, an organization opposed to conscription and to all other steps in preparation for war on the ground that such measures would inevitably lead to participation in the war. At neighborhood street corner meetings and at local schools and colleges, Thomas spoke in opposition to compulsory military training and to other measures the Wilson administration had ordered in mobilizing for war.

Thomas now found himself in opposition to his own church, contending against religious leaders who were moving inexorably toward positions that supported the war. He objected to a Presbyterian Sunday School poster depicting US soldiers firing off heavy field artillery under a huge banner calling for peace with honor and with God. He protested against church organizations such as the Federation of Churches because its leadership openly advocated war and the conscription of young men for the army. He asserted that the church was advertising its own failure when it gave its support to the training of soldiers for battle. He condemned the Church's "rush into advocacy of conscription and virtually of war in the name of Jesus of Nazareth."[3] The church's uncritical justification of and support for the war led to his

---

1 The sermon is quoted in part in Harry Fleischman, *Norman Thomas: A Biography* — *1884–1968* (W.W. Norton, New York, 1969), 55.

2 Thomas letter, dated 1/31/17, to Rev. Howard A. Walter.

3 Thomas letter, dated 3/15/17, to Dr. Laidlaw.

bitter disillusionment, and he became one of a small minority of Protestant clergymen who rejected the war even after the United States officially became involved in the spring of 1917.

The events in Europe drove Thomas to examine closely the role of Christianity in the time of war, and ultimately, he was constrained to adopt a narrow form of Christian pacifism. His inability to reconcile Christianity and war, on religious, ethical, or philosophic grounds, also resulted in his rethinking the relationship between God and man and between man and the world he lived in. This reevaluation of basic Christian concepts reaffirmed his newly formed belief that the Church had failed its people, and thus he began searching out an agency that would perform better and accomplish more than the Church. A few years earlier, he had shifted his economic views in the direction of socialism. Now he was about to adopt socialism as a guiding political principle as well.

Most peoples of the world at one time or another have adopted some form of socialism. Only in the United States has "socialism" always been a bad word.[1] For some Americans of Thomas' era, socialism barely even existed, and in fact Thomas was reared in a home that was essentially unaware of its existence. At Princeton he studied fundamental socialist principles, but his professor emphasized socialism's deficiencies and failings and recommended the reform of capitalism rather than the adoption of a socialist system. At the time, Thomas was sufficiently impressed with his professor's approach to consider writing a book exposing the errors of socialism, but years later, when he saw how Harlem's employers exploited their workers and reduced the level of their existence essentially to that of slaves, he began to see socialism, which then appeared to him to be a more efficient and equitable economic system, as an alternative to capitalism. He recognized that his own efforts in Harlem amounted to little more than "bailing out a tub while we kept the faucet running,"[2] and that the issues daily confronted by his parishioners would not be resolved by preserving the economic status quo. Perhaps socialism would lead to a better result.

He read again Rauschenbusch's exposition of the Social Gospel and his advocacy of a socialist economic system. He questioned friends living across the Atlantic about socialist trends in European countries. He spoke to socialists he encountered during the course of his parish activities, read their books and articles, and was impressed by their opposition to this nation's entry into the war. Still, he came to socialism slowly and reluctantly. He was engaged in a process of reevaluating the basic principles that had ruled his life to that point.

---

1 Michael Harrington, *Socialism* (Saturday Review Press, New York, 1972) 109.
2 Norman Thomas, *We Have a Future*, 11.

Many years later, while writing his autobiography, Thomas asked himself whether he would have become a socialist had it not been for World War I. It was only after the conflict was ended that he fully realized the degree to which the war had changed his life and work. But it was not the war alone that motivated him to turn to socialism. Undoubtedly, Rauschenbusch's Christian approach to socialism also influenced him greatly, but that which moved him the most was what he daily observed in Harlem — "grotesque inequalities, conspicuous waste, gross exploitation, and unnecessary poverty." These conditions pervaded the lives of his parishioners.[1] His sense of fairness and equity demanded change, but how to effect that change was an unanswered question. While searching for answers, Thomas grew steadily more impressed with socialism's approach to the resolution of basic economic issues.

Thomas' thoughts about socialism crystallized during New York City's mayoralty campaign of 1917 when he decided to support Morris Hillquit, the Socialist Party candidate. Hillquit, born in Russia, was a brilliant lawyer active in organizing workers in the city and in promoting public housing for the poor. He also was a prominent member of the Socialist Party, and at the party's national convention held in St. Louis earlier in the year, had authored a resolution condemning the war on the ground that neither the destruction of militarism nor the promotion of democracy could be achieved by force of arms. That resolution, adopted by the convention on the day after the United States declared war on Germany, cried out that since the working class of the United States had no quarrel with the working class of Germany or that of any other country the United States should not have gone to war.

The Socialist Party resolution on the war was one that Thomas had long thought the church should have adopted. When it came to the war, Thomas was more in tune with the Socialist Party than he was with his own church. In a letter which Thomas later made public, he assured Hillquit that although he had not joined the Socialist Party, he would support him in the mayoralty campaign. He went on to state that he believed that the future lay in a new social and economic order which required the abolition of the capitalistic system:

> War itself is only the most horrible and dramatic of the many evil fruits of our present organized system of exploitation and the philosophy of life which exalts competition instead of cooperation.... I am convinced that the hope of peace lies not so much in statesmen who have already shown themselves largely bankrupt of ideas but in people of all countries who demand the cessation of war in which they pay so horrible a price.

---

1 Thomas autobiography, 68.

To vote for you is to voice that demand and to express a hope in the sort of internationalism in which alone is our confidence for the future.[1]

The letter shocked family and friend alike. Theodore Roosevelt had previously called Hillquit a traitor and "a Hun inside our gates," and one of Thomas' Princeton professors had called for his hanging. Family members and friends protested that Thomas' support for the Socialist candidate together with his advocacy of the abolition of the capitalistic system was simply unthinkable for a man in his position. One of those who protested was Thomas' mother, who was greatly concerned that her son had compromised his position in the church. In response to her criticism, Thomas wrote to her at length:

> I did not know you would be so surprised at my supporting Hillquit. I am not a member of the Socialist Party but as I have told you I agree very nearly with many of their fundamental doctrines and I have for sometime admired Mr. Hillquit personally. When you were here last summer the issues of the campaign were not yet drawn. Mr. Mitchel [the incumbent mayor] had not called every man a traitor who disagreed with [his] most violent pro-war party.... On the so-called peace issue, I do not see that Mr. Hillquit's position is treasonable. . . .

As for the church, he thought he was rendering her a high service by showing that she was sufficiently universal in nature to accept radical as well as conservative ministers. But he had no doubt that he may have undermined his future with the church:

> For myself I believe that Christian ethics are impossible in the present order of society and that every Christian must desire a new social order based on cooperation rather than competition.... I believe that no opportunity has come to me as a minister greater than that which I have because my conscience has compelled me to come out on the radical side. It means something when a Christian minister can assure an enormous audience in Madison Square Garden, as I did the other night, that he takes the stand he does because he believes in the ethics of Jesus. Whether the church will tolerate me or not is for it to say. I hope it will. If it does not it will injure herself far more than it will injure me and I say this without conceit because her attitude toward me will be symbolic of her outlook for the future. I am perfectly aware that the stand I am taking is costing me many friendships; every possible chance of getting another church if I should leave here; and perhaps, though I think not, my present position. I can only say that if it costs me more than I fear, it is to my mind the only way for I could not maintain my self-respect and do differently nor could I serve the Kingdom of God as effectively.[2]

One month after the United States entered the war, Thomas wrote in an essay entitled "The Christian Patriot" that he could not accept the position advanced by the Wilson administration that America entered the war to make the world safe for democracy:

---

1 Thomas letter, dated 10/2/17, to Morris Hillquit.
2 Thomas letter, dated 11/2/17, to his mother.

> War demands that I give my conscience . . . into the keeping of my supe-
> rior officer. It knows no crime but disobedience. It sanctions deception and
> countenances the buying of treason. It organizes all the triumphs of science
> for the killing of men. It denies to me any force in dealing with the enemy
> save death and destruction and it sends me forth to kill, not individual
> criminals, but their dupes who seek my life even as I seek theirs, for ideals
> of patriotism and liberty.[1]

In this essay, the Church's position on the war also came under Thomas'
attack. He observed that while the Church maintained that a worker who
sees his children suffering from malnutrition, because he lacks the means to
adequately feed them, may not resort to violence in order to place food on
the family dinner table. But the Church then says to the worker that in the
name of patriotism he should go forth and wage warfare, utilizing a form
of violence and destruction far surpassing any force he might have used to
obtain food for his children.[2]

Violet's grandfather, then age 95, was incensed at Thomas' stand, but
Violet stood by her husband. Thomas' brothers, on the other hand, were split
on the war. Ralph immediately enlisted in the Army and later was severely
wounded in France. Arthur also enlisted but Evan, who had a hatred for war
and violence from childhood, refused to serve in the military when drafted
and later was imprisoned as a conscientious objector.

Thomas continued to lead the Harlem parish, but his heart was no longer
in the ministry. By the end of 1917, he was acting as the part time secretary of
the Fellowship of Reconciliation, and in the beginning of 1918 he agreed to
assume the editorship of *The World Tomorrow* a Christian Socialist and pacifist
magazine. He remained active in the American Union Against Militarism
and, together with a fellow member and friend, Roger Baldwin and other of
their acquaintances, founded the Civil Liberties Bureau which later evolved
into the American Civil Liberties Union.

His friends — among them Henry Sloane Coffin — began to desert him
on the war issue, concurring with President Wilson that the war had been
unavoidable. Some Protestant ministers who had joined the Fellowship of
Reconciliation prior to the war resigned their memberships after the United
States entered the war. While the Presbyterian Church and other churches
continued their support for the war effort, Thomas remained convinced
that Christianity and war were in complete opposition. "God," he felt, "was
certainly not the 'God and Father of our Lord Jesus Christ' if his servants
could only serve Him and the cause of righteousness by the diabolic means
of war."[3]

---

1 Norman Thomas, "The Christian Patriot," reprinted in Bernard K. Johnpoll, *Norman Thomas On
  War*, (Garland, New York, 1974) 44.

2 Ibid., 50.

3 Thomas autobiography, 66.

It was the war that carried Thomas outside the Protestant creed he had known since childhood. He now expressed a belief in a Christianity that was profoundly revolutionary. Christianity should offer cooperation, not competition. It should reject worldly gain and instead plead for service to mankind. He believed that the Church and each individual Christian were required to work for a social order that rejected conditions of extreme poverty and a business ethic of unlimited profit. Unchristian conditions required a definitive plan of opposition. Because the Church had no such plan, he grew increasingly critical of its leaders, accusing them of complacently accepting the status quo by ignoring, if not implicitly accepting, conditions that violently twisted the lives of men, women and their children living in his parish and throughout the country.

Thomas' work in Harlem was financed by the Home Missions Committee of the New York Presbytery as well as through private contributions, some of them obtained through Thomas' efforts. His stand on the war and his criticism of the Church now threatened that financing. The chairman of the Home Missions Committee — Dr. William Adams Brown, one of Thomas' teachers at Union Theological Seminary and a friend as well — summoned Thomas after he announced his support for Hillquit's candidacy for mayor. Brown asked Thomas to withdraw his support. It was bad enough, Brown argued, that Thomas was a pacifist and almost a socialist, but his public opposition to the incumbent mayor — the reform candidate, no less — was too much. Thomas' positions were causing financial strain on the Committee. He hinted at Thomas' resignation without demanding it.[1]

Thomas was aware that private contributions were falling off. One of Harlem's local merchants who each Christmas had contributed toys and dolls to Thomas' church announced that he would contribute no more as long as Thomas continued as pastor. Although many of Thomas' parishioners were friendly to his views, the merchant's stand was typical of those whose contributions financed activities in support of the parish's poor.

At the age of 33, after twelve years of service to the Church, Thomas resigned his position at the Harlem church. When he wrote to his mother, after announcing his support of Hillquit, he had predicted that the stand he was then taking would not cost him his position at the Harlem church but that it would probably bar any further church assignments. He was wrong with regard to the first prediction but right with regard to the second. His resignation was accepted by Dr. Brown and no discussion ensued regarding another assignment.

Thomas also felt compelled to withdraw his membership in several other organizations, including clubs and other groups with which he was associ-

---

1 Ibid., 69-70.

ated as a Princeton alumnus. He resigned from the local school board and gave up a part-time teaching position he held at Columbia University. This sudden break with friends and a way of life — conventional by accepted standards — was a cause of considerable shock and strain both for himself and for Violet. That the tension was not greater, Thomas attributed to the closeness of new friendships formed, a confidence that the future would bring better times, and above all, Violet's acceptance, taking in stride all that befell her and her family.[1]

One further step was necessary in order to effect a complete break with the past. When Thomas wrote to his mother in November 1917, he informed her that he was not yet a member of the Socialist Party, but that he was in agreement with many of its fundamental doctrines. Every Christian, he declared, "must desire a new social order based on cooperation rather than competition," and this is also the hope of the Socialist Party.[2] Now, a year later, Thomas joined the Socialist Party.

In applying for membership he made it clear that his participation in the party was not to be of the orthodox variety. He was joining the party because "these are the days when radicals ought to stand up and be counted." He advised party officials that he believed "in the necessity of establishing a cooperative commonwealth and in the abolition of our present unjust economic institutions and class distinctions," but that he had a "profound fear of the undue exaltation of the State.... The new world we desire must depend upon freedom and fellowship rather than upon any sort of coercion...." He made certain that they understood that his interest in Socialist Party principles extended only to those which were serviceable in gaining liberty for all men and women. Finally, although he accepted the general principles of the party's platform, he made it clear that he did not agree with all of its details.[3]

The Socialist Party accepted his conditions for joining and he became a member, as did Violet, the granddaughter of the founder and former President and Chairman of the Board of Trustees of the United States Trust Company.

---

1 Ibid., 72.
2 Thomas letter, dated 11/2/17, to his mother.
3 Thomas letter, dated 10/18/18, to Alexander Trachtenberg.

Chapter 4. Civil Liberties in Time of War

Little that occurred in Thomas' early life suggested that his political thinking would later turn radical. His father-inherited Republicanism meshed well with the political affiliations of his Princeton classmates, and at his graduation in 1905 his political orientation remained basically conservative. In the 1908 presidential election, he voted for the Republican William Howard Taft, and the following year he campaigned for the Republican candidate in the New York City mayoralty contest. At the time, he described his political views as "progressive," by which he meant he believed in the inevitability of human progress. He registered Bull Moose Progressive four years later and voted for Theodore Roosevelt, the first sign of a more liberal political bent. In 1916, he voted for Woodrow Wilson, the Democratic Party candidate for president, but only because he believed Wilson was more likely to keep the country out of the war than Charles Evans Hughes, the nominee of the Republican Party. Two years later when he announced that he had joined the Socialist Party, his family and friends were stunned, finding it nearly impossible to believe that he had made such a dramatic turn, shifting from a conventional to a radical political perspective.

The Socialist Party that Thomas joined in 1918 had failed to gain the appeal among Americans that Socialist parties had achieved in Europe. Thomas attributed this failing to two factors. Class consciousness — the foundation of all Socialist thinking at the time — was never as dominant a factor in the United States as it was in Europe. Living in a country with an over abundance of land, Americans were free of the control of a landed aristocracy, and this freedom tended to inhibit the development of an identification with any particular class of people. Secondly, immigrants to this country found it far easier as individuals to rise above the level of economic deprivation than to actively participate as members of a group in programs designed to improve economic conditions for the general population.[1]

The American Socialist Party had been organized in 1901 following a merger of Eugene Debs' Social Democratic Party with a wing of the older Socialist Labor Party led by Daniel DeLeon, once a lecturer in international law at Columbia University. From its inception, the party was an ecumenical organization of Marxist and Christian Socialist radicals. It advocated — to some extent inconsistently — the reform of the existing capitalist economy in the near term and revolutionary economic change, highlighted by the replacement of capitalism with socialism, in the not too far distant future.

The Party grew steadily, its membership increasing from less than 10,000 in 1901 to nearly 120,000 ten years later. In 1910, seventy-three socialist mayors were elected around the country, and for the first time voters selected a Socialist Party member to serve in Congress. In the 1912 presidential election, Socialist Party candidate Eugene Debs received just under 900,000 votes, representing 6 percent of the nation's total vote. In that year, more than one thousand members of the party served as public office holders. By that time, the Socialist press had increased to thirteen daily and nearly three-hundred weekly papers. Some writers portrayed this growth as the rising tide of socialism.[2]

Early in World War I, most Americans agreed that the United States should make every effort to remain clear of the conflict, but by 1915 they tended to favor undertaking measures to prepare for war. Socialists, on the other hand, rejected any measures intended to prepare the country for war as acts that would make war more likely. The Hillquit resolution adopted at the Socialist Party's St. Louis convention in 1917 urged people to demonstrate against the war, conscription, and military training, and called for the formation of a new society in which peace and fraternity would be its dominant ideals. The Hillquit resolution alienated many in the Party — Jack London and Upton Sinclair among them — and exacerbated anti-Socialist feeling. Nevertheless, the party still fared well at the polls. Hillquit, as candidate for New York City mayor in 1917, received 22 percent of the vote, five times the normal Socialist vote in the city to that time. Ten Socialists were elected to the New York State Legislature that year, and enormous gains in the vote were achieved in cities such as Chicago and Buffalo. Such was the status of the party when Thomas' name was added to its membership rolls.

---

1 Norman Thomas, *Socialism Re-examined* (Greenwood, Westport, Conn., 1963; reprinted, 1984) 115.
2 Richard Hofstadter, *The Age of Reform* (Vintage, New York, 1955) fn. 240-241.

Thomas, "in a vague sort of way," expected to return to the ministry once the war ended.[1] But he had lost favor with church leaders, having condemned them for failing to oppose the war and for abandoning fundamental Christian beliefs and principles. Contrary to his views on the church and its leaders, he perceived socialism as having remained true to its basic tenets in opposing the war. Socialism, rather than religion, thus became a more relevant factor in his life, and he turned from religious to economic and political solutions to the problems plaguing society's poor and oppressed. Economic and political issues also soon dominated his work with the Fellowship of Reconciliation and his editorship of its publication, *The World Tomorrow*. This change in direction proved fortunate for him, since for many years after the war, church leaders assiduously avoided him, thus barring his return to the ministry even if he had expressed a desire in resuming the life of a clergyman.

Socialism's primary goals, as Thomas then perceived them, included the end of economic exploitation, the establishment of justice, and the conquest of poverty. He viewed the economic order in which socialism arose and against which it struggled as totally dominated by capitalism. He maintained that throughout the world, the ascendancy of capitalism had been achieved, at least in part, through the grievous exploitation of the worker. Thus the capitalistic system carried within itself the seeds of opposition and revolution, and socialism was the principal expression of that opposition and revolution.[2] As Thomas noted, "The typical Socialist never dreamed of doubting the capacity of men freed from ancient tyrannies to triumph easily once and for all over poverty and injustice."[3]

In later years as a public figure, Thomas was primarily recognized and identified as a Socialist. His acceptance of Socialist premises, however, did not constitute the bedrock of his life-guiding principles. Late in his life he wrote that "work in a miserably poor tenement region of New York and the coming of World War I made me an ardent civil libertarian before it made me a Socialist."[4] He was first and foremost a humanitarian, perceiving socialism as the best available means of achieving the goals, as he perceived them, of eliminating the existing state of economic misery endured by the poor and the oppressed. His intensely activist humanitarianism required an institutional means of attaining his goals, and socialism was the vehicle that afforded him that means. The type of life he chose to lead at the Spring Street Church and Settlement House and in his East Harlem parish — devoting his entire being to altering the course of the misery that the poor and disenfranchised appeared destined to suffer — was a precursor of the type of life he

---

1 Thomas autobiography, 76-77.
2 Norman Thomas, *A Socialist's Faith* (W.W. Norton, New York, 1951), 22-23.
3 Ibid., 14.
4 Norman Thomas, *The Test of Freedom* (W.W. Norton, New York, 1954), 16.

would lead once he had chosen to become a Socialist and had entered public life.

After leaving the East Harlem parish, Thomas devoted most of his time to the Fellowship of Reconciliation and his editorship of *The World Tomorrow*. Under his leadership and that of Devere Allen, a colleague and friend, the magazine flourished, becoming a leading journal of liberal Christianity and Christian-motivated political radicalism.[1]

Along with his new work at the Fellowship of Reconciliation, Thomas confronted a family matter of consuming importance — the imprisonment of his brother Evan as a war time conscientious objector. Following in Norman's footsteps, Evan had attended Princeton with the intention of later preparing for the ministry, but soon after graduating he decided against living the life of a clergyman. Early in the war he traveled to Britain to evaluate the treatment of captive German soldiers. Returning to this country in 1917, he registered for the draft and later reported, as directed, to Camp Upton in New York. At that point, as a matter of conscience, he rejected all military orders and refused to undergo training for combat. War Department policy at the time was to offer noncombatant service to those who honestly objected to the taking of human life in war. When Evan rejected noncombatant service as an alternative form of service, he was placed under arrest, and the Army sent him along with other conscientious objectors to Fort Riley, Kansas. Since conscientious objectors were commonly looked upon as either cowards or slackers, they often were treated like criminals, and that is precisely what Evan confronted at Fort Riley.

Out of a draft army of 3,000,000, fewer than 4,000 claimed conscientious objector status. Most of the objectors were willing to accept noncombatant service, but a small minority rejected any form of service.[2] Evan was one of the latter — an "absolutist objector" — refusing any work required to be performed in response to a military command, even work having no connection with the war effort. As an absolutist objector, Evan adopted an uncompromising stand based on his belief that the performance of any function in the military amounted to approval and confirmation of the war's validity.

Conscientious objectors were often subjected to abuse. Long periods of manacling and solitary confinement were common. In protest of these practices, Evan entered upon a hunger strike. Army officials looked upon Evan as a leader of the conscientious objectors, and when he was convicted of refusing to obey the lawful order of a superior officer, he was sentenced to life imprisonment at hard labor. The authorities, as an "act of mercy," later

---

1 David A. Shannon, *The Socialist Party of America* (Quadrangle, Chicago, 1967), 191; originally published by Macmillan, New York, 1955.
2 Norman Thomas, *War: No Glory, No Profit, No Need* (Frederick A Stokes, New York, 1935), 51.

reduced his sentence to twenty-five years and sent him to Fort Leavenworth to serve his time.

At Leavenworth, Evan met a group of Molokans, an obscure Russian religious and pacifist sect whose members refused to obey military orders. Because their religion provided that they could not obey a military order under any circumstances, they refused to engage in any work in the prison since it was operated under military orders. As punishment for their refusal to work, the Molokans were held in solitary cells, manacled for the better part of the day and otherwise abused and subjected to the type of treatment often meted out to Quakers, Mennonites, and other religious groups.

The Molokans soon found themselves in even more desperate circumstances. Due to their religious scruples they rejected much of the prison food placed before them since it was not prepared according to their religious requirements. They spoke little English, had no one to plead their cause, and did not possess the means of communicating with the outside world. Other conscientious objectors, learning of their plight, drew up a formal complaint to the War Department, but prison officials refused to allow them to mail it. Evan then embraced the Molokans' cause, notifying the prison commandant that just as he had previously refused to obey any military commands he would now also refuse to obey all prison directives. Prison officials ordered that Evan be placed in solitary confinement.[1]

Evan managed to send a letter "underground" through the prison system to Norman, who released the letter to the press, thus disclosing to the public that these men, whose only offense was loyalty to conscience, were being held in dark cells, manacled nine hours a day in a standing position, and forbidden to read, write, or even speak. Responding to Thomas' pleas, newspapers including the *New York World* sent reporters to Leavenworth, and they verified Thomas' charges that imprisoned conscientious objectors were being treated cruelly. The newspaper then took up the cause of the Molokans and the other objectors and sought a general amnesty for them. Not long after, President Wilson ordered the Secretary of War to eliminate the most egregious practices used against conscientious objectors, and early in 1919, a Board of Inquiry ordered the release of the objectors imprisoned at Leavenworth.

Thomas did not dispute the commonly held view that the conscientious objector at times acted out of error, but he insisted that in a democracy each person had the right to decide for himself or herself what is morally right or morally wrong. Because he honored all men who stood firmly by their principles, he respected the stand of the conscientious objectors. He supported those who responded to pacifist principles, such as his brother Evan, and

---

1 Ibid., 50-55.

those who acted out of religious convictions, such as the Molokans, Mennonites, and Quakers, but also those who were motivated by less lofty reasons, as long as the objector acted on principle. His brother's suffering at the hands of governmental authorities undoubtedly deepened the intensity of his feeling for the conscientious objectors, and he was sufficiently moved to address in a public forum the basic issues underlying the positions they adopted.

Early in the war, in an article written for *The Nation* magazine, Thomas reminded Christians that in the history of the Church there had been those "whose consciences have made them believe that participation in war, even for a just end, was a denial of the Christ whom they were trying to follow."Although most Christians might think such believers to be wrong, individual consciences cannot be coerced in such a vital matter. "If conscientious objectors are wrong, a Christian must trust to the power of reason under God to set them right."[1] Later, as the war was nearing its end, Thomas again wrote for *The Nation* pleading for the pardon of those objectors still imprisoned.[2]

With the end of the war, Thomas hoped the church authorities would back his support of the conscientious objectors, but he was sorely disappointed as he received no help from that quarter. He later wrote:

> Conscription made the question raised by the war . . . even more acute. "Render unto Caesar the things that are Caesar's" was a popular text for justifying the Christian's obedience to the draft. But unfortunately there was an awkward second clause to Jesus' saying: "and unto God the things that are Gods." What is God's if not conscience and the direction of a man's life?[3]

Thomas charged the churches with beating the drums outside the recruiting office, preaching war and hatred of the Germans, all in the name of Jesus — a pacifist and a lover of all men, including the Germans.[4]

Although military and prison authorities committed grievous wrongs against conscientious objectors, Thomas felt that the Church, because of its Christian tradition of extending mercy to the oppressed, committed the greater crime by not speaking out in their behalf. He found it especially ironic that members of the clergy who refused to grant a conscientious objector the right to exercise his freedom of conscience were those who, without protest, accepted their own exemption from military service as ministers.[5] "If the state did not prove itself the exemplar of what many had thought were

---

1 Norman Thomas, "Conscience and the Church," *The Nation*, 8/23/17, 198.
2 Norman Thomas, "Justice to War's Heretics," *The Nation*, 11/9/18, 547.
3 Norman Thomas, *The Conscientious Objector in America* (B.W. Huebsch, New York, 1923), 11; later reissued under the title, *Is Conscience a Crime?* (Vanguard, New York, 1927).
4 Ibid., 273.
5 Ibid., 266-267.

American traditions of liberty of conscience, the Church did worse."[1] Thomas never forgave the Church for its refusal to support freedom of conscience in time of war.

Despite the absence of church backing, the conscientious objectors, in Thomas' mind, achieved a great victory:

> This insignificant fraction of the youth of America challenged the power of the state when it was mightiest and the philosophy of war when it was most pervasive. They said, "You may kill us but you can't make us fight against our will." They said it not as men who court martyrdom but as men who serve principle; not as those who despised the state but as those who refused to make it God. If enough of them had said that thing in every land there would have been no war.... [2]

Two years after the end of the war, after the last of the imprisoned objectors had been released, Thomas remained convinced that the very fact that the government had been forced to deal with these men created a significant precedent, and he hoped that the memory of their defiance would help the masses to break the spell of blind obedience to "the homicidal mania men call patriotism."[3]

The intensity of his feeling did not soon fade. Five years after the war, in his book *The Conscientious Objector in America*,[4] he dedicated its pages to "the brave who went for conscience's sake to trench or to prison." Setting forth in vivid detail the prison experiences of the objectors and the brutalities they suffered, Thomas again argued why conscientious objection matters:

> Men's affairs are in sorry plight if it serves society to compel the individual to be true to his fellows by being untrue to himself. In a world where conformity is easy and independent thinking is hard, where . . . heresy has always been the growing point of society; where governments of all sorts are often stupid and cruel, reasonable men are constrained to do some fresh thinking on the duty of civil disobedience."[5]

This theme underlies every aspect of Thomas' public life. Viewing himself a political heretic, he lived his life according to principles he derived or verified through his own thought. Throughout his life, he was constrained to rethink the underlying premises of a multitude of issues that commanded his attention.

While his brother Evan confronted governmental intervention in his life, Thomas was experiencing his own problems with governmental authorities. With the end of the war, nonconformist and radical publications such as *The World Tomorrow* fell under the increasingly sharp scrutiny of the US government. During the war, President Wilson expressed little patience with any

---

1 Ibid., 273.
2 Ibid., 284-285.
3 Ibid., 285.
4 Ibid.
5 Ibid., 9.

dissent. Shortly after the war began, Congress enacted the Espionage Act of 1917 that made it a crime for a person to interfere with or obstruct the draft or enlistments to the military forces, and it also granted the federal government the power to censor newspapers by banning them from the mails. Although the statute was not directed specifically at dissenters of administration policies, aggressive federal prosecutors undertook to attack every left-of-center utterance they came across. Attorney General Thomas Gregory expressed the opinion that 95 percent of the men in the country would die willingly for their country, but he warned the remaining five percent that the courts would act against any manifestation of disloyalty. "And may God have mercy on them, for they need expect none from an outraged people and an avenging government."[1] Apparently, for the Attorney General and other members of the Wilson administration, and for a majority of the members of Congress as well, dissent was a form of disloyalty. Less than a year after adopting the Espionage Act of 1917, Congress enacted the Sedition Act of 1918 which declared it unlawful for any person to publish any disloyal language intended to cause contempt or scorn for the government.

Eugene Debs, the Socialist Party's candidate for president in four previous elections, was indicted under the Espionage Act after he encouraged party members attending the 1918 convention of the Ohio State Socialist Party to obstruct the recruiting processes of the military services Actually what Debs said on that occasion he had said often before. He noted that the master class had always declared the wars, while the working class had always fought the battles, that the master class had all to gain and nothing to lose, while the working class had nothing to gain and all to lose — including their lives. The court determined that the natural effect of this language was to inhibit recruiting for the military services, an act in violation of the Espionage Act. Debs was convicted and sentenced to ten years' imprisonment.[2]

The Supreme Court followed the mood of the country. Jacob Abrams, a severe critic of Woodrow Wilson, printed and distributed a leaflet opposing Wilson's decision to send a military force to Russia during the civil war that followed the 1917 Communist revolution. The leaflet urged workers to leave their jobs in protest of Wilson's action. Abrams was arrested and indicted for violating both the Espionage and Sedition Acts. In affirming his conviction, the Supreme Court upheld the constitutionality of both Acts, ruling that though these statutes limited freedom of expression, they were necessary to protect national security in time of war. The court made it clear that those who spoke or wrote in opposition to the war could be prosecuted and imprisoned.[3]

---

1 *The New York Times*, 11/21/17, 3.
2 *Debs v. United States*, 249 U.S. 211 (1919).
3 *Abrams v. United States*, 250 U.S. 616 (1919).

Politicians and business leaders pressured the government to use the Espionage and Sedition Acts to repress labor unions and radicals, and subsequent prosecutions under the Acts specifically targeted Socialists and pacifists, triggering wholesale violations of their civil rights. The presence of uninvited government agents became a common occurrence at Socialist Party meetings and gatherings of the Fellowship of Reconciliation. Government agents considered Thomas dangerous and placed him under surveillance and tapped his telephone line. Thomas fought back. To thwart agents from making an intelligible record of his speeches (in an era before the arrival of recording devices) he learned to speak rapidly, a talent he employed throughout his life.

Postmaster General Albert S. Burleson proceeded to ban the *Milwaukee Leader* and other Socialist publications from the US mails, and then turned his attention to *The World Tomorrow*. The New York postal authorities considered Thomas' publication to be subversive, and for three months in the summer of 1918 they excluded it from the mails. They found several articles objectionable, including one written by Thomas where he, as did Jacob Abrams before him, protested American intervention in the emerging Soviet Union. In another issue, the well known and well respected Rev. John Haynes Holmes, in an article entitled "The Search — a Parable," sought to discover where Hatred resided. He described how he had searched for Hatred in many places, in the trenches, in the military hospitals, and at Army headquarters, but all in vain for it did not reside in any of those places. He continued his search and ultimately discovered Hatred residing in a beautiful garden, frequented by an elderly man and woman and a clergyman. Apparently, post office authorities considered Haynes' contention that Hatred dwelled among elderly and religious noncombatants, but not in the minds of the country's military, to be subversive.

Thomas complained about the post office ban of *The World Tomorrow* to Postmaster General Burleson who, as Thomas explained in another context, did not know "socialism from rheumatism."[1] Burleson told Thomas he held him to be more insidious than Debs, that he would not only continue the ban on *The World Tomorrow*, but would send Thomas to jail as well.[2] Thomas left Burleson's office in a rage. How could the Postmaster General presume to judge what was proper for citizens to read, even in war time?

> I am especially concerned because in this war for democracy, autocracy is growing so fast. I do not believe that democracy is a garment that can be taken off and put in moth balls for future use or that you can secure democratic ends by Prussian methods of which the latest example is the

---

1 Thomas autobiography, 73.
2 Ibid.

legislation which makes the Postmaster General judge of what the American people shall read.[1]

Undoubtedly the post office ban would have continued, and perhaps Thomas would have gone to jail, had it not been for one of Thomas' associates at the Fellowship of Reconciliation. John Nevin Sayre, brother to the husband of President Wilson's daughter, visited the White House and informed Wilson that Burleson was harassing Thomas and was inhibiting the distribution of his publication. Although Wilson was critical of the tenor of the articles published by Thomas, he instructed Burleson to remove the ban. He also told Sayre to inform Thomas that one could be guilty of an "indecent display of private opinions in public."[2] If this was meant as a threat, Thomas ignored it. Undeterred, he continued to produce provocative reading in *The World Tomorrow*.

The end of the war did not bring an end to civil rights violations. Rather, the attacks only intensified. A story that was circulated at the time — a tale Thomas believed to be true but was never able to verify — told of a man who publicly questioned the wisdom of the war. Eventually he was arrested by a local police officer who found in the man's pocket a document which the arresting officer instantly recognized as seditious. It spoke of self-evident truths about life, liberty, and the pursuit of happiness. "Now, I've got you," he exclaimed to his victim. "But I didn't write it," was the arrested man's response. "Who did?" asked the police officer. "A man named Tom Jefferson," the man answered." "Lead me to him," said the constable, "I'll take you both in."[3]

Apocryphal or not, the story well illustrated the tenor of the times. Massive violations of civil rights and attacks against dissidents of all sorts commonly occurred. Socialist Party meetings were disrupted across the country. A candidate for governor of Minnesota was so harried at his political rallies by state authorities that he conducted meetings of his supporters across the border in Iowa. Six Texans were beaten because they failed to subscribe to the Red Cross. A Socialist received a ten-year sentence for writing to a Kansas City newspaper condemning war profiteering. A Protestant minister in Ohio was kidnapped and horsewhipped because he spoke against those who expressed hatred of the Germans. An organizer for an antiwar group in Montana was lynched. In Hartford, Connecticut, where a group of suspected Communists was held in jail, those who visited them were also locked

1 Thomas letter, dated 10/2/17, to Morris Hillquit.
2 Thomas autobiography, 73.
3 Norman Thomas, *War: No Glory, No Profit, No Need*, 47.

up on the theory that only one who was a Communist would visit another Communist.[1]

Early in 1919, a Senate committee investigating pro-German propaganda in this country issued a *Who's Who in Pacifism and Radicalism*, a list of persons who allegedly were active in movements that failed to help in the war against Germany. The list of sixty-two men and women included such notables as Socialist Eugene Debs; Oswald Garrison Villard, publisher of *The Nation*; Harry Overstreet, a prominent psychologist at City College; Rufus M. Jones, leader of the Quakers; historian and former Columbia University professor Charles A. Beard; ACLU president, Roger Baldwin; Jane Addams, head of the Woman's Peace Party; Scott Nearing, a former Wharton School Professor of Economics; Jacob Panken, Judge of the New York City Municipal Court; Frances Kuno, former Harvard professor; Rabbi Judah L. Magnes; Rev. John Haynes Holmes; and Norman Thomas.[2] Although they were not accused of violating the law, the conclusion intended to be drawn from the publication of this list was clear — these people were disloyal. Thomas was considered so dangerous that for some time secret service agents followed him in the streets of New York.

A few months later, when *The New York Call*, a Socialist Party daily newspaper, invited guests to view its new headquarters, more than a hundred men in soldier and sailor uniforms brandishing clubs and sticks broke into the building, beat up staff members, injured several of those present, and halted the festivities.[3] The same mob then raided the Rand School, a Socialist adult education institution. The previous evening, a much larger mob had tried to break up a union meeting at Madison Square Garden.[4] Those involved in civil rights violations such as these were not punished and similar incidents continued with increasing frequency.

This time of suppression of civil liberties, often referred to as the "Red Scare" period, reached its apex when J. Mitchell Palmer, US Attorney General from 1919 to 1921, relied upon the Espionage and Sedition Acts to support the arrest and detention of political radicals, dissidents, anarchists, Communists, and aliens. Under Palmer's direction, in what became known as "Palmer Raids," Secret Service agents rounded up thousands of persons suspected of subversive activities, and in the process committed what has been called the worst violations of civil rights in American history.[5]

---

1 These events were reported in W. A. Swanberg, *Norman Thomas: The Last Idealist* (Charles Scribner's Sons, New York, 1976), 65.

2 *The New York Times*, 1/25/19, 1;

3 Ibid., 5/3/19, 3.

4 Ibid., 5/2/19, 1.

5 Samuel Walker, *In Defense of American Liberties: A History of the ACLU* (Southern Illinois University Press, Carbondale, Ill., 1999), 43.

The first raid occurred in November 1919 when Justice Department agents attacked the offices of the Union of Russian Workers in twelve cities and beat up and arrested 250 union members, many of whom were later deported. At the end of 1919, Palmer announced that during the coming year he would act against the leaders of organizations advocating radical proposals, and he urged the press, the churches, the schools, labor unions, and patriotic organizations to resolve to study, understand, and appreciate the "Red" movement in the country.[1] Two days later the Justice Department conducted a series of raids in thirty-three cities, arresting more than two thousand suspected radicals. During these raids, government agents committed broad-scale violations of law, including illegal searches, arrests without warrants, physical brutality, and unnecessary destruction of property.

In January 1920, *The New York Times* published an article entitled "Socialism as an Alien Enemy," purportedly written by a "Government Agent," who was not identified. The author wrote that the Socialist of the day had forgotten what it felt like to be an American because his head was full of Bolshevism. The author could remember days in the past when a person could consider becoming a Socialist "without first wiping his feet on America." He applauded recent instances where members of the American Legion had intervened to prevent Socialists from speaking at public forums. "Americans, in a new mood of their own, which the Socialists do not comprehend at all, are not only no longer good-naturedly tolerant of them, we are perfectly ready to face the drastic step of denying them any hearing at all." [2]

As the Palmer raids continued, socialism was clearly placed on the defensive. The New York Legislature voted to suspend five recently elected Socialist Assemblymen on the ground they were disloyal. The five were later placed on trial and Thomas testified as an expert witness on the relationship between socialism and religion. This was not a matter in contention within party ranks, since from its earliest days religion was considered solely a private concern. But the religious views of the five Socialists on trial grew to be matters of great interest for those who would ban them from the legislature, for apparently these legislators believed that all Socialists were anti-religious. Reflecting the political climate of the times, the five Socialists were ordered expelled from the Legislature.[3]

Socialists and radical groups were not the only objects of right-wing oppressive attacks. Liberals such as John Dewey and Felix Frankfurter came under suspicion. The Daughters of the American Revolution labeled *The Nation* magazine "subversive." Labor unions were prime targets of abuse. But the Red Scare hysteria failed to deter Thomas, especially when it came to

---

1 *The New York Times*, 1/1/20, 17, and 1/5/20, 1
2 Ibid., 1/11/20, 43.
3 Ibid., 1/11/20, 1.

preserving the right of free speech. When the mayors and other civic authorities of several New York and Connecticut towns adopted ordinances authorizing them to refuse to grant Socialists and other radical groups permits to hold public meetings on the streets of their communities, Thomas decided to test the validity of the ordinances. Along with Rev. John Haynes Holmes and a union organizer, Thomas advised the mayor of Mount Vernon, New York, that without the benefit of a permit the three would conduct a street meeting in that town, and they provided the mayor with the date, time and location of the planned meeting. On the designated day, the three arrived in Mount Vernon, where a group of residents had assembled on the main street to listen to their speeches. Holmes stood up and started to read from the US Constitution, but he was immediately arrested and taken off to the police station. Thomas followed by reading from the New York State Constitution, and he and the union representative also were arrested and carted off. On the following day, a Mount Vernon judge convicted all three of violating a town ordinance and ordered that they be fined. A higher court later reversed their convictions and Mount Vernon was thereafter open to speakers of all political types.

Within two weeks of the massive January 1920 Palmer raid, at a time when the concept of free speech was in total retreat, Thomas, along with Roger Baldwin and others, formed The American Civil Liberties Union. The ACLU was an outgrowth of the National Civil Liberties Bureau — also formed under the leadership of Thomas and Baldwin — created in 1917 to oppose governmental and super-patriot suppression of free speech, free press, free assembly, and liberty of conscience, and to act as a clearing house for complaints of injustice. Thomas later wrote that "We of the Bureau ... suffered at the strong hand of the state, but we were able to render some service as time went on to the thousands of victims of ... Palmer's obscene anti-red raids."[1] The ACLU immediately entered the fray and ever since has been involved in the preservation of individual constitutional rights.

At the end of 1920, Congress repealed the Sedition Act of 1918, and the government began to release from prison every person convicted under that Act and under the provisions of the Espionage Act of 1917. This would not be the last time, however, that Americans would experience wartime hatred and hysteria, leading to character assassination, suppression of genuine debate of public issues, and the curtailment of civil liberties in general. Thomas would appear in the midst of those battles time and again.

---

1 Norman Thomas, *The Test of Freedom*, 17-18.

Chapter 5. Running for Elective Office

The Bolshevik revolution in Russia threatened to destroy the Socialist movement in the United States. Led by Lenin, the Bolsheviks created an authoritarian dictatorship in Russia and proclaimed a Twenty-One Point program establishing the terms of affiliation of Communist parties throughout the world. All Communist parties were to be organized along rigidly centralized lines, controlled by an iron discipline established in Moscow. Communists were to disavow all forms of reformism, and Socialist democratic leaders of the past, such as Morris Hillquit of New York, were to be denounced as traitors.

Eugene Debs characterized the Twenty-One Points as a "policy of armed insurrection," dismissing it as "ridiculous, arbitrary, and autocratic."[1] Thomas agreed. He found particularly abhorrent Lenin's demand for absolute control of all Socialist parties. But this did not deter American Communists. They attacked Socialists and members of other left-wing political parties, viewing them as rivals and as greater threats to communism than Europe's rapidly growing Fascist parties. In 1919, the Communists in the United States abandoned the Socialist Party ranks and formed their own party, and the Socialist and Communist Parties from that point onward were the bitterest of enemies. In the public's eye, however, they were not always considered as separate political movements, and Thomas often found himself rebutting the charge that socialism and communism were of the same mold. As Thomas specified in his application for membership in the Socialist Party, he was not a Marxist:

---

1 Quoted in James Oneal and G.A. Werner, *American Communism: A Critical Analysis of its Origins, Development and Program* (Greenwood, Westport, Conn., 1947), 98.

> Perhaps to certain members of the party my socialism would not be of the most orthodox variety.... I have a profound fear of the undue exaltation of the State and a profound faith that the new world we desire must depend upon freedom and fellowship rather than any sort of coercion whatsoever. I am interested in political parties only to the extent in which they may be serviceable in advancing certain ideals and in winning liberty for men and women.[1]

Thomas' rejection of "any sort of coercion whatsoever" made it impossible for him to accept the Bolshevik concept of Soviet control and dominance. Moreover, the Twenty-One Points only increased his "profound fear of the undue exaltation of the State." He agreed with the Bolshevik call for "the democratization of industry," but fervently opposed Communist rejection of programs involving the concept of civil liberties. When Thomas insisted upon designating the American Socialist movement as "Democratic Socialism" the Communists ridiculed him and poured contempt on his absolute opposition to the use of violence in attaining socialistic goals. Moreover, they derided his reliance on constitutional change, rather than violent revolution, to effect the replacement of capitalism with socialism. Thomas and the Communists remained enemies for the rest of his life.

As the 1920 presidential campaign approached, Eugene Debs still languished in a federal prison in Atlanta. Debs had run as the Socialist Party candidate for president in four of the previous five presidential elections and remained very popular within party ranks. Socialist Party leaders decided that his incarceration was not reason enough to bar him from another run for the presidency, and they nominated him once again.

American Socialists held Debs in the highest regard, some elevating him to a status bordering on sainthood. In his youth, Debs had worked in the Indiana railway yards as a locomotive fireman and helped organize the American Railway Union, subsequently serving as its president. Viewing the labor movement as a struggle between classes, Debs converted to socialism. In 1900, the Socialist Party nominated him as its first candidate for president. Morris Hillquit, who knew Debs well, described him as a man of striking appearance. "Tall and lanky, with an air of infinite kindness shining through his limpid gray eyes and emanating from his whole being, he immediately attracted and fascinated."[2] He hated all forms of injustice and oppression. He was neither an intellectual nor an effective politician, but his personal warmth and sincerity, coupled with an uncompromising sense of integrity, won him the support of Socialist stalwarts as their presidential candidate.

Debs, however, was not without his detractors. Many objected to his participation in the 1920 electoral process as a convicted felon, especially since he still resided behind prison bars. Editorial writers of *The New York*

---

1 Thomas letter, dated 10/18/18, to Alexander Trachtenberg.
2 Morris Hillquit, *Loose Leaves from a Busy Life* (Macmillan, New York, 1934), 48.

Times, greatly dismayed by photographs of Debs dressed in prison garb as he accepted the Socialist Party nomination, called his candidacy "an outrage against the nation and against its heroic defenders."[1] Thomas did not feel that outrage. He campaigned extensively for Debs, despite the presence on the Republican Party ticket of his former fellow Marion, Ohio townsman, Warren G. Harding. On election day, Debs polled 3.5 percent of the total votes cast, considerably less than the 6 percent he received in 1912.

After the election, Thomas set out to obtain Debs' release from prison, asking the newly-elected Warren Harding to grant Debs a pardon. Harding was always cordial to Thomas — after all, he was a hometown boy and once worked for him. On one of Thomas' visits to the White House, Harding pointed to a huge pile of folders on the desk before him. "They're all pardon cases and no part of my work so troubles me. Only this morning I pardoned an old German-American, a victim of spite of some relatives, no more disloyal than old Fritz — you remember him, Norman, in Marion?"[2] Thomas used Harding's nostalgia for his Ohio hometown — and any other argument he could muster — to convince Harding to release Debs. Some months later, when Harding saw that it was then to his political advantage to free Debs, he ordered his release.

As the focus of Thomas' interests shifted in the direction of economic and political issues, he became less comfortable with his leadership role in the Fellowship of Reconciliation and his editorship of *The World Tomorrow*. Toward the end of 1921, he concluded that a person with a stronger Christian orientation than his should replace him in those positions. He had not abandoned Christianity, but his religious beliefs had grown increasingly inharmonious with the articles of faith of the magazine's readers. Therefore, he resigned both positions and joined the staff of *The Nation* magazine as an associate editor, a position he held for about a year before joining the League for Industrial Democracy as co-executive director.

The League was an outgrowth of the Intercollegiate Socialist Society, formed in 1905 to promote interest in socialism among college students and other educated men and women. Its first president was the author Jack London and its initial membership included Clarence Darrow and Upton Sinclair and it later added Heywood Broun and Walter Lippmann. Thomas joined the Society in 1914 and was active in promoting its goals, speaking at colleges and universities whenever his schedule permitted. In 1921, the Society was renamed the League for Industrial Democracy and its focus was redirected from college campuses to the general public. When in 1922 Thomas agreed to join the League with Harry Laidler as co-executive directors, it

1 *The New York Times*, 6/12/20, 14.
2 Thomas autobiography, 78-79.

marked the beginning of a long association of the two men in many activities and projects involving the Socialist movement.

Thomas often referred to his marriage as the greatest success of his life. Family members and friends agreed, always describing the marriage in idealistic terms. He was grateful for Violet's devotion to him and thankful that she shared his basic beliefs. She loved him deeply and was unquestioningly loyal to him, freely adjusting her life to accommodate his. Thomas lived by a strict moral code and expected the same of his children. Whether they should follow him on the road to socialism was another matter. He refrained from preaching socialism to them, determining early in their lives not to pressure them to adopt the causes that were to become so great a part of his own life. He recognized that a parent's appeal to affection as a guide to important decisions is difficult for young children to resist. Thus, he resolved to preserve their freedom by forbearing from influencing their political views. Later in life, he wondered whether he had succeeded too well.[1]

Though Thomas was frequently absent from the home, each of his children had a close relationship with him. They were aware that some people considered him as something of a pariah and by others as a dangerous revolutionary, but that knowledge did not undermine their love and respect for him. The public's fear of Socialists — a fear common to that era — was sometimes expressed by schoolmates and playmates. More than one of their peers voiced the concern that the child of a Socialist might place a bomb in their classroom. Thomas' biographer, Harry Fleischman — with whom Thomas cooperated in the writing of the biography — tells a story that reveals how Thomas' children coped with foolishness of that sort. A friend of his daughter Frances invited her home for lunch and they agreed upon a date. Later, the girl told Frances that she was sorry but had to withdraw the invitation because her grandmother, with whom she lived, refused to have a child of "that Socialist" in her home. Frances later told her mother and father that was "the nuttiest thing I ever heard of."[2]

Late in 1920, all six of Thomas' children were stricken with a streptococcus infection. In the oldest child, Norman Jr. — everyone called him "Tommy" — the infection centered in his ear. Antibiotics and other drugs now common were then unavailable to treat infections of this sort, and Tommy's infection grew worse. Doctors performed a mastoid operation but spinal meningitis developed, and at the age of nine Tommy died.

Norman and Violet were devastated. Apparently, Thomas never successfully dealt with the death of his first child. Twenty-five years later, while

---

1 Ibid., 21.
2 Harry Fleischman, *Norman Thomas, A Biography: 1884–1968* (W.W. Norton, New York, 1969), 88.

writing his autobiography, he managed to devote only one sentence to the tragedy: "Our beloved Tommy died of Meningitis."[1]

For several years, the streptococcus infection seemed to recur in the family in various forms. Violet, who had a heart condition, also fell ill on several occasions. Since leaving East Harlem, the family had lived in a rather large house on East 17th Street in Manhattan. To escape these recurring illnesses, Thomas decided they should leave the city, and he moved the family to Hartsdale, a small suburban town in Westchester County. There they resided for a year, with Thomas commuting daily to the city. Then the family moved back to the City to settle in a shabby house on East 18th Street, just north of that section of the city now called the "East Village," where they resided until 1939.

With his family's health in a state of flux, Thomas limited nearly all activities that took him outside the home. By the summer of 1923, however, his family appeared to be on the mend. Coincidentally, he was presented with a job offer he was anxious to accept. For many years the Socialist Party in New York City had published a daily newspaper named *The Call*. After the war, the paper began to flounder and its circulation all but disappeared. In mid-1923, two powerful labor unions in the city — the International Ladies Garment Workers Union and the Amalgamated Clothing Workers Union, both long-time supporters of Socialist causes — agreed to provide the financing for a new daily paper — to be named the *New Leader* — to focus on labor as well as Socialist issues. Morris Hillquit, who then spoke for the Socialist Party in New York, urged Thomas to accept the editorship of the new paper. Thomas' experience with the publication of a daily newspaper had been limited to his boyhood delivery of the afternoon paper in Marion Ohio, but he enthusiastically accepted the position. A remarkable staff was then assembled. The city editor was Herbert Gaston, later the Assistant Secretary of the Treasury. The cartoonist was Edmund Duffy, later a Pulitzer Prize winner on the staff of the *Baltimore Sun*. Herbert Brubaker subsequently wrote for the *New Yorker* and sportswriter Ed Sullivan later wrote for the *New York Daily News* and became a television celebrity with his own show in the 1960s.

As Thomas later put it, "We had a grand time for a few weeks," but the paper soon ran out of funds and it folded. It was the "most humiliating disappointment" of his life.[2] What went wrong? The paper's initial financial backing was inadequate, and its circulation and advertising revenue failed to increase rapidly enough to support the paper once they expended the initial funding. But Thomas attributed failure primarily to non-financial factors. By the fall of 1923, the Communists had marked all of the progressive unions

---

1 Thomas autobiography, 81.
2 Ibid., 83.

in the city for infiltration and capture. The fight was bitter, especially in the ranks of the International Ladies Garment Workers Union. Members of the staff of the *New Leader* were not Communists, but as newspaper people they believed their primary obligation was the straight reporting of the news. Thus, in the paper's pages, the Communist position was not always condemned in terms the unions would have liked. Union leaders failed to understand this editorial stance and felt the paper had failed adequately to support them in their battle against the Communists. When they learned that the paper could continue publication only with additional funding, they were content to let it die. Soon after, the paper ended publication. Harry Fleischman relates the story, undoubtedly told to him by Thomas, that as the staff was leaving the paper's offices for the last time, a sign painter was in the process of applying gold leaf to the front door, announcing it as the offices of the *New Leader*. When told to stop painting, that the newspaper was out of business, the painter refused and continued his work until the lettering was completed.[1] This was the last episode in a series of frustrating failures.

Thomas' frustration and disappointment were complete. At the time, he classified himself as a total failure. He later wrote:

> My own spirits were at low ebb. Here was I almost forty, father of a large family, well trained for a profession [the ministry] I couldn't honestly follow, a failure in meeting the great opportunity which had come to me. I envied men who earned their living by doing things like doctors and engineers rather than by lecturing and imparting ideas. They had objective standards of value and accomplishment.[2]

As one without employment, Thomas was more fortunate than most others in similar circumstances. If compelled to, he could have made a decent living merely by devoting his time to writing and speaking, and Violet was never reluctant to help, either by working in a part time nursing position or, as she did once, by operating a tea room or, as on still another occasion, by raising cocker spaniel puppies. In any event, Violet's inheritance was available.

In the early years of his marriage, his wife's inheritance tore at his conscience. He asked himself whether as a Socialist he could allow himself to support his family through income generated from investments in a capitalistic system? Could he allow his family to live on money he had not earned through use of his own hands or his own mind? Was it not inconsistent — if not dishonest and hypocritical — for him to advocate socialism for others at the very time the welfare of his family was dependent upon a thoroughly capitalistic institution? He long agonized over these issues before settling upon a solution. He reasoned that because the inherited income permitted

---

1 Harry Fleischman, *Norman Thomas, A Biography: 1884–1968*, 95.
2 Thomas autobiography, 85.

him to pursue a course of life that he otherwise could not follow without penalizing the welfare of his family, it was appropriate for him to rely upon the inheritance income. He decided that in good conscience he could rely upon Violet's money to support his family if it allowed him to continue his work with the League for Industrial Democracy, the American Civil Liberties Union, and the Socialist Party, and to assume leading roles in various other endeavors intended to aid the impoverished and others victimized by a capitalist system. If Violet's inherited income freed him to do the things that he thought ought to be done for the good of his fellow man, then it was reasonable for him to use the inheritance money to support his family.[1]

Following the *New Leader* fiasco, he returned to the League for Industrial Democracy. Thomas was always happiest when working with the young. Speaking for the League at campuses across the country, he grew in status and reputation with students and their professors, particularly with those of a liberal or radical political orientation. The League attracted as many, if not more, liberal minded individuals than it attracted Socialists, and thus Thomas became acquainted and associated with such well-known liberal figures as Paul Blanchard, writer and Protestant minister; John Dewey, philosopher, educator and founder of the philosophical school based on the principles of pragmatism; Bruce Bliven, editor of *The New Republic* magazine; Paul H. Douglas, Columbia University professor and later US senator from Illinois; Reinhold Niebuhr, theologian; Alexander Meiklejohn, dean of Brown University and subsequently president of Amherst College; and Freda Kirchwey, editor of *The Nation* magazine.

As Thomas became better known, and as his associations with persons of status grew in number, he developed into an increasingly valuable asset for the Socialist Party. Some co-workers in organizations such as the League for Industrial Democracy and the American Civil Liberties Union also were members of the Socialist Party, and many of them became devoted followers of Thomas and banded together to form a block of supporters within the party.

Thomas first ran for public office in 1924. That was also the year that the Socialist Party for the first time in its history decided not to offer a candidate in a presidential election. Instead, the party supported the third party candidacy of Robert M. LaFollette, then serving as a Wisconsin senator. LaFollette was not a Socialist, but a radical with political ideals modeled on the Populist Party of the late 19th century. Thomas and other Socialists gave their support to LaFollette in the hope that his candidacy could lead to the formation of an American farmer–labor party based on Socialist principles. Many Socialists favored such a party because they believed a political combi-

---

1 Ibid., 86.

nation of farmers and workers had a greater chance of success on the national level than their own Socialist Party. Thomas reasoned that even if a newly created farmer–labor party failed to elect its candidate to the presidency, it eventually, through the election of candidates to lower offices, would grow in strength sufficient to hold the balance of power on the national scene. Even if this third party movement was not immediately Socialist, he hoped that he and other Socialists could make it in fact Socialist if not in name.[1]

When the coalition of parties backing LaFollette decided not to run candidates for local offices, the Socialists held a convention to nominate candidates for several state offices. Though Thomas was not a delegate to the convention, the Socialists nominated him to run for governor of New York. The following day, *The Washington Post* reported the nomination under the headline: "Former Newsboy on Harding's Paper Nominated for Governor."[2] Thomas described his unexpected nomination as the "event which next to World War I did most to affect my own life,"[3] since in accepting the nomination, he assumed a responsibility to the Socialist Party he thereafter never neglected or evaded and only deepened over the years.

His opponent in the election was the incumbent governor, the liberal Democrat Alfred E. Smith. Smith had formulated a good record as governor and, since he was a friend of labor, many Socialists supported his reelection. Thomas knew he had no chance of unseating Smith, but that failed to deter him from speaking in virtually every city across the state, urging voters to support the LaFollette candidacy and his own as well. Of the political parties supporting LaFollette, only the Socialist Party was equipped to conduct a national campaign, and party members were generous in affording the LaFollette supporters with workers and financial support. Their generosity, however, worked to Thomas' disadvantage, since the party could then provide him with little funding for his candidacy for the governorship.

Thomas was unsparing in his support for LaFollette, but the Wisconsin senator's campaign staff gave him no support in return. He spoke at LaFollette campaign rallies where he was directed not to refer to his own candidacy for governor. At a campaign event in Syracuse, after he had given a powerful speech in favor of LaFollette, the rally's presiding officer rose to thank him and then told the audience that all that Thomas had said about LaFollette could also be said of Smith. With Thomas standing at his side, he urged the audience to vote for Smith for governor, apparently unaware that Thomas was himself a candidate for the office.

LaFollette polled 4,800,000 votes, representing 17 percent of the votes cast nationally for president. Thomas received less than 100,000 votes in the

1 Norman Thomas, *Socialism Re-Examined* (Greenwood Press, Westport, Conn., 1963), 124-125.
2 *The Washington Post*, 7/28/24, 3.
3 Thomas autobiography, 89.

governor contest, far less than the 467,000 votes New Yorkers cast in favor of LaFollette. Thomas, however, was not bitter. Rather, he perceived the large LaFollette vote as a successful first step in the formation of a national third party. But his hopes for such a party were short-lived. Soon after the election, LaFollette's backers decided against pursuing any further third party efforts. Thus, Thomas learned how difficult it is in this country — unlike in nations such as Great Britain — to build a national third party. But he never abandoned hope; he believed the failure of the LaFollette venture signaled merely a postponement of the formation of a viable third party in the future. That belief was never realized during his lifetime.

During the course of his public life, Thomas could have been elected to office as candidate of either major party, but he chose to remain in the Socialist Party. Unperturbed by his loss in the governorship election, Thomas ran for public office again in 1925, this time for Mayor of New York City. Tammany Hall's choice for the office was Jimmy Walker — described by everyone as "debonair" — and the Republican candidate was Frank Waterman, better known as the "fountain pen king." The Communist Party also ran a candidate, Benjamin Gitlow who later wrote in *I Confess: The Truth About American Communism* that as the Communist candidate his primary task was to undermine the Socialist Party and the Thomas candidacy.[1]

Throughout the campaign, Walker wisecracked that he enjoyed listening to Thomas' campaign speeches because Thomas wanted all the things that he wanted for New York City, but he was the person, not Thomas, who could get them for New Yorkers. Congressman Fiorello H. LaGuardia, who would later be elected mayor, supported Thomas, stating that he was the best qualified candidate in the race and the "only one who has a platform that is constructive and means something."[2] Thomas had asked for and received LaGuardia's endorsement, who was not a Socialist, but an independent and unattached liberal. Thomas wrote to LaGuardia: "With all my heart I wish that you with your record of service to the people, your political sagacity and personal following were a Socialist."[3] LaGuardia never moved to the Socialist Party but he did join a non-partisan committee supporting Thomas' candidacy.

Thomas was the first candidate in a New York City election campaign to advocate a program of municipally-owned housing to replace the slum-ridden areas infesting the city. He argued that the slum problem was insoluble without public housing, but even Thomas realized that he "was a

---

1 Benjamin Gitlow, *I Confess: The Truth About American Communism* (E. P. Dutton, New York, 1939), 364.

2 *The New York Times*, 10/19/25, 3.

3 Quoted by Arthur Mann, *LaGuardia: A Fighter Against His Times, 1882B 1933* (J. B. Lippincott, Philadelphia, 1959) 266.

voice crying in the wilderness."[1] The election results were not close; Walker won in a landslide, receiving 750,000 votes to 360,000 for Waterman, and a mere 39,000 for Thomas. The small vote was particularly disappointing for Thomas since in 1917, when Morris Hillquit ran for mayor, he polled nearly four times that number of votes.

For Thomas, losing an election was not as devastating an experience as it was for others who opted for public office. Winning for him was never a realistic possibility, and from the moment he decided to run for office, he knew he would lose. His campaigns were never about winning. Rather, he used election campaigns as occasions to address the electorate, to present the issues in clear and uncompromising terms — terms other candidates shunned.

Thomas used the electoral process to pronounce and advocate economic and political principles he deeply held. Because he had no chance of winning, he could present these issues without concern for how the electorate would view them — whether voters accepted them or not. This was a position his political opponents could never afford to take, and thus it nearly always appeared as if Thomas was the only candidate who addressed the issues directly and candidly.

With devastating losses in the governor's election in 1924 and the mayoralty election in 1925, the voters would not have been surprised if Thomas sat out the 1926 election. But Thomas was not one to choose to do what the public expected; instead, he chose to run for a seat in the New York State Senate.

Beginning with the mayoralty campaign of 1925, Thomas involved himself in seeking out solutions to the problems plaguing New York City. As a candidate from the lower east side of Manhattan running for a seat in the New York state senate, he had another opportunity to address issues crucial to city residents. This campaign was an especially joyful one for him. Street meetings conducted in overcrowded tenement neighborhoods attracted listeners numbering in the thousands. He was in top form, debating the issues before huge audiences long into the night. People listened to him, liked him, but did not vote for him. As expected, he again went down to defeat.

Even with his efforts in seeking public office, he still found time to reach out and help a group of striking textile mill workers in northern New Jersey. The strike began when mill owners in the town of Passaic announced a 10 percent cut in workers' wages. The workers, already overworked and underpaid, rebelled. More than 10,000 of them walked off the job and set up picket lines. In the weeks following, mill after mill in the area shut down, as their workers joined the strike. With their number growing, the strik-

---

1 Norman Thomas, *We Have a Future* (Princeton University Press, Princeton, 1941) 5.

ers increased their demands. Not only did they want the 10 percent pay cut rescinded, they now demanded a 10 percent salary increase, a reduction in their work week, and owner recognition of their union.

The mill owners responded with brutal suppression. They turned fire hoses on pickets in freezing weather. They fired tear gas bombs on picket lines, even when children were marching with their parents. New York City newspaper reporters were roughed up and their cameras smashed. The mill owners hired replacement workers and gunmen to protect them. The police and mill owners combined in ignoring the law, resorting to guns and clubs to crush the effort of the workers.

The strikers were desperately poor. Many of them were foreign-born and existed at the lowest level of society. They needed help. In response to their plight, the League for Industrial Democracy and the American Civil Liberties Union established relief committees who sent the strikers food and clothing. Thomas frequently spoke at meetings of strikers, encouraging them to stand firm and to refrain from any sort of violence.

Town officials, siding with the mill owners, ordered police officers to subdue and restrain striking workers, though the strikers had consistently acted peacefully. They barred striking workers from meeting among themselves, thus denying them their constitutional rights of speech and assembly. The county sheriff established what amounted to martial law. The chief of police explained the attitude of law enforcement authorities: "We gotta keep order. We can't let them strikers march all over the place. Why, that last picket line was a disgrace — kids hammerin' tin pans! A stranger comin' into town would of thought he was in a lunatic asylum."[1]

The strikers realized they needed legal assistance; the sheriff's denial of their constitutional rights of free speech and assembly had to be tested in a court of law. The striking workers asked the American Civil Liberties Union to intercede on their behalf. The ACLU decided to test the limits of the sheriff's powers, calling for a meeting of strikers in violation of the sheriff's order not to hold such meetings. When ACLU officials tried to rent a hall suitable for such a meeting, Passaic building owners refused to rent them any space. After a futile search for an indoor location, they settled on an open field, and word of the time and place of the meeting went out to the strikers.

Thomas and a small group of ACLU faithfuls were chosen to speak at the meeting. Each of them was aware they faced arrest for violating the sheriff's directive. Thomas was the first scheduled speaker. "I don't know how the little group of my companions felt," Thomas later revealed, "but . . . I went to [that] place with much apprehension." On his arrival at the field, his apprehension was not much relieved when he noted the presence of several

1 Freda Kirchwey, "New Jersey Under 'The Terror,'" *The Nation*, 4/28/26, 470.

police officers and deputy sheriffs, accompanied by a group of hired strike-breakers, toting sawed-off shot guns, and appearing to look for an excuse to use them.[1]

There was no speaker's platform from which Thomas could speak. Fearing that he could not be seen or heard by all of the several hundred strikers present, Thomas mounted a nearby tree stump and started to speak:

> This is the first stump speech I've ever made from a stump. We have come here to test our rights as American citizens to hold a peaceful meeting for a legal and legitimate purpose. Yesterday, [we celebrated the day] Thomas Jefferson was born. You may have heard the name. His birthday is being celebrated in Passaic by a shameful desecration of the cause of liberty for which he strove so valiantly. I want to urge upon the strikers here that they continue their fine record of peaceful endeavor to win just demands. You strikers have shown a wonderful spirit of self-control. The violence in this strike is not of your making. You have had nothing to do with violence except to be the victims of it. This has been a legal and orderly strike. Your leader . . . is in jail. He is being held in $30,000 bail. This excessive bail is a mockery of American justice.[2]

At that point a whistle shrieked and police officers quickly moved in to surround Thomas. They dragged him down from the stump and placed him under arrest. Fortunately, none of the strikers were carrying weapons and they quickly dispersed. No one was hurt.[3]

Police hustled Thomas into the back seat of a squad car and drove him over back roads to the county seat at Hackensack. The police officer who drove the car said to Thomas, "What you was doing was moral all right, but maybe it wasn't legal. Some things is moral that ain't legal and some things is legal that ain't moral, and what's a cop to do about it?"[4]

The police brought Thomas before Louis Hargreaves, a Justice of the Peace, to be charged. Hargreaves had made a name for himself as a bitter antagonist of the strikers, condemning them as enemies of God, home and country. He denied arrested strikers the right of counsel and ordered them held on unusually high bail. Unable to determine what to charge Thomas with, Hargreaves telephoned the county prosecutors for advice. They decided that the appropriate charge was "inciting to riot" — even though Thomas had urged the strikers to refrain from violence. Hargreaves fixed bail at $10,000. As it was late in the evening, Thomas could not possibly raise that sum, as Hargreaves well knew. Thomas was not allowed to contact counsel or his friends, and nobody knew where he was. In fact, some of those present at the meeting of strikers believed he had been kidnapped. Thomas spent the

---

1 Thomas autobiography, 104.

2 The speech is quoted in Harry Fleischman, *Norman Thomas, A Biography: 1884–1968*, 105-106.

3 *The New York Times*, 4/15/26, 1.

4 Norman Thomas, *Human Exploitation in the United States* (Frederick A. Stokes, New York, 1934), 285.

night in the county jail. He later described this experience in rather low-key terms:

> So to the county jail I went for the night. I've been in several jails in similar tests but only once over night. That was supposed to be a modern jail but the noise, the quality of guards, the poor food, the indiscriminate herding together of all sorts of cases, are typical of the low order of our County prisons. I'm not sure that a night, at least, in one of them ought not be a prescribed part of the education of ... judges.[1]

While Thomas was trying to get some sleep in the county jail, League and ACLU loyalists were frantically searching for him, but the Passaic chief of police and the county sheriff refused to disclose where they had taken him. Violet was home ill at the time, and her friends were afraid to tell her that her husband was missing. However, when he failed to arrive home at a reasonable hour she surmised that he had been arrested and was spending the night in jail. She would not permit herself to panic.

On the following afternoon, a bail hearing was conducted by Hargreaves and, as expected, he ordered the $10,000 bail continued. By that time, Thomas' friends had located him. They raised the bail and he was released. Thomas immediately called for another meeting of the strikers, again violating the sheriff's ban on such gatherings.[2] ACLU lawyers filed a petition with a local court to enjoin the sheriff from treating others as Thomas had been treated. The court granted the injunction and thus a dangerous attack on liberty through the misuse of New Jersey's inciting-to-riot law was ended. Charges against Thomas were then dismissed.

The strike continued. A few days after spending the night in jail, Thomas attended a meeting of Protestant ministers in Passaic. Local clergymen were generally opposed to the strikers, and they rejected Thomas' request to speak to the group. Without their permission, he stood up, and raising his voice so as to be heard, spoke to them about the strike:

> The 10,000 men and women who are on strike here may be successful [or] they may be defeated.... If they are defeated, they will always bear in mind that the Protestant churches here have stood by while methods were invoked against them such as prevailed in the Russia of the Czars.... While you talk of Christian idealism, you did nothing. On the other hand, a Jewish rabbi went so far as to discuss the situation in a Catholic Church. [He then cited figures demonstrating the high profitability of the mills.]. Christian ethics demand that you pay attention to this! ... The church must properly consider a Christian wage. You gentlemen are aware that I am a Socialist. Under some conditions it is easier to be a Socialist than a Christian.[3]

At this point, they shouted him down.

---

1 Thomas autobiography, 105.

2 *The New York Times* 4/29/26, 25.

3 Thomas' speech is quoted in W.A. Swanberg, *Norman Thomas: The Last Idealist* (Charles Scribner's Sons, New York, 1976) 103.

While Thomas was engaged in trying to enlist the aid of the church, the ACLU sought another injunction against the sheriff, this time to bar him from enforcing a ban on meetings of the strikers. Again, the court granted the strikers injunctive relief and they resumed their meetings and continued the strike.

In the end, the strikers returned to work. The strike leaders had made mistake after mistake. They started the strike in the dead of winter, at a time when the workers were totally unorganized and lacking the resources to support a lengthy work stoppage. Still, the workers, demonstrating amazing endurance, managed to extend the strike for several months. Once Thomas and the ACLU entered the battle, the courts acted to protect the rights of the workers to meet in support of the strike, thus enabling them to extend the strike even longer. Ultimately, the mill owners met the demands of the strikers in part, and then claimed victory.

This was the first of many labor strikes in which Thomas intervened on behalf of the workers. Thomas abhorred corrupt unionism, and forcefully spoke out in condemning it, but throughout his life, he always sided with and supported the workers. What he saw in Passaic, he recognized as a pattern of conduct workers confronted across the country:

• Workers are paid wages insufficient to afford them a decent living.

• They go on strike, but then are deprived of their civil rights by local governmental authorities sympathetic to the employer.

• Church leaders, as they are aligned with capital, oppose the workers.

• Forbidden to assemble, and by that time, generally hungry and exhausted, the workers abandon the strike.

• They return to work, and again are paid inadequate wages.

The role of local government in this pattern of conduct generally arose out of fear that the strike would lead to public disorder. But Thomas earlier observed that the fear of disorder rendered local governmental officials the blind allies of the employer, serving as agents of injustice.[1] Thomas tried to break this pattern in the Passaic mill strike, but was only partially successful. He would try again in later labor disputes.

The New York and New Jersey newspapers reported Thomas' involvement in the strike. His participation in other efforts to protect civil liberties was making him well known, inside and outside the ranks of the Socialist Party. He was preparing himself to assume a larger role in the party, in politics, and in the country.

While Debs was in prison, cut off from events occurring in the party, he unexpectedly expressed strong support for the Bolsheviks, a sentiment for-

---

1 Norman Thomas, *The Christian Patriot* (The William Penn Lectures — 1917), 40, reprinted, Bernard K. Johnpoll, *Norman Thomas on War: An Anthology* (Garland Publishing, New York, 1974), 66.

eign to nearly all party members. He declared, "I am a Bolshevik from the crown of my head to the soles of my feet."[1] He later realized his mistake and shifted his position to one more attuned with that commonly accepted in the party. But party leaders now did not trust him, fearful of what he might say on impulse in public. Thomas described Debs' participation in party meetings in his later years as "emotional orgies on the order of old home week, and his speeches, for the most part, were merely repetitions of what he had said before the war, thus fitting "the pattern of pious remembrance of the past rather than an attempt to shape the future."[2] It was time for new leadership in the Socialist Party.

Thomas did not at first appear as the likely successor to Debs. Unlike Debs, he was an intellectual, not a blue-collar worker, and had not risen from the ranks of labor. Although no longer active in the ministry, he was negatively looked upon by some as a "sky pilot." But he had one advantage — he was one of a mere handful of native-born intellectuals remaining in the party, most others having resigned to support the war or to join the Communists. Earlier contenders for a leadership position, such as Hillquit, spoke with heavy accents (a distinct disadvantage for an aspiring politician in the era of Harding's "normalcy") and, as they were foreign-born, were not eligible for the US presidency. Thomas, on the other hand, was born of an old American family, spoke impeccable English, was highly educated, and was known to have sacrificed a career in the church on the ground of principle. No one else in the party could claim these advantages. Thus, Thomas rose to a leadership position in the party largely through default. He had little competition.

Debs died in the fall of 1926. At a service in Debs' memory, Thomas lauded him as a prophet. "The secret of his greatness lay in love for the individual as well as for humanity. Debs had the soul of a prophet and the kindliness of a lover of men."[3] At the time it is unlikely Thomas anticipated he would become as commanding a figure in the Socialist movement as had Debs, nor is it likely he foresaw that while Debs ruled during a time of growth of the Socialist Party, he would rule during its demise.

---

1 Thomas autobiography, 100.
2 Ibid., 101.
3 *The Washington Post*, 11/29/26, 7.

Chapter 6. Running for President

Thomas' speaking skills were said to be comparable to those of William Jennings Bryan, Woodrow Wilson, Franklin D. Roosevelt, and Eugene Debs. He had a "booming, virile, organ-roll voice that he could modulate from a roar to a whisper," complemented by gestures, such as "the pointing finger, the out flung arm, the shaking of the head."[1]

The debating clubs at Princeton had provided Thomas with his first training in public speaking. His friend and fellow debater at Princeton, Raymond B. Fosdick, spoke of Thomas as the most brilliant student in his class, but rated his speaking and debating skills only as "effective."[2] Neither Fosdick nor Thomas particularly distinguished himself as a speaker or a debater at Princeton.

Thomas later sharpened his speaking skills while preaching to his Harlem parishioners. Immigrants, able to speak and understand only a little English, could still feel Thomas' compassion in his sermons, making them aware that he was one of them. He also gained experience by addressing college students, speaking often for the Intercollegiate Socialist Society. By the time he spoke out for Morris Hillquit in the 1917 New York City mayoralty campaign, his speaking skills were well-honed.

In February 1917, just before the United States' entry into World War I, Thomas spoke at a Wesleyan University branch of the YMCA, whose president, an army officer of six years' standing, had offered to drill students in preparation for entering military service. After listening to Thomas, he ad-

---

1 *The New York Times*, 12/20/68, 1. This description appeared in Thomas' obituary written by Alden Whitman.

2 Raymond B. Fosdick, *Chronicle of a Generation: An Autobiography* (Harper, New York, 1958), 52.

---

vised YMCA officials that he was withdrawing his offer to drill the students. "Fellows, after last night's . . . talk, I am an out-and-out pacifist and I can't take this job."[1]

Over time, Thomas spoke to every imaginable grouping of citizens — at clubs and associations of nearly every description, at strike rallies, farmers' picnics, conferences of academics, teachers' conventions, protest meetings, political campaign events, and college commencements. He addressed audiences of all sizes, from small street corner gatherings to huge political rallies conducted at Madison Square Garden. He generally spoke to those who freely chose to listen, but on occasion he found himself speaking to captive audiences — students required to attended chapel services or the incarcerated residing in jails or prisons. He addressed military and civilian audiences, and groups of all ages, including children, from kindergarten to graduating high school seniors. He experienced his greatest success — and joy and satisfaction — in speaking to college students, always appreciating their lively responses and the give and take between speaker and audience.[2]

He spoke in every state except Alaska, and in most states dozens of times. His compulsion to reach as many people as possible led to thousands of speeches and most of them without receipt of a fee, often without reimbursement of his traveling and other expenses. If the circumstances demanded it, he could have earned a substantial income from his speaking endeavors.

H. L. Mencken, critic and journalist, characterized a Thomas campaign speech that ran on for more than an hour as one seeming to last no longer than an ordinary political speech of twenty minutes:

> It was full of adept and memorable phrases.... It shined with wit and humor. The speaker poked gentile but devastating fun at all the clowns in the political circus, by no means forgetting himself. There was not a trace of rancor in his speech, and not a trace of Messianic bombast . . . His voice is loud, clear and a trifle metallic. He never starts a sentence that doesn't stop, and he never accents the wrong syllable in a word or the wrong word in a sentence.[3]

The *Washington Post* once commented that Thomas' speeches in "candor and pertinacity far surpass those of any other presidential candidate."[4]

Thomas brought an enthusiasm to his speeches that at times was infectious. W. A. Swanberg, one of Thomas' biographers, was present at a speech Thomas gave at the University of Minnesota in 1932: "He bounded to the rostrum and spoke with vigor, fluency, conviction, and charisma that linger in

1 This story has been reported in many works including Harry Fleischman, *Norman Thomas, A Biography: 1884–1968* (W.W. Norton, New York, 1969), 58.

2 Norman Thomas, *Mr. Chairman, Ladies and Gentlemen: Reflections on Public Speaking* (Hermitage House, New York, 1955), 12.

3 Murray B. Seidler, *Norman Thomas: Respectable Rebel* (Syracuse University Press, Syracuse, 1967), 91, quoting Mencken's article appearing in the *Baltimore Sun* 10/18/48.

4 *The Washington Post*, 10/19/48, 12.

my memory forty-four years later. I was a Socialist at the time, but Thomas may have got my vote even had he been a Bolshevist or Falangist."[1]

Thomas often won over his audiences with humor, especially in his presidential campaigns. He more than once joked that "While I'd rather be right than President, at any time I am ready to be both."[2] In the 1932 campaign he told audiences that they should not hold President Herbert Hoover responsible for the country's economic plight because "such a little man could not have made so big a depression."[3] In the 1948 campaign, he described Republican candidate Thomas E. Dewey as a man who is "clad each day in a pair of platitudes."[4] He generally delivered barbs of this nature with a smile, but always directly on target.

Although some characterized his eloquence as "irresistible," his conviction and earnestness counted most with those he addressed. He had the talent to express vividly what his audience hungered to hear.[5] He believed in what he said and worked hard to find the best way of conveying his beliefs. Whether engaged in a speech or a debate, he was always fully prepared, generally having more knowledge about the subject at hand than anyone else present. One commentator was not guilty of exaggeration when he wrote that the man who takes on Norman Thomas in a debate "is monkeying with a buzz saw."[6]

He knew, of course, that he possessed the power to move a group of listeners, but he also was aware that the power to persuade was one easily abused. Commenting on the subject of misuse, he once said: "On occasion a competent speaker is tremendously tempted to get the kind of response that comes when he deliberately appeals to the emotions and prejudices which unify a large assemblage into a crowd, a herd, or a mob . . . which he can play as a musician on an instrument."[7] Yet, he consistently refrained from exploiting his powers of persuasion to elicit wholly emotional responses from his listeners. He wanted to persuade by establishing the reasonableness of his position. Moreover, he understood that an emotional response is generally fleeting, while a response based on reason is one that is more likely to endure. And yet, a good speaker for an honorable cause must enlist the emotional sympathy and support of his audience. Thomas illustrated the point:

> It is easy to sense but not easy to define by formula the difference which makes Churchill's famous speech exhorting his country to blood, sweat

---

1 W. A. Swanberg, *Norman Thomas: The Last Idealist* (Charles Scribner's Sons, New York, 1976), 136.
2 *The New York Times*, 12/20/68, 1.
3 Murray B. Seidler, *Norman Thomas: Respectable Rebel*, 92.
4 Ibid., 93.
5 Devere Allen, "Presidential Possibilities: Norman Thomas — Why Not?" *Nation*, 3/30/32, 365.
6 Ibid., 366.
7 Thomas autobiography, 122.

and tears one of the world's classics while a similarly emotional appeal on the lips of a demagogue or fanatic exhorting a crowd turned into a mob. . . is abhorrent. The difference lies in the honesty and responsibility of the speaker, the nature of the issue, and a fair statement of the cost of the action to which a devoted company or a whole nation is urged.[1]

Thomas enjoyed reading news reports of his speeches such as the "guests at the banquet found it hard to realize that Thomas spoke for well over an hour," or that "Thomas used his keen wit to temper his fervent convictions."[2] He wrote that "in all the world there are few satisfactions greater than a speaker finds in a sense of identification with an audience whose mind and heart he, temporarily, possesses."[3]

In 1928, Thomas decided to use his talent and skills as a public speaker to run for president. This decision did not come easily. A third party equivalent of the LaFollette coalition clearly would not emerge that year. The Socialist Party would have to stand alone, but it was not blessed with potential presidential candidates. Two of the party's most powerful leaders — Morris Hillquit, head of the party in New York, and Victor Berger, a member of Congress elected from Wisconsin — had not been born in the United States and thus were barred by the Constitution from serving as president. Milwaukee's Socialist mayor, Daniel Hoan, was content serving as a mayor of a major city and was not inclined to seek higher office. James Maurer, a union labor leader long associated with Socialist causes in Pennsylvania and a local office holder, ruled himself out as a candidate. That left Norman Thomas.

Thomas at first attempted to avoid the party's nomination. He favored Maurer and urged him to reconsider his decision not to run. Maurer, however, resisted Thomas' pressure and that of other party leaders. Eventually, he offered a compromise. He would accept the party's nomination for vice-president provided Thomas accepted its nomination for president.

Still, Thomas resisted. Two days before the opening of the party's national convention, *The New York Times* reported that the delegates were prepared to draft Thomas.[4] Morris Hillquit spent the days leading up to the convention pleading with Thomas to accept the nomination. Thomas wavered and in the end relented. He advised the convention, "I did not want to be in a position to have to accept this nomination for various reasons, including the duty I owe to my family. I have been forced to change my mind against my inclinations."[5] He remained convinced that Maurer would have been the better choice, but the party nevertheless went on to nominate him for president and Maurer for vice-president.

---

1 Norman Thomas, *Mr. Chairman, Ladies and Gentlemen: Reflections on Public Speaking,* 87.
2 Ibid.
3 Ibid.
4 *The New York Times,* 4/13/28, 15.
5 Ibid., 4/17/28, 31.

In his acceptance speech, Thomas made what the convention delegates considered an egregious error — he admitted that he did not expect to be elected. Many raised their hands in horror; this is not what a party nominee announces to those who are about to dedicate a segment of their lives to getting him elected. But Thomas was not deterred: "I have no illusions concerning the present condition of the party.... We are not building for this election but for education and for the future. Today we cannot risk world convulsions. We are too interdependent.... Our task is to bring a better world into being without revolutionary and catastrophic woe."[1]

He advised the party he would not support revolutionary changes in the country's economic system. He argued that Socialists should not measure success in terms of vote totals. More important than winning elections was the party's task to educate men and women to the possibilities of peace, freedom, justice, and brotherhood.

His acceptance speech reflected his basic political beliefs. Rather than viewing the Socialist Party as a potential major political party, he thought of it as a forerunner to a mass political movement. The party's role was to inspire or spearhead a major national third party rather than to become one itself.[2] His political views paralleled those underlying his support for the LaFollette candidacy four years earlier. He envisioned a major third party movement that joined workers and farmers across the country in a single cause.

His perceived limited role for the party reflected reality. Party membership had decreased in the preceding ten years from 118,000 to less than 8,000 as the 1928 campaign began. Thirty years after its birth, the Socialist Party barely existed. Thomas approached these facts with eyes wide open. Most of the convention delegates did not.

Thomas never abandoned this perception of a limited role for the Socialist Party in national politics, but he held to it with varying degrees of intensity. In narrowing the party's role, he did not intend to denigrate his own candidacy, since he believed that the Socialist Party could fulfill its role as precursor and educator only by fielding a presidential candidate. Nearly twenty years later, he questioned whether he had misconceived the proper role of the party and whether another approach would have been more fruitful. He asked himself then whether attempts to organize the party for a presidential campaign every four years had been the most productive approach? He wrote in his autobiography:

> Maybe I should have done better if I had not always been so keenly appreciative of the point of Lincoln Steffens' conversation with the devil. He and Satan were walking down Fifth Avenue when a man in front of them

picked up a chunk of truth. "Big enough" said Steffens, "to put you out of business." "Yes," said Satan. "What are you going to do about it?" asked Steffens.

"Oh," replied the devil, "that's easy. Get him to organize it."[1]

He tended to ignore the party's day-to-day internal problems. He was less interested in organizing the internal functioning of the party to win elections than he was in planning the party's efforts to disseminate its message. Some commentators later maintained that this attitude contributed to the diminishing results achieved by the party in national elections and ultimately to the demise of the party.

The Democrats nominated Alfred E. Smith as their presidential candidate while the Republican Party named Herbert Hoover. From the outset of the campaign, one issue dominated all others — Smith's Catholicism. Beneath the surface of the campaign, religious bigotry ran rampant — Smith's election would bring the Pope to America who would annul all Protestant marriages and declare all children born of those marriages to be bastards. Thomas vigorously attacked those who implied that Catholics were un-American. He lashed out at all aspects of anti-Catholicism, warning the voters that religious prejudice would undermine the validity of the election results. In an open letter to Protestant churches he argued that in many instances their support for Hoover merely masked their religious partisanship, that they were guilty of dragging religious prejudice into the campaign. He attacked not only the Protestant churches but also all others who introduced the subject of religion into national politics while openly participating in religious bigotry.[2]

In his campaign speeches, Thomas spoke of "peace, freedom, and plenty," a slogan he repeatedly used to express the Socialist agenda. For him, the "peace" issue in 1928 related to the use of the Marines in Nicaragua and the perception among many Americans that the United States was illicitly involved in an expanding imperialism.[3] To preserve the peace, he advocated reductions in military appropriations, cancellation of war debts, and the entry of the United States into the League of Nations. The most pressing "freedom" issues related to racial discrimination, fairness in taxation, child labor, and justice for the poor. In addressing the "plenty" issue, he expressed concern about rising unemployment and accompanying poverty, and argued in favor of Federal old-age pensions. The overriding presence of religious bigotry in the campaign, however, diverted attention from these issues, and the other candidates for the most part failed to address them.[4]

---

1 Ibid., 107-108.
2 *The New York Times*, 9/30/28, 9.
3 Ibid., 5/20/28, 18.
4 Ibid., 11/4/28, 26.

Thomas reminded campaign crowds that the roaring capitalist prosperity of the 1920s had failed to resolve the basic issues underlying conditions of poverty that continued to plague a large portion of the populace. Although catastrophic unemployment had yet to surface, he advocated steps to deal with the problem of unemployment to the extent it then existed. Thomas exhibited a greater awareness than either Hoover or Smith of the economic problems associated with unemployment and poverty, although even he did not fully understand the depth and extent of these problems and thus failed to anticipate the total collapse of the national economy that occurred one year later.

Thomas contended — as he would in campaigns of later years — that there was little that differed between the Republican and the Democratic parties. "The Democratic Party . . . has been a kind of second [railroad] car for the business interests to ride in. This year Salesman Al Smith is trying to make it the first or preferred car."[1] Thomas frequently told his audiences that greater differences existed among individual members of each of the parties than existed between the parties themselves.

The campaign was long and hard. Thomas traveled mostly by train, spending his nights in overheated and stuffy sleepers. The days were filled with countless speeches — given in labor halls, at Socialist Party rallies, and before most any other group of voters he could find gathered in one spot. When he was not speaking, he was attending party conferences and newspaper interviews. Thomas appears to have enjoyed it all. Reading his description of a typical campaign trip, one wonders how he could have experienced anything but discomfort and frustration:

> Certain features [were common to these trips]. Traveling in all sorts of vehicles, from busses and automobiles to air planes, but mostly in trains taken at all sorts of hours, sometimes in coaches and sometimes in Pullmans, often with an upper berth for space. The problem of clothes, wet with perspiration, in a berth after [attending] meetings on hot nights. Arriving in strange cities in the early morning; wondering who will meet you; what sort of press interviews and above all what sort of meetings there will be. The extra strain of poorly attended meetings. The disappointment of the result after such hard work even though it was expected.[2]

Contrary to some reports, Thomas encountered little animosity from those attending his speeches. There was little heckling in his presidential campaigns, and he remembered only one egg hurled in his direction. At first, he was unable to detect whether it was voter tolerance or voter apathy that operated to suppress active opposition to the views expressed in his speeches. Some years later when he looked back at his campaigns, he felt that perhaps he would have fared better in an atmosphere of open op-

---

1 Ibid., 8/5/28, 7.
2 Thomas autobiography, 108-109.

position. The real foe was indifference, not opposition. "Apathy is a terrible enemy."[1] He had no liking and little aptitude for the gold fish bowl existence of a presidential candidate or for the strutting and posturing that voters and party leaders expected of him. Again, looking back, he wondered whether he might have been more successful as a candidate if he "had been a little more of a fanatic or demagogue."[2]

Thomas' first presidential campaign in 1928 was his most difficult. Because family matters required Violet's presence at home, she was unable to be at his side during the campaign. In later campaigns, she accompanied him on most of his lengthy trips, taking on the role of his secretary. Her presence on the campaign trail was of particular value in turning out press releases. She was always "a constant marvel and joy" to him, rendering the discomforts and frustrations of a national election easier to endure.[3]

Newspaper coverage of Thomas' speeches and other campaign events was far less than Thomas hoped for. Although individual reporters assigned to interview Thomas were generally fair and friendly, they usually arrived at the interview unprepared and ignorant of Socialist principles and theory. This forced Thomas to spend considerable time explaining that Socialists were neither Communists nor anarchists. He attributed distorted accounts of his campaign speeches that appeared in print from time to time to Communists who were powerful in some chapters of the Newspaper Guild.

The 1928 presidential campaign was the first in which the candidates made substantial use of radio. Apparently, the people who operated these early radio stations held the electorate in general contempt. On the few occasions that Thomas was given the opportunity to broadcast a political speech, he was told to keep in mind that he would be speaking to a million morons and that he should keep his talk simple. Thomas kept it simple, not because of contempt for his radio audience, but because he was skilled in presenting complex ideas in lucid and understandable form.

The Socialist Party lacked the funding to buy more than token amounts of radio time, thus forcing Thomas to rely upon personal appearances throughout the campaign. Traveling greater distances than either Smith or Hoover, he delivered more than 150 major speeches, speaking in all but three states, and in some states, several times. He found that people often voted *against* one of the two major candidates rather than *for* one of them, and that voting for a third party candidate was considered a wasted vote. Thomas grew tired of hearing: "This time I cast my vote against the greater evil. Maybe the next time I'll vote Socialist." The next time never came. Shortly after the 1928 campaign, a well-known woman of society rushed up to him and said, "Mr.

1 Ibid., 112.
2 Ibid., 107.
3 Ibid., 111.

Thomas, I had my mind all made up to vote for you, for I thought you were the best candidate and had the best platform. But at the very last minute I went into the polling booth and voted for Al Smith, just because I didn't want to throw my vote away." "And so you did," Thomas said, interrupting her little homily.[1]

When the election was over, many voters expressed to Thomas regret that they had not voted for him, as surely he was the best candidate. "Thanks for the flowers," Thomas responded, "But I wish you hadn't waited for the funeral."[2] A Republican party official once told Thomas: "I'll . . . support you Socialists . . . as soon as you're the second party,"[3] apparently never occurring to him that the Socialist Party would never become a major party unless he and others first gave it their support by voting for its candidates, thus elevating it to a major party status.

The 1928 campaign saw a major shift in the type of voters attracted to the ranks of the Socialist Party. For some time working-class members had been defecting from party ranks. Out of necessity, party leaders turned to the educated classes to replace the defectors, and they for the first time targeted intellectuals for party membership. The intellectuals responded enthusiastically. Thomas-for-President clubs emerged on college campuses, particularly in New England and the Atlantic states. A number of leading university educators announced their support for Thomas, and newspaper articles subsequently presented long lists of prominent professors who had declared for him.[4] With this kind of success, the party gradually turned from its labor-oriented origins to a middle class, college graduate orientation. The shift worked to strengthen Thomas' leadership role in the party.

The final vote proved a disaster for the party — the worst presidential showing ever. Hoover won over Smith, 21,000,000 to 15,000,000 votes, with Thomas bringing up the rear with a paltry 267,000 votes. Thomas' less than 1 percent of the vote was the smallest percentage recorded by the Socialist Party since its inception in 1900. The extent of the debacle is made apparent when contrasted with Eugene Debs' candidacy of 1920 when, as a prison inmate, he received nearly 1,000,000 votes.

The New York Times attributed the party's poor showing to two factors. The temporary submergence of the Socialist Party to the LaFollette standard four years earlier made it difficult for its leaders to revive a national campaign organization in so short a time, particularly in light of the paucity

---

1 Devere Allen, "Presidential Possibilities: Norman Thomas — Why Not?" *The Nation*, 3/30/32, 365, 367.

2 This story has been reported by many, including Harry Fleischman, *Norman Thomas, A Biography: 1884–1968*, 116.

3 Thomas autobiography, 110.

4 New York Times, 9/18/28, 5.

of its financial backing. Secondly, the existence of general prosperity in the country militated against a ground swell of support for a political party advocating economic and social protest. "Whenever the ticket of most violent dissent polls so slight a percentage of the total as the Socialist Party polled in 1928, the lesson of contentment with existing things is plain."[1]

But all had not been lost. During the course of the campaign, Thomas became a national figure, carrying the Socialist message throughout the country. Henceforth, when he spoke out, he would be heard. Thomas, therefore, was on track to fulfill his goal of turning the Socialist Party into a force for educating the public.

At the age of forty-four, Thomas was about to become the symbol of American Socialism; the party of Eugene Debs would be the party of Norman Thomas. Non-Socialists often accused Socialists of living in another world, but in 1928 Thomas spoke directly to the people about the world they knew and lived in. He examined their problems and offered explicit remedies. He urged adoption of constitutional amendments prohibiting child labor and requiring a shortening of the work week commensurate with recent increases in productivity. He argued for federal old-age pensions and unemployment insurance, financed through increased corporate taxes and taxes assessed against wealthy individuals. In foreign relations, he advocated a strengthened and more democratic League of Nations that the United States would join to effect international disarmament.[2]

The Socialists placed in their platform a demand for the socialization of the economy: "We stand . . . for the collective ownership of natural resources and basic industries and their democratic management for the use and benefit of all instead of the private profit of the privileged few."[3] By 1928, however, the United States, as a capitalist nation, had already achieved a high level of economic development, and any move to a system of Socialist collective ownership would have required its leaders to recast basic economic structures. Recognizing this, Thomas subordinated this provision of the party's platform, thus de-emphasizing the party's demand for collective ownership. Without such a demand, the party stood in the position of advancing political positions that differed little from those espoused by left-wing reformers of capitalism. Socialists and reformers both advocated practical measures undertaken to eliminate poverty and raise the American standard of living. The reformers and the Socialists, however, used similar programs for different purposes, the reformers to save capitalism and the Socialists to move the economy in the direction of democratic socialism. With this altered

---

1 *The New York Times*, 12/15/28, 16.
2 David A. Shannon, *The Socialist Party of America: A History* (Quadrangle, Chicago, 1967), 191-195; first published by Macmillan, New York, 1955.
3 Ibid., 195-196.

approach to the advancement of the Socialist cause, Socialists found a new leader in Norman Thomas, a person who could command the attention even of non-Socialists. The election of 1928 showed Socialists that with Thomas' leadership they could earn the country's respect, even if they could not persuade the electorate to give the party its votes.[1]

1 Ibid., 199.

Chapter 7. The Depression Years

Following the 1928 presidential election, the League for Industrial Democracy — in which Thomas had become increasingly active — held a series of meetings to consider the formation of a third national political party. Thomas played a leading role in these meetings, but he no longer thought in terms of a farmer — labor coalition. He now envisioned a new party based on the unification of his own Socialist Party with the nation's leading liberals, including John Dewey, Oswald Garrison Villard, Morris Ernst, Paul Douglas, and W.E.B. DuBois, to form the League for Independent Political Action.

A number of New York Socialists — especially those close to Morris Hillquit — were less than enamored with the new organization. Members of the Hillquit group, later known as the "Old Guard" segment of the party, were mostly self-educated, European-born Jews, closely allied with the *Jewish Daily Forward*, the most important Yiddish language daily newspaper in the United States. For the first thirty years of the Socialist Party's existence, the New York Socialists and the Jewish Daily Forward were mainstays of the Socialist movement in the United States. Early in the century, the *Forward* was the key instrument of Socialist education, and the financial aid it provided to the party enabled the Socialist cause to survive. Although they eschewed radical revolutionary rhetoric, Old Guard Socialists were Marxist in orientation.[1]

In contrast to the Old Guard, the group of Socialists then gathering under Thomas' leadership was for the most part American-born, middle class, university educated, and far less Marxist in orientation. While these Social-

1 Murray B. Seidler, *Norman Thomas: Respectable Rebel* (Syracuse University Press, Syracuse, 1967), 105-106.

ists welcomed the liberals, the Old Guard feared that an association with a non-Marxist group could lead to the adulteration of party principles. Thus, was born a factionalism that by the mid-1930s would tear apart the Socialist Party.

Changes in party structure intensified Old Guard doubts about Thomas and his plans for the Socialist Party. The party's national executive committee named twenty-seven-year-old Clarence Senior — a recent University of Kansas graduate and a Thomas protégé — to the post of national secretary. His appointment represented a new trend in the administration of party affairs; younger members, cast in the Norman Thomas image, were replacing older members in important party posts. Senior's appointment also reflected a change in the party's basic constituency, a shift from a working class to an intellectual middle class and this change, the Old Guard suspected, would in turn lead to the abandonment of long-held party policies. Shortly after Senior's appointment, the fears of the Old Guard were realized when the party voted to eliminate its long-established rule that required applicants for membership to affirm his or her belief in the concept of the class struggle. With this change — long-favored by Thomas — an aroused Old Guard cried out that the party was departing from its Marxist roots. They were right. The party was moving closer to a non-ideological socialism favored by Thomas. Under Thomas' leadership, the party was about to be remade. Instead of advocating revolution, as it had in the past, the party turned its focus to gaining social justice for the poor and the oppressed. The Old Guard now asked whether Thomas was truly a Socialist or merely a liberal progressive masquerading as a Socialist.

Old Guard fears of Thomas' ascendency in the party were exacerbated when the League for Independent Political Action gave its support to Thomas in the New York City mayoralty contest of 1929. After the 1925 mayoralty election, Thomas closely followed the proceedings of the city's various governing agencies. Through these efforts and his contacts with various labor unions, he learned firsthand about corruption in the city. He thus entered the 1929 mayoralty campaign possessing a substantial body of knowledge relating to the way Mayor Jimmy Walker and Tammany ran the city. New Yorkers who found themselves adversely affected by the inertia of corrupt city officials now turned to him in increasing numbers for help.

At the outset of the 1929 mayoralty campaign, Thomas set forth his program in an article that appeared in *The New York Times* under the title, "Where the Socialists Stand":

> We Socialists look at this city of great luxury and greater poverty, a little beauty and immense ugliness, this market place where everything, even justice, is bought and sold and we say: Nevertheless those who toil with hand and brain can ... make this marvelous city the dwelling place of com-

fort and beauty, justice and peace. It will be a long struggle but it can be done.[1]

He offered the public an explicit program for the reformation of the city's political institutions. First, he pledged to end "the complex alliance of politicians, fixers, racketeers, the Police Department, and magistrates," an alliance that he maintained undermined the business operations of small merchants and large builders and contractors. Second, he advocated a constructive housing program that would transfer people from run down tenements to municipally-financed garden apartments. "Good housing is essential for good citizenship, and the war against crime and disease." Third, he recommended the unification of the subway system and the creation of a citywide system of public markets. In advancing these elements of change, he frankly admitted that the Socialist Party could not achieve such an ambitious program in a single administration and, moreover, that the State and the Federal governments would have to offer their cooperation for the plan to succeed.[2]

One of the primary goals of his campaign was to expose corruption. He specifically identified city magistrates whose conduct he alleged was corrupt. In this respect, his campaign was successful since, as he later reminded anyone who would listen, every magistrate he had charged with corruption had subsequently resigned, was removed, or was not reappointed.[3]

With Tammany Hall support, incumbent Mayor Jimmy Walker felt confident of his reelection and thus declined to debate his opponents. The Republicans offered Fiorello LaGuardia as their candidate, but because his progressive political views did not sit well within party ranks, his candidacy was fatally flawed. In an endeavor to strengthen LaGuardia's position, his supporters asked Thomas to withdraw from the race. Thomas was quick to respond: "Politics is going crazy when a Republican organization wants a Socialist to withdraw on the ground that the Republican candidate will give a pale imitation of a Socialist program."[4]

Thomas and LaGuardia later met to debate the issues. LaGuardia argued that the Socialist and Republican Parties had identical goals — the defeat of Jimmy Walker and the ouster of Tammany Hall from power. LaGuardia claimed, however, that Thomas was running a hopeless race; he could not win and his continued presence in the election only drained votes from him, thus rendering it less likely he would defeat Walker. Thus, to achieve their mutual goal, LaGuardia again asked Thomas to withdraw. Thomas was not persuaded. He responded that he saw no hope for better city government

---

1 *The New York Times*, 9/29/29, XXI.

2 Ibid.

3 Thomas autobiography, 127.

4 Arthur Mann, *LaGuardia: A Fighter Against His Times, 1882–1933* (J. B. Lippincott, Philadelphia, 1959) 275-276.

with either the Democrats or the Republicans in power. Moreover, he had entered the race to offer new ideas for the resolution of city issues that neither of the major parties had addressed. He believed his candidacy was in the public's interest, and he rejected all overtures to withdraw in favor of LaGuardia.[1] Despite these differences in view, Thomas and LaGuardia more often than not agreed on the main issues of the election.

Through a chance meeting, Thomas received better press coverage than he had in previous elections. Thomas and Adolph Ochs, publisher of the *The New York Times*, and a group of city dignitaries were named to serve as a welcoming committee to greet the visiting Ramsay MacDonald, the British prime minister. As the committee members sailed out into the harbor to meet MacDonald's incoming ship, Ochs commented to Thomas, "I see that you're running for mayor. I hope you'll really discuss issues." Thomas responded that he always discussed issues, but that in the last presidential campaign the *Times* had barely covered his speeches, merely reporting some of his jokes made on the campaign trail. Ochs seemed surprised and said that he would look into the matter. He was true to his word, and throughout the remainder of the campaign the *Times* provided daily coverage of Thomas' campaign events, and other leading city newspapers followed suit.[2]

The New York Times later noted that many people inside and outside the city were reading Thomas' speeches and discussing their vigor and intelligence. Interest in Thomas' views led to the formation of a group of nonpartisan supporters made up of artists, clergymen, business people, lawyers, educators, and doctors. The group, chaired by John Dewey and John Haynes Holmes, included a number of the rich and famous — Edna St. Vincent Millay, Paul Blanshard, Devere Allen, Fannie Hurst, Reinhold Niebuhr, Heywood Broun, and Morris Ernst, among more than 300 others.[3] Other groups, including the Citizens' Union, comprising both Republicans and Democrats, also endorsed Thomas.

On election day, Walker handily defeated LaGuardia. The vote recorded in favor of Thomas was the highest ever attained by a Socialist in a New York City election. Thomas tallied more than four times the vote he received in the 1925 contest, and his vote tally exceeded that of Morris Hillquit in the 1917 mayoralty race. Even the Socialists were amazed. Applications for membership in the Socialist Party rapidly flowed into party headquarters.[4] As one

---

1 *The New York Times*, 10/14/29, 2.
2 Thomas autobiography, 128.
3 *The New York Times*, 10/14/29, 2.
4 Ibid., 11/8/29, 12; 11/13/29, 21.

of Thomas' biographers put it, "as of that moment, Thomas was the white-haired boy of American socialism."[1]

Not one to rest on his laurels, with the election barely over, Thomas encouraged a non-partisan attack on corrupt practices in city affairs, and led the way in establishing the City Affairs Committee, later headed by Paul Blanshard, his good friend and Socialist associate. The Committee immediately began a broad-based investigation of the Tammany-led city administration, and subsequently Thomas and Blanshard made the Committee's views known at city government hearings and meetings. On more than one occasion, their vociferous objection to corrupt practices led to their ejection from city agency hearings. Undeterred, they brought charges against Mayor Walker in 1931, and in the year following, state officials ordered an investigation of the Walker administration, designating Judge Samuel Seabury for the task. Soon after, Thomas and Blanshard co-authored *What's the Matter with New York*, a 360-page summary of the City Affairs Committee's investigations of Tammany, together with a catalogue of recommendations for structural changes in city government to contend with corrupt practices.[2] Unfortunately for the sale of the book, on the day it was published, Walker resigned as mayor. Although Thomas was not responsible for causing the demise of the Walker administration, he surely contributed to it.

Socialist Party leaders anticipated neither the stock market crash of October 1929 nor the ensuing Depression, but then neither were they wholly surprised by these calamitous events. Six months before the crash, the party's national executive committee expressed concern that unemployment across the country had risen to dangerous levels, and it warned government officials that mass suffering was likely to occur unless they undertook immediate action to confront the problem.

The economic crash brought massive unemployment to every part of the country. The number of those unemployed grew rapidly, soaring to eight million by 1931. A year later, the number of workers without jobs increased to 12 million, and still the unemployment rolls continued to grow. At one point, the unemployment rate stood at 25 percent. Unemployment of that magnitude had not been previously known, and national, state and local governments had no programs in place adequately to combat it. By 1934, 11 percent of all Americans were receiving some form of relief, and it was estimated that twice that number were living at or below the level of extreme poverty.[3]

1 W.A. Swanberg, *Norman Thomas: The Last Idealist* (Charles Scribner's Sons, New York, 1976), 119.

2 Norman Thomas and Paul Blanshard, *What's the Matter with New York; A National Problem* (Macmillan, New York, 1932).

3 These statistics come from Thomas himself. Norman Thomas, *Human Exploitation in the United States* (Frederick A. Stokes, New York, 1934), 183-184. See also, David A. Shannon,

Thomas related a story he felt was especially pertinent to and descriptive of the problems that confronted the unemployed during the Depression years. A woman living in New England advertised in her local newspaper to hire a full time cleaning person and domestic helper, offering as compensation room and board, and two dollars per week. She received eighty applications. Among those who applied for the job were unemployed school teachers and nurses, as well as other professional workers who had lost their positions.[1]

Thomas did not stand idly by as the ranks of the unemployed wildly expanded. More persistently perhaps than any other New Yorker, he harangued the New York City mayor, the New York governor, and the president to help unemployed workers, insisting that all levels of government had a responsibility to initiate programs to create jobs and extend financial relief to the families of the unemployed. He pressured the city and the state to authorize job-creation construction projects. He repeatedly visited Washington to urge Congress to appropriate vast sums to assist the suffering poor and to underwrite public works projects to provide sorely needed employment. President Hoover rejected such programs as financially unsound as they would unbalance the national budget, but Thomas countered that to allow millions of workers to remain without jobs and their families without food was worse than unsound — it was inhuman.

Thomas helped organize Unemployed Workers Leagues to provide hope for those desperately in need of hope. Some of these Leagues were operated on a barter system where men and women worked for food, clothing and other necessities. If nothing else, the Leagues tended to restore a sense of dignity to those who had lost their identity and self-esteem along with their jobs. Thomas spent many hours speaking to groups of unemployed workers, expounding not only the merits of socialism but urging them to grasp the power obtainable by them through union organization. He offered the unemployed hope for the future.

Thomas raged against a society that allowed workers to be turned out of work as easily as a person turns out a light:

> Henry Ford can discharge 30,000 at a clip as he could not discharge 30,000 mules. Mules would kick and mules can't graze on city streets. In this respect the wage system is even more heartless than chattel slavery. The owner of slaves could scarcely afford to let them starve when he had no work for them. But our industrialists expect to hire and fire with precious little corporate responsibility.[2]

The Socialist Party of America, A History, Chicago, Quadrangle, 1967; originally published by Macmillan, 1955.

1 Norman Thomas, *Human Exploitation in the United States*, 146.
2 Norman Thomas, "A Program for Unemployment," *The World Tomorrow* 5/30, 215.

He offered specific proposals for resolving the national unemployment problem:

- public works projects.
- unemployment insurance.
- a shorter work week.
- a coordinated system of public employment offices.
- the retraining of workers employed in obsolete positions.
- the compilation of accurate statistics on unemployment.
- minimum wage laws.
- abolition of child labor.[1]

Each proposal was attainable within the existing capitalistic system. Here, Thomas was preaching capitalism's reform, not its replacement with socialism. His advocacy of governmental responsibility for the unemployed appealed generally to many voters, and after Franklin D. Roosevelt succeeded Herbert Hoover as President, he persuaded Congress to consider each of these proposals and most were adopted.

Speaking night after night to unemployed workers across the nation, Thomas was swelling the ranks of the Socialist Party. Party membership more than doubled during the first years of the Depression. In Wisconsin, eleven party members were elected to the state legislature and two were elected in Pennsylvania. In 1931 alone, nearly one hundred new Socialist Party locals were formed. But despite the opportunities for Socialist Party growth, Thomas' first concern was the unemployed. He directed his efforts to the improvement of the conditions confronted by the families of those who had lost their jobs. Dealing with the inhumanity of the Depression was a far more pressing matter for him than was the advancement of Socialist goals. The replacement of capitalism with socialism would have to wait.

The Depression also found Thomas involved in bitterly contested labor disputes in North Carolina, West Virginia and New Jersey. Intolerable working conditions and starvation wages sent many workers into the streets in strikes against their employers. With the proliferation of such strikes, Thomas created strikers' relief funds through the League for Industrial Democracy. When textile workers in North Carolina went on strike, their union lacked the funds to support the work stoppage, and they called upon Thomas for help. He responded with funds sufficient to feed the strikers and their families until the nine-week strike was settled in favor of the workers. But then the mill owners failed to abide be the terms of the settlement, refusing to re-employ more than one hundred of the strikers who had joined the union. The workers again went out on strike, but this time matters turned violent. The local sheriff and his deputies ordered the strikers to disperse, and when they

---

1 Ibid., 216-217.

refused, they fired tear gas canisters, followed by gun fire. Six strikers were killed, and many more wounded, most shot in the back. One of the arrested strikers died on the operating table, still handcuffed. [1]

Another strike that did not end well involved West Virginia coal miners. By 1931, one third of the miners were out of work and close to one half those remaining on the job were working only one or two days a week. With contributions raised by Thomas and others, the United Mine Union organized the workers, and not long after, 23,000 miners went on strike, demanding improved working conditions and higher pay. The mine owners responded by evicting strikers and their wives and children from company-owned homes. Thomas worked tirelessly to raise funds to support the strikers but eventually they were forced to return to work without prevailing on any of their demands.

When 6000 silk workers struck their plants in Patterson, New Jersey, Thomas and many others sympathetic to the demands of the strikers walked the picket lines. In the sixth week of the protracted strike, Thomas and forty-five others were arrested and held in a local jail until they raised bail. Included among the forty-five were two clergymen and a college president. [2]

In a period of a little more than a year, Thomas wrote two books directed to resolving Depression era issues. In *America's Way Out: A Program for Democracy*,[3] he set out to correct a mistaken perception of socialism that was then current. He indicted capitalism on four counts: the whole system was planless and chaotic; it bestowed wealth upon some who exerted no effort; it divided industry's product irrespective of need or ability; and because it accentuated luxury and competitive spending, it was socially wasteful. He stressed the need for a Socialist program and organization based on social ownership of natural resources and means of production, the preservation of the democratic state, and the use of constitutional means of social transformation.[4]

He presented an accurate picture of existing economic conditions and suggested methods of dealing with them through the implementation of practical programs. He wrote of his conviction that capitalism was incapable of succeeding without ultimately enslaving the workers. Thomas departed from orthodox Marxism, however, by offering again a proposition he had long supported — that socialism was attainable through peaceful and democratic means. This was the only road to salvation. Thomas hoped the book would serve as a stimulus to a discussion of a more comprehensive phi-

---

1 *The New York Times*, 10/3/29, 1: Harry Fleischman, *Norman Thomas, A Biography: 1884–1968* (W.W. Norton, New York, 1969), 124-125.

2 *The Washington Post* 9/4/31, 1.

3 Norman Thomas, *America's Way Out: A Program for Democracy* (Macmillan, New York, 1931).

4 The book was summarized in *The World Tomorrow*, 4/31, 119.

losophy and plan for the nation's future, and it was well received. A review of the book that appeared in the *Nation* magazine put it succinctly: "Here is an honest book by an honest man."[1]

In the second book, *As I See It*,[2] written in the midst of the Depression, Thomas wrote with a greater sense of urgency. "If we are to avoid catastrophe there is no time to lose." While reconsidering the recommendations set forth in *America's Way Out*, he suggested additional ways of resolving the problems of persistent unemployment and resulting poverty.

While writing about the Depression and the hordes of unemployed workers, Thomas disclosed a great deal about himself and of his views concerning socialism, war, and religion. He examined his relationship with Marxism, a matter he understood needed clarification. He continued to believe in the existence of a class struggle between an owning and a working class, a struggle that tended to explain the bitterness of labor disputes and glaring deficiencies in the justice system. But he protested proclamations by Marxists that a clear understanding and enunciation of the class struggle concept were in themselves sufficient to teach and inspire workers to deal with everyday workplace problems and prejudices. More was needed — a philosophy of cooperation for the common good. Such a philosophy does not require a Socialist creed that compels every speech and every speaker to shout class conflict in Marxist language. Other roads leading to the Socialist ideal should not be dismissed merely because they fail to emphasize class conflict.[3] Then, as throughout his life, he emphasized the value of a philosophy of cooperation, rather than a dogmatic Marxist creed, as the best path to an ascendant socialism.

Thomas viewed worldwide economic problems as a prelude to war. He predicted — accurately as it turned out — another world war within a decade. His World War I pacifism had not weakened:

> [World War I] left a legacy of broken men and women, ill nourished children, all ripe for perpetuating endless fear and hate. It did not end war, make the world safe for democracy, vindicate forever the rights of small nations, or give a new soul to men. Not a single one of the idealist hopes wherewith the war was gilded for the suffering nations has been fulfilled.... There is not the slightest reason to think that in terms of results the history of any future world war will be different. Modern war is loss and only loss for every combatant.... [In the next war] there can be no non-combatants. Women and children are the inevitable victims of warriors of the air and cities the necessary goals of the destruction [the warring nations] will rain down from the very heavens to which men have reached up hands for blessing.[4]

---

1 Henry Raymond Mussey, "An Honest Socialist," *The Nation* 4/15/31, 418.
2 Norman Thomas, *As I See It* (Macmillan, New York, 1932).
3 Ibid., 17-18.
4 Ibid., 17-18.

If there was any hope for avoiding war, it lay in the concept of non-violence. He viewed Gandhi's concept of non-violence with some optimism. Perhaps it could be employed on a broader scale to world events at large:

> There are times when honest men must explain why they are not in jail, and when a willingness to endure without flinching is more effective than the will to fight. The final and most difficult revolution will not be in the ends men seek but in the means they use. To cling blindly to violence is in our day close to a reactionary counsel of despair.[1]

Fifteen years had elapsed since he resigned his Harlem ministry, protesting the Church's position on the war. In *As I See It*, he returned to a consideration of this issue, while questioning the Church's role in the social order. Thomas recalled that some years before, in a discussion concerning the fate of the World War I conscientious objectors, a Jewish judge had commented that it was "the greatest irony in history that the most militaristic and acquisitive nations in the world should have chosen a pacifist Jewish peasant not only as their prophet but as their God."[2] Thomas agreed; the Church had always blessed war and he was convinced it would bless the wars to come.

Thomas rejected a form of Christianity that sanctioned Christians killing other Christians or peoples of other faiths. Similarly, Christians who gave the appearance of being able to live at peace with a social order whose god was profit always troubled him. He cited as an example a group of Protestant churches in Danville, Virginia who fell woefully short of the principles of Christianity by which they claimed to live. A group of workers went out on strike against their Danville employer. The strikers were members of local Protestant churches, and from all appearances took their religion seriously. The owner of the company that employed them also was a Christian and also a member of a local Protestant church. The church attended by the company owner supported his position in opposing the workers' strike demands. Almost without exception, all the other churches in Danville also stood by the company owner as he fought all attempts of his workers to organize and achieve an improved standard of living. Thomas accused the Danville churches of adopting a position that was wholly indifferent to the cause of justice espoused by their own members. The God of the Danville churches was the god of profit: "A very gallant struggle was lost, and with the defeat the hope of peaceful social progress . . . grows dimmer. Fine voices in the church were raised in the crisis, but the church was impotent or indifferent on an issue involving not primarily economics but human justice and liberty."[3]

---

1 Ibid., 60.
2 Ibid., 140.
3 Ibid., 150-151.

He saw little hope for a meaningful role of the Church in the Depression's economic struggles. Although the influence of the Church was waning, Thomas believed that religion would not die with the major churches. A minority of churches still existed who zealously campaigned for justice and liberty. "Of that minority there cannot be too many, and to that minority, though I cannot share its faith and give my allegiance, I offer my admiration and respect."[1]

As has been noted, at the time Thomas left his Harlem parish in 1917, his criticism of the Church centered on its failure to condemn the war. He chose socialism over the Church because Socialists perceived the war as evil and refused to sanction it. Fourteen years later, he was convinced that the Church also had failed to play a meaningful role in the social order. He persisted in holding that the ethics of Christianity at its best, and the kind of God Christians professed to believe in, are incompatible with capitalism. In a world where god is profit, Christianity had no program to guide its adherents. Socialism, on the other hand, had a definitive plan for a new society. While Christianity should have been a mighty force for justice, it failed to offer a viable plan for change. Thus, Thomas' perception of Christianity's place in the workplace was severely limited:

> If a man's Christianity makes him a Socialist, well and good. But let him remember it does not absolve him from an understanding of economic forces and programs in which non-Christians may unite with him. Let him prove the values [of] his Christianity ... by his service in the Socialist movement, not by trying to substitute Mark for Marx.... The generalizations [of Christianity] are meaningless unless worked out in a world where there is one justice for the rich and another for the poor, where gross inequalities of wealth and poverty have little relation to need or deed and none at all to brotherhood.[2]

Even so, Thomas still thought that Christianity could play a meaningful role in the workplace if it inspired men and women to seek a human interpretation of its conception of the Kingdom of Heaven. The Kingdom of God is here on earth, not in some far off place. The social gospel movement still stirred Thomas' soul.

Thomas could no longer accept the religion of his childhood, as he equated any attempt to return to it with a desire to escape from life and its problems. His father had centered his religion on the goodness or badness of individual men and women but, as Thomas was not hesitant to point out, had neglected to take into account the nature of the social system in which those men and women lived and worked. Thomas, however, recognized the strength of that aspect of his father's faith that focused on the nature and existence of God and on man's relationship to the universe. "Are our noblest

---

1 Ibid., 152.
2 Ibid., 149.

aims and ideals and hopes but the illusions of this strange animal man cursed with consciousness in a world essentially alien to his dreams?"[1] His father's answer was simple. God had his own in his care; God's universe was man's home.[2] Thomas' answer was not as simple. He had lost his father's faith, but beneath it all, he wished he had not.

---

1 Ibid., 161.
2 Ibid., 163.

Chapter 8. The 1932 Presidential Election and the New Deal

The Socialist Party expanded rapidly between the 1928 and 1932 presidential elections, with party membership doubling during those years. In the first five months of 1932 alone, new membership resulted in the formation of more than one hundred new locals. A concomitant growth in the party's influence was reflected in the increased circulation of Socialist-oriented periodicals, also more than doubling in number during that time.[1]

Morris Hillquit, as he had for many years, continued to serve as the party's national chairperson. Socialists viewed Hillquit as the party's leading theorist. He had authored three works on socialism, was an excellent speaker, and was fluent in five languages. The party faithful held him in high esteem, unofficially designating him as the grand old veteran of the party. Hillquit and Thomas, however, differed on certain fundamental issues. Hillquit denounced capitalism as historically and philosophically wrong, while Thomas impugned America's capitalist system primarily because of its exorbitant demands upon the worker.[2] Hillquit considered the core of the party to lie with its blue-collar laborers, whereas Thomas looked to and drew support from the intellectual side of the party. It was during these years that the mantle of leadership began to shift to Thomas.

Outside the party, Thomas was already viewed as the spokesperson for socialism; inside the party, his position was not yet secure. Hillquit and his Old Guard followers resented Thomas' rise to leadership, while the progres-

---

1 James Weinstein, *The Decline of Socialism* (Monthly Review, New York, 1967), 338; Bernard K. Johnpoll, *Pacifist's Progress: Norman Thomas and the Decline of American Socialism* (Greenwood, Westport, Conn., 1970), 88.

2 Bernard K. Johnpoll, *Pacifist's Progress: Norman Thomas and the Decline of American Socialism*, 85.

sive, Social Gospel-oriented party members enthusiastically supported him. Thomas' influence within the party was greatest among the younger, university educated, middle-class members, while older party members who had lived through the successes and failures of the party's earlier times were less accepting of his new role in the party. They viewed him as a Liberal rather than as a Socialist, since his non-Marxist stance on many issues fell short of socialism as they perceived it.

While Thomas' non-Marxist positions alienated the older party members, the Old Guard's rigid Marxist dogmatism repelled Thomas and his followers. When Thomas elicited support from the intellectuals in the party, thus elevating their party status over that of the blue collar laborer, the Old Guard looked upon Thomas as a heretic. They correctly viewed their leadership roles to be in jeopardy, as the party intellectuals — many of whom were clergy and divinity students — set about to recast the party more to their mode of thinking.

One issue that deeply divided the party was the nature of its response to the emergence of the Soviet Union and American communism. Most American Socialists had been sympathetic to the Russian revolution of 1917, but over time the Old Guard membership grew critical of Bolshevik denials of elementary civil rights of Soviet citizens. Newer and younger members of the party, on the other hand, advocated a friendlier attitude toward the Soviet Union and they tended to place less emphasis on its totalitarian ways. Moreover, they wanted to create an all-inclusive party, welcoming even ex-Communists as long as they accepted Socialist principles and were not subjected to the control of any outside group. The Old Guard rejected this position, fearing that it could lead to their loss of control over party machinery. Having been present twelve years earlier when the Communists left the party, they were suspicious of any attempt of Communists to return to the party, even if they disavowed their Communist affiliation.

Thomas favored a coalition of Socialists and other liberal and radical minded groups, but Hillquit rejected the idea. Following the 1929 mayoralty election, reform-minded New Yorkers suggested that Socialists, trade unionists, independents and liberals form a coalition with Thomas as its leader. Thomas was interested, but Hillquit would have none of it. He adamantly opposed a coalition with non-Socialists that might result in the dilution or abandonment of the Socialist Party program or its identity.[1]

As party members assembled for their national convention in Milwaukee in May 1932, their ranks were split. A group of the more progressive members were convinced that Old Guard traditionalism would ultimately retard

---

1 Norma Fain Pratt, *Morris Hillquit: A Political History of an American Jewish Socialist* (Greenwood, Westport, Conn., 1979), 237.

the growth of the party, and they urged basic changes in party doctrine. Old Guard members remained inflexible, opposing any change. A third group, consisting of mostly younger members — calling themselves "Militants" — espoused a radical Marxism. They rejected gradualism and reformism as avenues of approach to capitalism's replacement by socialism and demanded immediate, remedial action to resolve the problems of poverty and unemployment wrought by the Depression. Members of an extreme wing of the Militants embraced the concept of a working-class party led by a leadership that would not make a "fetish of democracy."[1]

The differences between the Old Guard and the militants were largely generational. Old Guard members were mostly in their fifties and sixties, while the Militants generally were much younger, many of them in their twenties and thirties, some young enough to be the grandchildren of oldest of the Old Guard. The Old Guard held important positions in the party hierarchy, while the Militants who had joined the party in the late 1920s and the early 1930s held few party positions of importance. Spanning both groups in age and philosophy were the Progressives. Adopting a centrist position; on the one hand the Progressives rejected the Old Guard's aversion to action, and on the other hand were suspicious of the rigid Marxism of the Militants.

As Marxists, the Militants opted for a working-class party with strong, centralized leadership. At best, the Progressives accepted a diluted Marxism. They were far more interested in the realignment of the national political parties. If the Socialist Party were unable to achieve major party status, they would be happy with a third party coalition of farmers, workers, and Socialists. Thus, the Militants and the Progressives had little in common, but were unified in their opposition and distaste for the Old Guard. The Militants were more vocal of the two, but the Progressives were more numerous and yielded greater influence in the party.

Thomas disagreed with many of the basic tenets of the Militants' program, but he perceived an advantage in identifying with the party's younger and more aggressive element. He wanted to be able to intensify and concentrate opposition to the older and bureaucratic elements represented by the Hillquit followers. Fratricidal warfare appeared imminent. It was evident to all factions that the Socialist Party could not continue divided in this fashion.

At the outset of the 1932 convention, a sharp clash between the Hillquit and Thomas camps set member against member. Hillquit and Thomas had been closely associated since 1917 when Thomas, still in the active ministry, spoke out in support of Hillquit's run for New York City mayor. In 1928, it

---

1 Ibid., 238.

was Hillquit who first moved to name Thomas as the party's presidential candidate, arguing that Thomas could provide new leadership while attracting younger people to the party. A year later, however, they were at odds. Hillquit objected to Thomas' turn to non-Socialist support for his mayoralty candidacy in 1929. As Hillquit opposed a coalition with non-Socialist forces, he also opposed the involvement of the Socialist Party in any form of third party movement. Thomas, of course, remained receptive to these concepts.

Thomas accused Hillquit and the Old Guard of exhibiting a grossly negative attitude toward the Soviet Union. Hillquit countered that the party should not act puppet-like in approving all things done by the Soviets. Following an acrimonious debate, the convention delegates voted in favor of a posture of friendly neutrality toward the Soviets, while demanding the release of all Soviet political prisoners and the restoration of civil rights for all Soviet citizens.[1]

The adoption of the Soviet resolution represented a tactical victory for the Thomas forces, and they immediately combined with the Militants to attempt to unseat Hillquit as the national chair and replace him with a more aggressive spokesperson. As his successor, they favored Daniel Hoan, the Socialist mayor of Milwaukee. A Milwaukee delegate, rising to speak in opposition to Hillquit's reelection, ill-advisedly criticized the New York delegation, openly suggesting that the position of national chairperson should not be filled by a New Yorker. The New York delegation was largely Jewish, and they instantly interpreted his remarks as anti-Semitic. Another delegate followed with the comment that the national chairperson should be someone unmistakably recognizable as "American." Hillquit's followers leapt to their feet, charging the Progressive and Militant factions with discriminating against those born Jewish or on foreign soil and condemning both groups for initiating a campaign to rid the party of "foreign elements."[2]

The anti-Semitic charge was bogus, and many well-connected Jewish members immediately rejected it. B. Charney Vladeck of the *Jewish Daily Forward* defended the Militants and Progressives and urged party members to turn to the real issue at hand — would the Socialist party benefit from a change in leadership? But Vladeck failed to calm the waters. Accusations of discrimination grew more vehement and the divisions between groups of delegates widened — New York City Socialists versus Socialists residing in the rest of the country; foreign born members versus American born; young versus the old.

---

1 *The New York Times*, 5/22/32, 3.
2 Ibid., 5/24/32, 1.

Finally, Hillquit rose to speak. He apologized "for being born abroad, for being a Jew, and for living in New York."[1] There the debate ended. Socialists, traditionally opposed to anti-Semitism and racism, unsurprisingly proceeded to vote in favor of Hillquit's reelection. As Thomas later noted, under the circumstances it was better that he was reelected.[2] But the vote in his favor did not eliminate factionalism within party ranks. Intra-party warfare would continue below the surface and — as we will see later — would arise again and all but destroy the party.

Since none of the American-born Old Guard members had the stature to contend with Thomas for the party's presidential nomination, he again was selected as the Socialist candidate. For the moment, all factions in the party united behind the Thomas candidacy. The bitterness that had developed at the national convention was suppressed — at least for the moment — as the party members turned to the election campaign at hand.[3]

The convention delegates adopted an expansive platform that anticipated much of the legislative action of the early days of Roosevelt's New Deal:

- Appropriation of Federal funds for the immediate relief of the poor and unemployed.
- Appropriation of Federal funds for public works, construction of roads, reforestation, slum clearance, and homes for workers.
- Legislation providing for the reduction of the length of the work week without reduction in pay.
- Adoption of adequate minimum wage laws.
- Legislation providing for compulsory Federal unemployment insurance financed by contributions by employers.
- Establishment of free public employment agencies.
- Adoption of old-age pensions for men and women sixty years of age and older.
- Legislation providing for health and maternity insurance.
- Enactment of workers' compensation and accident insurance laws.
- Abolition of child labor.
- Protection for farmers and small homeowners against mortgage foreclosures.
- Legislation facilitating the organization of labor unions, while prohibiting "yellow-dog" contracts.
- Enactment of laws steeply increasing inheritance, income, and corporate taxes.

---

1 David A. Shannon, *The Socialist Party of America, A History* (Quadrangle, 1967; originally published by Macmillan, New York, 1955), 217.
2 Thomas autobiography, 160.
3 David A. Shannon, *The Socialist Party of America, A History*, 218.

- Modification of immigration laws to permit the reuniting of families and to provide for the refuge of those fleeing political persecution.
- Constitutional guarantees of economic, political, and legal equality for African-Americans.
- Strict enforcement of anti-lynching laws.
- Nationalization of basic industries to be effected by transfer from private to government ownership with compensation to be paid to affected business owners through the issuance of Federal bonds.[1]

Despite demonstrations of unity as the convention concluded its business, the Socialist Party entered the 1932 election campaign as a deeply divided political entity. The intra-party anger and bitterness had been subordinated, but the appearance of unity was little more than a facade. If the party had been truly unified, it would have been better prepared to grasp the opportunity presented at the time, an opportunity to grow significantly closer to achieving major political status on the national stage. Millions of workers were without jobs, banks were closing, and the country wallowed in the depths of its severest economic depression. Untold millions suffered in misery. Capitalism was on the decline; socialism was on the ascent. Americans were receptive to new political formulas and new ideas for salvaging the economy. In 1932 the Socialist Party was in a position to offer the country new formulas and new ideas.

Despite Thomas' record of losing elections and, as a consequence, his lack of experience serving in a public capacity, he was considered as well qualified for the office of president as any other American of the time. Since first running for New York City Mayor in 1925, he had attained a tighter grasp on the workings of city, state, and national politics. Paul Douglas, later US senator from Illinois, viewed Thomas as one of the most appealing political personalities of the 1930s:

> Thomas' whole career is evidence of what one brave, sensitive and able man can do. The last decade was in many ways disgraceful for both its corruption and the vulgarities of materialism. That in such a decade one man could grow in stature as Thomas has is indeed proof of the spark which lies within men and of what happens when idealists master realities.[2]

Even Thomas' opponents spoke well of him, as illustrated by a story related by Felix Frankfurter. In the 1932 campaign, before his appointment to the Supreme Court, Frankfurter led a group of independent voters supporting Roosevelt in the election. On one occasion he was present at a Roosevelt campaign speech, and afterward a man in the audience advised Roosevelt

---

1 Daniel Bell, "The Background and Development of Marxian Socialism in the United States," *Socialism and American Life*, Vol. I, Edited by Donald Drew Egbert and Stow Persons (Princeton University Press, Princeton, 1952), 372; *The New York Times*, 5/25/32, 3.

2 Paul H. Douglas, "An Idealist Masters Realities," *The World Tomorrow*, 5/32, 151. These comments were made in the course of a review of Thomas' *As I See It*.

that although he agreed with much that he had heard, he remained convinced that Norman Thomas was the candidate to whom he should give his
vote. Apparently Roosevelt was not offended, for he told the listener:

> Norman Thomas is a fine man. I have only one thing against him. I asked
> him to go on my unemployment commission shortly after I became gover-
> nor [of New York] to deal with the unemployment problem . . . when the
> depression really hit us, and he refused. I thought he should have gone on
> [the commission], but he is a fine man.[1]

Murray B. Seidler, author of *Norman Thomas: Respectable Rebel,*[2] knew Thomas well. He described Thomas as having the bearing of a leader. His towering
size and "strongly etched patrician features," gave him a unique appearance,
a distinct political asset.[3] Thomas was self-confident, but not arrogant, and
possessed an innate sense of dignity. He seemed always thoroughly in command of himself. While keenly aware of the life and death problems confronting the whole of society, he often focused on personal problems of individuals who sought his help. "He has an abundance of charm and an unfailing
sense of humor, which endear him even to persons who meet him once or
know him only slightly."[4] Attributes such as these undoubtedly would have
qualified Thomas for a leadership role in any political organization. He might
have been elected president had he been a Republican or Democrat.

At the outset of the 1932 campaign, the Socialist Party claimed a membership of slightly more than 15,000, spread across the country in 1600 locals. As
in past elections, the party faced formidable obstacles to the election of its
presidential candidate. A few states — including Illinois and Ohio — had
enacted legislation making it difficult for Socialist Party candidates to appear on their ballots, thus introducing impediments to any of the electorate intent on casting a Socialist vote. Little money was available to finance
Thomas' campaign. The party looked to independent sources for additional
funding but achieved little success in raising more than token sums. Severely
under funded, Thomas entered a national campaign that would take him to
thirty-eight states.

Thomas made up for a lack of financial support with an enthusiasm for
campaigning that seemed never to wane. His unremittingly energetic approach to the campaign trail was legendary. Literally, he never stopped. A
day on the campaign with him was known to those who attempted to follow
him as a "Thomas Track Meet." His schedule was not scripted as is typical
in out times. Rather, it developed as the day proceeded. He accepted nearly
every invitation to speak, and thus was forced to rush hectically from one

1 Harlan B. Phillips, *Felix Frankfurter Reminisces: Recorded Talks* (Regnal, New York, 1960), 240.
2 Murray B. Seidler, *Norman Thomas: Respectable Rebel* (Syracuse University Press, Syracuse, 1967).
3 Ibid., 79.
4 Ibid., 79-80.

event to another, delivering speeches seven, eight, or even nine times in a day. Those attempting to follow him on his daily trek usually lacked the energy or perseverance to continue at his pace. And yet Thomas pursued such an agenda day after day.

As noted earlier, Thomas was less interested in winning elections than in spreading Socialist principles, but this did not deter him from vigorously attacking the Republican and Democratic Party candidates — Herbert Hoover and Franklin D. Roosevelt — and their platforms. He condemned the major parties because they failed to offer any real plan for relief from raging unemployment and also ignored the multitude of other problems brought on by the Depression. Thomas dismissed the Democratic and Republican Party programs as wholly inadequate for dealing with the Depression: "There are those who say, 'Never mind the parties, they aren't much good, but . . . vote for the best man.' But the best man living couldn't help prevent [continuation of present conditions] if he followed the Democratic or Republican platforms." In contrast, Thomas pointed out that the Socialist Party platform offered sensible, straightforward policies — a five-day work week, national unemployment insurance, and immense public works programs. Thomas repeatedly argued that neither the Republican nor Democratic candidates could succeed in curing the nation's ills since each relied on a platform that failed to provide meaningful relief for the poor and unemployed.[1]

Thomas declined to discuss the Republican Party platform; he simply dismissed it. Promises of "a chicken in every pot," "a car in every garage," and "prosperity is just around the corner" did not warrant serious discussion. The real Republican platform was the record in office of President Herbert Hoover, and his record was mistake after mistake. "His only idea of restoring prosperity is to lend some more money to those who have already borrowed too much. He vainly waits for some Santa Clause to restore prosperity while he . . . fights to the last ditch against what he calls doles to unemployed workers."[2] In Thomas' view, the Democratic Party platform that Roosevelt offered was hardly better. In many respects it was worse, since Democrats used their platform to conceal their role in furthering "outrageous racial discrimination and . . . the most flagrant corruption in the cities."[3]

In his speeches, Thomas often appeared to be advocating the reform of capitalism, not its abandonment. Contrary to fundamental Marxist precepts, his primary approach to resolving pressing economic issues was to reform the existing economy, an economy that operated within the confines of a capitalist system. Consequently, some members of the Socialist Party accused him of merely paying lip service to Socialist doctrine. They noted that

1 *The Washington Post*, 9/4/32, 2.
2 *The New York Times*, 5/23/32, 1.
3 Ibid.

during the campaign he refrained from stressing Socialist dogma that held that capitalism was no longer viable. Nor did he call for a Socialist economy — an economy that did not rely upon the profit motive — as capitalism's replacement. Thus, in some respects, Thomas' plans for dealing with the Depression were more readily accepted outside the Socialist Party than inside it.

While Hoover and Roosevelt tended to speak in generalities, evading detailed discussion of the issues facing a country in crisis, Thomas confronted those issues head on. When he spoke in Los Angeles to the Interdenominational Ministers Association, he did not soft-pedal his attack on the Church's alliance with capitalist forces and its negative role in resolving Depression-era problems. He accused the ministers of sitting idly by, watching the capitalistic system negate every Christian ideal. He charged them with having allowed the Church to succumb to offering a religion of nationalism allied with capitalism, and consequently ending on the wrong side of every issue of importance.[1] Nor did he moderate his pointed criticism of other groups. He was constantly on the attack. Since he had no hope of election, he had no fears of taking positions that would cost him votes. He never offered compromise. He presented positions with a directness other candidates could appreciate but could not afford to emulate.

The lack of strong labor union support plagued the Thomas campaign, and his supporters turned to forming *ad hoc* "Thomas-for-President" clubs. His supporters also placed greater reliance on the 1600 Socialist Party locals to organize get-out-the-vote campaigns. Later analyses of the vote revealed that Thomas fared far better in middle-class than in blue-collar neighborhoods and that a large segment of the labor vote went to Roosevelt. In one Philadelphia ward where unemployment was rampant, Thomas polled only 166 of the 23,000 votes cast.[2] Thomas' showing in other heavily blue-collar districts was equally dismal.

While labor support was lacking, intellectuals stepped in to back Thomas. Independents — most of them intellectuals — formed a "Thomas Committee of Ten Thousand," and as support grew rapidly, its leaders optimistically renamed it the "Thomas Committee of One Hundred Thousand." Paul Douglas was its leader and its membership included the well known from all professions and occupations: John Dewey, Reinhold Niebuhr, the radio newscaster Elmer Davis, W.E.B. DuBois, George Gershwin, Edna St. Vincent Millay, Stephen Vincent Benet, and author and critic Alexander Woollcott.[3]

---

1 *The Washington Post*, 10/11/32, 8.

2 Irving Bernstein, *The Lean Years: A History of the American Worker, 1920-1933* (Houghton Mifflin, Boston, 1960), 511.

3 David A. Shannon, *The Socialist Party of America, A History*, 222.

Thomas campaigned tirelessly, delivering 214 speeches in thirty-eight states, drawing huge crowds in New York City, Philadelphia, Indianapolis, Milwaukee, Los Angeles, and Hartford. Where in 1928 he addressed gatherings of a few hundred, in 1932 he drew crowds of 10,000 and more. When Thomas appeared before 22,000 in a packed Madison Square Garden in New York City, another 10,000 who were unable to gain entrance stood in adjacent streets, listening to his speech over a loud speaker system.

In Philadelphia, Thomas' followers scheduled a speech in one of the city's public parks, but city officials refused to sanction the event on the ground that longstanding regulations permitted educational meetings but not political speeches in public park areas. Even after these officials were reminded that they had granted approval for a speech by President Hoover, scheduled to be presented a week later in the same park, they persisted in barring Thomas' speech. Thomas circumvented the ban by conducting an "educational meeting," designating his speech as a "history lesson." "Now pupils," he began in addressing the throng that had gathered to hear him, "the first lesson in history we will take up will be about [city corruption]." He then proceeded to castigate Republicans and Democrats in Philadelphia and elsewhere, and to excoriate Mr. Hoover: "He will tell you of all the chickens in the pot of the Republican Party and of all the cars in the garages. But do not forget they had to kill the chickens because they could not feed them, and they keep the cars in the garage because they have no gas."[1]

Thomas was especially popular with collegians and their professors, and they formed nearly 300 Thomas-for-President clubs on college campuses. Forty-six members of the Harvard faculty publicly announced their support for him. He was highly praised by several publications — *Vanity Fair*, the *Christian Science Monitor*, the *Christian Century*, among others — and his portrait appeared on the cover of *Time* magazine.

He also received support in strange places. He liked to tell the story about a little girl who, after participating in her class' mock election, told her teacher that she had voted for Norman Thomas because he was the father of her dog. Her teacher later learned that the girl's parents had purchased her dog from Violet, then engaged in raising cocker spaniel puppies to supplement the family's income. Thomas commented that "the little girl's reason was only a little crazier than some adults' I have heard."[2]

Thomas hoped that his vote count would reach two million, doubling that achieved by Debs in his best showing. To his great disappointment, the huge crowds and the enthusiasm of his followers and supporters failed to convert to votes. Thomas related the story of a prospective young supporter

---

1 *The New York Times*, 10/29/32, 10.,
2 Thomas autobiography, 95.

who approached him following a speech in Milwaukee. With tears in his eyes, the young man said, "I believe in everything you say and I agree entirely with your principles, but my wife and I can't vote for you. The country can't stand another four years of Hoover."[1] Thomas was aware, of course, that he could lose thousands, if not hundreds of thousands, of votes if others were to reason similarly. But he understood this was a dilemma the voters confronted whenever they considered voting for a third-party candidate. He could only sympathize with the young man.

Roosevelt's 22,800,000 votes far surpassed Hoover's 15,800,000. Thomas' vote total of less than 900,000 was hardly worth counting. In fact, some commentators claim that a large portion of the Thomas vote was not counted. In districts lacking voting machines, election officials often ignored the vote of third-party candidates. The Socialist Party rarely had enough poll-watchers present at the vote count, and this often led to an undercounting of the tally for the Socialist candidate. A Socialist Party poll-watcher assigned to a south side Chicago polling district reported an incident that lent support to those who claimed an undercounting. The Communist Party had no poll-watchers in this polling district, and the Socialist poll-watcher noticed that the Democrats and Republicans were not recording the Communist votes. When confronted, they told him: "When you Socialists have no poll-watchers, we do the same to you. But since you're here, we'll split up the Communist vote among the three of us."[2] If all the votes cast for Thomas had been recorded, his total may have been as high as 2,000,000 — the target set by Thomas. Still, in comparison with the vote of the major candidates, his vote was relatively insignificant. Even when reminded that he had more than tripled his 1928 vote, Thomas was disappointed with the final result.

On the day before Roosevelt's inauguration, Thomas spoke to a large student audience at the University of North Carolina in Chapel Hill. He told the students that the collapse of the country's economic system required radical steps of the new administration, and that Roosevelt should refrain from any half measures. He then proceeded to outline the initiatives he believed Roosevelt should immediately undertake to resolve the financial crisis. On the day following, Roosevelt announced to the nation his program for resolving the crisis. It was immediately apparent to those who had been present at Thomas' speech in Chapel Hill that Roosevelt's program paralleled Thomas' proposals of the day before. Thomas himself was vastly surprised by the tone and content of Roosevelt's address.

In proclaiming the New Deal, Roosevelt undertook to enact reforms of the economy long advocated by the Socialist Party. Socialists had called for

---

1 Harry Fleischman, *Norman Thomas, A Biography: 1884–1968* (W.W. Norton, New York, 1969), 136.
2 Ibid., 136-137.

a reduction in the work week; the New Deal did also. During the campaign, Thomas had advocated a vast public works program to provide relief for those forced into unemployment; Roosevelt called for Congressional appropriation of such funds. Socialists had demanded the abolition of sweat shops and of child labor; the New Deal abolished most sweat shop conditions and child labor in all but a few industries. Many other reforms backed by the Socialist Party — the adoption of adequate minimum wage laws, Federal unemployment insurance, and old-age pensions — would later become keystones of New Deal reforms. Thomas and others viewed Roosevelt's program for reform of the economic system as far more reflective of the Socialist Party platform than of his own party's platform.

Shortly after his inauguration, Roosevelt welcomed Thomas and Hillquit at the White House, where both pressed upon the newly-elected President more radical reforms, such as the nationalization of the banking system. Roosevelt listened attentively, giving his Socialist visitors far more attention than any previous President. But not all Democrats were pleased with the welcoming of Socialists to the White House, nor were all happy with the New Deal's Socialist slant, sometimes referred to as "creeping socialism." A few years later, Alfred E. Smith, former New York governor and Democratic Party presidential candidate, went so far as to equate the New Deal with socialism, accusing the new administration of carrying out the reforms specified in the Socialist Party platform. "It is not the first time in recorded history that a group of men have stolen the livery of the church to do the work of the devil." To establish his point, he suggested that his fellow Democrats lay Socialist Party doctrines along the side of those of the New Deal and note how they tallied. "How do you suppose all this happen?" he asked. "Here is the way it happened. The [New Dealers] caught the Socialists in swimming and they ran away with their clothes." He did not object if members of the administration wanted "to disguise themselves as Norman Thomas or Karl Marx or Lenin or any of the rest of that bunch, but what I won't stand for is to let them march under the banner of Jefferson, Jackson, or Cleveland." [1] Thomas rejected Smith's claim that Roosevelt had carried out the Socialist Party platform. The only way he carried it out, Thomas said sarcastically, "was on a stretcher." [2] Thomas did not dismiss, however, the commonly accepted wisdom that both major parties eventually accepted Socialist principles, at least in part. He approved the measures Roosevelt undertook to reduce unemployment and his endeavors to assist those in dire need. He also recognized that the successes achieved through New Deal programs showed that democracy could be made to work in the worst of times, even when

1 *The New York Times*, 1/26/36, 1.
2 Harry Fleischman, *Norman Thomas, A Biography: 1884–1968*, 171.

capitalism appeared to be at a stage of self-destruction. He nonetheless remained adamantly opposed to labeling the president's program as a form of socialism. It was true that the New Deal was in some respects progressive, but it failed ultimately to resolve basic economic obstacles. Roosevelt saved the banks, not by nationalizing them, but by turning them back to the bankers. Through enactment of a series of reforms, Roosevelt secured a temporary capitalist recovery, and thus buttressed an economy geared to the production of profit for private owners. Again, Thomas asserted, this is not socialism. Rather, it was an experimental attempt at reformed capitalism.[1]

Throughout the early days of the New Deal, Roosevelt led Congress to enact a series of acts intended to reform some of the more inefficient and unjust features of capitalism. If Roosevelt did not creep toward socialism, he surely undercut actual and potential support for the Socialist Party.[2] Thomas was quick to recognize the problems Roosevelt's program presented for the Socialists:

> We have an immensely bold attempt to stabilize capitalism by means of a partnership between industry, the workers, and the government. The terms of this partnership . . . have been far more hopefully affected by Socialist teaching and Socialist immediate demands than seemed possible prior to [Roosevelt's inauguration]. It was not the Democratic but the Socialist program that demanded great-scale public works, federal unemployment relief, federal action to abolish child labor, etc. Nevertheless, all these things . . . may be not only consistent with. . . capitalism, but a necessary condition of its continuance.[3]

Thus, Thomas was dually motivated in attacking the New Deal. He sincerely believed it was structurally inadequate to resolve all the issues confronting the nation. But, in addition, because Roosevelt's programs of social reform continued to undermine the foundation of the Socialist party, Thomas had to demonstrate to the Socialist Party membership that substantial differences still remained between the New Deal and Socialist programs. He recognized, however, that Roosevelt had become "the idol of the masses." He noted in his autobiography that Roosevelt's first one hundred days in office "wrought marvels in the restoration of hope, confidence in democracy, and a beginning of recovery.... Roosevelt's great and deserved fame began . . .with his first inaugural and early fireside chats. The courage with which he surmounted his physical handicap always commanded admiration."[4]

As early as a year after Roosevelt took office, Socialists holding leadership positions in the party began to gravitate toward the New Deal. In 1936, two major labor unions — the Amalgamated Clothing Workers, under the

---

1 Norman Thomas, *After the New Deal, What?* (Macmillan, New York, 1936), 16.
2 David A. Shannon, *The Socialist Party of America, a History*, 229.
3 Norman Thomas, "New Deal or New Day," *The World Tomorrow* 8/31/33, 488.
4 Thomas autobiography, 133, 134.

leadership of Sidney Hillman, and the International Ladies Garment Workers Union, led by David Dubinsky — organized a mass defection from the Socialist Party to the Democratic Party. The desertion of party members threatened to cause the party's disintegration. If party leaders were unable to keep members from leaving, the continued existence of the Socialist Party was very much in question.

Chapter 9. Arkansas Sharecroppers

A letter sent to Thomas by a small town businessperson in Arkansas ushered in a new phase in his life. The letter writer was H.L. Mitchell, a Socialist and the operator of a dry-cleaning store in the small town of Tyronza,[1] located in the northeastern part of the state. In 1933, the people living in and around Tyronza were barely surviving. As the Depression deepened, Mitchell witnessed the worsening of conditions of those who lived and worked on neighboring farms. He wrote to Thomas to elicit his help in addressing the extensive rural poverty then prevailing in Arkansas.

The farmers living in the Tyronza area were mainly sharecroppers, tenants, not owners of the land they worked. Thomas later described a sharecropper as a "man who owns . . . as near to nothing as any man in the United States."[2] A sharecropper typically tended a twenty or thirty-acre tract of land planted with cotton. His tract was merely one of hundreds of others, each worked by a sharecropper, on a huge plantation of many thousands of acres, each sharecropper bound to the plantation owner in a semi-feudal relationship. The land owner staked the sharecropper to a mule, tools, seeds, food and clothing, all furnished through the owner's commissary or by arrangement with a local merchant. The owner also furnished the sharecropper a house, usually little more than a shack. The sharecropper's debt thus incurred accumulated interest, sometimes at rates as high as 40 percent. During the course of the year, the sharecropper could obtain additional supplies from the commissary or local merchant, generally at inflated prices.

---

1 Tyronza remains a small town. The 2000 Census reported a population of 918.
2 Norman Thomas, *Human Exploitation in the United States* (Frederick A. Stokes, New York, 1934), 44.

The sharecropper and his family lived in his assigned, run down shack on his designated parcel of land, and he, his wife, and children planted, cultivated and then picked the cotton grown on his small plot. At the end of the growing season, the plantation owner arranged for the sale of the harvested cotton, deciding on the time and place of sale, as well as the sales price. The owner did not permit the sharecropper to participate in any way in setting the terms of the sale. After subtracting the cost of the materials furnished to the sharecropper during the course of the year, the owner paid him his share of the proceeds of the sale. In computing the sharecropper's share, the owner often worked with a "crooked pencil."[1] If the sharecropper was illiterate, as he often was, he had no means of checking the owner's computation. If he was African-American, he dared not protest.

A piece of folk humor expressed sharecropper perception of the financial relationship with the land owner:

> Teacher: "If the landlord lends you twenty dollars and you pay him back five dollars a month, how much will you owe him after three months?"
>
> Young student: "Twenty dollars."
>
> Teacher: "You don't understand arithmetic."
>
> Young student: "You don't understand our landlord."[2]

A sharecropper had little recourse against a land owner's bookkeeping machinations. If he questioned the accuracy of the owner's accounting or objected to the cost of the commissary food, clothing, and other materials, his only recourse was to move onto another plantation, where he would most likely again confront similar circumstances.

A sharecropper could live on the same plantation all his life and acquire no rights outside the terms of his annual contract with the owner. Owners made it a rule not to take on a sharecropper who had failed to pay his debts to the owner of the plantation where he last lived and worked, thus creating a system of peonage nearly impossible to break out of. A sharecropper could not protest these conditions through participation in the electoral process as a poll tax effectively disenfranchised him. From planting to harvesting, the sharecropper lived a life of near total despair.

The sharecropper was an essential element of a system of tenant farming that had spread throughout the South. In the 1930s, three-quarters of the farmers in Southern states did not own the farms they worked. They were tenant farmers, and a vast majority of these were sharecroppers. The Depres-

---

1 Ibid., 45.

2 Howard Kester, *Revolt Among the Sharecroppers* (University of Tennessee Press, Knoxville, 1997), 28-29 of the Introduction by Alex Lichtenstein. This work was first published by Covici-Freide, New York, 1936.

sion expanded the prevalence of tenancy farming even farther. More than a million white families and seven hundred thousand African-American families living in the South — over eight million people in all — were trapped in this system that compelled them to live in a state of poverty and deprivation so horrible that most people who witnessed the enveloping context of a sharecropper's life had difficulty convincing others that people actually lived in those conditions.[1]

The typical sharecropper family lived in a two-room shack, usually unfit for human habitation, having no plumbing, perched on wooden posts and without a cellar. A few chickens generally made their homes beneath. Except for a small patch of trampled down dirt, cotton fields surrounded the shack. Some shacks had outhouses; most did not. The shack was generally unpainted, its roof leaked, and its windows were unscreened, thus affording no protection from flies and mosquitoes. If a sharecropper made any improvements to his shack, he received no compensation for his labor, and if he moved to another farm, the improvements automatically passed to the owner.

Inside the shack stood a wood-burning stove, rigged from an old oil drum, a bed, three or four rickety chairs and a table, and perhaps a few other pieces of beat up furniture. Sharecroppers did not need closet space as family members had no clothes other than what they wore. The children had no underclothes; some had no shoes. Local county fairs offered prizes to young girls who made the nicest dresses from fertilizer sacks. The family usually had only one bed. Where the children slept was a mystery. If they slept on the floor, they could catch an occasional glimpse of the stars through the cracks in the roof. If it was about to rain, they had to calculate where the water would not fall before settling in.[2]

Disease was rampant; pellagra and malaria were common. Advertisements touting cures for malaria were posted throughout eastern Arkansas. For some families, a contaminated creek was their sole source of drinking water. The family elders fell ill and the babies died. They ate meal, molasses, and fat-back — three times a day in the best of times, two times when matters were worse. Pellagra was prevalent because a sharecropper would plant every inch of soil with cotton, leaving no room for a vegetable garden. Even if a sharecropper had a garden, there was no time left in a day to tend to it. Cotton was king, and must be served irrespective of the human consequences.[3] One of the consequences was a multitude of human bodies scarred by insufficient and unbalanced diets.

---

1 Arthur M. Schlesinger, Jr., *The Coming of the New Deal: The Age of Roosevelt* (Houghton Mifflin, Boston, 1959), 374-376.

2 Norman Thomas, *Human Exploitation in the United States*, 5-6.

3 Howard Kester, *Revolt Among the Sharecroppers*, 41.

A day in the life of a sharecropper family rarely varied — work from dawn to dusk, or as the sharecroppers expressed it, "from can to can't." Every member of the family, even children as young as six, labored in the cotton fields. Sharecropper children received little schooling. The schoolhouse was likely to be far off, and most often not served by a school bus. Howard Kester, a committed Socialist and devout Christian engaged in organizing the sharecroppers, wrote *Revolt Among the Sharecroppers*, in which he described a typical Arkansas school located in sharecropper country:

> The schoolhouse . . . is likely to be a dilapidated one-room frame building with an ancient stove for heating purposes, rough-hewn seats . . . and broken window panes. Sometimes there are holes in the floor large enough to permit a small boy's swift escape . . . from an exasperated, underpaid teacher who tries to impart some notion of the three R's to her motley brood. Sometimes logs are placed against the sides of the rickety structure to keep it from toppling over and . . . rough lumber or tin roofing may serve to patch a broken window. . . . Many a sharecropper's child . . . would not know a school bus from a Rolls-Royce. Thinly clad, often without shoes, trudging to school with no books, paper or pencil, to be there all day without anything to eat is not a very pleasant thing for a normal youngster.[1]

The land owner, as sole source of credit, controlled the choice of the sharecropper's family diet, the place where he and his family lived and worked, the extent and kind of education afforded his children, and his annual earnings. The sharecropper's status demanded complete dependence on the owner. Thomas characterized the place of the sharecropper in this system as "the most stark serfdom and exploitation . . . left in the western world."[2]

The sharecropper of the 1930s was no better off than his grandparents of the 1880s. Vast profits had been earned from cotton production over the years, but the sharecroppers had not shared in them. After years of continuous struggle, the average sharecropper remained mired in the depths of a system that rarely provided him anything more than a bare subsistence. A Protestant minister serving in Arkansas vividly portrayed this system of generational deprivation:

> The sharecropper of today is no more literate, no more wealthy, no more cultured, no more privileged than was his grandfather of fifty years ago. Hope, ambition and incentive have through the years been killed.... It is stupid to condemn them as idle, shiftless and immoral. If they are so, the responsibility is not theirs. The [sharecropper] is today the product of a vicious, stifling environment into which he was born. He is condemned at birth to grow up in a poverty-stricken home, guided by illiterate parents who themselves are without ambition, without incentive. Idealism is a word unknown. Such a child matures, marries and in turn establishes a

---

1 Ibid., 46.
2 Thomas was quoted by Kester in *Revolt Among the Sharecroppers*, 17.

home no better, no worse, than his father's. So generation after generation, the tragic fate of the [sharecropper] is repeated.[1]

This system could not be rationally defended; it was wholly indefensible. Yet there were those who nonetheless attempted. Thomas noted that a local newspaper editorially argued that the sharecroppers were "shiftless," otherwise they would buy the land and fix up their homes. Thomas was wholly unconvinced:

> An extreme form of the argument runs to the effect that what the Negro gets is plenty good enough for him and probably also for the white sharecropper. Here again the whole tone of the argument is reminiscent of old arguments in support of slavery. A Government investigator who whitewashed conditions near Tyronza called upon the most active Socialists in town and requested that there be "no more complaints or disturbances," adding this word of advice: "The landlords are all your friends and these sharecroppers are a shiftless lot. There is no use of being concerned about them as they really don't count. They are here today and gone tomorrow."[2]

In 1934, Socialists residing in Arkansas initiated action to end this system of peonage. Twenty-five years earlier, when Eugene Debs was at his peak, socialism had taken root in parts of Arkansas, Louisiana, Oklahoma, and Texas. Debs had fired the imaginations of workers and farmers of that area of the country, and by 1912 the Socialist Party had 12,000 members in Oklahoma alone, and many pockets of members were active in the other three states. From this grass roots socialism had sprung enthusiasts such as H. L. Mitchell of Tyronza. Mitchell talked socialism to everyone who came into his dry-cleaning establishment, and one of his converts was Clay East, scion of an old local family, owner of a gasoline station next to Mitchell's dry-cleaning store. Mitchell and Clay were both respected as honest business people. They chartered a local branch of the Socialist Party and became active in enlisting aid for sharecroppers in the area. In the closing months of 1933, Mitchell wrote the letter to Thomas that alerted him to the tragedy unfolding in Arkansas.

In response to Mitchell's letter, Thomas visited Tyronza and toured the surrounding area. For many years Thomas had lived in the slums of New York City among people existing in the most distressing conditions, but none of what he had seen on Spring Street or in Harlem prepared him for what he found in Arkansas. Shocked and horrified, he walked among the sharecropper shacks, muttering, "deplorable, deplorable." Never had he laid eyes on such an ugly state of affairs. "It is a feudal system . . . under which the

---

1 Rev. Alfred Loring-Clark, quoted in the *Memphis Press-Scimitar* 9/28/35; reprinted in Howard Kester, *Revolt Among the Sharecroppers*, 24.

2 Norman Thomas, *The Plight of the Share-Cropper* (League for Industrial Democracy, New York, 1934), 11-12.

sharecroppers live." He had discovered what he described as the "Forgotten Man." [1]

After the tour, Thomas spoke to an overflow audience at a school in Tyronza and denounced the system of semi-slavery he had just observed. He advised a group of local Socialists that they could crush this system only if the sharecroppers organized as a labor union. He pledged his assistance. He left Arkansas, his indignation aroused, determined to awake the public to the existence of a million and a half farm families living in conditions of utter deprivation, illiteracy, disease, and starvation.

Throughout his life he advocated socialism as the general means of ending human exploitation, but he was always quick to act personally, to throw himself into the midst of a situation where the issues were immediate and personal. If through his action he believed he could prevent individual acts of inequity and unfairness, or could contribute to eradicating conditions of injustice and oppression, he did not hesitate. He acted. That is precisely what he did in Arkansas.

A few weeks after Thomas' visit to Tyronza, twenty-seven sharecroppers, black and white, gathered in a schoolhouse just south of the town to discuss their common problems. The discussion immediately turned to Thomas' recommendation that they form a union, and nearly everyone was in favor. "Are we going to have two unions, "one of those present asked, "one for the whites and one for the colored?" Total silence. It was not a question easy to answer, but it was a question that had to be answered. One of them rose to remind the group that the churches had divided the races; perhaps the union should also. Another expressed the opinion that it would be dangerous to mix the races as the owners would not stand for it. A black man rose to speak:

> We colored people can't organize without you, and you white folks can't organize without us. Aren't we all brothers and ain't God the Father of us all? We live under the same sun, eat the same bread, wear the same kind of clothing, work on the same land, raise the same crop for the same landlord who oppresses and cheats us both. For a long time now the white folks and the colored folks have been fighting each other and both of us have been getting whipped all the time. We don't have anything against each other but we got plenty against the landlord. The same chain that holds my people holds your people too. If we're chained together on the outside we ought to stay chained together in the union. It won't do no good for us to divide because there's where the trouble has been all the time. The landlord is always betwixt us, beatin' us, and starvin' us and makin' us fight each other. There ain't but one way for us to get him where he can't help himself and that's for us to get together and stay together.[2]

He then sat down, and thus was born the Southern Tenant Farmers' Union (STFU), with a black and white membership.

---

1 *The Washington Post* 2/18/34, 3.

2 Howard Kester, *Revolt Among the Sharecroppers*, 56.

Socialists were prominent in the union from its inception, but the STFU was not an adjunct of the Socialist Party, as detractors later charged. Suffering and bitterness motivated the sharecroppers to unionize. Conversely, satisfaction with the world as it existed motivated the opposition of the landowners. They opposed the newly organized union at every turn and resorted to acts of intimidation against the small group of union organizers. The sharecroppers, experiencing a sense of unity, fought back. Their number increased daily.

Mitchell became a marked man in northeastern Arkansas. As the union's field organizer, he successfully recruited hundreds of new members for the union, but then Tyronza residents, urged on by the land owners, boycotted Mitchell's dry-cleaning business — and it soon failed. When threats of violence were made against him and his family, he moved his wife and children across the Mississippi River to Memphis, forty miles distant. Thomas and Mitchell visited the Arkansas governor to inform him — as if he were unaware of the circumstances — of the horrendous conditions then existing in the cotton fields of his own state. The governor rejected their plea for help and warned them, "You can't go around preaching social equality in the state of Arkansas."[1]

Despite widespread owner opposition and acts of intimidation, the union continued to grow and gain strength, enrolling more than six thousand members in less than a year. Sharecropper enthusiasm for unionization was high, and union locals were established in nearly every small town in the region. For some, advancing the goals of the union amounted to a crusade. Howard Kester moved into the state to help Mitchell. Thomas traveled the eastern part of the state delivering fiery, uplifting speeches in support of the union. He spoke to thousands, many of whom had walked for miles to hear him. Reporters from *The New York Times* and *The Washington Post* were drawn to the area and the entire country became involved.

Union members frequently held meetings in church halls, and Thomas often spoke at those meetings urging the sharecroppers to hold firm and not succumb to the intimidating tactics of the land owners. Following one of these meetings, Thomas stayed the night at a nearby hotel and paid his room bill with small change collected at the meeting. The hotel desk clerk seemed transfixed by the number of nickels, dimes, and quarters Thomas handed him in payment for the room. A short time later one of those who had been present at the church meeting heard the desk clerk call the Police Department. "That you, Chief? Listen. Watch out for a traveling dice game operated by a tall fellow going by the name of Norman Thomas."[2]

---

1 John Herling, "Field Notes from Arkansas," *The Nation* 3/29/35, 419.
2 Harry Fleischman, *Norman Thomas, A Biography: 1884–1968* (W. W. Norton, New York, 1969), 148.

Owner opposition to the union, at first merely vocal, turned physical and vicious. In midwinter, some owners evicted the families of sharecroppers active in the union. Visitors to Arkansas at the time described scenes resembling wartime. The roads were clogged with the evicted. Local residents were reminded of photographs of fleeing World War I refugees. Seeing entire families sitting by the roadside in the cold surrounded by their few scraps of belongings was not uncommon.[1] "Riding bosses" who worked for plantation owners attacked STFU meetings with whips and guns, and union members were warned against "outside agitators like Norman Thomas."[2]

In March 1935, sharecroppers confronted a new eruption of violence initiated by the land owners. Shareholder shacks were riddled with machine gun fire, union organizers mobbed, beaten and jailed.[3] Two sharecroppers were shot during a raid of a union meeting. Still, the union continued to grow.

W. H. Stultz, a local sharecropper, joined the union and later became its president. Subsequently, he spent time in jail for signing up members for the union. He was charged with "interfering with labor."[4] His landlord then evicted him, his wife, and six children. Riding bosses and a band of vigilantes threw their belongings onto the road and warned him that if he failed to leave the county within twenty-four hours, they would see to it that 'his brains were blown out and his body thrown into the . . . river."

The sharecroppers went out on strike, and Thomas enthusiastically backed them. When he was not speaking to meetings of union members, he was leading a campaign in the north to raise money, food, and clothing for the striking sharecroppers and their families. Thomas tirelessly traveled about the country raising funds for the strikers. The strike would not have long continued had it not been for the financial aid received from outside Arkansas.

As the owners' campaign of violence and terror intensified, Thomas grew increasingly resolved to help the sharecroppers. He was nearly overwhelmed with rage, his sense of justice and fairness inflamed, when on one of his speaking tours he witnessed an eviction of a shareholder family. He came upon the sharecropper, a fellow named McCullough, his wife, and his five children, ranging in age from four to seventeen, sitting by the roadside. The summer before, two riding bosses had raped McCullough's fourteen-year-old daughter. He filed a criminal complaint against the rapists, but instead of arresting them, town officials jailed McCullough, supposedly for having stolen a couple of eggs. The rapists were never prosecuted. After he was re-

---

1 *The New York Times* 4/20/35, 5.
2 David M. Kennedy. *Freedom from Fear: The American People in Depression and War, 1929-1945* (Oxford University Press, New York, 1999), 209.
3 Arthur M. Schlesinger, Jr., *The Coming of the New Deal: The Age of Roosevelt*, 378.
4 John Herling, "Field Notes from Arkansas," *The Nation.*

leased from jail, McCullough was brutally beaten.[1] Now he had been evicted from his home. Thomas' dedication to the ideals of equity and justice was never more directly challenged than it was in Arkansas.

The small town of Marked Tree, located not far from Tyronza, became the focus of much of the mob-induced violence against union members. Marked Tree was a community of about two thousand, half of whom were African-Americans. It was typical of towns of that part of the country. The tracks of the St. Louis & San Francisco Railroad ran along one side of its main street and one-story brick commercial buildings were located along the other. One of the brick buildings was occupied by the Chapman-Dewey Lumber Company, the owner of the largest plantation in the county and also of a commissary store. A.C. Spellings was farm manager for Chapman-Dewey and also a town leader. Spellings told a *New York Times* reporter that if he were on a jury trying a man charged with killing "an outside agitator," he would vote for acquittal despite the evidence.[2]

The largest building in Marked Tree was the First Methodist Church, whose pastor was the Rev. J. Abner Sage, known locally as "Brother Sage." Brother Sage's sympathies were with the plantation owners in their battle with the sharecroppers, who he claimed had "only themselves to blame if they are not as well blessed with this world's goods as they would like to be."[3] He spent the good part of every day conferring with A.C. Spellings about the local "red menace" and what could be done to confront it. Brother Sage also felt strongly about the way northern union organizers shook hands with African-Americans, addressed them as "Mister," and "gave them ideas about social equality." He conceived of a plan to relieve serious unemployment in the town by raising money from land owners to put men to work beautifying the town. Any of the unemployed who wished to gain such employment could do so merely by renouncing the STFU. Otherwise, these positions were barred to them.[4] Brother Sage was unsuccessful in reducing the union membership.

Local law enforcement in Marked Tree fell under the purview of Fred H. Stafford, Deputy County Prosecutor. Stafford prided himself on having discovered that students from a nearby college who had "poked their noses into the sharecropper situation" had been subjected at the college to the "Communist viewpoint."[5] Along with Spellings and Sage, Stafford ran the town. Undoubtedly, a word of disapproval from any of the three would have halted

---

1 Ibid. This event was also reported in Harry Fleischman, *Norman Thomas, A Biography: 1884–1968*, 148.
2 *The New York Times*, 4/16/35, 18.
3 Ibid.
4 Ibid.
5 Ibid.

the night-ridings and other acts of violence against the sharecroppers. That word of disapproval was never uttered.

On one evening, a band of more than forty masked night-riders shot up the home of C.T. Carpenter, the attorney representing the STFU. The fact that Carpenter, whose father had fought for the Confederacy under Robert E. Lee, was a fixture in the community and was long active in Democratic Party politics, did not deter his attackers. Similar attacks were later made upon the homes of African-American members of the union. A mob of armed vigilantes accosted a group of African-American men and women returning home after attending evening church services, beating them with pistol butts and flashlights. On the same night, another group of night-riders shot out the lights of a small church in a neighboring town, terrorizing the women and children that were present.

In the midst of this campaign of terror, Thomas decided to challenge the land owners. On the evening of March 15, 1935, he and a group of supporters approached the neighboring town of Birdsong to speak to an assemblage of union members at the town's African-American church. Thomas and his supporters were in physical danger, and they knew it. Here, in gun-toting country, more than one thousand miles from New York City, he was looked upon as "an interfering Yankee," having no legitimate purpose in speaking to poor sharecroppers in rural Arkansas.

About 500 sharecroppers and family members — a huge crowd for that area — came to the church to hear him speak. The church was not large enough to accommodate them, so they congregated on a grass plot in front of the church. As the meeting was about to begin, about thirty white men, armed and drunk, forced their way through the crowd to the steps and platform fronting the church. Thomas afterward described them as a "terrifying mob of white planters and riding bosses."[1] Standing on the church steps, Howard Kester started to speak. He got as far as "Ladies and gentlemen," when a drunken chorus prevented him from speaking further: "There ain't no ladies in the audience and there ain't no gentlemen on the platform." The gunmen violently pushed Kester off the steps, and one of them screamed at him, "You ain't got no invitation." Thomas stood up to speak, waving a letter inviting him to address union members. Also clutching a copy of the Arkansas Constitution, he directed the attention of the gunmen to that document's Bill of Rights and demanded of them to declare by what authority they were preventing the meeting from proceeding. "Is this a legal meeting?" he shouted. They had to admit it was legal, but they persisted. "There ain't goin' to be no speakin' here. We are citizens of this county and we run it to suit ourselves. We don't need no God-damn Yankee bastard to tell us

---

1 Thomas autobiography, 144.

what to do with our niggers and we want you to know that this is the best God-damn county on earth." Another gunman shouted that "[they] weren't afraid of any God-damned nigger-loving Yankee even if he did speak over the radio." Even as the drunken men brandished their guns, Thomas spoke on, but he then was struck from behind and dragged from the church steps. One of the union officials also was struck on the head. Thomas had never seen an uglier group. At that point one of the attackers, identifying himself as a deputy sheriff, warned Thomas that if he persisted in speaking, many of those present were going to get hurt. They then threw Thomas, Kester, and two others into their automobile and told them to get out of the county and never return. Several carloads of gunmen followed their car to the county line.[1] Thomas later wrote, "I should have enjoyed the trip better if we had [bullet] proof glass in the rear window!"[2]

A reign of terror followed the Birdsong incident. Six days after Thomas had been barred from speaking, a mob attempted to lure the union chaplain, the Rev. A. B. Brookins, from his home, apparently to lynch him. When they failed in their purpose, they riddled the Brookins' home with bullets. Brookins and his wife escaped injury but their daughter was wounded. On the same day, the Rev. T. A. Allen, an African-American preacher and organizer for the union, was shot and his body, weighted with chains, was cast into a river. The day following, Mary Green, wife of a union member then active in organizing the sharecroppers, was said to have died of fright when armed vigilantes came to their home to lynch her husband. That same evening, a mob prevented Clay East from addressing a meeting of union members in Marked Tree, and an armed band escorted him out of the county and told him that if he ever were to return he would be shot on sight. Five days later, John Allen, secretary to a union local at one of the larger plantations, escaped a mob of riding bosses and deputies intent on lynching him. While he was in hiding, several African-Americans were beaten, including a woman whose ear was severed, because they refused to reveal his hiding place. Three days afterward, an armed band of vigilantes mobbed a group of African-Americans returning home from church services. Men and women were beaten and scores of children were injured in their struggle to escape the attackers. That same night another church, in which the union members had been conducting meetings, was burned to the ground. Two days later, machine gun fire struck the home of Rev. E. B. McKinney, vice-president of the union.[3]

---

1 The Birdsong event is recorded in several works, including Howard Kester, *Revolt Among the Sharecroppers*, 80-81. Thomas also wrote of it in some detail in autobiography, 144-145-A.

2 Thomas autobiography, 145-A.

3 Howard Kester, *Revolt Among the Sharecroppers*, 82-85.

Following the incident in Birdsong, Thomas returned to New York shaken but nonetheless determined to awaken the national conscience to what was happening in Arkansas. He addressed the nation by radio:

> There is a reign of terror in the cotton country of eastern Arkansas. It will either end in the establishment of complete and slavish submission to the vilest exploitation in America or in bloodshed, or in both.... The plantation system involves the most stark serfdom and exploitation that is left in the western world.[1]

He then took another tack. Well aware of his own limitations in effecting a reform in Arkansas, he turned to a higher authority. He called upon President Roosevelt to come to the aid of the sharecroppers.

1 Ibid., 85.

CHAPTER 10. THE SHARECROPPER PROBLEM AND THE ROOSEVELT
ADMINISTRATION

Thomas insisted that the most pressing human problem facing the United
States in the mid-1930s was that involving the sharecroppers.[1] The Roosevelt
administration, though not unaware of the torment and oppression suffered
by the sharecroppers, viewed their plight from another perspective. Secretary
of Agriculture Henry A. Wallace argued that tenant farming had grown to
such an extent that it had become an undesirable characteristic of rural life.
He noted that because the average period of tenancy was less than five years,
an unusual degree of instability and the lack of a well-knit social life existed
among the sharecroppers, and thus it was nearly impossible for sharecropper families who moved from place to place every few years to meaningfully
participate in school, church, and other social activities.[2] The only way to
introduce a stable community was to render it possible for sharecroppers to
become owners of the land they worked. Wallace was more a visionary than
a practical politician and his proposed solution to the issue had no immediate effect upon the life of the suffering sharecropper.

The depression-induced decline in the price of cotton added to the prevailing misery of the sharecropper population. While resisting the coercive
tactics of his landowner, the sharecropper was further devastated by a rapidly deteriorating economy. The precipitous drop in cotton prices meant
that the proceeds of sale at the end of the growing season covered a smaller
portion of a sharecropper's debt incurred to the landowner during the year.

---

1 The Washington Post, 2/23/35, 3.
2 Henry A Wallace, "Wallace Points to Dangers of Tenancy," The New York Times, 3/31/35, SM-4.

When the bottom dropped out of the cotton market, the sharecroppers were those most adversely affected.[1]

The New Deal's solution to falling farm prices was the enactment of the Agricultural Adjustment Act (AAA) which by design drove up the price of farm products by reducing the acreage placed in production. In anticipation that the reduction of the acreage planted in cotton would lead to widespread unemployment of sharecroppers, Department of Agriculture officials directed farm owners:

> to *endeavor in good faith* to bring about a reduction of acreage . . . in such manner to cause *the least* possible amount of labor, economic and social disturbance, and to this end . . . , *insofar as possible*, maintain [on their farms] the normal number of tenants and other employees.

In addition, the law allowed displaced sharecroppers to remain in their shacks rent free *"unless any such tenant shall so conduct himself as to become a nuisance or a menace"* to the landowner.[2]

The Roosevelt Administration's general intent in requiring landowner compliance with these demands was to minimize the displacement of sharecroppers when the owner took acreage out of production, but that intent was not realized. The obligations imposed upon the landowners — couched in such terms as "endeavor in good faith" and "in so far as possible" — were so weak and ambiguous as to be meaningless, and landowners looked upon them as more in the nature of goodwill gestures than binding obligations. In designing the cotton acreage reduction program, Henry Wallace's Department of Agriculture failed to obligate the landowners, in any real sense, to undertake any action to protect their sharecroppers from the havoc and depredation that would flow from implementation of the program.

The negative aspects of the acreage reduction program did not end there, since the law inadvertently empowered landowners to use other provisions of the program to further disadvantage their sharecroppers. The program permitted a displaced sharecropper to remain in his shack rent free for a period of up to two years unless he conducted himself in such manner as to become "a nuisance or a menace" to his landlord. Many landowners relied on that provision to evict sharecroppers who supported the union, reasoning that a union member surely was a nuisance as well as a menace.

Thus, the United States government, through mistaken notions evolved in the Department of Agriculture, inadvertently joined the landowners in oppressing the sharecroppers. It intensified sharecropper misery by allowing the introduction of a form of exploitation nearly as vicious as that yielded

---

1 Howard Kester, *Revolt Among the Sharecroppers* (University of Tennessee Press, Knoxville, 1997), Introduction by Alex Lichtenstein, 29.

2 Agricultural Adjustment Act of 1933 and Section 7 of the Cotton Acreage Reduction Contract.

---

by the landowners over the years before the Federal government intervened with the acreage reduction program. Under the AAA, huge numbers of share-croppers lost their status as tenant farmers and thereafter were reduced to hiring themselves out as day-laborers, workings for landowners for as little as seventy-five cents for a day's labor. But those who became day-laborers were the fortunate ones; thousands of other sharecroppers, at the time their plots of land fell within the acreage reduction program, found themselves unemployed, and their families without a place to live.

Thomas wrote to Wallace describing sharecropper frustrations and blighted hopes, and portrayed the sharecropper system as "one of the most abominable and indefensible systems of landlordism in the world":

> Now under the operation of the AAA hundreds of thousands of [sharecrop-pers] are either driven out on the roads without hope of absorption into industry or exist without land to cultivate . . . in shacks scarcely fit for pigs.... Has the Administration any plans. . . other than pious hopes. . .? Shall they starve quietly so as not to interrupt our much predicted return to prosperity?[1]

Thomas then initiated a series of scathing attacks against the Department of Agriculture and its cotton acreage reduction program. To strengthen his position, he undertook to gather more compelling evidence of the program's direct, adverse effect upon the sharecroppers. He asked Professor William R. Amberson of the University of Tennessee Medical School to conduct a study of a group of five-hundred Arkansas sharecropper families to learn how they fared under the cotton acreage reduction provisions. Following a detailed examination, Amberson concluded 1) that the cotton acreage reduc-tion program had indeed been responsible for the decline in the number of families living and working on cotton farms, 2) that landowners had used the program to minimize their reliance on sharecroppers, and 3) that 20 per-cent of all sharecroppers had been forced to turn to day-labor work in order to survive. The overall effect of the acreage reduction program was to fur-ther disadvantage the sharecropper population.[2] Thomas then published the findings of the Amberson report and his own observations and conclusions in a pamphlet entitled "The Plight of the Share-Cropper."[3]

With the Amberson report in hand, Thomas descended upon Henry Wal-lace and the Department of Agriculture. Wallace was not one to act quickly, no matter the urgency of the issue at hand. In another matter, he rebuffed a petitioner who had urged him to immediate action: "When you see some-thing you think is wrong, you want to do something about it right away. You

---

1 Thomas letter, dated 2/22/34, to Henry Wallace. The letter is quoted in part by W.A. Swanberg, *Norman Thomas: The Last Idealist* (Charles Scribner's Sons, New York, 1976), 159.

2 William R. Amberson, "The New Deal for Share-Croppers," *The Nation*, 2/13/35, 185.

3 Norman Thomas, *The Plight of the Share-Cropper* (League for Industrial Democracy, New York, 1934).

want to act quickly. I'm not like that. I'd rather sit under a tree and let the cycle of time help heal the situation."[1] Wallace was prepared to let "the cycle of time" resolve the sharecropper problem. Thomas was not.

Wallace refused to meet with Thomas. Thomas then appealed to Under Secretary of Agriculture Rex Tugwell and AAA Administrator Chester Davis, but neither agreed to undertake any action to help the sharecroppers. He conferred with other Department of Agriculture officials, but soon was convinced that powerful senators, such as Joseph T. Robertson of Arkansas, were inhibiting Department officials from initiating any meaningful action to assist the sharecroppers.

Despite pleas by the Socialist Party and the Southern Tenant Farmers' Union — and even by some in Roosevelt's administration — urging the Department of Agriculture to move to amend the cotton acreage reduction program, Wallace remained unmoved. He attributed the violence in Arkansas to Socialist and Communist agitation, and refused to give credence to claims that his own policies were in part responsible for the continuing turmoil. Eventually, Wallace ordered a Department investigator into Arkansas, but after reviewing her report, he refused to publish it. He enlisted a Duke University professor to study the problem, but still took no action when the professor confirmed the findings of the Amberson report.

Wallace tried to persuade the public of the efficacy of his approach of allowing the passage of time to resolve issues, including those confronting the sharecroppers. In an article written for *The New York Times*, he declared that AAA programs were incapable of resolving the problem. Anything the Department of Agriculture might do would, at best, be merely a temporary palliative:

> It seems to me that it will be virtually impossible for America to develop a rural civilization which affords security, opportunity and a fully abundant life for our rural people unless she acts to convert tenants of this sort into owner farmers. It is extremely unlikely that a satisfactory and stable rural civilization can be developed in communities where the land is owned by absentee landlords interested primarily in profit and farmed by tenants who are willing if not encouraged to mine the soil and allow the buildings to decay, with the thought that they can move on to a different farm every two or three years.[2]

In the long run, Wallace never varied his belief that the sharecropper issues would be resolved *only* by converting their status from tenants to landowners, and that a Federal program of long-term loans could assist in accomplishing this. He steadfastly advocated such a program, arguing that it constituted a thoroughly sound and justifiable procedure for creating

---

1 Arthur M. Schlesinger, Jr., *The Coming of the New Deal: The Age of Roosevelt* (Houghton Mifflin, Boston, 1959), 77.

2 Henry A Wallace, "Wallace Points to Dangers of Tenancy," *The New York Times*, 3/31/35, SM-4.

greater security and more desirable homes for the rural population. His proposal provided a long-term solution but offered no immediate relief. Wallace seemed not to realize that thousands of sharecroppers could very well starve to death before his ambitious program could be brought to fruition.

Frustrated by Wallace's failure to comprehend the urgency of the sharecropper plight, Thomas turned to governmental officials and others outside the Department of Agriculture. He was unsuccessful in arranging a meeting with Eleanor Roosevelt. He then turned to Felix Frankfurter, then a professor at Harvard Law School. Although Frankfurter was one of Roosevelt's closest advisors on New Deal legislation, he told Thomas he had much less influence with Roosevelt than the newspapers generally made people believe, and consequently he was unable to advance the sharecropper cause. Thomas also wrote to powerful members of the US Senate, and appealed in a radio broadcast to his listeners to bring immediate pressure on the Administration to act. He pressured newspaper editors to send reporters to Arkansas to witness for themselves the sorry state of the dispossessed sharecroppers. Here he achieved a degree of success. Among the newspapers who responded to his entreaties was *The New York Times*, who sent Raymond Daniell to Tyronza, Marked Tree, and the surrounding area. Daniell subsequently wrote a series of articles for the *Times* vividly portraying the plight of the sharecroppers and the vicious acts the landowners directed against them.[1]

Thomas also tried to persuade Senator Robert F. Wagner of New York to include protections for the sharecroppers in his proposed National Labor Relations Bill. Wagner, however, had already concluded that to ensure the bill's passage, he would have to exclude all agricultural workers from its coverage. Thomas then appealed to the labor unions for their assistance, and while the American Federation of Labor adopted resolutions deploring the conditions to which the sharecroppers had been reduced, it failed to offer any significant aid to the STFU.

Though Thomas failed to secure a meeting with Wallace, he ultimately succeeded in arranging a meeting with President Roosevelt. Having met with the President on previous occasions, Thomas was prepared to deal with Roosevelt's favorite tactic of turning a conversation in a direction that he, but not necessarily other parties to the conversation, wanted to pursue. On this occasion, Thomas, seizing control of the conversation, set out to describe the scenes of deprivation he had witnessed in Arkansas. He then asked Roosevelt whether he had ever read the Department of Agriculture contract that governed the rights of the landowners and sharecroppers in the cotton acreage reduction program. When Roosevelt responded that he had not, Thomas handed him a copy, highlighting those clauses that provided that

---

1 *The New York Times*, 4/16/35, 18; 4/18/35, 24; 4/19/35,18; 4/20/35, 3.

farm owners were required 1) merely to act in good faith in bringing about a reduction of acreage, 2) in such manner as to cause the least possible amount of labor, economic and social disturbance, and 3) only insofar as possible to maintain the same number of tenants and other employees. After reading the contract, Roosevelt said, "Well, that can mean anything or nothing." Apparently, Thomas asserted, insofar as the leadership of the Department of Agriculture is concerned, it means "nothing." Roosevelt moved to regain control of the conversation: "Norman, I'm a damned sight better politician than you are," at which Thomas interposed, "Certainly, Mr. President, you're on that side of the desk and I'm on this." Thomas never got to complete his thought, as Roosevelt interrupted to tell Thomas how certain US senators from Southern states could savage his New Deal programs if he were to attempt to run roughshod over their interests while attempting to resolve issues related to the sharecropper situation. Matters were changing in the South, Roosevelt said; Thomas had to be patient.[1] This was advice Thomas found impossible to accept. How could he, when sharecroppers and their families daily confronted obstacles that placed their very survival at stake?

Newspaper accounts of the meeting reported that Thomas has pressed Roosevelt in three areas, asking:[2]

> 1. That the Federal government open an investigation into what had happened in Arkansas, especially regarding the reign of terror, the night riders, and the murder of a minister and others.

> 2. That the President require the Department of Agriculture to alter the cotton acreage reduction program to provide meaningful protection for the sharecroppers.

> 3. That Roosevelt ask Congress to amend the Agriculture Adjustment Act to specifically guarantee the right of sharecroppers to organize as labor unions.

Roosevelt was persistent in advising patience, but Thomas was equally persistent in demanding immediate action. *The Sharecropper's Voice*, a publication of the Southern Tenant Farmers' Union, stated that, under Roosevelt, "too often the progressive word has been the clothing for a conservative act. Too often he has talked like a cropper and acted like a planter."[3] But Roosevelt realized his options were limited. Congressional enactment of his New Deal proposals was heavily dependent upon the support of cotton state spokespersons in the Senate and the House of Representatives. Roosevelt had gained passage of New Deal programs by working with the Democratic Party leadership, and one of those leaders was Senator Joseph T. Robinson of Arkansas. Robinson favored the Arkansas landowners, and displayed little

---

1 Thomas autobiography, 142-143.

2 *The Washington Post*, 5/3/35, 11.

3 Quoted in Arthur M. Schlesinger, Jr., *The Coming of the New Deal: The Age of Roosevelt*, 379.

sympathy for the sharecroppers in his own state. Roosevelt feared that any proposal of his to help the sharecroppers would alienate Robinson, thus placing the entire New Deal program in jeopardy.

The President declined to order an investigation of allegations made by Thomas and the Southern Tenant Farmers' Union that a massive number of sharecroppers had been dispossessed by the Department of Agriculture's implementation of the cotton acreage reduction program. Rather than acceding to Thomas' request that the Federal government initiate a program providing immediate relief for dispossessed sharecroppers, Roosevelt asked Arkansas Governor Futrell to appoint a committee of local citizens to investigate the existing conditions of the sharecroppers. Futrell, acting essentially as a tool of the landowners, had already publicly established a position that was antithetical to the sharecroppers, who he identified as a "shiftless bunch." Thomas likened Roosevelt's involvement of the Arkansas governor as comparable to asking Al Capone to investigate conditions in Chicago's underworld. Subsequent to a speech later delivered by the president in Arkansas, Thomas unmercifully condemned Roosevelt's failure to act more forcefully in favor of the sharecroppers:

> The President was dissuaded from action in Arkansas by consideration of the possible adverse effect of such action upon the political forces of his Administration. It is an Administration in which Southern Senators by virtue of seniority hold very high place. . . .The President in his . . . address in Arkansas. . .avoided all references to the terrorism which a few days later added a Southern woman and a clergyman to its list of victims of flogging and other brutalities. He contented himself with praising Senator Robinson. . . .[1]

Thomas' reference to "victims of flogging" related to three beating incidents. In the spring of 1936, three thousand sharecroppers, reduced to working as day-laborers, went on strike, seeking a higher daily wage. Led by the STFU, the strikers sought to double the prevailing 75 cents daily rate. Emotions ran high among striking cotton field workers and landowners.

In the midst of the strike, Willie Sue Blagden, of Memphis, and the Rev. Claude C. Williams, of Little Rock, were beaten by a group of six men near the small town of Earle, in northeastern Arkansas. The target of still another beating on the same day was Roy Morelock, a sharecropper working with the strikers as a messenger. Miss Blagden, a writer and social services worker, and Reverend Williams, a Presbyterian minister and a vice-president of the American Federation of Teachers, had gone to Earle after hearing reports that a sharecropper in that town had been fatally beaten. When they arrived in the town, they were dragged from their car and pushed and shoved into a deeply wooded area where they were chastised for their "socialistic lean-

---

1 Norman Thomas, *After the New Deal, What?* (Macmillan, New York, 1936), 50.

ings" and then lashed with a heavy leather harness strap studded with metal brads. Their attackers accused them of traveling to Earle to "stir up trouble," and they were told to leave the town or be killed. Morelock later reported that he had been detained by a group of night riders and beaten with a small sledge hammer.

When he heard of these beatings, Thomas cabled Roosevelt appealing to him "to act in this monstrous perversion of everything decent in the American tradition," and Roosevelt ordered the Attorney General and the Department of Justice to investigate.[1] Thomas doubted the efficacy of a Federal investigation, but agreed it was better than a state investigation involving local Arkansas authorities who in the end would do nothing. Indeed, the sheriff of the county in which the floggings occurred later announced that "the only trouble we have . . . is from a bunch of foreign agitators. . . . All I know about the . . . floggings is what the newspapers carried."[2] The Earle newspaper reported that the floggings had produced results in that they eliminated foreign agitators where less drastic action had failed.[3]

As Thomas had anticipated, later that summer the Attorney General announced that the investigation of the floggings had failed to disclose any violations of Federal law.[4] A few weeks later the Democratic Party selected Arkansas' Senator Robinson as its National Convention Chair. Thomas criticized the appointment, calling Robinson the "beneficiary and protector of the cotton plantation system, the most shameful form of exploitation in America":

> The President and his Party knew of peonage, terrorism, the flogging of men and women. . . and they were silent. Friends of the Southern Tenant Farmers' Union, especially outraged by the whippings of the Reverend Claude Williams and Miss Willie Sue Blagden, picketed Senator Robinson's hotel. The result was silence — not even a specific platform reference to the rights of agricultural workers. The Convention listened without gasping while Joe Robinson, Senator from one of the most backward of our states in social legislation, protector of night riders and floggers, apostrophized liberty and justice.[5]

The sharecropper strike produced mixed results. The union maintained that it obtained higher wages for thousands of day-laborers and that a number of plantation owners had recognized the Southern Tenant Farmers' Union as bargaining agent for their workers. Landowners, on the other hand, claimed that the strike had been ineffective and little had changed since labor remained plentiful at 75 cents a day.[6]

---

1 *The New York Times*, 6/17/36, 3: *The Washington Post*, 6/17/36, 1, and 6/21/36, B-4.
2 *The New York Times*, 6/18/36, 9.
3 Ibid., 6/24/36, 19.
4 *The Washington Post*, 8/13/36, XI.
5 Norman Thomas, *After the New Deal, What?*, 4.
6 *The New York Times*, 7/10/36, 1.

President Roosevelt ultimately took action, but it was too little and too late. By executive order, he established the Resettlement Administration to administer projects involving the resettlement of destitute families from rural to urban areas and to provide loans to finance the purchase of farm land by farm tenants, sharecroppers and day-laborers. Those representing sharecropper interests in Arkansas characterized the programs envisioned by the administrators of the new agency as "utterly inadequate" and "purely palliative," that failed to strike at the root of the problem.[1] Unfortunately, they were right. The successes of the Resettlement Administration were few, and in 1937, it was absorbed by another Federal agency.

In the end, all of Thomas' efforts failed, since the life of the average sharecropper did not change in any material way. The union won small pay increases for its day-laborer members but failed to achieve any fundamental changes in the sharecropper system and this system remained intact for years after. But Thomas was the first person to alert the country to the plight of the sharecropper, and it was through his dogged determination that the issue remained in public view for several years. Thomas spoke so frequently about the sharecroppers that when one Socialist heard that he was coming to his area to speak at a dinner meeting, he remarked, "Oh, Lord, that means we'll have sharecroppers again for dinner."[2]

One of Thomas' biographers referred to him as a "successful failure."[3] That description may be aptly applied to that period of Thomas' life devoted to helping the sharecroppers and their families. Although he ultimately failed to resolve their problems, the very fact that this sophisticated New Yorker traveled half way across the country to assist a group of farm workers and their families — existing at society's lowest economic level — endeared him to those people. In the nearly eighty years that the sharecropper system had effectively bound families in peonage to a land owning class, no one of his stature had ever come to their aid. That he willingly placed his own life in jeopardy in furtherance of their interests, and then on their behalf personally petitioned the President of the United States, was for these people — all but ignored citizens of a backward state — simply incredible. Under Thomas' leadership the Arkansas sharecroppers had joined together — black as well as white — and established in a Southern state, in a pre-civil rights era, a racially integrated labor union that continued from that time onward to represent members of both races. The sharecroppers realized that Thomas truly believed that they — despite their lack of education and horrendous

---

1 Howard Kester, *Revolt Among the Sharecroppers*, 89-90.

2 Harry Fleischman, *Norman Thomas, A Biography: 1884–1968* (W. W. Norton, New York, 1969), 153.

3 Murray B. Seidler, *Norman Thomas: Respectable Rebel* (Syracuse University Press, Syracuse, 1967), 294.

lives lived in abject poverty — were worthy of the focus of his attention. If nothing else, Thomas' presence in their midst tended to restore their faith in themselves, and — one can only hope — he thus made their lives more bearable.

Chapter 11. The Decline of the Socialist Party

Thomas had rejoiced in the downfall of the Russian czarist government in 1917, but later had serious doubts about Lenin and the Bolshevik government that followed. In 1919, he made his home available for meetings of the unofficial delegation of Bolsheviks to the United States, but his willingness to cooperate with the Russian delegation did not immunize him from subsequent Communist attacks. The Communists set out to capture or, if that proved unsuccessful, destroy the Socialist Party. They considered Socialists betrayers of the working class and they unmercifully attacked Thomas, Hillquit and other Socialist Party leaders, using any criticism that might occur to them, regardless of how false or contrived.

Throughout Europe, Socialist parties gained dominant roles in the politics of their nations, but not in the United States. The American Socialist Party never exercised national political power, since its primary role in American society — though not by design — was educational. The Communists, who hated and feared democracy, targeted the American Socialists because they championed the cause of democratic progress. Leon Trotsky once sarcastically said of Thomas that he was a Socialist "as the result of a misunderstanding."[1] Earl Browder, leader of the American Communist Party in the 1930s, denounced Thomas and other Socialists as "left social-fascists" and described them as "the most dangerous enemies of the workers' struggles today."[2] Communists branded Thomas, their chief target among Ameri-

---

1 W. A. Swanberg, *Norman Thomas: The Last Idealist* (Charles Scribner's Sons, New York, 1976), 193.

2 Arthur M. Schlesinger, Jr., *The Politics of Upheaval: The Age of Roosevelt* (Houghton Mifflin, Boston, 1960) 198.

can Socialists, as "yellow," "a fake," "a traitor," "a reactionary," and — in their minds, the ultimate vilification — "a sky-pilot," a reference to his former life as a clergyman.[1]

Hurling invectives at his critics was not Thomas' style. He was loath to respond to the Communists in kind, but nonetheless was sorely tempted. At first, he tried to cooperate with the Communists, but to his dismay found that the notion of reasonable fair play was foreign to them. Under instructions from Moscow, Communists were consistently on the attack, always placing Communist Party interests above those of all others. They would not hesitate to break up a labor union in the midst of a strike if they could not control the striking workers, all the time protesting that they were the only friends the workers ever had. The Communist Party press claimed that Thomas was a supporter of lynching, that he favored war, and that he once stood by laughing while police beat up an unemployed worker.[2] When Thomas testified before a Congressional committee regarding legislation authorizing preparations for war, Communists denounced his testimony while deliberately distorting it.[3] Actions of this type reflected Lenin's precept that any lie or deceit was justified if it advanced the Communist cause.

Communists frequently tried to disrupt Socialist meetings and rallies. In February 1934, the Socialists held a rally in New York City to protest the violent attack and slaughter by Austrian officials of a group of Socialists in Vienna. More than 15,000 Socialists and members of various local trade unions gathered at Madison Square Garden for the rally, but before the proceedings got under way, more than 5,000 uninvited Communists marched into the building. Handbills distributed by the Communists outside the Garden denounced the Socialists as having engaged in the fostering of fascism in the United States. When leaders of the meeting called it to order, the Communists started screaming and hooting, thus preventing any of the speakers from being heard. The Socialists and trade unionists were so stunned by the spectacle that at first they sat silent and confused as the Communists continued to outshout each other. Then fist fights erupted throughout the hall. Communists hurled chairs from the balconies down upon those sitting below. They attacked Socialists with knives, scissors and beer bottles they had concealed in newspapers. The leader of the Communist mob rushed to the speaker's platform but Socialists barred him from speaking and quickly ejected him from the building. Socialists on the speakers' platform tried in vain to silence the mob and restore order, but each time a speaker attempted

1 Devere Allen, "Presidential Possibilities: Norman Thomas — Why Not?" *The Nation* 3/30/32, 365.

2 Norman Thomas, *The Choice Before Us: Mankind at the Crossroads* (Macmillan, New York, 1934), 151-153.

3 Norman Thomas, *The Test of Freedom* (W. W. Norton, New York, 1954), 51-52.

to address the crowd, the Communists would shriek and yell. Ultimately the rally had to be canceled, as the Communists intended from the outset.[1] Thomas later said that the reaction of Germans to similar tactics used by Communists in that country paved the way for Hitler's rise to power.

The fear of being tarnished by association with the Communists had no hold on Thomas. While recognizing the impossibility of an organic unity of Socialists and Communists, he nevertheless believed that common action was possible, that under certain circumstances Socialists and Communists could co-operate on specific issues, such as in resisting all forms of fascism,[2] the enemy above all others of both groups. But events similar to that which occurred at the Madison Square Garden rally ultimately persuaded him that any sort of co-operative effort was unlikely to succeed as long as the Communists continued to act in bad faith.

In spite of the many personal attacks upon him and despite his misgivings about Communist lack of good faith, Thomas retained a modicum of hope that the two groups could at some point present a united front, at least in some narrow areas. Thus, in the latter part of November 1935, Thomas agreed to participate in a debate with Earl Browder, Chairman of the Communist Party of the USA, to discuss the merits of the doctrines advanced by each party. More than 20,000 Communists and Socialists attended the event, again staged in Madison Square Garden, the site of the Communist-induced riot less than two years earlier.

Browder hailed the occasion as speeding the way toward the goal of united action by the two parties, but Thomas was far more cautious in projecting any form of co-operative effort. He insisted, as he had many times previously, that the Communists must first show through convincing evidence that they intended to act in good faith before the parties could undertake common action. "I favor the maximum possible amount of joint action by all who are opposed to war or fascism," he said, but in face of the destructive record of the Communists, he added, "We are justified in asking for proof of sincerity of the changed position of the Communists." He expressed skepticism regarding Communist aims and goals, but remained hopeful they would prove themselves fit to participate in a unified front.[3]

During the debate, Browder unwisely alluded to Socialist Party internal disputes then roiling the party. The most pressing of those disputes arose out of Old Guard opposition to any joint activity with the Communists. Most recently, leaders of the Old Guard faction had expressed unhappiness that Thomas had agreed to meet publicly with Browder. Noting that Old Guard members were absent from the debate, Browder congratulated Thomas on

1 *The New York Times* 2/17/34, 1.

2 Norman Thomas, *The Choice Before Us: Mankind at the Crossroads*, 151.

3 *The New York Times* 11/28/35, 36.

his continued opposition to that faction of the Socialist Party. Thomas icily responded that Browder was unqualified to stand as a judge of an internal Socialist Party dispute.

Browder had touched a raw nerve. Old Guard members had openly opposed all efforts to form a united front with the Communists. Thomas, on the other hand, contended that the Socialists dare not ignore any group or political faction that would join with them in opposing fascism, war, or capitalistic exploitation of the workers. Even while recommending limited co-operation with the Communists, Thomas repeatedly condemned Communist Party advocacy of violent class warfare. He made clear to the Old Guard members that he feared a Communist dictatorship, condemning it as the antithesis of democratic freedom, and that he was well aware that American Communists willingly subjected themselves to the rule of Moscow, thus precluding a unification of the two parties.

The readiness of the Communists to resort to violence to achieve their ends was totally foreign to Thomas' view and that of the Socialist Party. He was convinced that violence begat violence, and that it should be avoided in America's transition from capitalism to socialism. Socialism should replace capitalism through democratic means and without violence. But, strangely, this fundamental difference in Socialist and Communist principles failed to deter Thomas from continuing attempts to persuade others that Socialists and Communists could co-operate in attaining that goal.

The Old Guard, inalterably opposed to any form of co-operative effort with the Communists, portrayed Thomas as the conscious or unconscious tool of the Communist Party. Some less caustically vocal members of the Old Guard held that Thomas' failure to realize that the Communists were engaged in a deliberate policy of treachery reflected his "turn the other cheek" approach to life held over from his days as a clergyman, and that he really was unfit for the role as a leader of the Socialist Party.

Thomas did not waver in opting for an inclusive Socialist Party. He wrote in his autobiography that his plan for an inclusive party was comparable to his planning a trip from New York to Philadelphia with a group of individuals who did not agree with him on traveling to any point beyond Philadelphia. In planning the trip, Thomas would be satisfied in deferring a decision on their ultimate destination. During the trip to Philadelphia, he and the group could discuss traveling beyond that city, and if they came to an agreement before their arrival in Philadelphia, they would be able to continue their trip together. Otherwise, they would go their separate ways.[1]

Thomas was not alone among party members in believing that the Socialists should make an effort to deal with the Communists and perhaps even

---

1 Thomas autobiography, 162-164.

work with them within the confines of existing civic organizations, but there was not a great deal of support for his position. Why he continued to advocate co-operation with the Communists for as long as he did is something of a mystery. Nearly every one of his contacts with the Communists had been negative, and he had been the subject of their most foul acrimony. Later in his life he admitted he had held a more favorable view of the Communists than that warranted by the facts, and that the Old Guard views were nearer the truth than had been his.[1] Ultimately he concluded that communism was little better than fascism. Unfortunately for the Socialist Party, Thomas arrived at this view too late to avert the disaster that was about to strike the party.

The simmering Old Guard– Militant dispute foreshadowed a split in the Socialist Party. Two factors hastened that split — the death of Morris Hillquit and the increased involvement of Norman Thomas in activities outside the Socialist Party. Hillquit died in October 1933. Had he lived, he might have brought about an Old Guard–Militant rapprochement. As the party's National Chair, he had long been a dominant figure in the National Executive Committee and, despite his identification with the Old Guard, his influence with the rest of the party membership remained considerable. Even after the 1932 national convention– with Thomas serving as the leader of the party outside New York — Hillquit retained a leadership role in New York and remained active in party affairs until his death. At that point, the leadership of the Old Guard faction passed to a triumvirate of his close advisers, but of those, one was in poor health, another was an ineffective public speaker, and the third was unpopular within party ranks. The Old Guard had no leader of the stature of a Morris Hillquit or of a Norman Thomas. Strong, assertive, and effective leadership of the Old Guard faction died with Hillquit.

Thomas' involvement in activities outside the Socialist Party left him little time for participation in internal party matters. His efforts expended on behalf of the Arkansas sharecroppers was a prime example. He became known as an easy mark for those in trouble because he never rejected a request for assistance. That was especially the case if the request came from someone in distress resulting from governmental action or inaction. These occasions took him far afield from party matters. Moreover, Thomas was inclined, whenever possible, to avoid party squabbles. He probably would not have allowed himself to become involved in the factionalism generated by the dispute between the Old Guard and the Militants had it not been for his growing frustration with the procrastination and inaction of Hillquit and his Old Guard followers. He might have mediated the dispute had he

---

1 Ibid.

not sided with the Militants, and unfortunately, the party had no one else to assume that role.

The Old Guard and Militant members of the party were contrasts in age, background, education, and political philosophy. Old Guard members had long been loyal to the party, viewing it as their own preserve, and by virtue of their seniority, occupied most of the party's leadership positions. Not of an activist mode, they assumed that the revolution culminating in the replacement of capitalism with socialism would occur in due course, probably without Socialist Party intercession. In contrast, the Militants adopted a radical political orientation, looking upon themselves as revolutionaries. Neither group had much respect for the other. The Old Guard considered the Militants as a group of irresponsible dilettantes, while the Militants looked upon the aging members of the Old Guard as a collection of pompous stuffed shirts.[1] On the eve of the 1934 Socialist Party national convention, the Old Guard–Militant factional dispute reached its climax.

At the convention, the Militants attacked the Old Guard as "the apologists of gradualism," and demanded that the Socialist Party immediately and vigorously press for national political power. They rejected any further effort by the party to engage in actions designed to reform the current political and economic landscape.[2] Because Thomas believed the Old Guard to be sterile, holding no promise for the future advancement of the party, he exhibited more sympathy to the general aims of the Militants. He never joined the Militants, but clearly he co-operated with them.

As mentioned earlier, the existence of a third group further complicated matters. The Progressives, a vague grouping of mostly members new to the party, were united in their dissatisfaction with the Old Guard's posture of inaction. "The Progressives wanted no more of the funereal, dragging steps that had characterized the party since [the end of World War I]; they demanded a quick march rhythm."[3] Their general goal was the creation of a national political party representing labor and farm workers. If the electorate selected the Socialist Party as that third party, well and good, but if another party were to achieve that status, then the Socialist Party should merge with it and attempt to direct it toward Socialist goals. Of course, this concept was totally foreign to Old Guard scripture that if a third party were to rise to a major political status, it had to be wholly Socialist.

---

1 Arthur M. Schlesinger, Jr., *The Politics of Upheaval: The Age of Roosevelt*, 177-178.
2 Daniel Bell, "The Background and Development of Marxian Socialism in the United States," *Socialism and American Life* , Vol. I, Edited by Donald Drew Egbert and Stow Persons (Princeton University Press, Princeton, 1952) 370; David A. Shannon, *The Socialist Party of America, A History* (Macmillan, New York, 1955), 211, 212.
3 David A. Shannon, *The Socialist Party of America, A History*, 214.

Most Progressives were convinced that only Norman Thomas could lead them to achieve their goals. Their goals and his were similar, and Thomas reflected their general philosophy that political leaders and their parties should act on principle rather than act as ones thirsting for political power.[1]

Socialists convened their 1934 national convention in Detroit in May of that year. As the delegates assembled, conditions existing in the economically depressed country were less than optimal for the party. Roosevelt, through his advocacy of New Deal measures directed to bringing about an economic recovery, had won over most of the country's progressives and labor union officials. These were the very people upon whom the Socialists relied upon to support them at the polls. As if that were not enough for the party to deal with, many Socialists also were turning to the New Deal.

All party factions came to Detroit prepared for battle, and the battle began when the Militants presented to the convention for its consideration a newly drafted Declaration of Principles. The document had been prepared by Devere Allen, a young Protestant minister, an editor of *The World Tomorrow*, and a Norman Thomas supporter. Overall, it was a statement of principles meant to guide Socialist behavior in the troubled times of the Depression. Words of revolutionary drive and force opened the document:

> The Socialist Party is the party of the workers, regardless of race, color, or creed. In mill and mine, shop and farm, office and school, the workers can assert their united power, and through the Socialist Party establish a cooperative commonwealth forever free from human exploitation and class rule. If the workers delay and drift, they will prolong their period of enslavement to a decadent capitalism.[2]

The most controversial section of the Declaration purported to require Socialists to accept certain responsibilities in case of war, the collapse of capitalism, or the onset of fascism. It reiterated Socialist Party positions that opposed militarism, imperialism, and war, and proposed to eradicate the perpetual economic warfare of capitalism which it claimed was the fruit of international conflict:

> War cannot be tolerated by Socialists.... Moreover, recognizing the suicidal nature of modern combat and the incalculable train of war's consequences which rest most heavily upon the working class, they will refuse collectively to sanction or support any international war.... They will meet war and the detailed plans for war...by massed war resistance.... [The Socialist Party] will do all in its power to fight fascism of every kind all the time and everywhere in the world, until fascism is dead.

The Declaration proclaimed anew the Socialist Party's faith in economic and political democracy, and pledged the party to act to replace capital-

---

1 Ibid., 213.

2 The Declaration of Principles is quoted at length in Murray B. Seidler, *Norman Thomas: Respectable Rebel* (Syracuse University Press, Syracuse, 1967), 128-131.

ism with a genuine workers' democracy: "Capitalism is doomed. If it can be superseded by a majority vote, the Socialist Party will rejoice. If the crisis comes through the denial of majority rights after the electorate has given us a mandate we shall not hesitate to crush by our labor solidarity the reckless force of reaction and to consolidate the Socialist state.[1]"

Those who supported the Declaration argued that war and fascism were imminent, and that the Socialist Party should declare its policies for contending with such catastrophes before they occurred. To circumvent a fascist coup, they argued it would be appropriate for the Socialists to seize power, by force if necessary.

Those in opposition to the Declaration responded that the document appeared to be Communist-inspired and its adoption could result in governmental prosecution. Some dissenters labeled it "communism, pure and simple."[2] Thomas appeared to straddle the issue. He spoke in support of the adoption of the Declaration, but with little enthusiasm, and in fact, minimized the significance of the document. He reminded the convention delegates that it merely repeated what Socialists had always held — that they would be justified in using violence only when all other means had been denied them. He later appeared more supportive when he wrote in *The World Tomorrow* that:

> The Declaration reiterates Socialist allegiance to peaceful and orderly methods of struggle, and to democracy in industry and politics. War and violence are neither blessed nor accepted as inevitable. On the contrary, it is because war is such a monstrous evil that Socialists are determined to offer "massive resistance" to it.... To establish peace means to change the system which breeds war. To prevent particular wars while we change the system depends more upon the firm opposition of masses of workers.... than upon any panacea a capitalist world will consider. I have repeatedly said and written that socialism and democracy each requires the other for the perfection of either. But we cannot afford to put or seem to put loyalty to a mechanical, nose-counting type of capitalist democracy ahead of loyalty to socialism. It is this which the Declaration says in its own words.[3]

At the convention, Thomas' focus was on opposition to war. He spoke vigorously against American participation in all wars. The task of the Socialist Party was to persuade the masses to adopt an uncompromising opposition to war. The only way to prevent war was to announce to "the lords and masters of the world" that "we will not fight."[4]

As historian Arthur M. Schlesinger, Jr. has observed, to the nation at large "it could not have mattered less what the American Socialist Party decided to

---

1 Ibid., 129-131.
2 Arthur M. Schlesinger, Jr., *The Politics of Upheaval: The Age of Roosevelt*, 178.
3 Norman Thomas, "What Happened at Detroit," *The World Tomorrow*, 6/28/34, 320, 321.
4 *The New York Times*, 6/4/34, 1.

do in case of war or economic collapse."[1] From the perspective of one outside the party, the Socialists appeared to be acting without regard to reality. But from the perspective of one standing within party ranks, the Declaration's tacit advocacy of the use of force and violence symbolized the gaping divide between Old Guard conservatism and the revolutionary radicalism of the Militants.

Despite Old Guard opposition, the delegates adopted the Declaration by a wide margin. Thomas and his followers then acted quickly to gain control of the National Executive Committee, electing eight of the committee's eleven members. The following day *The New York Times* reported that these developments marked Thomas' definitive ascendancy to party leadership, and that he had achieved what he barely failed to attain in the battle with Morris Hillquit two years earlier. Norman Thomas had captured complete control of the Socialist Party.[2]

Though Thomas' support for the Declaration of Principles was far from spirited, the Old Guard soundly criticized him, as did many observers outside the party. Louis Waldman, the party's New York State Chair, described the Declaration of Principles as "perhaps less frank, but not one bit less dangerous than the doctrines of the Communists."[3] *The New York Times* editorialized that Thomas apparently had felt compelled to go along with the radical element of his party. It compared him with a French political leader who said, as he saw his people rushing off to join the revolution, "I must follow them, since I am their chief."[4] *The Washington Post*, on the other hand, applauded Thomas' skill in saving the party from being swallowed by the Socialistic swing of Rooseveltian democracy on one hand while diverting it from surrender to communism on the other. But it also noted that in the process Thomas had encouraged a factionalism that in the future would likely split the party.[5]

And the party did split — irreversibly. Thomas continued to alienate the Old Guard through his advocacy of co-operation with the Communists. He agreed to a joint gathering of Socialists and Communists to celebrate May Day in Union Square in Manhattan. For the Old Guard, Thomas had gone too far. This proved that he had become a "tool of the Communists." They refused to attend the Union Square rally and arranged separately for their own May Day celebration.

Militant members living in New York City then seceded from the New York State party, long controlled by the Old Guard. When Thomas endorsed

---

1 Arthur M. Schlesinger, Jr., *The Politics of Upheaval: The Age of Roosevelt*, 178.
2 *The New York Times* 6/4/34, 1.
3 Ibid. 6/5/34, 10.
4 Ibid., 22.
5 *The Washington Post* 6/5/34, 8.

the secession movement, the Old Guard threatened Thomas with expulsion, asserting that he was attempting to establish a dictatorship role in the party. The National Executive Committee, with Thomas in control, proceeded to revoke the Old Guard charter and recognized instead the Militant secessionist group as the newly organized New York State Socialist Party.

When the party's 1936 national convention opened in Cleveland, both the Old Guard and the secessionist delegates were on hand, each group claiming to represent the Socialist Party in New York. When the Old Guard delegates were not formally seated at the convention, they walked out of the convention hall and out of the Socialist Party. Among those who left were party members who had been present thirty-five years earlier at the formation of the party, and they left with tears in their eyes. They were primarily from New York, but the group also included other state delegates who opposed the left wing of the party led by Thomas. Thomas expressed little sympathy for them, predicting — wrongly, as it turned out — that they would soon return to the party.[1]

The Old Guard charge that the Party was turning Communist proved unfounded. The day following the departure of the Old Guard members, the remaining delegates soundly rejected a Communist Party proposal that the two parties present a united front in the 1936 presidential election by jointly naming Thomas as their presidential candidate and Earl Browder as his running mate. In response to the Old Guard claims, Thomas stated that the "implication that the Socialist Party...advocates violent insurrection and dictatorship is, of course, false."[2]

Thomas remained unapologetic about his role in remaining aloof of any attempt to prevent a party split. Apparently, he felt no remorse for failing to have done little to keep the Old Guard members within party ranks. The Old Guard charge that he had become a tool of the Communist Party was of course unfounded, and he never forgave them for this calumny. Some years later he wrote in his autobiography:

> It is especially ironic that the right wing of the Old Guard who left us in 1936 because they felt that we were falling under the influence of Communist ideology and intrigue were by the end of the year working side by side with Communists in New York in the newly formed American Labor Party in support of Roosevelt while we were running our own ticket. And I, rather than any of them, remained the chief object of Communist wrath and abuse.[3]

With the withdrawal of the Old Guard, Thomas confirmed his leadership role and was free to redirect the path of the party along lines the Old Guard theretofore had proscribed. But his victory had come at a great cost. Between

---

1 *The New York Times*, 5/25/36, 1.

2 Ibid., 5/26/36, 1.

3 Thomas autobiography, 158.

the 1934 and 1936 national conventions, the Socialist Party lost nearly 40 percent of its membership, and the departure of the Old Guard resulted in additional significant depletions of membership in New York, Connecticut, Massachusetts, and Pennsylvania. The party was in the midst of an unremitting decline.

Thomas, more than any other person, had the standing and stature to have mediated the disputes that tore the party apart, but instead of serving as an arbiter between the Old Guard and the Militants, he sided with the Militants. Some commentators have argued that in favoring one side rather than maintaining a position of neutrality, Thomas, instead of saving the party, participated in its destruction.[1] Others point out that even if the Old Guard had not left, the Socialist Party would not have survived. Ultimately, right-wing members of the Old Guard joined left-wing Militants in flocking to the New Deal. It was Roosevelt and the New Deal, not the departure of the Old Guard, that undermined the Socialist party.[2]

The abandonment of the party by the Old Guard also has been described as the *coup de grace* to an already declining party."[3] Party membership fell below 6,500, an all-time low. But even with the departure of the Old Guard, crass factionalism continued to plague the party. Thomas' inclination to favor an all-inclusive party led to still another tragedy. He welcomed as new members former Communists, including a large group of followers of Leon Trotsky. Trotsky, one of the leaders of Russia's 1917 revolution, had later served the Soviet government as Commissar of Foreign Affairs and War, but following the death of Lenin, had lost a power struggle with Joseph Stalin who forced him into exile. He then tried to establish his own Communist party, with branches in various parts of the world, including one in the United States.

Before being admitted to the Socialist Party, the Trotskyites were required to agree that they would refrain from endeavoring to create a party within the party. Although they purported to join as individuals, in fact they entered party ranks as a coherent group, and once admitted, formed a subdivision in the party, even going so far as to publish their own newspaper. They later made it clear that they had joined the party either to assume control over it, thus establishing a base of operations for Trotsky or, failing that, to destroy the organization they felt was their primary opponent in the United States.

With the entry of the Trotskyites into the party, all turned to bedlam. In their public utterances the Trotskyites referred to Thomas as a great Social-

---

1 Bernard K. Johnpoll, *Pacifist's Progress: Norman Thomas and the Decline of American Socialism* (Greenwood, Westport, Conn., 1976), 177.

2 Murray B. Seidler, *Norman Thomas: Respectable Rebel*, 302.

3 David A. Shannon, *The Socialist Party of America, A History*, 250.

ist leader, but in private they repeated Trotsky's portrayal of Thomas as a Socialist "as a result of a misunderstanding." Within six months of their arrival, with the party in a state of near anarchy, it was clear that if the Socialist Party were to survive as a viable entity, the expulsion of the Trotskyites was an absolute necessity. Their number was small, but when the Trotskyites were expelled a thousand of the party's youngest members departed with them. This ended Thomas' dream of an all-inclusive party.

When Thomas first ran for president in 1928, party enthusiasts retained the hope — remote as it may have been — that the Socialist Party would in time develop into a powerful force in politics. By the time Thomas began his presidential campaign in 1936, that hope had all but vanished.

CHAPTER 12. BETWEEN ELECTIONS

How it would have been possible for Norman Thomas to have accomplished more than he did during the four-year period between the 1932 and 1936 presidential elections is difficult to conceive. Besides his longstanding efforts to aid the Arkansas sharecroppers and his involvement with a host of internal disputes that were then punishing the Socialist Party, he still had the time, determination, and energy to confront the Ku Klux Klan, enmeshed in a corrupt city government in Florida, and a dictatorial governor in Indiana. With all that going on, he still found time to write four books.

The elective office Thomas most wanted to win was that of Mayor of New York City. He had made himself an expert on city matters and was confident he could successfully fill the mayoralty position. He came close to achieving that goal in 1933 when the leaders of the Fusion movement — a coalition of New York City's Republican and Liberal parties — approached him about running for mayor as their candidate. Thomas was greatly tempted, but he felt that his responsibilities to the Socialist Party, so overwhelming at the time, did not permit a full time commitment to city affairs. Thus he refused the offer, and Fiorello LaGuardia, subsequently chosen to run on the Fusion ticket, was elected mayor. In relating the incident in his autobiography, Thomas wrote longingly that he "always regretted that of necessity [his] public role [had] been one of criticism and advice with no chance for constructive performance."[1]

LaGuardia, fully aware that Thomas' decision to decline the Fusion nomination had led to his own election, offered Thomas a high position in his

---

1 Thomas autobiography, 130.

administration. Again, Thomas decided he had to decline. But a year later, he changed tack. Although nearly overwhelmed by his commitments to the Arkansas sharecroppers and by his efforts to move the Socialist Party in a direction more to his liking, he agreed to run for the US Senate. Why he decided to run for office in 1934 but not a year earlier is difficult to fathom, especially when one considers that he might very well have won the mayoralty race but had no chance of election to the Senate.

Thomas' campaign for the Senate was unsuccessful, but he had the time of his life. Due to his long festering contest with the Old Guard, he all but disregarded New York City during the campaign, concentrating instead on the rest of the state. In beautiful autumn weather, with his wife at his side, he drove thousands of miles up and down and across the state in their rumble-seated automobile. In the larger cities he spoke in high school gymnasiums and city auditoriums, but in smaller towns, he would park his car near the center of town, and after Violet had placed signs in and around the car and attracted something of an audience, he would stand on the rumble seat and give his speech. He usually started his address by asking the fifty or so persons present to gather closer to the car, assuring them that he was not suffering from small pox or any other disease and they could catch nothing worse than socialism. He never enjoyed a campaign more. In the end, he achieved the highest upstate vote ever recorded by a Socialist candidate.[1]

In the years before his 1932 run for president, Thomas had written three books. In *The Conscientious Objector in America*, published in 1923, he analyzed what for him was an issue of far-reaching importance — the conflict that arises when a person's conscience tells him that he must do one thing and the state requires him to do another. When the demands of conscience conflict with the demands of public authority, which should a man obey — his own conviction as to what is right and what is wrong or the demands of the state. The brutal incarceration of his brother Evan as a conscientious objector in World War I rendered the issue even more poignant for him.[2]

Thomas had two objectives in writing *America's Way Out: A Program for Democracy*, published in 1931. First, he was determined to correct absurd misunderstandings of socialism then held by much of the non-socialist population. Second, in recognition of the weaknesses in positions asserted in defense of American socialism, he recommended to the party faithful that they enter upon a reexamination of socialist doctrine and of the stereotypical generalizations Socialists were accustomed to proffer as solutions to national and local issues. After completing his own re-examination, he continued to advocate public ownership and control of land and of the nation's other

1 Ibid., 165.
2 Norman Thomas, *The Conscientious Objector in America* (B.W. Huebsch, New York, 1923); reissued as *Is Conscience a Crime?* (Vanguard, New York, 1927).

natural resources, but emphasized that such ownership and control were to be attained through a constitutional transformation of the state, a concept unlikely ever to be accepted by orthodox Marxist socialists.[1]

The third book written prior to the 1932 campaign was a joint effort with his good friend Paul Blanshard. They analyzed the difficulties then plaguing New York City as a consequence of the massive corruption of the Jimmy Walker administration. Although Blanshard wrote most of *What's the Matter with New York?*, Thomas analyzed seemingly unresolvable issues that any re-formist government would have to confront, and he contributed ideas reflecting his own experiences as an expert on city affairs. As earlier noted, Thomas and Blanshard suffered the misfortune of seeing their book published on the same day that Jimmy Walker resigned his position as mayor, thus rendering much of the book irrelevant.[2]

In the first of the four books Thomas wrote between the 1932 and the 1936 presidential elections — *The Choice Before Us: Mankind at the Crossroads*[3] — he conducted another of his many re-examinations of Socialist doctrines and their applications to US economic and political structures. Socialism always starts with the notion that the great natural resources ought to be owned and managed as the common possession of the people. Thomas argued from that premise that the Socialist Party should not encourage the delusion that the existing scheme of government, even if fundamentally re-formed, would be suitable for a new society. The mandate for Socialism must be one for change, not reform. If Americans were to start anew with a clean slate, no one would consider constructing so cruel and crazy a world as the one they lived in. But we cannot start with a clean slate, since the dominant class will not willingly abandon its power, wealth, and prestige for an adventure in renewal. Although starting with a clean slate is impossible, a fresh start, embodying changes in the perception of basic political, cultural, and economic institutions, is possible. As an example, they must be persuaded that the country's great natural resources ought to be their common possessions, owned and managed for the common good, and not for profit of the few. But again, it is clear that owners of those resources will not willingly relinquish them to common ownership and management. How then is this to be accomplished?

Thomas admitted that the demands of the transitional period between capitalism and socialism — how to survive while struggling to create a better life — stretched the imaginations of the Socialists. But for certain, the

---

1 Norman Thomas, *America's Way Out; a Program for Democracy* (Macmillan, New York, 1931; also published by Rand School Press, 1931).

2 Paul Blanshard and Norman Thomas, *What's the Matter with New York; A National Problem* (Macmillan, New York, 1932).

3 Norman Thomas, *The Choice Before Us: Mankind at the Crossroads* (Macmillan, New York, 1934).

New Deal was not the answer. Roosevelt wanted to reform capitalism, not replace it. Thus, the New Deal programs did not serve as models for Socialist planning of the transitional period. Socialists would have to continue their struggle to find ways to guide the country through this difficult period. Thomas refused to offer "pie in the sky" formulas as substitutes for unanswered questions in the Socialist agenda.

Six months after *The Choice Before Us* appeared in the book stores, Thomas published another work — *Human Exploitation in the United States.*[1] Thomas began this work with an account of the exploitation of Americans brought about through the use and misuse of the nation's natural resources, forests, and minerals, and in this work he focused on the exploitation of certain groups, especially women and African-Americans. A Communist critic condemned Thomas for entitling his book *Human Exploitation* rather than *Capitalist Exploitation.* But Thomas' book title reflected his broader interest in the economy, an interest that extended even beyond capitalism's systemic exploitation of men and women. It should be noted here that broad as Thomas' passion was for a system of justice — a system he believed would be accomplished only through fundamental economic and political change — still he was very much attentive to individual instances of exploitation and injustice. In fact, he appeared happiest whenever he was able to eliminate an injustice or prevent further sufferings of an exploited group of persons or even a single individual.[2]

Thomas' work on war — *War: No Glory, No Profit, No Need* — reflected his continuing pacifist views.[3] The pacifism he expressed prior to and during World War I had its basis in Christian principles, but by 1935 his pacifist perspective was grounded almost entirely on his view of the world as seen through the eyes of a Socialist:

> The condition of secure peace is shared abundance. Shared abundance implies more of the good things of life which we need — the food, the shelter, and a hundred and one other things. The condition of our having them is that at last we shall begin to plan for abundance. Such planning must rest upon social or cooperative ownership of the great natural resources.... We must end the profit system. Our ancestors could afford to isolate themselves in comparatively small groups as we cannot. We may begin the sharing of abundance within America's borders; we cannot end there if peace or prosperity is to be secure.... In our modern world we are not as much independent as interdependent. The more civilized we are the more truly we depend on one another. . . .Nevertheless, if world organization ignores the fact that for some nations to live at all, and for all nations to live well, we

1 Norman Thomas, *Human Exploitation in the United States* (Frederick A. Stokes, New York, 1934).

2 Daniel Bell, "The Background and Development of Marxian Socialism in the United States," *Socialism and American Life* , Vol. I, Edited by Donald Drew Egbert and Stow Persons (Princeton University Press, Princeton, 1952), 370, 399.

3 Norman Thomas, *War: No Glory, No Profit, No Need* (Frederick A. Stokes, New York, 1935).

must plan in terms of interdependence rather than independence, [then] we shall not escape war.[1]

Thomas gave a strange title to his fourth book written between the 1932 and 1936 elections. *After the New Deal, What?*[2] was published as he was entering his third presidential election campaign. He wrote it at that particular time because he wanted to satisfy his own need to think through his approach to persuading Americans that the programs advanced by socialism, rather than those offered by the New Deal, were appropriate for confronting the issues then facing the nation, and he felt he could more readily argue his case in a book rather than in a series of campaign speeches. He wrote for readers who understood that mere emotional enthusiasm for liberty, peace, and democracy was insufficient for survival in the critical times in which they lived, and he invited them to seek out the forces available to protect and insulate them and their neighbors from poverty, exploitation and war.

In reality, it was a campaign book, arguing that the New Deal's form of capitalism failed to resolve the economic issues that then beset the country. Many had argued that the New Deal was actually engaged in carrying out the 1932 Socialist Party platform, and some of Roosevelt's critics had accused him of allowing "creeping socialism" to corrupt New Deal programs. Thomas had to concede that Roosevelt's programs had in fact partially fulfilled certain of the Socialists' immediate demands, but he continued to argue that the New Deal measures were primarily of an ameliorative nature and failed to confront the real business at hand — the need to nationalize the country's basic industries. He contended that the New Deal was already of the past. It was dead, and thus Roosevelt needed to invent a Newer Deal."[3] The existing New Deal had neither secured a firm recovery from the Depression nor brought about an effective reform or a fundamental change in the capitalist system. In Thomas' view, socialism was a reasonable alternative to a failed capitalism, especially in an age of interdependence and increasing collectivism.

Thomas preached the glory of the triumph of socialism, but realistically recognized the supreme difficulties the nation confronted in attaining that triumph. He urged Americans to accept the concept that Socialism is the condition of true democracy:

> [Socialism] is the fulfillment of the prophet's dream of brotherhood.... To establish socialism requires struggle.... It requires the development of new and noble loyalties. The socialist society is not for fools or cowards. There is no foreordained assurance that man will have the wisdom to use for the social good the machinery which he had the intelligence to invent.[4]

1 Ibid., 130, 133.
2 Norman Thomas, *After the New Deal, What?* (Macmillan, New York, 1936).
3 Ibid., 8.
4 Ibid., 156-157.

Thomas' book writing endeavors were often interrupted. In 1935, two in-stances of outrageous violations of civil rights demanded his attention — one in Indiana and the other in Florida — and required of him the expenditure of an inordinate amount of time and effort. The first occurred in Eugene Debs' hometown of Terre Haute, Indiana. After the workers of a local manufactur-ing plant that made enameled cooking utensils elected to go on strike, the company hired sixty private guards, purportedly to maintain order. When the workers learned that most of the sixty were thugs and gunmen, recruit-ed from the underworld from nearby cities, they demanded their removal, but the company refused to change course. The leadership of the American Federation of Labor then called a general strike of all unionized employees in Terre Haute and this prompted Indiana Governor Paul McNutt — once the National Commander of the American Legion — to declare martial law in the city and the surrounding county and, although no violence had fol-lowed, to march in the National Guard. After two days of living under mili-tary control, the workers ended the general strike, but the original strikers continued their work stoppage. Terre Haute remained under military law, but the governor reduced the number of troops in the city to a few officers and a handful of soldiers, headed by a certain Major Weimar.

Major Weimar maintained strict military control over the city, suspend-ing nearly all civil rights of its citizens. Picketing by the strikers was banned. All public meetings were prohibited. Those who tried to speak in public were jailed. Scores of townsmen were placed under military arrest and detained in the county jail for weeks without charges levied against them. Other resi-dents were arbitrarily ordered off the streets, and some from their own front porches. A professor at a local college was held *incommunicado* for thirty-six hours simply because he asked an innocent question of one of Weimar's soldiers.

The Socialist Party sent one of its national organizers to Terra Haute to protest these conditions. He tried to conduct a meeting on the courthouse steps, but was arrested and held without bail. While in jail, Weimar de-nied him contact with a lawyer as well as his family. The Socialist Party sent another organizer and he also was arrested. Then it was Thomas' turn; he scheduled a mass meeting to be held on the courthouse steps. The meeting, widely advertised, was set up as a test case that would enable the people of Terre Haute to pursue a civil rights case in the Federal Court against Gov-ernor Mc Nutt and Major Weimar. Thomas expected to be arrested, but as he mounted the courthouse steps, the military authorities announced to the surrounding crowd of more than 2000 that the governor had revoked the ban on the meeting, and Thomas was free to speak. The crowd roared. Following Thomas' speech, the governor ordered a relaxation of all martial law provisions, and picketing and public meetings resumed.[1]

In speaking against the imposition of martial law, Thomas portrayed the governor's action in allowing Major Weimar to exercise absolute military control over the city as one of the worst offenses against civil liberty ever committed by an American governor. Subsequently, Thomas repeatedly referred to McNutt as the "Hoosier Hitler," a nickname that stuck to him and later undermined his presidential ambitions.[2]

The civil rights violations that occurred in Florida culminated in a murder. It happened in Tampa, where the Ku Klux Klan was powerful and where illegal gambling had long prospered, protected through bribery of public officials. The Ku Klux Klan maintained social order against the poor and discontented of the city, seeking to enforce its own standards of morality against all persons considered as offenders of the social mores.

The city had developed into a haven for bootleggers and other racketeers who in turn became a force for political corruption. City officials enrolled Klan members as poll watchers in municipal elections to make certain that incumbent office holders retained their positions. The Klan relentlessly persecuted those who challenged corrupted officials. Flogging was the favorite instrument of punishment for dissenters and agitators. Nevertheless, a small group of courageous residents were determined to clean up the city. They formed a reform group called "Modern Democrats," and on the evening of November 30, 1935, met at a private home to plot a course of action to clean up the city. Tampa police raided the meeting and, without a warrant, arrested six of those present and took them to a local police station for a "communistic investigation."

Later that evening, the police released the six men, but a mob seized three of them outside the police station and took them to a remote wooded area outside the city. The three — Joseph Shoemaker, Eugene Poulnot, and Samuel Rogers — were stripped, held over a log, repeatedly beaten with chains and rubber hoses, and then tarred and feathered. The mob targeted Shoemaker for special treatment — they tortured him by holding his leg over a fire until his flesh was charred. The mob then left. Shoemaker was dying, and Poulnot and Rogers were badly injured. After struggling through wooded areas for several hours, Poulnot and Rogers made their way to Tampa to secure help for Shoemaker. Shoemaker, in great pain, was taken to a hospital where armed guards were stationed at the entrance to his room to inhibit further attack. Shoemaker was near death and could not speak, was horribly

---

1 Thomas autobiography, 139-142; Norman Thomas, "Hoosier Hitlerism," *The Nation* 9/18/35, 324.

2 Milton S, Mayer, "Men Who Would Be President: Pretty Boy McNutt," *The Nation* 3/30/40, 415.

mutilated and paralyzed on one side. He lived on for nine days before dying in agony.[1]

Shoemaker had once been a Socialist but with the election of Roosevelt had become an ardent New Dealer. Apparently, his only crime was in organizing a local group of Socialists and liberals to confront the corrupt politicians running the city.

A Florida Socialist notified Thomas of the floggings. An outraged Norman Thomas immediately spread news throughout the country of Shoemaker's beating and murder. Tampa became the focus of national attention and newspaper reporters flocked to the city from across the country. Thomas accused the Ku Klux Klan of having committed the floggings, but Dr. Hiram W. Evans of Atlanta, the KKK imperial wizard, denied the Klan had been involved.

Within three weeks of the floggings, a grand jury indicted eight men for second degree murder, kidnapping, and assault with the intent to kill. Six of the eight were Tampa police officers, and four of the officers were members of the Ku Klux Klan.[2] A few weeks later, the former Tampa Chief of Police also was indicted. When one of his friends, a member of the Ku Klux Klan, was questioned about the floggings, he committed suicide.[3]

Tampa residents doubted that city officials would vigorously pursue the prosecution of those indicted. They sought Thomas' help and arranged for a mass meeting to be held at the city auditorium. Warned that the Klan intended to meet his train, Thomas left it two stations before Tampa, and then a body guard escorted him to the auditorium. Although threats had been made that the auditorium would be bombed when Thomas spoke, the hall was packed with more than 2000 men and women and another 1000 stood outside the hall to listen. *The Tampa Times* described Thomas' speech as a "verbal flogging [of the floggers] more lacerating than their own lashes, more scorching than their own tar," adding that, "the visit and the speech of Norman Thomas will have a helpful effect in heartening the sentiment of the community and strengthening the arm of officials. We are glad that he came and that he spoke."[4]

Thomas felt that he made "one of the most effective speeches of his life." Apparently the attorneys representing the eight indicted defendants agreed, as they immediately applied to the court for a change in venue of the case,

---

1 Thomas autobiography, 147-148; *The Washington Post* 5/24/36, M-4.

2 *The New York Times*, 12/25/35, 14; *The Washington Post*, 12/23/35, 10.

3 *The New York Times*, 1/25/36, 32.

4 Quoted in Harry Fleischman, *Norman Thomas, A Biography: 1884–1968* (W.W. Norton, New York, 1969), 157.

arguing that because of the speech the defendants could no longer receive a fair trial in Tampa. Thomas was skeptical; the speech was not that good.[1]

Tampa residents then selected Thomas to head a *Committee for the Defense of Civil Rights in Tampa*. The Committee immediately brought pressure on city officials, thus forcing city prosecutors to vigorously investigate the beatings and to search out witnesses who could corroborate the testimony of Poulnot and Rogers. A prospective witness questioned about the case committed suicide. His family claimed that it had been murder not suicide, and the circumstances of his death seemed to support that view.

The subsequent investigation revealed that the kidnapping of Shoemaker, Poulnot and Rogers matched a pattern of previous occurrences — the arrest of victims by Tampa police officers followed by their release and delivery to a mob. Evidence mounted that the floggings had not occurred impromptu but that the police had planned them in detail. This case was worse than previous ones in that no effort had been made to conceal the participation of police officers in the mob kidnapping. The three victims were taken from police headquarters and forced into automobiles parked directly outside.[2]

At the outset of the trial, defense counsel questioned prospective jurors concerning their attitudes toward Thomas, describing him as the "nationally known communist and propagandist." This blatant attempt to poison the minds of the jurors failed. After a six-week trial, with thirty-four witnesses testifying for the prosecution, a jury convicted five of the indicted police officers on the kidnapping charge. Thomas declared that the trial outcome was a step forward in the fight to restore civil liberties in Tampa and to oust the Ku Klux Klan from control of the municipal government.[3]

Thomas' friends in Florida had warned him that a conviction of any Klan member would be set aside by the Florida Supreme Court, and that proved to be the case. The convictions were reversed on the ground that the indictments had been improperly worded and thus were legally deficient.[4] Thomas later remarked that if the decision of the appeal court was legally sound, then it was difficult "to escape the conviction that some . . . official in the prosecutor's office had deliberately given an escape to his Klan friends by a faulty framing of the indictment."[5]

In the 1930s, the State of Florida advertisements directed to the tourist trade bade them come to Florida "where life at its best is cheap." As Thomas noted, "the Shoemaker case gave a grim meaning to the words." The long

---

1 Thomas autobiography, 148.
2 *The New York Times*, 3/22/36, 42.
3 Ibid., 5/24/36, 1.
4 Thomas autobiography, 149.
5 Norman Thomas, *Mr. Chairman, Ladies and Gentlemen: Reflections on Public Speaking* (Hermitage House, New York, 1955), 16.

struggle to attain justice in Florida left Thomas without any desire to retire there in his old age.[1]

A sense of outrage led Thomas to intervene in Terre Haute and Tampa just as it had moved him to engage in the struggle to obtain relief for the Arkansas sharecroppers. Throughout his life, the inequities and injustices he witnessed around him greatly angered him. He was so often involved in eliminating injustice and inequity that his threshold of anger must have been very low since it did not take a great deal to move him to action when he saw others suffering.

Thomas brought a boundless energy to civil rights cases such as these. Men and women thirty years younger found it difficult to keep up with him. He was driven, but appeared not to be so. He could always focus on the problems at hand as he had no private interests, aside from his family. He had no hobbies or avocations and very few non-political friends. That he devoted his energy almost exclusively to public affairs is illustrated by a story told by Roger N. Baldwin, a friend and leader of the American Civil Liberties Union. Baldwin owned a small farm north of New York City where he often spent his weekends. On one occasion Baldwin invited Thomas to spend a few days at the farm, hoping to afford him a change of pace and some distance from his daily schedule of pressing commitments. Trimming apple trees appeared a good way to divert Thomas' attention, so Baldwin got Thomas to climb a tree with a saw and clippers in hand. But even while holding to a precarious perch three quarters of the way up the tree, Thomas never for a moment stopped talking politics. That was the last time Baldwin had him up for a weekend visit.[2]

Thomas appeared to possess a personal need to do battle for a good cause.[3] He was driven to eliminate every injustice. After he graduated from Princeton and assumed responsibility for the Spring Street parishioners, he was never at any point during the remainder of his life without some involvement in one dispute or another. He liked people, was interested in their problems, and could express warmth and friendliness, but his interest in the masses never made him one of them.[4] He always stood outside their personal problems, but this did not prevent him from making a total commitment to resolving their problems. It was his commitment that counted most.

He did not seek respectability and thus often championed unpopular causes. He was intent on fighting injustice, wherever it might appear. His enthusiasm was near endless. When introduced at political gatherings as

---

1 Ibid.

2 Roger N. Baldwin, "Norman Thomas: A Combative Life," *The New Republic*, 1/13/68, 11.

3 Murray B. Seidler, *Norman Thomas: Respectable Rebel* (Syracuse University Press, Syracuse, 1967), 213

4 Ibid., 80.

the defender of lost causes," he customarily responded, "Not lost causes — causes not yet won."[1] Whatever the chances of success, he viewed all battles fought to protect the civil rights of his fellow citizens as causes not yet won.

1 W. A. Swanberg, *Norman Thomas: The Last Idealist* (Charles Scribner's Sons, New York, 1976), 279.

Chapter 13. Opposing a United States President and a New Jersey Mayor

Thomas once described his relationship with President Roosevelt as "not close, but personally friendly."[1] On occasion they met in the White House to discuss matters important to them both, and Roosevelt nearly always answered Thomas' letters. Thomas' admiration and high regard for the President, however, did not deter him from criticizing New Deal policies, at times, quite severely. When Thomas wrote complaining that Roosevelt should not have supported the newly adopted Smith Act[2] as it was a strike against civil liberties, the President responded with some of his own sharp criticism:

> Sometimes even you, like the best of us, get things a bit twisted! . . . You and I may disagree as to the danger to the United States — but we can at least give each other credit for the honesty that lies behind our opinions. Frankly, I am greatly fearful for the safety of this country over a period of years, because I think that the tendency of the present victorious dictatorships is to segregate us and surround us to such an extent that we will become vulnerable to a final attack when they get ready to make it."[3]

After Roosevelt won election to a third term in 1940, he responded to Thomas' letter of congratulations with a general invitation for him to come to Washington to talk things over:

> Dear Norman:
>   That is a mighty nice note of yours and I appreciate it. Do run down here some day soon. I want to have a good talk with you. I

1 Thomas autobiography, 135.
2 The Smith Act — the Alien Registration Act of 1940 — made it a criminal offense to advocate the violent overthrow of the government.
3 Roosevelt letter, dated 7/31/40, to Thomas.

am really a bit worried about the trend of undemocratic forces in the country.[1]

Thomas ignored the invitation, and their relationship seems to have soured.[2]

Despite Roosevelt's repeated expressions of friendship, Thomas' attitude toward the president was one of formality and reserve, and he did not attempt to conceal his contempt for some of Roosevelt's New Deal policies. In the 1936 presidential campaign — and in later campaigns as well — Thomas launched critical attacks against Roosevelt, while leaving his Republican candidate unscathed. Except for Communists and Fascists, Thomas' criticism of his adversaries was generally free of animosity and bitterness, but when it came to Roosevelt and his policies, Thomas frequently was far more caustic.

The New Deal was destroying the Socialist Party. Roosevelt's left-leaning policies attracted many liberals and radicals to his cause, and hundreds of leading Socialists abandoned the party to support him. Among the defectors were James Maurer, Thomas' vice presidential running mate in the 1932 election, Abraham Cahan, editor of *The Forward*, the country's largest Socialist newspaper, New York City Judge Jacob Pankin, author Upton Sinclair, and Paul Blanshard, with whom Thomas co-authored *What's the Matter with New York?* and one of his best friends.[3]

The political success of the New Deal paralleled the decline of the Socialist Party.[4] Thomas disparaged the notion that Roosevelt's New Deal programs could accurately be described as creeping toward socialism. He reminded the country that Roosevelt was engaged in the process of saving capitalism, not in advancing socialism. But in saving capitalism, Roosevelt in effect reduced Thomas and the Socialist Party to near irrelevancies, and over time Thomas increasingly grew more negative with regard to that person he held most responsible for the desertion of his own followers.

Clearly, Thomas viewed Roosevelt as having stolen his thunder and that of the Socialist Party. True, Roosevelt's programs were closer to those advocated by the Socialists than those advanced by his own Democratic Party, but Thomas argued that the New Deal brought changes that were more of a bureaucratic than a fundamental nature. Moreover, Thomas held that Roosevelt adopted and adapted Socialist ideas to prop up a decadent capi-

---

1 Quoted in Harry Fleischman, *Norman Thomas, A Biography: 1884–1968* (W.W. Norton, New York, 1969), 198.

2 Thomas autobiography, 135.

3 *The New York Times*, 8/21/36, XI; David A. Shannon, *The Socialist Party of America, A History* (Quadrangle, Chicago, 1967; originally published by Macmillan, New York, 1955), 234.

4 David A. Shannon, *The Socialist Party of America, A History*, 229.

talistic system.[1] The result was still capitalism, not socialism. In an interview with *The New York Times*, Thomas pointed out the vast differences between a New Deal that exhibited socialistic tendencies and socialism itself:

> Last year (1935) there was a 36 percent increase in the profits of the great corporations. The increase in employment was exactly 2-1/2 percent. This could not happen under a Socialist government. There are twelve million men and women out of work. A sixth of our population is on relief. There has been no increase at all in the... wage of the average worker. This is not socialism. No, indeed. I would hate to think of a socialism which sanctioned a steadily increasing burden of debt.... In my wildest flights of imagination I cannot imagine a Socialist government closing its eyes to the exploited peons of the cotton fields or to the slaves of Florida's flogging belt....[2]

Thomas never departed from arguing that the New Deal failed to offer adequate solutions to the nation's chronic economic problems, and that the New Dealers never even considered socialism's fundamental tenet, that ultimately capitalism had to be replaced by socialism.

But Thomas "protested too much." He had to have been pleased with the New Deal's record of success in initiating programs long advanced by the Socialist Party. During Roosevelt's first term, the country saw innovations that did not fall within what some referred to as creeping socialism; rather, it witnessed a virtual torrent of new social programs. Thomas could not realistically have expected Roosevelt to have gone farther, to have ushered in a program of collective ownership of the country's natural resources. The country was not ready for that as Thomas well knew. His criticism of New Deal programs had its genesis in doubts about his own relevancy and that of the Socialist Party. His criticism was an act of self-preservation. If he failed to take a stand in opposition to the New Deal, the country would readily dismiss him and his Socialist Party.

Thomas was not convinced that the Socialist Party would gain any advantage by entering the 1936 presidential campaign. Because Roosevelt had been successful in implementing many of the immediate demands of the Socialist party platform, many party members would be voting for him rather than the Socialist candidate. He was certain that the party's national vote would shrink, thus depressing and discouraging its membership. But did the party have an alternative? What would happen to the party if it did not field a presidential candidate?

Socialists believed that if socialism had any chance of ultimately prevailing across the country, the Socialist Party would need always to maintain a national presence, and it could accomplish that only by running candidates for national office. It was widely believed that a failure to enter the 1936 presidential election could ultimately lead to the ruin of the Socialist Party.

1 S.J. Woolf, "Thomas: If I Were President," *The New York Times*, 6/7/36, 107.
2 Ibid.

Since Thomas was the Socialist Party's only credible candidate, a decision on his part not to run could lead to disaster for the party. Thomas had little choice but to give in to the pleadings of the party leaders, and at the national convention in Cleveland, he allowed himself to be offered as the Socialist Party candidate. This would be his third run for the presidency. His pledge to work to bring about" socialism in our time" — unrealistic as that may sound to us today — excited and encouraged the party's membership.[1]

Two years earlier, after the Old Guard members had left the party, they organized themselves as the" Social Democratic Federation." Subsequently, right wing elements of many of the Socialist Party state delegations, including Massachusetts, Connecticut, Pennsylvania, Maryland, Rhode Island, Washington, and Montana, also threatened to withdraw from the party in favor of the new Social Democratic Federation.[2] One delegate to the Cleveland convention noted at his departure that," Norman Thomas won a nomination and lost a party."[3]

With the defection of the Old Guard, the party entered the campaign badly divided. But Thomas, displaying the energy, spirit, and determination of a candidate who really believed he could win the election, proceeded immediately to attack his opponents. Roosevelt, he claimed, had failed to deliver the country from poverty and exploitation. "It is not the old deal . . . or the New Deal that has failed. It is the principle of capitalist nationalization, of which both are the expression, that has completely fallen down."[4] Rather than belittling Roosevelt's accomplishments, however, he emphasized the president's failures, his failure to end racial discrimination, as well as his failure to initiate programs guaranteeing full racial equality. Roosevelt's administration had allowed the plight of the sharecroppers and tenant farmers to critically worsen while it initiated acreage reduction plans that mainly benefitted landowners. The New Deal had done nothing to improve housing conditions, even as many Americans continued to live in hovels unfit for human habitation. It had failed to deal adequately with existing massive unemployment, and consequently more than 12 million men and women remained out of work.

During the campaign, newspaper reporters asked Thomas, assuming he were elected president, to list his priorities. His first step, he responded, would be to mobilize the country to wage war on unemployment. In order to win such a war, we would need to amend the Constitution to deprive the Supreme Court of the power to declare social legislation unconstitutional. Additional amendments would be necessary to give the Federal government

---

1 Ibid., 5/26/36, 22.
2 Ibid., 5/31/36, E-7.
3 *The Washington Post*, 5/31/36, B-4.
4 S.J. Woolf, "Thomas: If I Were President," *The New York Times*, 6/7/36, 107.

the power to acquire and operate the nation's basic industries, such as the coal mines, railroads and power plants. He would propose a Federal unemployment system, old-age insurance, and socialized medicine. He would move to abolish all laws that interfered with free speech, free press, and free assembly.[1]

Reporters also called upon him to distinguish Socialist Party doctrine from that advanced by the Communist Party. He observed that both parties opposed the capitalistic system, and both sought to found a new system based on use rather than profit. But the similarities ended there. Communists believed nothing would be accomplished until a Communist dictatorship was established, while the Socialists emphasized the value of freedom and political and economic change accomplished in a peaceful, legal, and democratic manner.[2]

In his closing speech of the campaign, Thomas approached a subject that was to increase in importance for him over the remaining years of his life — the imminent threat of war. He noted that the recent rise of Nazism and Fascism threatened war in Europe:

> The skies over Europe and eastern Asia are black with the clouds of war. No one knows when they may break in floods of devastation or what will be the consequences to America of this fresh carnival of death. Yet the discussion in this political campaign has scarcely touched the issue of peace except in terms of platitudinous generalities.... It is only we Socialists who have urged American leadership in disarmament, the complete denunciation of imperialism, genuine neutrality and a program for taking profit out of war and preparation for war.... Our general policy may be summed up in the phrase "cooperation in what makes for peace, isolation in what makes for war."[3]

In this final campaign speech, Thomas also emphasized the country's need to preserve the civil liberties of all its citizens. He reminded his audience that Socialists were committed to the preservation of all civil liberties, to the expansion of the rights of workers to organize and bargain collectively, and to the elimination of racial discrimination from the workplace, the school, and the courthouse.

The Socialist Party 1936 presidential campaign was a disaster. In several states, party regulars were unable to gather sufficient signatures to put Thomas' name on the ballot. In those states, a voter wishing to vote for Thomas had to resort to a write-in ballot. Some state organizations sat out the election, believing there was little to gain by their participation. Virtually every labor leader in the country backed Roosevelt.

---

1 Ibid.
2 Ibid.
3 Ibid., 11/2/36, 10.

He might have advanced his candidacy by attacking Alfred Landon, the Republican Party candidate, as many in his party urged. They wanted him to brand Landon a Fascist, but Thomas refused, since he knew Landon to be a Liberal, standing to the left of mainstream Republicanism, and he recognized Landon's sincerity and honesty. Following the campaign, Landon and Thomas formed a lasting friendship.

The attitude of one of Thomas' friends typified the mood of those who had voted for him previously, but not in this election. "You haven't seen me around much lately, have you? You see, I had made up my mind how I was going to vote and I didn't want to be disturbed by listening to you."[1] A disastrous campaign led to disastrous results. Thomas received 187,000 votes compared to nearly 900,000 in 1932. Not since 1900 had a Socialist presidential candidate received so few votes. The votes received on the Socialist line in New York, where the Old Guard was strongest, fell far below the vote cast in 1932. Apparently many Socialists voted for Roosevelt on the American Labor Party line, which far out polled the Socialist Party. Only the most optimistic Socialists held firm to the hope that their party had any future in the elections to come.

While dealing with Roosevelt, Thomas also was forced into confrontation with a despotic figure of enormous proportions — Frank Hague, Mayor of Jersey City. It was often noted in the 1930s that the position of the Statue of Liberty, standing in New York harbor with her back to Jersey City, was eminently appropriate, because the city behind her had a record of suppression of civil liberties unsurpassed by any other municipality in the United States.[2]

Frank Hague had been Mayor of Jersey City since 1917, heading a political dynasty that ruled the city and the entire state of New Jersey. Exercising vast power in both the Democratic and the Republican Parties, he was as powerful and as ruthless as any big city mayor in the country's history. No political machine had ever perfected control over an American city as completely as that accomplished by the Hague organization. A prominent New Jersey lawyer once told Thomas that there were not three judges in New Jersey who would dare to decide a case contrary to Hague's wishes. To the end of his life, Roosevelt appointed and the Senate confirmed only those candidates for the Federal bench that the Hague machine endorsed.[3] Even Tammany Hall, which dominated New York City for decades, failed to achieve the level of control over its citizenry as Hague achieved in Jersey City.[4] In his introduc-

---

1 Thomas autobiography, 170-171.

2 Dayton David McKean, *The Boss: The Hague Machine in Action* (Russell & Russell, New York, 1940), 227.

3 Thomas autobiography, 151.

4 Dayton David McKean, *The Boss: The Hague Machine in Action*, xv.

tion to his 1940 study of the Hague machine, historian Dayton David McK-
ean explained how Hague achieved that control:

> The Hague organization, alone among American city machines, has system-
> atically and successfully utilized the methods of terrorism, the infiltration
> of groups and associations, the suppression of criticism, and the hierar-
> chal principle of leadership that have characterized the Fascist regimes in
> Europe.... The thoughtful citizen who may be curious about daily life in a
> police state, where telephone lines are tapped and mails are tampered with,
> need not go abroad. He can observe [Jersey City] where there are as many
> spies as there are in a Balkan kingdom, where the police arrest persons
> on suspicion or on trumped-up charges, where citizens are searched, de-
> ported, or beaten at the whim of a policeman.[1]

The concepts of civil and constitutional rights were wholly foreign to Jersey City. Hague simply denied city residents the right to criticize his regime.
He stated his position bluntly: "We hear about constitutional rights, free
speech and free press. Every time I hear these words, I say to myself, 'that
man is a Red, that man is a Communist.'"[2] This was not merely a chance re-
mark; Hague really believed it. He once testified in a court case that "Whenever [you] hear a discussion of civil rights and the right of free speech and the
rights of the Constitution, always remember you will find the [advocate of
civil rights] with a Russian flag under his coat."[3] In Jersey City, you heard no
"nonsense" about constitutional rights. Unlimited discussion and criticism
were not allowed in Hague territory. This was the environment Thomas entered in December 1937.

Hague was then engaged in an extended campaign to persuade out-of-
state businesses to move to Jersey City. As an enticement to the business
community, he suppressed the activities of any labor union that tried to establish a collective bargaining unit in a business located within the city's
borders. He targeted the newly formed and militant Congress of Industrial
Organizations (CIO) for special acts of intimidation and was determined
that it would not gain a foothold in his domain. Among the tactics he employed was to denounce the CIO as Communist-controlled. He was thus
justified, he argued, in undertaking all measures necessary to keep it out of
Jersey City. He refused to allow the CIO to conduct meetings anywhere in
the city. He denied it permits for outdoor meetings and pressured owners
of auditoriums and meeting halls to refuse to rent their facilities for indoor
meetings of union members. He harassed the union at every turn.

Thomas came to the union's defense. He and some of his League of Industrial Democracy associates conducted a meeting at a Methodist church
in downtown Jersey City. Three hundred labor sympathizers attended, and

---

1 Ibid., xv-xvi.
2 Samuel Walker, *In Defense of American Liberties: A History of the ACLU* (Southern Illinois University Press, Carbondale, Ill., 1990), 110.
3 Dayton David McKean, *The Boss: The Hague Machine in Action*, 227.

Hague designated them all as "interlopers of a Communist color." The meeting, ostensibly held to observe the 150th anniversary of New Jersey's signing of the United States Constitution, gave Thomas the opportunity to denounce the mayor for having barred the CIO from conducting a meeting it had planned for that same evening. He attacked Hague personally. Hague was far more than a local political boss, he said:

"He is the man who chooses your governor . . . and your United States senator."

"And the judges too," someone in the audience shouted.

"I was coming to them," Thomas said.

"I was going to give them a separate paragraph."

Thomas noted that Hague had not interfered to prevent their meeting in the church, thus conceding the weakness of his own position. No CIO speaker would have said anything of a more threatening or subversive nature than what Thomas said that evening, and the CIO had as much right to say it as he did. Thomas concluded that, "If we have the right to speak here, the CIO has a double right. The CIO will not come [to Jersey City] to raise the red flag. It will come here to redeem the American flag."[1]

The Socialists decided to follow up the Methodist Church meeting with a May Day celebration in Jersey City's Journal Square, the site where large public events often were conducted. City officials required any organization planning to conduct a public event in the Square to first apply for a permit. When Hague henchmen denied the application submitted by a group of Socialists, Thomas decided to go ahead with the meeting without a permit. On the evening of the event, Thomas, accompanied by a few colleagues, his wife and his brother Evan[2] drove in several open cars to Journal Square, where a large crowd of several thousand had gathered to await his appearance. Thomas no sooner stepped out of the automobile when a group of police officers accosted him and roughly pushed him into a waiting squad car. In the melee that followed, an arresting policeman struck Violet. (Thomas later claimed she was slugged). The police drove Thomas at high speed to the Jersey City docks, and forced him to board a ferry boat about to depart for Manhattan. When he refused to walk aboard, policemen carried him onto the vessel, and then warned him against returning. Apparently, incidents of this nature were common in Jersey City; it was the customary method of dealing with "agitators."

Thomas was not one readily deterred from a course of action once he had decided to pursue it. When the ferry reached Manhattan, he phoned his home and left a message that he was immediately returning to Jersey City

1 *The New York Times*, 12/22/37, 23.

2 His brother, Evan, a physician and a bachelor, lived with Norman and Violet from 1920 until he married in World War II.

by train. While Thomas was being ferried to New York, Evan and Violet were trying to locate him. When the police told them he had "gone home," they called and learned that Thomas was returning to Jersey City. They and others decided to stay in Journal Square to await his arrival. On his return, he told the crowd remaining that he had not been arrested; rather, he had been kidnapped and then deported. "He had returned," he told them, "to find out what happened to my wife and other American citizens in Hitler-Hague fiefdom."[1] The crowd was delighted to hear that he was planning to sue their "Fascist" mayor. By that time, the police had heard enough, and they escorted him, his wife and brother to a nearby train station and placed them on an express bound for Manhattan.[2] Thus, for a second time that evening, Hague's police "deported" Thomas from Jersey City. Some years later, in describing his return to Journal Square after the first deportation, Thomas said: "In . . . anticipating General MacArthur, I said, 'I will return.' And I did."[3]

Thomas angrily denounced his "kidnapping" and "deportations," and charged Hague with exercising "sinister power" over the residents of Jersey City, reducing them to a form of slavery not exceeded by anything in Fascist Rome or Berlin in the 1930s. Thomas was not the only one to express anger over the event. *The Washington Post* editorially referred to Hague as "the Fuhrer of Jersey City," to his police as "storm troopers" and "the Gestapo," and to his rule as mayor as "utterly un-American."[4]

Thomas, the ACLU and the CIO filed legal actions against Hague in the New Jersey State and Federal Courts. Five weeks after his deportation, Thomas scheduled a speech in a municipal park in the nearby city of Newark, intending to present the speech he had been prevented from giving in Jersey City. He would attack Hague, charging him with violating the CIO's constitutional right of free speech and assembly and with illegally interfering with its rights to organize workers laboring in Jersey City.

A permit for the event in the Newark park was granted, but city officials refused to give permission for the use of sound equipment. Since a small crowd was anticipated, the absence of sound equipment was not looked upon as a serious problem. Although Hague's Jersey City domain was located close by, problems with the police or a crowd were not expected.

On the evening of the event, a small crowd of five hundred assembled in the Newark park. When Thomas arrived, he mounted a small speaker's platform. He had spoken only a few words when a parade of about two hun-

---

1 *The Washington Post*, 5/1/38, M-1; *The New York* Times, 5/1/38, 1.

2 Thomas autobiography, 150-153; Dayton David McKean, *The Boss: The Hague Machine in Action*, 236; *The Washington Post*, 5/1/38, M-1; *The New York Times*, 5/1/38, 1.

3 Norman Thomas, *Mr. Chairman, Ladies and Gentlemen: Reflections on Public Speaking* (Hermitage House, New York, 1955), 111.

4 *The Washington Post*, 5/7/38, X-6.

dred men, dressed in various forms of military garb, led by a band of thirty musicians blaring their instruments and beating their drums, marched out of a side street and into the park, and headed in the direction of the speaker's platform. Some bystanders later described the marchers as local gangsters and hooligans. As the band played on, others marching in the parade shouted, "We want Americanism, not Reds." Some marchers carried signs: "The working people of our city are contented. Reds keep out," and "Let all Russian radicals and Red foreigners go back to Russia." Four mounted policemen and a score of officers on foot surrounded the speaker's platform, apparently to protect Thomas in the event the crowd got ugly. The band halted immediately in front of the platform. When Thomas tried to speak, the band started anew. When Thomas tried again to speak, the band started again. Cheers, boos, jeers, and hisses mingled with the band music. Then missiles began to fly. Electric light bulbs, rotten eggs, overripe tomatoes, pears and apples bombarded the speaker's platform and many hit Thomas.[1]

Trying to ignore the continuing shower of eggs, fruits, and vegetables, Thomas pleaded to be allowed to speak. Above the din, he shouted, "In any city of the United Stated man has the right to present both sides of the story. Won't you please let me present mine?" The band then struck up a marching song and began encircling the platform. The horse of a mounted policeman suddenly bolted and lunged toward the speaker's platform. As the platform collapsed, Thomas leapt aside, barely averting being crushed beneath horse and debris. Others standing near the platform were injured and ambulances were summoned. The police protection may have been nothing more than a facade, as Thomas later contended, but in any event, it surely was inadequate.

The police called for reinforcements. By that time, the crowd had increased to more than four thousand. Eventually, police headquarters dispatched four hundred policemen to the scene. Fist fights broke out between Thomas loyalists and those in the parade. Police arrested and dragged from the park several Thomas supporters. Thomas mounted a park bench and tried again to address the crowd. During a break in the music, he shouted, "How many of you believe in fair play?" They would have none of it. He yelled at the band, "I hope you are being paid union wages." Several of the mob took up pieces of the fractured speaker's platform and rushed at Thomas. Two of those accompanying Thomas also were attacked. At that point the police surrounded Thomas and escorted him from the field of battle. He asked the police to accompany him to the train station so that he could return to Manhattan. "I expect to be given safe conduct back to America." He later added,

---

1 A photograph of eggs hitting Thomas in the face was selected as one of the most important news photographs of 1938. The photograph appears in Harry Fleischman, *Norman Thomas, A Biography: 1884–1968* (W.W. Norton, New York, 1969).

"This is the way tyranny grows in the guise of patriotism. I certainly shall add the name of Newark to that of Jersey City."[1]

Sporadic fighting continued in the park for some time and the police made several more arrests. Two of those injured by the charging mob alleged that the police had refused to arrest their assailants. Thomas later that evening charged city officials with having created the mob. "Who else," he asked, "would pay for the band?"

> This whole thing had the marks of connivance . . . with the police. The police could have prevented violence . . . I watched the disturbance for ten minutes and at any time the police could have broken it up.... Most [of the mob] were just bums and drunks.... It is up to the people of Newark to make amends for tonight's trouble.[2]

Two days later, Hague led an "Americanization" parade through the center of Jersey City. Waving a small American flag and bowing to bystanders, Hague announced that the parade was a demonstration of his city's stand against communism and that his admirers had arranged it to serve as a sign of their appreciation for his stand against Communists and other radicals.[3]

Thomas was not finished with Mayor Hague. He requested the City Commission of Newark to investigate the park riot. The Commission complied and assured him full protection if he chose to speak in Newark again. Two weeks later, Thomas spoke before a Newark audience of four thousand, accusing Hague of heading a regime guilty of acts of corruption, violence, and repression. On the night before, Roosevelt had addressed the nation by radio. Without mentioning Hague by name, the president said: "The American people will not be deceived by anyone who attempts to suppress individual liberty under the pretense of patriotism."[4]

The CIO sued Hague, alleging that he had unlawfully refused to issue the union permits to conduct meetings of its members within city limits. In response, Hague maintained he had acted lawfully, since a city ordinance authorized the denial of a permit to any person or organization that intended to conduct a public meeting to advocate a change in the government of the United States by other than lawful means. Hague claimed the CIO was a Communist organization, and thus he rightly denied its applications for permits. The mayor's position faltered on the claim that the CIO was Communist. It was not. In any event, the CIO argued that the ordinance was unconstitutional, that it deprived the union of its rights of free speech and peaceable assembly, secured by the Fourteenth Amendment.

---

1 *The Washington Post*, 6/5/38, M-1.

2 *The New York Times*, 6/5/38, 1.

3 *The Washington Post*, 6/7/38, X-3.

4 Harry Fleischman, *Norman Thomas, A Biography: 1884–1968*, 161-162.

Ultimately, the case reached the Supreme Court, which agreed that the Jersey City ordinance was unconstitutional. The court then granted the union a great victory by enjoining Hague from interfering with union meetings held in Jersey City.[1] The case established a significant precedent. The Supreme Court warned cities and towns throughout the country not to use local ordinances as tools to deny persons or organizations their constitutional rights of free speech and assembly. For Mayor Hague, the decision constituted a rare defeat in his long career of dictatorial control of Jersey City.

---

1 *Hague v. Committee for Industrial Organization*, 307 U.S. 496 (1939).

CHAPTER 14. FASCISM, COMMUNISM AND PACIFISM

Fascism haunted Thomas; he feared its violence and disavowal of personal freedom. For a time, he believed that a Fascist takeover was a possibility in the United States. He was among the first Americans to realize the dangers the Fascist regimes in Europe presented for the United States. He held that the triumph of fascism in Germany was not only an expression of rampant nationalism, but also wholly out of line with conditions of peace in an interdependent world.[1] As early as 1934, he had led Socialists in anti-Nazi demonstrations, urging shoppers not to buy German goods. At the time, he felt Socialists had few other options to express their opposition to Fascist dictatorships.[2]

Thomas' fear of the rise of an American fascism dated from the early Depression years. In his book *The Choice Before Us*, written in 1933, he noted that Fascist methods appeared congenial to certain aspects of American life, such as gangsterism, lynching, and racism. He warned his readers that the failure of the government to meet the unemployment crisis could inspire Fascists to attempt to resolve that crisis on their terms, using their methods.[3] It was possible that segments of middle-class America would even welcome fascism. Anxious to hold on to what they possessed, or what they could reasonably expect to possess, they could very well grow resentful of blue-collar worker aspirations to attain middle class status. Thus, he was fearful that fascism

---

1 Norman Thomas, "If War Is to be Averted," *The World Tomorrow*, 10/26/33, 585.
2 *The Washington Post*, 1/28/34, 3.
3 Norman Thomas, *The Choice Before Us: Mankind at the Crossroads* (Macmillan, New York, 1934), 42-62.

would be especially appealing to that section of the American middle class that opposed socialism and was barely tolerant of labor unions.[1]

Despite warnings from some quarters, Thomas had no concern that Roosevelt might harbor Fascist leanings. "Mr. Roosevelt is no Fascist.... Your Fascist leader will have a different accent from Mr. Roosevelt's."[2] During the Depression years, Roosevelt arrested any drift to an American fascism by using his oratorical powers and popularity with the masses to extol democracy. He awakened hope and gave the masses new confidence in a duly constituted government. Thomas feared, however, that Roosevelt's leadership was insufficiently reflected in the New Deal's reorganization of the Federal government, and that the roots of a Fascist movement had been left intact. A demagogue, such as a Huey Long or a Father Coughlin could come along and gain from those roots a renewed life for fascism.[3]

Thomas' concerns about an incipient fascism were not relieved when the Supreme Court issued its ruling in a case involving the refusal of Jehovah's Witnesses to salute the American flag. In 1936, the principal of a Pennsylvania elementary school expelled two children of Jehovah's Witness parents for refusing to salute the flag, a ceremony that customarily began each school day. Jehovah's Witnesses believed that saluting the flag was equivalent to worshiping a graven image, an offense against God. The parents of the expelled children sued the school board and the case eventually led to the Supreme Court decision that State authority co-opted religious liberty, as long as the State did not directly promote or restrict religion. The court expressed the view that since national unity is the basis for national security, a local school board that believes a compulsory flag salute promotes national unity, acts within the law when it orders children to salute the flag.[4]

Thomas depicted the court's decision ordering the children to salute the flag as one "Hitler might have applauded."[5] For some, however, the decision inflamed mob patriotism. In more than three hundred instances in the months immediately following the decision, Jehovah's Witnesses were subjected to acts of violence, some savagely brutal. For Thomas, the Supreme Court's decision and the mob violence that followed showed clearly that fascism was on the rise. But the reaction of a good part of the public demonstrated the exact opposite. Newspapers across the nation condemned the Court, as did a significant portion of the legal profession. Three years later, with a change in its membership, the Court reversed its earlier decision and

---

1 Norman Thomas, *After the New Deal, What?* (Macmillan, New York, 1936), 188.
2 Norman Thomas, *The Choice Before Us: Mankind at the Crossroads*, 164.
3 Norman Thomas, *We Have a Future* (Princeton University Press, Princeton, 1941), 77-78.
4 *Minersville School District v. Gobitis*, 310 U.S. 586 (1940).
5 Norman Thomas, *We Have a Future*, 81.

ruled that the children of Jehovah's Witness parents had a constitutional right to refuse to participate in flag salute ceremonies.[1]

In retrospect, Thomas' fears of an American fascism appear to have been overblown. In the years just before World War II, however, these fears still loomed large in his mind. He believed that the event most likely to introduce fascism to the country would be America's entry into another European war. Conceivably, Americans would adopt a form of fascism in response to the confusion and despair wrought by another major conflict.[2] Since fascism was likely to arise out of war, opposition to war was a priority. This thought coincided with his pacifist principles. His fears relating to the rise of an American fascism and his persistent opposition to involvement in any foreign military conflict traveled on parallel tracks. In all events, war must be avoided.

Thomas was acutely aware that the fascism of Hitler, Mussolini, and Franco posed mortal threats to world democratic institutions. The problem for Thomas — and for the Socialist Party — was how to confront fascism and destroy it without resorting to war. Neither Thomas nor the Socialist Party ever completely resolved that dilemma.

It was the Spanish civil war that severely tested Thomas' dedication to the pacifist principles that twenty years earlier led him to join the Socialist Party. When Franco led the revolt against the Spanish government in 1936, the United State, France, Great Britain, and other democratic countries imposed an arms embargo on both sides of the conflict. Germany and Italy, however, continued to supply arms to Franco's Fascist forces throughout the war. The arms embargo effected by the democratic countries cut off all military supplies to the Loyalist forces, materially undermining their efforts to oppose and defeat the Fascist forces.

From the outset of the war, Thomas supported the Spanish Loyalist forces, accurately viewing the rebellion as a Fascist military venture, not an uprising of the exploited masses. A Fascist victory would culminate in the annihilation of Spanish democracy and would end any possibility that the Spanish people would turn to democratic socialism. When Hitler and Mussolini rejected the arms embargo and instead supplied the rebel Fascist forces, Thomas called upon Roosevelt to permit American arms manufacturers to sell their products to the Loyalists. Roosevelt was not persuaded, insisting on maintaining strict US neutrality. Thus the embargo continued to tip the military advantage in favor of the Fascists.

Thomas' position on the appropriateness of the United States policy in the Spanish civil war was inconsistent with positions he assumed in prior

---

1 *West Virginia State Board of Education v. Barnette*, 319 U.S. 624 (1943).
2 Norman Thomas, *After the New Deal, What?*, 186-187.

conflicts. He had previously favored the imposition of an arms embargo on both sides of a conflict, always questioning a US policy that allowed unilateral sales of arms to one side of a conflict, as frequently occurred in Latin American civil wars. In Spain, he favored a genuine, all inclusive, hands-off policy for all nations. Such a policy, he was certain, would bring about a Loyalist victory, but when Germany and Italy continued to furnish arms to the Fascist forces, the defeat of the Loyalists appeared imminent. At that point, Thomas abandoned his position of strict neutrality, and argued in favor of arms sales to the Loyalists.

He and many others saw little risk that the sale of arms by American companies to the Spanish government would result in a United States' involvement in that war. In any event, Thomas argued, the defeat of Franco and the Fascists was necessary if peace in Europe, and in the world as well, were to prevail. Thus, in his mind, the sale of military supplies to the Loyalist forces was wholly justified, even if it violated his pacifist principles.

Though opposed to all wars, Thomas understood that fascism in Spain could be defeated only by war. "Is it any wonder," he wrote, "that in this kind of world, consistency among peace lovers is not a common virtue?"[1] He now rejected a pacifism that made mere abstention from war the supreme command, since it no longer could deliver humanity from new cycles of war and oppression. He held that it was unrealistic to say that it did not matter who won in Spain if only the guns were stilled. Rather, it mattered profoundly not only for Spain, but for the democratic world that the Fascist aggression be defeated. "Persons who believe this must support the gallant resistance of the workers and other Loyalists."[2] Thomas thus reasoned that the United States was justified in abandoning its position of strict neutrality, at least to the extent of permitting arms sales to the Loyalist government. He concluded that he had to reject strict pacifist principles, since in these circumstances, they were no longer relevant or meaningful.

Thomas did not limit his retreat from pacifist principles solely to arguments in support of arms sales to the Spanish Loyalists. He went further. Jack Altman, a prominent member of the New York branch of the Socialist Party, proposed that the party raise $50,000 to support a "Eugene Debs Column" of five hundred volunteers to fight in Spain at the side of the Loyalists. Giving his support to Altman's proposal, Thomas arranged for the party's National Executive Committee to establish a new group, called the "Friends of the Debs Column," to raise the funds required to send the volunteer force to Spain.

---

1 Norman Thomas, "The Pacifist's Dilemma," *The Nation* 1/16/37, 66.
2 Ibid.

Thomas' support for the Debs Column was too much for the pacifists in the party. They reacted with revulsion at the sight of the Socialist Party caught up in the recruitment of soldiers for battle. The Rev. John Haynes Holmes, one of Thomas' closest friends, wrote to Thomas, charging him with abandonment of his bedrock pacifist principles:

> Times have changed apparently since you and I were young, and in 1917 saw the Socialist Party refuse to support a war in which not a foreign but our own country was involved!. . . By what right does any Socialist today profane the sacred name of Debs by using it to designate a regiment of soldiers enlisted for the work of human slaughter?. . . Let us send food, clothing, medical supplies in abundance, but not a gun, not a bomb, not an airplane, to prolong the war, and extend the area of devastation and death. You and I, Norman, have been through this business before. We stood fast when Belgians lifted cries as pitiful as those lifted by Spaniards today, and when Paris was beset no less terribly than Madrid.... Are we to stand by idly now when a new generation . . . yields to the appeal for another fight to save democracy. . . ?[1]

Thomas' response to condemnation of his position regarding the Spanish conflict revealed the extent to which he had altered his pacifist beliefs. He wrote to friends that for many years he had found it impossible to recognize the type of religious pacifism he had accepted during the First World War. Life had forced him to change in many respects his philosophy of those years, and he now argued with himself and with others in an endeavor to justify this new stand. For him, an enormous gulf separated a policy that lent support to the Loyalists, in the hope that their victory would make the coming of another world war less likely, and a policy that could result in a far more extensive war, in which the US government would become involved in wholesale killings.[2] Responding to those who failed to accept that distinction, he argued that in any event support for the Loyalist cause was justified as the lesser of two evils.

He later wrote that after the First World War he greatly modified those of his pacifist beliefs that were based on Christian philosophy: "For many years now I have been deeply concerned to find a substitute for war . . . while at the same time I have been unable to say categorically that under every circumstance I must oppose wholesale violence."[3] Holmes responded to Thomas' letter in sadness and disbelief:

> I must be frank . . . and say that your letter saddened me beyond all words to describe. Had this been reported to me and not set down over your signature, I would not have believed it. I stand where I have stood from the beginning, moved by the same religious convictions that held me a quarter

---

1 John Haynes Holmes letter, dated 12/23/36, to Thomas.
2 Thomas letter, dated 12/24/36, to John Haynes Holmes.
3 Thomas autobiography, 181.

of a century ago, and it devastates my soul to think that any change for any reason should have come to you.[1]

The sadness that Thomas experienced in parting with his many friends over Spanish civil war issues failed to weaken his support for the Loyalist cause. He sought to establish yet another basis for justifying his support for the Eugene Debs Column by sharply distinguishing between the right of individuals to aid a cause in which they believe and the right of a government to involve an entire nation in a military intervention.[2] The Debs Column volunteers willingly placed their lives at risk in the struggle to free Spain from Fascist control. This was a matter far different from war time conscription of young Americans to fight in the trenches in France. The volunteers freely invested their own lives; their government's conscription laws did not force them to offer their lives in sacrifice. "They are of a long line of men who have said with Tom Paine: 'Where liberty is not, there is my fatherland.'"[3] Convinced of the rightness of his position, he renewed with President Roosevelt the issue of arms sales to the Loyalists, but again his appeal was ignored.[4]

In 1937, leaders of the Socialist Party arranged a twentieth anniversary celebration of Thomas' first active connection with the party. For Thomas, it was a day of considerable joy as friends, dating from his days at Princeton, Spring Street and Harlem, were on hand to greet him, along with those he later worked with in the Socialist Party. A large purse was collected for the many causes with which he was closely associated, and an anonymous group, the identity of which he was never able to ascertain, presented him with a fund sufficient to defray the cost of a European trip for him and his wife. He later wrote in his autobiography that he felt he had never properly thanked all the people who had made the occasion a success. "If this ever meets their eyes I hope they will accept this tribute of gratitude."[5] Not long after, Thomas and Violet sailed aboard the SS Aquitania bound for Europe, with England the first stop of an itinerary that included Austria, Czechoslovakia, Poland, Russia, Finland, Sweden, Denmark, Belgium, Spain, and France.

In Moscow, Thomas and Violet observed that Russians were afraid to be seen with Americans. From the time they entered Russia from Poland, until they departed the country by passing over the border to Finland, a State-appointed guide accompanied them on every step of their tour. Based on visits to Moscow, Leningrad, Kiev and cities and towns in between, he formulated a favorable opinion of the Communist efforts to conquer illiteracy and improve education, but was impressed with little else. Consumer goods were

---

1 John Haynes Holmes letter, dated 12/28/26, to Thomas.
2 Norman Thomas, *A Socialist's Faith* (W.W. Norton, New York, 1951), 311.
3 Norman Thomas, "The Pacifist's Dilemma," *The Nation*.
4 Thomas autobiography, 183-184.
5 Ibid., 170.

scarce and inferior. New construction was shoddy, and slave labor worked under armed guards. There were no signs of individual freedom and the prisons were full.[1]

On one evening in Moscow, Norman and Violet, accompanied by Col. Faimonville, an American military attaché, attended the ballet, as did Joseph Stalin (who sat in a box formerly reserved for the czars and their families). Just before Stalin's arrival at the theater, a Russian army officer sitting in the box above Stalin's stood up and appeared to carefully inspect the audience as if he expected a would-be assassin were present. "That's my old friend, General Feldman," Faimonville noted. "He's very high up and very close to Stalin." Thomas thought little of the matter until about a month later when in France he read a newspaper account of the trials of some Russian army generals. In a series of purge trials ordered by Stalin, many prominent old members of the Communist Party and of the military were convicted of acts of treason on evidence largely fabricated by the secret police or on the basis of confessions obtained under pressure or torture. General Feldman's name appeared on the list of generals caught up in these purges and who ultimately were executed. Thomas later wrote in his autobiography that whatever Feldman's offense had been, "he was no vulgar assassin for I had seen him pass up a chance such as John Wilkes Booth never had."[2]

Thomas concluded that Russian communism could never be conceived as democratic socialism. Instead, Russian communism had subverted socialism; at best, it was a degenerate form of socialism. He accused Stalin of using the purge trials to murder his opponents. Rather than a successor of Lenin, Stalin was more accurately described as the successor of Ivan the Terrible. There was no hope for a political system that supported institutions that the purge trials stood for.

Arriving in Spain, Norman and Violet again were subjected to the "guided tour" approach. Their days were always mapped out for them in specific detail, and consequently Thomas met few of the people with whom he wanted to confer. He visited the war front and was amused to see on a dugout wall a Marxian photo — not of Karl, but of Groucho and his brothers. When they arrived in Valencia early one evening, the moon was bright and their guide remarked that it was a good night for bombing. In fact, search lights were already at work. But the skies over Valencia had been quiet for several weeks and Norman and Violet went to their hotel bed without much fear. Near dawn, a blinding flash and a deafening crash of what appeared to be thunder awakened them. Fascist planes were bombing Valencia. Three bombs fell

---

1 Norman Thomas, *Socialism Re-examined* (Greenwood, Westport, Conn., 1963), 72-73.

2 Thomas autobiography, 190. In his autobiography, Thomas referred to a "Col. Faimonville" and a "General Feldman," while in *Socialism Re-examined*, 73, he referenced a "Col. Famonville" and a "General Friedman."

---

within a few hundred feet of their hotel. The bombing killed more than two hundred townspeople and demolished nearly fifty buildings. Panic gripped the city for several hours.[1]

Thomas' first thought after the bombs began to fall was how angry his children would be with him for allowing their mother to visit war-torn Spain. Norman, Violet and the other hotel occupants hurried down from their rooms to a darkened hotel lobby, hoping to find there some protection from the bombs. When the lighting was later restored, they discovered they had gathered for safety under a stained-glass dome.[2]

Interviewed a few days later in Paris, Thomas condemned Hitler and Mussolini for waging war on the Spanish people. The bombardment of Spanish cities served no military purpose since women and children were primarily those who suffered death or injury:

> I saw devastation of the working class quarters at Barcelona and can testify that its principal effect was not to weaken morale but to increase bitterness and hate to a degree that might give even Hitler, Mussolini and... Franco reason to fear for the future.... It has only been German and Italian intervention which made and is making a long war out of what would have been a short, unsuccessful revolt.[3]

He also attacked the democratic powers, who by their inaction tacitly approved of the slaughter inflicted by the bombers.[4] Thomas returned home in the summer of 1937, resigned to the inevitability of continued war in Spain and convinced that only the United States could save what remained of democracy in Europe.[5]

While in Spain he observed that the Communists were not hesitant to use murder and treachery to dominate the Loyalist government. When he discovered that the Debs Column volunteers had been attached to the Communist controlled Abraham Lincoln Battalion — comprised mostly of Americans students, commanded by a twenty-eight-year-old Communist and former lecturer at the University of California[6] — he withdrew his support for the venture.[7]

What he had seen in Russia and Spain ended any hope that he previously had for cooperative efforts between the Socialists and the Communists in this country. As observed in earlier chapters, Thomas' initial reaction to the Communists in the early 1920s was notable for its ambivalence. As late as the early Depression years, he had been impressed with the economic progress

---

1 *The Washington Post*, 5/29/37, 1.
2 Thomas autobiography, 185-186.
3 *The Washington Post*, 5/31/37, 7.
4 Ibid.
5 Thomas autobiography, 191.
6 Hugh Thomas, *The Spanish Civil War* (Harper, New York, 1961), 377, 380.
7 Norman Thomas, *A Socialist's Faith* (W.W. Norton, New York), 311-312.

achieved in Russia, but he never accepted the Communist dogma that only violent revolution would bring down capitalism. Moreover, he consistently condemned Communist suppression of civil rights as a tool to consolidate power as in the Soviet Union. Until 1934, however, he was one of a minority of Socialists who still believed that under limited circumstances cooperative efforts of the Socialists and Communists were possible.[1] He now realized he had been wrong. The Communists would never cooperate in good faith with the Socialists, and any expectation to the contrary would be foolishly held.

Although he condemned the Communist agenda in the United States, he never wavered in arguing that it was incumbent on Americans to fully protect the civil rights of Communists, as well as any other group. On one occasion, he urged a Princeton University dean to permit Communist Earl Browder to speak to the students, arguing that tolerance establishes its virtue when it successfully deals with intolerance. But even Thomas began to lose patience with the Communists when it became increasingly evident in the late 1930s that their thirst for power would lead only to totalitarianism. The executions of many of Russia's top leaders in the purge trials conclusively confirmed that which he long suspected — the principles of democratic socialism would never take root in that country. Rather than moving toward a classless society, the Russians were creating new class divisions in which the Russian workers were denied all political freedom. On his return from Europe, he wrote in *The Socialist Call* that Socialists must insist that what was happening in Russia was not socialism, and that it certainly was not what Socialists hoped to establish in America.[2] He now became a severe critic of Russian communism. Again writing in *The Socialist Call*, he set forth an explicit condemnation of the Russian experience:

> What has happened in Russia represents the degeneration of Socialism, the complete subversion of revolutionary idealism, and an all but fatal wound to working class integrity and confidence in its own destiny. There is no hope for socialism, which indeed deserves no support, unless it can divorce itself completely from everything that the Moscow trials stand for.... The only important thing that is left for us to do is correctly learn the lesson of these Russian tragedies. To my mind it is clear. No society can be decent, certainly no society can be Socialist, under the regime of the totalitarian state ruled by the iron hand of the dictator of a monolithic party, which... from the beginning professed to believe that the end justifies the means and that good faith is a contemptible bourgeois virtue.[3]

1 Norman Thomas, *A Socialist's Faith*, 311-312.
2 *The Socialist Call*, 12/25/37, 4; referred to in Murray B. Seidler, *Norman Thomas: Respectable Rebel* (Syracuse University Press, Syracuse, 1967), 184.
3 *The Socialist Call*, 3/19/38, 5: quoted in Murray B. Seidler, *Norman Thomas: Respectable Rebel* (Syracuse University Press, Syracuse, 1967), 185.

For Thomas, the Stalin–Hitler Pact of August 1939 was anticlimactic. The pact only rendered more evidently than ever that communism did not stand as an opponent of fascism. To the contrary, both communism and fascism stood in opposition to democracy and socialism. Writing to a friend, he excoriated Stalin's duplicity, which forever revealed the falsity of Communist claims that they were the arch enemies of the Fascists. "Communism and fascism will be enemies only to the extent that both are rivals for power in a totalitarian society."[1] Thomas now proclaimed, and would continue to proclaim for the remainder of his life, that while socialism represented democracy's perfection, communism represented democracy's utter and complete failure.

Thomas turned to frontal attacks on American Communists. Seven members of the national board of the ACLU were Communists and pro-Stalinists. Accusing them of favoring the denial of civil rights for those they opposed politically and of giving blanket approval to all things Russian, he moved to oust the seven from the board. His stand created internal disputes within the ACLU, which he proceeded to air in the press, while continuing to engage in direct attacks against the seven he had targeted. Almost overnight, removing Communists from leadership roles in the ACLU had become a holy war for him. He won that war when the ACLU soon afterwards barred from all its leadership positions anyone supporting any form of totalitarianism, Communist or Fascist. [2]

Following upon the turmoil of the 1936 Socialist Party national convention, the desertion of the Old Guard membership, and the fiasco of the 1936 presidential election, Thomas decided the time was ripe to reexamine the positions he had been advancing over the past two decades. He recognized that socialism, then more than ever, was on the defensive, and its continued existence in this country was a matter of serious concern. The book he then wrote he entitled, *Socialism on the Defensive*.[3]

In this work, Thomas introduced the premise that collectivism, in one degree or another, was here to stay. Increasing governmental controls over economic processes as well as over many aspects of social life was an increasingly common occurrence around the world. Thus, the issue the nation then confronted was unrelated to the question whether collectivism should be accepted or opposed. Rather, the primary issue was how much collectivism was appropriate and who should control it — a totalitarian state or a cooperative commonwealth? He emphasized that collectivism, in and of itself,

---

1 Thomas letter, dated 8/25/39, to Morrie Ryskind; quoted by W. A. Swanberg, *Norman Thomas: The last Idealist* (Charles Scribner's Sons, New York, 1976), 234.

2 Samuel Walker, *In Defense of American Liberties: A History of the ACLU* (Southern Illinois University Press, Carbondale, Ill., 1990), 119, 128, 130-131.

3 Norman Thomas, *Socialism on the Defensive* (Harper, New York, 1938).

was not socialism, nor did it automatically lead to socialism. Collectivism under a totalitarian state may give the workers greater security but not liberation, abundance or peace. These are the values, however, that Socialists held dear.

Although socialism relies upon well-established principles of guidance, Thomas observed that it must remain experimental in outlook and temperament. No infallible blueprint exists to plot the most effective Socialist organization. Solutions to human problems require continuing creative thought. In general, the Socialist task is to enlarge contacts with the workers through the presentation of a philosophy and a program that educates and guides:

> The acceptance of that philosophy and program must be a conscious act. It will require the believers in socialism to win the power of the state and to use it consciously to establish the new society.... A minority may lead the way, but to win a Socialist victory it must gain the support of the workers.... It is not impossible work for men who are convinced . . . that only in socialism is there plenty and peace, freedom and fellowship for mankind.[1]

He concluded his re-examination of Socialist principles by reiterating a position he had long held — that the United States had to reorganize the economy to meet human needs, and socialism presented the best means of accomplishing that reorganization.

---

1 Ibid., 298-299.

Chapter 15. Opposing the United States' Entry into World War II

The imminent threat of war and loss of young American lives dominated Thomas' life and thought during the period between the Spanish civil war and America's entry into World War II. He later wrote that he found it impossible to express in words the effect that the impending war had on his innermost life, and he was incapable of depicting adequately his feelings of frustration and guilt. "War has been the principal preoccupation of most of my mature years; to help to banish it from the world, or at least to keep my country from involvement in it, my fondest ambition. And in that ambition I have utterly failed."[1]

The Spanish civil war had compelled him to qualify his long-held, uncompromising, pacifist point of view, especially since his pacifist frame of reference had been grounded on religious convictions he no longer accepted. Although he had deviated from his pacifist principles in urging support for the Spanish Loyalists, he remained as much opposed to war in general as earlier in his career. As discussed in the last chapter, he justified active support for the Spanish Loyalists on the ground that a Fascist victory in Spain would inevitably lead to a far more expansive war — a second world war far worse than the first — entrapping and engaging all democratic nations, including the United States. Viewed in this larger context, his insistence on aiding the Loyalists was consistent with another of his convictions — that the United States should always formulate a foreign policy that rendered its involvement in a foreign war less rather than more likely.

---

1 Thomas autobiography, 172.

His antiwar beliefs led him to organize and later lead the Keep America Out of War Congress (KAOW). Eminent pacifists and anti-Fascists and more than one thousand delegates from union, religious, fraternal, farm, and political groups assembled over the 1938 Memorial Day weekend in Washington, D.C. to express their opposition to President Roosevelt's increasingly active support of measures aimed at preparing the country for war. A few months later, more than six thousand supporters gathered at a KAOW event in New York City to hear Thomas and others inveigh against Roosevelt's "war" policies.

Thomas carried his campaign against war into the 1940 presidential election. Earlier in the year he made it known that he preferred not to run for the presidency a fourth time, but again it was apparent that the party had no one of comparable status to offer the electorate. If he held to his position not to run, the Socialist Party would be without a presidential candidate for the first time in forty years. This, many Socialist Party members held, would amount to abdication in the face of the enemy.

At the party's national convention held in Washington, D.C., Thomas "consented" to be drafted, but only after the delegates had agreed to adopt a platform adhering to his antiwar views. In formulating the party's platform, a group of convention delegates, in face of the resistance of a vocal minority, moved to include a provision opposing US economic assistance to the European democratic powers then engaged in war. The minority opposition, equally opposed to war, believed that the defeat of the Fascist powers would be hastened if the nations resisting them were provided with economic assistance. Thomas disagreed — steps taken short of war were still steps taken toward war. He argued — inconsistently with the position he advanced during the Spanish civil war — that lending economic assistance to belligerents would inevitably turn to military assistance, and thus would constitute a significant step in the direction of America's entry into the war.[1] With Thomas' support, the measure opposing economic assistance to Allied countries was added to the party platform.

After his nomination, Thomas stated his goals in running for president a fourth time and then offered his agenda for the forthcoming election: "I make no prophecy of the size of our vote. But this I affirm: If we can make our fellow citizens stop and listen to our program for keeping America out of war; ...if we can make our words like a burr stick on their consciences in this hour of darkness, doubt and confusion, we shall not have failed."[2] Thomas would devote his presidential campaign to issues relating to war and peace.

1 *The New York Times*, 4/8/40, 1.
2 Ibid.

Thomas tied his election campaign to the work of the Keep America Out of War Congress. By then, the war in Europe was in full progress, and Thomas declared repeatedly throughout the campaign that the United States must not intervene in that war. While Thomas was highly critical of steps undertaken by the administration in preparing for war, Roosevelt persisted in telling the voters that he would not send soldiers to Europe, and Wendell Willkie, the Republican Party candidate, echoed Roosevelt's position when he told the electorate that Americans must always remain clear of that conflict. Thomas believed that neither Roosevelt nor Willkie sincerely held to his position. Both supported legislation providing for a peacetime draft, the first in American history. Roosevelt, moreover, proposed an agreement with Great Britain calling for the exchange of Navy destroyers for leases on naval bases in this hemisphere, and although Willkie declined to endorse the exchange, he refrained from making it a campaign issue.[1] Thomas viewed the transaction as an additional step edging the United States closer to the European conflict.[2]

Thomas argued that although an arms economy tended to reduce the national unemployment rate, it simply accelerated the country's drift toward war. In pursuing the point, he accused Roosevelt of advocating steps in preparation for war as a means, not only of resolving the unemployment problem, but of enhancing his own power as well. Roosevelt, finding this extremely offensive, responded in a letter to Thomas with an unusual display of anger.

> I think that knowing me you will want to withdraw the grossly unfair suggestion . . . that I am in favor of some form of conscription because of the executive power which it gives me personally. That is unworthy of you. You and I may . . . disagree . . . but we can at least give each other credit for honesty that lies behind our opinions.... Incidentally, though you are a student and a thinker, I cannot help feeling that my sources of information are just as good and probably better . . . than yours are. With a sincerity and an honesty equal to yours, I believe that we ought this Autumn to take some kind of action which will better prepare Americans by selection and training for national defense than we have ever done before.[3]

Presidential anger failed to deflect Thomas from continuing to offer fierce opposition to all measures undertaken to prepare the country for war. He persisted in questioning the integrity of Roosevelt's position. Writing to his friend Senator Burton K. Wheeler, Thomas expressed the bitterness he

---

1 David M. Kennedy, *Freedom from Fear: The American People in Depression and War, 1929 - 1945* (Oxford University Press, New York, 1999), 459-461.

2 Winston Churchill viewed the deal as Thomas did. He said it signified the deepening of a process whereby "the English-speaking democracies ... will have to be mixed up together in some of their affairs for mutual and general advantage. For my part,... I do not view the process with any misgivings. I could not stop it if I wished; no one can stop it. Like the Mississippi, it just keeps rolling along." Quoted in David M. Kennedy, *Freedom from Fear*, 461.

3 Franklin D. Roosevelt letter , dated 7/31/40, to Thomas.

held for the president: "It burns me up to discover the attitude of so many people who wait with resignation to find out whether the president will put us all the way into war or halfway into war or what. Is there nothing at all that you folks in Washington can do to some degree to take the play out of his hands?"[1] Thomas implied that America's entry into the war depended on a decision solely made by Roosevelt, apparently discounting the possibility that matters beyond the President's control, occurring outside the United States, could draw the country into the war.

Many in the Socialist Party disagreed with Thomas' antiwar position, and they began to quit the party ranks in large numbers. Ironically, many Militants joined former Old Guard members in supporting Roosevelt and his position on preparing for war. Their defection left the party severely weakened, and its 1940 election campaign ended in as great a disaster as its campaign four years earlier. In fact, Thomas' vote was even smaller — 70,000 fewer than 1936. But his campaign succeeded in attaining widespread distribution of his antiwar message. *The New York Times, The Washington Post,* and several other large newspapers reported his campaign speeches, and national magazines such as *The Nation, The Christian Century,* and *The New Republic* provided forums for the views he expressed while campaigning.

Following the election, Thomas continued his attacks on Roosevelt. He appeared before several Congressional committees, testifying in opposition to conscription and to the production of war armaments. In January 1941, he testified before the House Foreign Affairs Committee, opposing adoption of the Lend-Lease Bill to render assistance to Great Britain. Under existing American law, Great Britain was required to pay cash for its arms purchases in the US, but by the end of 1940, it was having difficulty meeting the payment in cash provisions. Roosevelt reacted by proposing the adoption of the Lend-Lease Bill, whereby the president would be given authority to aid Britain by allowing payment for its arms purchases to be made in any manner acceptable to him. This gave Roosevelt a free hand to lend (or in effect, make a gift of} arms to Britain in furtherance of his policy of helping Britain in its war effort against Germany.

Thomas was sympathetic to Britain's plight in confronting an invasion by the German Nazi forces, and thus he altered his antiwar position so as not oppose the sale of arms to Britain, but argued that the adoption of the Lend-Lease measures moved beyond that and would inevitably involve the United States in direct participation in the war. This he continued to oppose because, as he perceived it, American security was not dependent upon a defeat of the Fascist powers. Moreover, he argued against any legislation

---

1 Thomas letter, dated 3/10/41, to Burton K. Wheeler, quoted by Murray B. Seidler, *Norman Thomas: Respectable Rebel* (Syracuse University Press, Syracuse, 1961), 209.

that would in effect place in the hands of the president the power to commit the United States to a state of war, without first obtaining the consent of Congress. In this instance, however, he refrained from attacking the president personally:

> In no sense, then, do I make a personal or partisan attack on Mr. Roosevelt when I say no man, not even an angel from heaven, who asks for such breath-taking powers of war or peace, with such vague limitations, should be trusted with them. If democracy in this crisis gives sole control of peace or war to one man, it has already surrendered the front line trenches to the principle of totalitarian dictatorship.[1]

Socialist party stalwarts were incensed. They immediately petitioned the House Committee requesting the opportunity to testify in support of the proposed Lend-Lease legislation. Contrary to Thomas' position, they expressed confidence that the powers proposed to be given to President Roosevelt were appropriate and could be granted without destroying democracy in this country. Striking directly at Thomas, they asserted that Socialists could not remain neutral in a world conflict "involving the fate of human values built up over centuries." A policy of isolation in the face of the Hitler menace represented "purely provincial selfishness."[2]

The Old Guard, now appearing under the banner of the *Social Democratic Federation*, also attacked Thomas:

> There are some 900,000 Socialist voters in the nation. Only 100,000 voted for Thomas [in 1940] and for the views he expresses. Eight hundred thousand campaigned and voted for Roosevelt because of his foreign policy. Democratic Socialists are wholeheartedly in favor of the Lend-Lease bill and for all aid to Britain as the best means of national defense today.[3]

Thomas' opponents, in and out of the party, now defined him as an isolationist. But Thomas insisted that his negative views of Roosevelt's war preparations were not isolationist, but were more accurately characterized as those advocating "the maximum American cooperation for peace; the maximum isolation from war"[4] But the isolation charge stuck, and the public continued to think of him as a hard-core isolationist. He was becoming increasingly isolated from just about everyone. In his antiwar cause, he had few followers or supporters. His was a voice "crying in the wilderness."His cause was unpopular, but as in the past, he was willing to sacrifice his political future to support a principle.

Despite the persistence of the charge, Thomas never considered himself an isolationist. More than once he said, "I am not and never was an isolationist."[5]

---

1 *The New York Times,* 1/23/41, 1.
2 Ibid., 8.
3 Ibid.
4 Norman Thomas, *We Have a Future* (Princeton University Press, Princeton, 1941), 72.
5 Norman Thomas, *What Is Our Destiny* (Doubleday, Doran, Garden City, N.Y., 1944), 36.

In words that today's Americans may find poignant, he set forth the basis of his non-interventionist position:

> I believed that, in a dangerous world, America as a nation . . . could better be protected out of a war than in it. More than that, I believed that the real America, a country which I loved without attributing to her a wisdom and power to do for the world what God himself had not done, could better serve herself, and in the long run mankind, by remaining an area of rela-tive sanity and peace, a place where the success of a peaceful democracy might develop an ever-more contagious power, a wellspring of healing and strength to nations broken by war. That would require a positive policy which our government never got around to trying.[1]

He continued to contend, even after the 1940 election, that America's drift toward war was furthered by Roosevelt's program of military preparedness, a program Thomas again claimed achieved greater success in resolving the nation's unemployment problem than had the cures advanced by the New Deal. He condemned Roosevelt's assertions that steps in preparation for war led to peace, and for assuring mothers and fathers that he would not send their sons to fight in a foreign war.[2]

Thomas' non-interventionist policy alienated nearly all American liber-als and radicals. After passage of the Lend-Lease bill, Thomas continued to oppose any United States action that bordered on a more direct participa-tion in the conflict. He urged Congress to consult with the people through a referendum before sanctioning the direct involvement of the nation in the war.[3] Three of the thirteen members of the Socialist Party National Execu-tive Committee resigned, protesting Thomas' "isolationist opposition" to large scale aid to Britain.[4] Another group of party members quit the party and formed the Union for Democratic Action. This group, later transformed into the Americans for Democratic Action, was enormously influential in the Democratic Party in later decades. Historians make a good case for the proposition that Thomas' antiwar frame of reference significantly under-mined the national standing of the Socialist Party, and that he bore direct responsibility for the party's continuous deterioration during the months immediately preceding America's entry into World War II.[5]

Even his close friends were deserting him. Dissenting views came from all sides, but a particularly painful dissent came from his friend Henry Sloane Coffin, then head of the Union Theological Seminary. Coffin wrote to him: "I cannot see how any intelligent American can fail to see that the wise course for this country to follow is to arm at once, and meanwhile give Britain ev-

---

1 Ibid., 34.

2 Norman Thomas, *A Socialist's Faith* (W.W. Norton, New York, 1951), 313-314.

3 Norman Thomas, *We Have a Future*, 75, fn.

4 *The Washington Post*, 3/10/41, 1.c

5 Murray B. Seidler, *Norman Thomas: Respectable Rebel*, 211; Bernard K. Johnpoll, *Norman Thomas on War: An Anthology* (Garland Publishing, New York, 1974), 205.

ery possible aid."[1] Appalled, Thomas perceived the church as again abandoning its Christian principles in favor of another bloody conflict, repeating its World War I error of lending support to America's entry into war.

Despite the ever increasing opposition to his views, Thomas persisted in advancing a non-interventionist point of view. Until June 1941, the American Communists also favored a non-interventionist stance, and Socialists who opposed Thomas' antiwar perspectives accused him of following the Communist line. But when Hitler turned on Stalin and sent his tanks into Russia, the Communists reversed course and urged the United States to intervene on the side of the Soviet Union. Thomas, however, did not alter his non-interventionist outlook, and those Socialists who had accused him of associating with Communists now found themselves paralleling the Communist position. Thomas had felt no need to defend himself against charges that his views reflected Communist Party dogma, but he must have felt some vindication when his critics were proved wrong and found themselves in the very circumstances that had evoked their criticism of his point of view on the war.

Thomas sympathized with the Russian people but offered only scorn for Stalin. "In every way his cruelty and duplicity have equaled Hitler's own.... The lion has now turned on the jackal." [2] He looked upon the German — Russian conflict as unworthy of the blood of American soldiers, and so he persisted in preaching nonintervention.

While in the end Thomas readily distinguished his antiwar policies from those advanced by the Communists, he never was able to dissociate himself entirely from the views of the America First Committee. America First, clearly isolationist, right wing, Roosevelt hating, and opposed to any involvement in World War II, was led by such notables as Col. Charles A. Lindbergh, Henry Ford, and General Robert Wood. Lindbergh's speeches on behalf of America First were emphatically isolationist, and some considered him as pro-Nazi. Secretary of the Interior Harold Ickes, in a speech presented to the Jewish National Workers Alliance of America, branded Lindbergh "the number one United States Nazi fellow traveler." He accused Lindbergh of preferring fascism to democracy, of agreeing with Hitler that Christianity was foundering in a state of decay, and of condoning the brutalities perpetrated by the Nazi regime. Ickes claimed that the connection between the America First Committee and the Fascists and anti-Semites was "clear and scandalous," and he expressed his dismay that America First had been accorded the respect of a whole host of fellow travelers, including "decent Socialists, such as Norman Thomas."[3]

---

1 Henry Sloan Coffin letter, dated 8/3/40, to Thomas.
2 *The New York Times*, 6/23/41, 9.
3 *The Washington Post*, 4/14/41, 24.

Although Thomas never formally became a member of the America First Committee, he often spoke under its auspices. Despite warnings that he would severely damage his reputation and would be looked upon as a Nazi sympathizer, Thomas on several occasions spoke from the same platform as Lindbergh. Thomas viewed the America First program as inadequate in advancing the cause of nonintervention, but rejected charges that the organization itself was pro-Nazi or Fascist. Lindbergh attracted vast audiences, and Thomas was willing to overlook Lindbergh's failings if it provided him with a forum to present his own views.

Lindbergh eventually made statements Thomas could not ignore. In a speech given in Des Moines, Iowa, Lindbergh claimed that the British and the Jews had formed an alliance with Roosevelt to force United States' entry into the war. "If any of these groups — the British, the Jews or the administration — stop agitating for war . . . there will be little danger of our involvement." He stated that he understood why American Jews desired the overthrow of the Nazi regime, but they were better advised to resist intervention in the war since they would be the first to feel its consequences. "Their greatest danger to this country," he said of the Jews, "lies in their large ownership and influence in our motion pictures, our press, our radio, and our government."[1]

Thomas immediately joined the public in condemning Lindbergh's speech. He noted that Lindbergh was not so much an anti-Semite as he was misguided, and he called upon America First to dissociate itself from Lindbergh and to repudiate anti-Semitism:

> Many groups and elements in this country are attempting to drive us into war. This issue cuts across all racial lines. No one race is responsible. The Socialist Party has many Jews in its ranks and these take their stand with the party against American involvement. No race or people can be made the scapegoat for this crime.[2]

Thomas instantly separated himself from Lindbergh and America First, but it was too late. He was now tagged by some as an anti-Semite, a charge that greatly irritated him. For years, he had urged United States asylum for Jews uprooted by German Fascism, and he continued throughout the war to plead with Roosevelt to open America's doors to Europe's Jewish refugees. Some prominent Jews and many others came to his defense. James G. McDonald, president of the Brooklyn Institute of Arts and Sciences, and later America's first ambassador to Israel, expressed shock when he heard that

---

1 *The New York Times*, 9/12/41, 2.
2 Ibid., 9/13/41, 2.

anti-Semitism had been attributed to Thomas. He publicly stated that it was wholly absurd to accuse Thomas of intolerance and anti-Semitism.[1]

Thomas persisted in his attacks on Roosevelt, and as late as October 1941, accused the president of trying to force an unwilling country into war.[2] He argued that under Roosevelt's leadership, the United States was giving Britain the amount and kind of aid which Americans, assuming they were to exchange places with the Germans, would regard as a cause for war. He never forgave the president when, speaking to mothers and fathers of boys of a military age, he asserted that: "I have said this before, but I shall say it again, and again, and again — your boys are not going to be sent into any foreign war."[3]

In November 1941, Thomas' son, Evan, a senior at Princeton, left school and joined the English forces in Egypt as an ambulance driver. Thomas wrote to Evan praising him for having chosen what for him — who also hated war — was the best possible course of action. He also tried to assure Evan that all was not wrong with this world: "I suspect that you will find much that makes for cynicism about us men and our ways, but I've found it a help to consider that if God must be disappointed in us, so must the devil in the presence of such courage and comradeship as plain people show."[4]

On the morning of December 7, 1941, Norman and Violet drove to Princeton to retrieve some of the belongings Evan had left behind. It was at Princeton that they heard the news of the Japanese attack on Pearl Harbor. For Thomas, this was an irreparable defeat of his hopes that his children would not know a world war.[5] As late as the day before, Thomas had written a letter to *The New York Times* again opposing any involvement of the United States in the war.[6] Now he had to face the fact that he had met defeat "of the single ambition of his life: that [he] might have been of some service in keeping [his] country out of a second world war."[7]

The Pearl Harbor attack forced upon him the need to again alter his anti-war policies. Prior to formulating a new perspective, he had to look back and review the evolution of his pacifist views over the past twenty-five years. As a clergyman during World War I, he had been unable to reconcile Christianity and war, either on philosophic or ethical grounds. Following that war,

---

1 Harry Fleischman, *Norman Thomas, A Biography: 1884–1968* (W.W. Norton, New York, 1969), 200.

2 *The Washington Post*, 10/15/41, 16.

3 Norman Thomas, *What Is Our Destiny*, 16.

4 The letter is quoted at length in Harry Fleischman, *Norman Thomas, A Biography: 1884–1968* , 201-202; and W.A. Swanberg, *Norman Thomas: The Last Idealist* (Charles Scribner's Sons, New York, 1976), 256-257.

5 Harry Fleischman, *Norman Thomas, A Biography: 1884–1968*, 202.

6 After hearing of the Pearl Harbor attack, Thomas withdrew the letter and it never was published.

7 *The New York Times*, 12/20/68, 1.

after leaving the church and modifying his thinking about God, man, and the universe, he found he could no longer advocate an absolute opposition to all wars. In the years following, as his admiration for Mahatma Gandhi grew, he tended to favor the concept of nonviolent resistance, but he never attained a complete confidence in the power of nonviolence, recognizing that although Gandhi was effective, given the conditions then prevailing in India, against a Hitler or a Stalin, he would have met an early death in some secret dungeon.[1]

Early on, he had high hopes for the League of Nations, but was quickly disillusioned. The rise of fascism and Hitler greatly disturbed him, but he failed to recognize, along with a good part of the rest of the world, that vigorous action of France and Britain, backed by the United States, could have checked Germany's rearmament. His fear of fascism led him to oppose the US embargo on arms to the Spanish Loyalists, especially when Roosevelt refused also to impose a ban on the sale of military supplies to Germany and Italy, who were supplying Franco's forces. By this time, while lending support to the Debs Column volunteers, he described himself as a "former pacifist."[2]

Dedicating himself to advancing the goals of the Keep America out of War Congress, Thomas spent the years immediately preceding Pearl Harbor in a last-ditch effort to stem the steady drift toward war. Ethically, he contended that sidling into war could not be justified, and he rejected Roosevelt's assertions that measures undertaken in preparation for war were steps leading to peace. He remained adamantly opposed to America's readying for war until the morning of December 7, 1941. By that afternoon, he knew his non-interventionist stance was no longer tenable or relevant.

What tortured him most was the conviction that he now had to accept the reality of a war that included the United States as a participant. His country was at war. As much as he wanted to oppose that war, he knew there was no conceivable political alternative but to support it. The nation had been attacked and Americans had no choice but to respond militarily. To sue for peace immediately after Pearl Harbor would have required submission to the Fascists and, of course, that was unthinkable.[3] "Caught between the circles of hell," Thomas chose what he thereafter referred to as "critical but active support of the war effort." He would support the war effort at least to the point where a decent peace could be achieved.[4]

His use of the term "critical support" was not without ambiguity. As a politician, his support was no longer sought by the Roosevelt administration — or by anyone else, for that matter. With most of the Socialist Party

---

1 Norman Thomas, *A Socialist's Faith* (W.W. Norton, New York, 1951), 308-309.
2 Ibid., 311-312.
3 Thomas autobiography, 202-203.
4 Norman Thomas, *A Socialist's Faith*, 315.

membership having deserted the party during the years immediately prior to the war, the party, now with fewer than one thousand members, was near extinction. Thomas no longer commanded a following. So what did he mean by "critical support" and how was his support at all relevant?

Shortly after Pearl Harbor, Thomas proposed to the Socialist Party National Executive Committee the adoption of a five-point program defining the policies the party should pursue during the course of the war:

• The party should continue to reiterate its position that America could have avoided the war.

• It should continue to deny that the war was democratic in its origins, aims, or alliances.

• The party should admit that the only alternatives following Pearl Harbor were an Allied or Fascist victory, and that the latter would be the greatest possible calamity.

• The party should refuse to support any peace offensive made early in the war because a peace agreement at that juncture could be had only on terms favorable to the Fascist powers.

• The party should devote itself primarily to working during the war for the expansion of civil liberties, racial justice, workers' rights, and rights for conscientious objectors.[1]

Thomas' proposed "critical support" of the war effort was based on these five declarations. For Thomas and the Socialist Party, the first four points proved meaningless, but Thomas would devote himself during the war years to carrying out the precepts of the fifth point. For the duration of the war, he would involve himself in working to protect the civil liberties of all Americans.

---

[1] Bernard K. Johnpoll, *Pacifist's Progress: Norman Thomas and the Decline of American Socialism* (Greenwood, Westport, Conn., 1970), 233.

CHAPTER 16. THE INTERNMENT OF JAPANESE-AMERICANS AND OTHER
WARTIME CIVIL RIGHTS VIOLATIONS

Historians examining the life of Norman Thomas affirm that his constant battles fought to protect the civil liberties of minorities, the disadvantaged, and the oppressed played as significant a role in his life as did socialism. In acting in defense of Americans subjected to civil rights violations, Thomas rightfully gained the reputation as one of the greatest advocates of civil rights of the twentieth century.[1]

At the beginning of World War II, Thomas was convinced the government would be less inclined than it was in the First World War to deprive its citizens of their civil liberties. After the Pearl Harbor attack, the public expressed little opposition to the war, and thus governmental officials had less reason and fewer occasions to suppress dissenting opinion. Thomas nevertheless continued to hold to his initial reaction to Pearl Harbor — that the most important service he could render during the war years would be to remain vigilantly on guard against occurrences of civil rights violations. He had not forgotten the repressive measures undertaken by Postmaster General Burleson and others in the Wilson administration, all under the pretext that such actions were necessary when a nation is engaged in war. But with the country united behind the war effort, the public for the most part showed little concern about repressive governmental action. That was not the case, however, with Japanese aliens and American citizens of Japanese ancestry living along the Pacific coast.

---

1 James C. Duram, *Norman Thomas* (Twayne, New York, 1974), 85.

Shortly after the beginning of the war, President Roosevelt issued an Executive Order authorizing certain designated Military Commanders to exclude persons from prescribed geographical areas as a protection against espionage and sabotage. Lieutenant General John L. DeWitt, the Military Commander of the Western Defense Command, embracing the western most states, designated the entire Pacific coast as an area possibly subject to an invasion by Japan and thus an area that could very well be targeted for espionage and sabotage. In May 1942, DeWitt ordered military personnel to remove all Japanese aliens and persons of Japanese ancestry from the area.

Longstanding racial animosity against the Japanese was a salient feature of prewar attitudes of whites living along the West Coast. The evacuation order followed several months of blatant anti-Japanese sentiment expressed by newspaper columnists, radio commentators and California politicians who agitated for some form of proscriptive action against persons of Japanese ancestry living in the United States.

Fred Korematsu, a native-born American, lived in the town of San Leandro, California. Six months before Pearl Harbor he tried to enlist in the US Navy, but was rejected because of health reasons. He then gained employment as a shipyard welder. No one questioned his loyalty as a United States citizen, but in June 1942 police authorities arrested and charged him with having committed a crime. What was his crime? Only that his mother and father had been born in Japan, and when military authorities ordered him to leave his home and move to an internment camp, he refused.

Korematsu had never visited Japan, had little knowledge of the Japanese way of life, and was about to marry a woman who was not of Japanese ancestry. Having no desire to be separated from his future wife, and reasoning that since he was a native-born American, the evacuation order was not applicable to him, Korematsu ignored the order and remained in San Leandro. It was not long before FBI agents arrived and marched Korematsu away in handcuffs.

Korematsu later related that at the time he had felt no guilt, that he had done nothing wrong. "Every day in school we said the pledge to the flag, 'with liberty and justice for all,' and I believed all that. I was an American citizen, and I had as many rights as anyone else."[1]

Over the next eight months, 120,000 men, women, and children of Japanese descent were forced to leave their homes in California, Oregon, Washington, and Arizona and were transported to internment camps. More than 80,000 of them were US citizens. The government did not charge them with criminal activity and it conducted no trials or hearings prior to their evacua-

[1] *The New York Times*, 4/1/05, C-13.

tion. The military authorities did not tell these people why they had to leave their homes nor how long they would be barred from returning to them.

Military commanders had no reasonable basis for selecting this group of people for evacuation and internment. Their action was motivated solely by racial bias. Army officers referred to persons of Japanese ancestry as "subversives," as "potential enemies," as a people belonging to "an enemy race," whose "racial strains were undiluted." They further claimed, without substantiating evidence, that persons of Japanese lineage were accustomed to practice "emperor worshiping ceremonies."[1]

These people were condemned simply because they constituted a large, unassimilated, tightly knit racial group, allegedly bound to an enemy nation by strong ties of race, culture, custom and religion. Especially damning for certain of them, their homes were located adjacent to military installations. The reasons alleged by the military as justifying these evacuations were based on misinformation, half-truths, insinuation, bias, and the assumption that because a few persons of Japanese ancestry may have tried to aid the Japanese war effort, the entire group could not be trusted to be or remain loyal to the United States.

The evacuation order forced innocent Japanese aliens, not charged with the commission of a crime, and Japanese-Americans, in violation of their constitutional rights, to leave their homes, businesses and jobs, and required them to sit by idly, without useful occupation, while the rest of the country was fighting the war.[2] The internment camps — later described by Supreme Court Justice Roberts as "concentration camps" — were located in isolated desert areas of the country. The internees were housed in barracks type buildings, surrounded by ten-foot, barbed wire fences and guarded by the military police. Those detained remained in these camps for three or more years, until close to the end of the war.[3] The program was ill-advised and wholly unnecessary. In Hawaii, where over one-third of the population was either Japanese or Japanese-American, no similar action was undertaken.

When compared with the Nazi concentration camps in Europe, the treatment of the Japanese internees was, for the most part, humane. The government established schools for the children and saw that they were decently fed, clothed and cared for in general. Robert T. Matsui, who later was elected to Congress and served in the House of Representatives for twenty-six years, was less than a year old when he and his second generation Japanese-American parents were forced from their Sacramento home and moved to an

---

1 *Korematsu v. United States*, 323 U.S. 214 (1944).
2 Tetsuden Kashima, *Judgment Without Trial: Japanese-American Imprisonment During World War II* (University of Washington Press, Seattle, 2003), 131.
3 Ibid., 120.

internment camp. There the family remained until he was four years old. A younger sister was born in the camp, as was his future wife.[1]

Thomas immediately raised his voice against the internments, comparing the military evacuation of the west coast areas to the Nazi transport of Jews to German concentration camps. Thomas was not one to mince his words. He saw the internments for what they were — racial acts violating the civil liberties of people of Japanese ancestry living in this country. Germans living in the United States were not rounded up, though some evidence showed that some of them had attempted acts of sabotage. The general thesis — that the imposition of suffering upon those who might undermine the war effort was justifiable — was immoral by all standards.

With these massive evacuations and detentions of thousands of innocent people, Thomas was convinced that civil liberties were then in greater danger than at any time during World War I. "Our disease was like a rash then, conspicuous, painful and perhaps for that reason more easily curable. It is now more like a cancer, deep seated and scarcely recognized by the average citizen."[2] The cancer had grown out of the totalitarian control the president had placed in the hands of the military. People of Japanese ancestry were the innocent victims of a distorted policy. Thomas was incensed, but he was unable to persuade others to protest the treatment of these people. In his three decades of experience dealing with issues of civil liberties, he had never found it more difficult to arouse public opinion. Americans chose to ignore the facts, and despite information to the contrary, denied that such camps even existed. At first, even the ACLU expressed reluctance to become involved.[3]

Thomas never tired of trying to awaken the public to acts of injustice occurring in their midst. No one became more involved than he in working to return the internees to their homes, but initially he met with little success. He wrote to the Attorney General, the Secretary of War, and finally to the president himself, but failed to move them. He prepared a pamphlet, "Democracy and Japanese Americans," and raised the issue in countless speeches around the country, alerting his audiences to what later became known as the United States' "worst wartime mistake."[4]

Fred Korematsu appealed his conviction and eventually his case reached the Supreme Court, where a majority of the justices agreed with the government's contention that the mass evacuation of all persons of Japanese ancestry was necessary to separate the disloyal from the loyal. The justices

---

1 *The New York Times*, 1/3/05, A-17.
2 Norman Thomas, "Dark Day for Liberty," *The Christian Century* 7/29/42, 929.
3 Ibid.
4 Murray B. Seidler, *Norman Thomas: Respectable Rebel* (Syracuse University Press, Syracuse, 1967), 214.

cavalierly dismissed opposing arguments that the overwhelming majority of those interned were innocent of any acts of disloyalty, commenting that "hardships are part of war, and war is an aggregation of hardships." They rejected charges of racial discrimination, asserting that casting the cases into "outlines of racial prejudice, without reference to the real military dangers that were presented merely confuses the issue."[1] The court affirmed Korematsu's conviction and gave its sanction and approval to the evacuation and the internments.

Three justices dissented from this ruling. Justice Frank Murphy stated that the internment order passed beyond what is constitutional and fell into "the ugly abyss of racism." He stated that the judicial test as to whether the government can validly deprive an individual of any of his or her constitutional rights is whether that deprivation is reasonably related to a public danger that is so "immediate, imminent, and impending" as not to permit any delay and not to permit the intervention of ordinary constitutional processes to alleviate the danger:

> [The internment order] clearly does not meet that test. Being an obvious racial discrimination, the order deprives all those within its scope of the equal protection of the laws. . . . It further deprives these individuals of their constitutional rights to live and work where they will, to establish a home where they choose and to move about freely. In excommunicating them without benefit of hearings, this order also deprives them of all their constitutional rights of due process. . . .[The internment order] is one of the most sweeping and complete deprivations of constitutional rights in the history of this nation in the absence of martial law.[2]

Agreeing with Justice Murphy and the other dissenters, Thomas condemned the majority ruling. "No act of any American court in any war so completely nullified effective protection of civil liberty."[3] Writing some year later in *Harper's Magazine*, he agreed with those who had denounced the evacuation and internments as this country's worst wartime blunder, noting that nothing wrought by the Wilson administration during World War I "equaled this departure from well-established principles of civil liberty in the number of people that it affected or in its danger as a precedent."[4]

Thomas continued throughout the war to speak out on behalf of the internees and eventually, with the end of the war in sight, public opinion shifted against the internment program. But it was not until 1988, forty-six years after the initial evacuation order, and twenty years after Thomas' death, that Americans finally sought to atone for these wartime racial acts. Congress then apologized on behalf of the government and authorized the payment of

---

1 *Korematsu v. United States*, 223.
2 Ibid., 234-235.
3 Norman Thomas, *The Test of Freedom* (W.W. Norton, New York, 1954), 39.
4 Norman Thomas, "What's Right with America," *Harper's Magazine*, 3/47, 237.

reparations to the surviving victims.[1] The courts ultimately vacated Fred Korematsu's conviction,[2] and in 1998, President Clinton presented him with the Medal of Freedom, likening his stand against the internment of Japanese-Americans to Rosa Parks' battle to maintain her civil rights as an African-American in the 1950s.[3]

Japanese-Americans remembered Thomas' efforts to gain them their freedom, and in later years they wrote letters of appreciation and sent him boxes of freshly grown lettuce, celery, and avocados from the farms they returned to after the war. Thomas had the satisfaction of having engaged in a battle well fought. He experienced additional satisfaction when years later he read the memoirs and autobiographies of the government officials who were directly involved in the evacuation and internment program. Francis Biddle, US Attorney General during the war, wrote in his autobiography that he had advised President Roosevelt that the actions directed against those of Japanese descent were unnecessary:

> [The evacuation] subjected Americans to the shame of being classed as enemies of their native country without any evidence indicating disloyalty....
> American citizens of Japanese origin were not even handled like aliens of the other enemy nationalities — Germans and Italians — on a selective basis, but as untouchables, a group who could not be trusted and had to be shut up only *because* they were of Japanese descent.[4]

Americans of Japanese descent were not the only citizens that Thomas helped during the war. As he had in the First World War, Thomas questioned the Government's treatment of conscientious objectors, though little evidence existed that World War II conscientious objectors suffered the type of maltreatment that his bother Evan had been subjected to during his imprisonment in 1917-1918. Thomas opposed, as he did in the earlier conflict, the policy that exempted from combat those conscientious objectors who objected to killing their fellow men because of religious beliefs, but refused to exempt those who objected to combat on philosophic, ethical, or other nonreligious grounds. Although the Roosevelt administration recognized, in principle, that conscientious objectors were entitled to remain out of combat if they agreed to participate in a program of alternative service, it regarded alternative service programs as semi-penal, and some conscientious objectors, in fact, were imprisoned for varying periods. The services of the conscientious objectors — many of them highly educated individuals — were thus not adequately used in the war effort, as most of those objectors who were not incarcerated were assigned work of second-rate or insignificant importance. Thus, at a time of severe work force shortages, potentially useful men

---

1 102 Stat. 903, Public law 100-383 (8/10/88), codified at 50 U.S.C., Section 1989 (b) (1996).

2 *Korematsu v. United States*, 584 F. Supp. 1406 (N.D. Calif. 1984).

3 *The New York Times*, 4/1/05, C-13; 1/9/98, A-16.

4 Francis Biddle, *In Brief Authority* (Doubleday, Garden City, N.Y., 1962), 212.

were kept under a form of discipline intended for criminals. From Thomas' view, "It [did] no credit to the supposed zeal of Americans to fight for liberty if, in order to persuade them to fight, the lot of the conscientious objector must be made contemptible."[1]

Following Pearl Harbor, Thomas disbanded the Keep America Out of War Congress and in its place established the Post War World Council, dedicated to encouraging America's participation in a postwar world federation committed to world peace and universal disarmament. Thomas first used the Council to express opposition to Roosevelt's plan to require the Fascist powers to agree to an "unconditional surrender" as the basis for ending the war. He considered this concept as "a major disaster to peace."[2] It provided the peoples of the Allied nations with a war-ending goal based on vengeance rather than on one calling for a peaceful rebuilding of Europe and the rest of the world. Worse, it united the peoples of the Fascist nations with a unity of despair, as the mere absence of hope of any reasonable terms of surrender compelled them to remain at war. It was, in short, a slogan leading to disaster. In place of unconditional surrender, Thomas would have established reasonable terms for the cessation of combat. The announcement of such terms, he believed, would engender popular revolts against the leaders of the Fascist powers, thus weakening if not ending further resistance, and saving thousands of lives.[3]

The Communists and much of the political left criticized Thomas for his opposition to Roosevelt's policy calling for unconditional surrender. Some years later, he felt somewhat vindicated when Winston Churchill admitted that he first heard the "unconditional surrender" concept from President Roosevelt without any prior consultation with him, and that he had never supported the president's position in that regard.[4]

In the presidential election of 1944, Thomas continued to press for concrete surrender terms instead of Roosevelt's demand for "unconditional surrender." He would rather have presented his views in the capacity as a non-candidate, but that was not to be the case. In each successive presidential election, Thomas expressed greater reluctance to stand as the Socialist Party candidate, and on each occasion the party membership pressured him to run. Thomas' choice for the party's 1944 presidential nominee was Maynard Krueger, who had previously run with him as the party's vice-presidential candidate. When Thomas arrived at the national convention in Reading, Pennsylvania, he announced he was not a candidate. Newspaper reporters

---

1 Norman Thomas, *What Is Our Destiny* (Doubleday, Doran, Garden City, N.Y., 1944), 162.

2 Thomas autobiography, 209.

3 Ibid., 209-210.

4 Norman Thomas, *A Socialist's Faith* (W.W. Norton, New York, 1951), 315-316, citing an Associated Press dispatch from London, dated 7/21/49.

---

laughed, pointing out that he sounded just like Roosevelt, who always said he was not inclined to run but always did.

When Krueger declined the nomination, electing instead to run for Congress, the convention delegates nominated Thomas, for the fifth time. The party went on to adopt a Thomas-inspired platform that explicitly criticized the unconditional surrender policy. Alleging that Roosevelt's policies were unnecessarily prolonging the war, the platform called for a peace offensive that offered armistice terms on four conditions:[1]

1. The peace must be organized on two fundamental principles: (a) the right of peoples of every race to live their lives without subjection to any race or nation; (b) the establishment of political and economic arrangements for removing the causes of war, settling disputes, guaranteeing security, and conquering poverty.

2. The German and Japanese people must replace their governments, disarm, and withdraw their forces from all occupied territory.

3.The United Nations must pledge itself to freeing all European nations overrun by Fascist forces and guaranteeing their independence by refraining from interference in their internal affairs.

4. The member states of the United Nations must pledge themselves to ending their own armaments and military conscription.

Thomas described the 1944 campaign as "a grim experience."[2] He traveled the country with only Violet at his side, receiving little assistance or money from party officials. He received a fair hearing in halls across the nation. People listened, but he again feared that the electorate would vote, as it had in the past, for either the Democratic or Republican Party candidate, depending upon which one they perceived as the lesser of two evils. An experience he had during one of his many train trips further aroused his fears. Thomas found himself sitting next to a young Texan soldier on leave and on his way home to surprise his mother. During their conversation, the young man said: "Sir, if you don't mind a personal question, who are you going to vote for? I've been away and don't know the score." Thomas answered, "Myself." "Well," said the soldier, "of course I know any man can be President, but . . ." Thomas interrupted and told the young man that he was the Socialist Party candidate. After a moment's thought, the soldier turned to Thomas and asked, "If you weren't running yourself, who would you vote for?"[3] Thomas probably laughed, but not without a degree of pain and bitterness, for he recognized that the encounter epitomized the general public's automatic exclusion of third party candidates from serious consideration.

---

1 A. Craig Baird, *Representative American Speeches: 1943-1944* (H.W. Wilson, New York, 1944), 277.
2 Thomas autobiography, 212.
3 Ibid., 109.

Thomas did not expect nor did he receive any more than token support for his candidacy. Again, all the major labor union figures backed Roosevelt, and liberal newspapers ignored Thomas while committing themselves to Roosevelt. The party failed to secure a place on the ballot in major states such as California, Illinois, and Ohio. Neither Roosevelt nor the Republican Party candidate, Thomas E. Dewey, would engage him in discussion of the issues. On election day, the Socialist Party suffered its worst defeat in its history. Of the nearly 48 million votes cast, Thomas polled just over 80,000. Roosevelt's vote was more than three hundred times that received by Thomas.

Five months later Roosevelt was dead. Thomas had been both an admirer and critic of the president, but following Roosevelt's first term, on balance, he was more critical than admiring. For Thomas, Roosevelt's greatest accomplishment was in guiding the country out of the depths of the Depression, while restoring Americans' confidence in themselves and in the power of the ballot box to achieve democratic action. Nearly all of Roosevelt's legislative victories occurred during his first term when much of the Socialist Party program was adopted in one form or another. Thomas viewed the enactment of Social Security as a particularly significant triumph, and he also gave Roosevelt credit for providing status and bargaining rights to labor. But in foreign affairs, Thomas was far more critical. He repeatedly condemned the president for assuring the people that he was pursuing the path of peace at the very time he was initiating policies that logically led to war. In this respect, Thomas believed that Roosevelt had deceived the people. "To put it more bluntly . . . the President and spokesmen for him lied to us . . . "[1] Morally, Thomas argued, Roosevelt should have forthrightly advised the populace that his policies were interventionist and would probably lead to war.

Writing of Roosevelt after his death, Thomas reiterated the views he had expressed throughout the twelve years of Roosevelt's presidency, but on this occasion he expressed them with unusual bitterness:

> [Roosevelt's] skill in the political game, his opportunism unguided by any deep philosophy, diverted him from paths of true statesmanship. More and more he showed his love of power. This and his essential lack of understanding of the conditions of democracy and peace made him a protagonist of . . . peacetime military conscription. The efficiency and even the integrity of some parts of the bureaucracy Roosevelt set up are yet to be judged. His reputation as a friend of the people actually tended to advance among the masses policies and attitudes which in Europe had contributed to the coming of the totalitarian state.[2]

Thomas' charge that Roosevelt was unguided by "any deep philosophy," and that he was thus diverted from the paths of true statesmanship to the

---

1 Ibid., 201.

2 *The Call*, 4/23/45, 1: quoted at length in Murray B. Seidler, *Norman Thomas: Respectable Rebel* (Syracuse University Press, Syracuse, 1967), 228.

advocacy of policies common to a totalitarian state, had no basis in fact. They were untrue of Roosevelt then and the intervening years have not altered that judgment.

This virulent attack on Roosevelt at the time of his death appears to be particularly out of character for Thomas. In later years, his view of Roosevelt mellowed to a degree, but he never wavered from his basic negative assessment of Roosevelt's accomplishments. His negativity arose in part from the fact that he looked upon Roosevelt as the savior of capitalism. In the early Depression years, Thomas wrote that the "Marxian prediction of the collapse of capitalism by forces inherent in it . . . is being astonishingly fulfilled before our eyes."[1] Thomas had been wrong; Roosevelt checked the disintegration of capitalism, and it did not collapse.

Some commentators argue that Roosevelt's New Deal tilted in the direction of socialism, but in fact his administration never accepted socialism's fundamental propositions. In rescuing capitalism, Roosevelt's first achievement was symbolic. He could have nationalized a broken-down banking system as the Socialists advocated, but instead, as Thomas put it, he "patched up the system and gave it back to the bankers . . ."[2] Governmental control over the nation's economy increased, but it did not amount to the control advocated by the Socialists. Other measures undertaken by Roosevelt changed capitalism, but not fundamentally, though some of his major achievements reflected, in part, commonly accepted Socialist principles. Thomas had to admit that certain features of the Roosevelt program resembled Socialist demands, but he sought to distinguish Socialist goals from Roosevelt's:

> Socialists ask for certain things in order that the workers may have strength to go on to take power away from private owners of productive goods. The Roosevelt program makes concessions to workers in order to keep them quiet a while longer and so stabilize the power of private owners.... It was, the President's admirers told us, his virtue that he was not cumbered with a philosophy and therefore he could more easily find out what play would work. These eulogists did not share the Socialist fear that, lacking in philosophy and a sense of direction, the quarterback might make some bold play only to discover that he had scored points for the enemy team behind the wrong goal line.[3]

Thomas hated capitalism on other grounds. He insisted that competitive aspects of capitalism made it inevitable that it would more readily accept war as a legitimate exercise of power. This probably led to Thomas' heightened suspicions about Roosevelt's prewar role. While charging the president with abandoning his pledge of neutrality, he noted that Roosevelt had at the same time failed to resolve the nation's unemployment problem. Thomas

---

1 Norman Thomas, *The Choice Before Us: Mankind at the Crossroads* (Macmillan, New York, 1934), 15-16.
2 Ibid., 89.
3 Ibid., 93-94.

reasoned that Roosevelt may have entered the war as a means of resolving that problem. If true, that was a particularly egregious use of capitalistic power.

We have already touched on the ways the New Deal tended to destroy the Socialist Party, and we will return to the subject in a later chapter (Chapter 24). Thomas was well aware of the attraction the New Deal had for Socialists, an attraction that culminated in massive defections in favor of the Democratic Party. He also was well aware that Roosevelt was a major, albeit indirect, cause of his own political demise. No one person did as much to undermine Thomas' public position as did Roosevelt, and even if that were not Roosevelt's intent, it was a natural consequence of his advocacy of positions similar to those advanced by Thomas.

Barred from looking into Thomas' mind to discover the source of his bitterness toward Roosevelt, we must rely on what we know of each of their lives and the ways they intersected There appears to be ample evidence that Thomas looked upon Roosevelt as an enemy, as one who rejected the causes he supported throughout a lifetime. In opposing Roosevelt as the savior of capitalism and the enemy of socialism, Thomas did not prevail. His bitterness toward Roosevelt resulted from that defeat.

Chapter 17. Taking Stock

Several publishing firms encouraged Thomas to write his autobiography, but he was not interested, once remarking that autobiography too often is a form of fiction touched with a small amount of history.[1] Nonetheless, on Christmas night 1944, after spending the day with his family, he began to write the story of his life. Having recently celebrated his sixtieth birthday, he considered a recorded summing up at this point in his life would have some value for his children, even if it were not published. In fact, in the end, his autobiography was never published.[2]

On that Christmas he experienced "a strange mingling of deep disappointment and unusual happiness." In a letter addressed to his children, later adopted as a foreword to the autobiography, he wrote: "I have been familiar with despair and with hope prolonged and lost, yet I think few men have been happier than I or had more reason to bless their own particular fortune — and mostly that means blessing your mother and you."[3]

One of his reasons for taking time from his hectic life to write his autobiography was to examine, for his own satisfaction, the underlying reasons for the paradoxical thoughts that passed through his mind that Christmas night — the intermingling of happiness and despair. Another reason was to restate, for his own consideration, those ideals in which he most believed. But he was driven neither to a public confession nor to defense of positions taken.

---

1 Foreword to Thomas autobiography, 2.

2 The autobiography, along with Thomas' other papers — copies of letters sent and received, the manuscripts to his later books, comprising one hundred and ninety-three cartons — are now housed with the New York City Library at its main branch at Fifth Avenue and Forty-second Street in Manhattan.

3 Foreword to the Thomas autobiography, 1.

He warned prospective readers that they would be sorely disappointed if they expected a complete record of the events of his life or of all the persons whom he loved or was closely associated. "It won't even contain a catalogue of our friends — the family dogs!"[1]

It was well that Thomas wrote with the expectation that the document would not see publication, since no publisher would have consented to offer it to the public in the form it was written. It really is not an autobiography at all. Thomas began with a detailed narrative of his youth, his student days at Princeton, and his early days at the Spring Street Church and Settlement House, but following those early periods of his life, he devoted the greater part of the work to a study of the issues he confronted during his public life, while alluding only occasionally to events in his private life. "I have inserted few and passing references to my private life which is dearer to me because it is private" [2] – hardly a formula one follows in writing the story of a life. Clearly, Thomas did not undertake to write a conventional autobiography, but it would not have been in character for him to have done so. At times, issues affecting the lives of others tended to have greater significance for him than issues affecting his own life, and his autobiography reflects that attitude.

Thomas looked upon his marriage to Violet as his greatest success in life. They had an especially close and loving relationship, and because Violet wanted to share her husband's life fully, she made certain that their home also served as his headquarters in his dealings with the world. When not caring for the children, she was usually at his side, actively engaged in his ventures, apparently happy to share the life of a heretic and an antagonist against injustice.

When family duties permitted, Violet accompanied her husband in his many election campaigns. She probably never made a speech in her life, but was accustomed to distributing leaflets and Socialist Party flyers at campaign events. She served as Norman's secretary on the road and at home as well, but also was his confidant. Harry Fleischman, one of Thomas' biographers and a close friend, recounts an incident that discloses the extent that Thomas relied upon his wife in political matters. On a visit to the Thomas home, Friedrich Adler, an Austrian Socialist, described for them the brutalities the Socialists suffered in World War I at the hands of the Austrian government. When the Socialists pressed the Prime Minister to convene the Austrian Parliament, he refused. Adler then shot and killed him. Adler was given the death penalty, but his sentence was commuted and eventually he was released and made his way to the United States. In detailing the event for Norman and Violet, Adler noted that he had shot the Prime Minis-

---

1 Ibid., 2.
2 Ibid., 3.

ter without advising anyone in advance. Incredulous, Violet asked: "Do you mean to say that you assassinated the Prime Minister without even talking to your wife about it beforehand?"[1] One may assume that Thomas invariably consulted his wife before undertaking any matter of significance.

In fact, Thomas was accustomed to discussing with Violet all the issues he confronted, large or small. Where Thomas perceived matters in terms of principle, Violet saw more clearly the sufferings of the individual persons involved. While he was fighting injustice, she quietly and personally served the oppressed and the poor who came to the Thomas home seeking help. The focus and direction of the one complemented the focus and direction of the other.

On Christmas Eve of 1943, the year before he began his autobiography, Norman felt moved to write a note to Violet expressing his love for her:

> This . . . is the first Christmas since Tommy was born that we've been without chick or child. And it won't matter much to me because I still have you. And that's a blessing so great I should like to thank some personal God very personally for a boon that makes a dark world bright. For, you see, it's you, but it's you and the children and the grandchildren for whom you seem to me to be so much responsible, not just biologically, but as the nicest kind of matriarch! So together we'll face life tomorrow and I hope for many more tomorrows and that will be life's richest Christmas gift to me.[2]

Violet suffered a heart condition that from an early age frequently incapacitated her. She suffered a major heart attack at the age of 48, and subsequently, on more than one occasion, doctors diagnosed the occurrence of other attacks. Although they considered these episodes as only moderately severe, the state of Violet's health was always a matter of grave concern for her husband. On August 1, 1947, during a telephone conversation with her daughter-in-law, Violet suffered her final heart attack and died. Norman was attending a meeting of the Socialist Party National Executive Committee in Reading, Pennsylvania when he received word that his wife had passed away. She was sixty-six years old.

Shortly after Violet's death, Thomas wrote to his children, endeavoring to portray what Violet had meant for him:

> I'd like to try to tell you in writing what I've said inadequately in speech .... I want to try to explain to myself and you why I am peculiarly lost without Mom. Parting is the common lot of men and I've had 37 wonderful years. I'm not fool or ingrate enough to say 'no sorrow is like unto my sorrow.' But circumstances as well as her own character made me unusually dependent on Mom — or should I say made us mutually dependent? — for strength and joy. Her love and loyalty, her interests in life, her resourcefulness made for me a peculiar haven of happiness and security in a storm tossed world.

1 Harry Fleischman, *Norman Thomas, A Biography: 1884–1968* (W.W. Norton, New York, 1969), 218-219.
2 Ibid., 218.

Just living with her and doing things together was fun.... I have kept love of life and much faith in human fellowship. And that's largely due to Mom. Her wisdom ... and her comradeship in the routine of living kept me aware of the fun of life and the variety of its interests. She'd let me talk about problems and worries and often helped me by her shrewd common sense.... I am rich in memories and your constant affection. I have friends and causes and some strength still to serve them. But if I seem to live in a dream it will be no lack of affection and interest in the strange and wonderful stream of life in which we are caught but because something rare and for me entirely irreplaceable is gone.[1]

Their marriage of thirty-seven years obviously, was an extraordinarily happy one. He later wrote that not only his marriage but his entire life had been happy, noting that he could not recall any hour of his life, extending back to his youth and passing through his college days, ministry, and marriage, in which he did not experience the presence of love, affection and friendship. And because he felt he had been blessed with a life of happiness, he felt obliged to work for a better and a more secure world, where more of its citizens could experience the type of love, affection, and friendship that he had enjoyed.[2]

As with many older men, Thomas had a closer and more intimate relationship with his grandchildren than he did with his children. His grandchildren, fifteen in all, called him "Big Dad," in part, no doubt, because of his height. To them, and to others as well, Thomas gave the impression of being an elder statesman. One biographer, who knew Thomas well, described him as "tall and thin, inclining toward the gaunt [looking] every bit the Old Testament prophet, as he denounced the sins of society."[3]

As he grew older — he was sixty-three when Violet died in 1947 — his hair turned snow white and he became a bit stooped, but he never lost the boundless energy that others found infectious. His towering height was a political asset, as were his patrician features that caused many to describe him as "handsome." He had a quick and warm smile and easily communicated warmth and friendliness. He exhibited an abundance of charm, and was the type of man that most of his associates felt comfortable in addressing as "Norman."

Thomas' powerful weapon was his skill as an orator. Strangely, people remember his voice differently, almost as if they had heard it from different men. One of his contemporaries said that "His commanding voice matched his commanding presence.... [As] one of America's most brilliant orators, . . .

---

1 Ibid., 220-221.

2 *The Socialist Call*, 2/10/50, 10, quoted at length in Murray B. Seidler, *Norman Thomas: Respectable Rebel* (Syracuse University Press, Syracuse, 1967), 248.

3 Bernard K. Johnpoll, *Pacifist's Progress: Norman Thomas and the Decline of American Socialism* (Greenwood, Westport, Conn., 1970), 9.

he spoke eloquently, and earnestly, indeed passionately. . . ."[1] But others in his audiences heard Thomas differently: "His voice is loud and a little harsh; he speaks rapidly and extemporaneously; his thoughts are sometimes too complicated to be fully grasped at such speed."[2] But even those who were critical of his oratorical skills had to admit that he was a successful speaker — he always won over his audiences.

> Yet he is enormously popular with audiences partially because he has a good sense of humor and does not take himself too seriously, partly because of his obvious, passionate sincerity, but chiefly . . . because you get the sense that he is holding nothing back for political reasons, that he is doing the best to tell the truth as he sees it.[3]

Thomas skillfully wove humor into his oratory. In the 1944 presidential election campaign, hampered by the paucity of Socialist Party funds, he reminded his radio audience that he had to speak rapidly because he had only minutes to discuss what Roosevelt and Dewey would take hours to evade.[4] Near the end of his life, crippled with arthritis, he walked with great difficulty and obviously in severe pain. He nonetheless continued to speak at public events around the country. On one occasion, after the chairperson had introduced him, he rose from his seat on the stage and slowly and laboriously made his way to the podium. The audience waited anxiously, fearing he might not make it. Finally arriving at the podium, he paused, caught his breath, and announced in a loud and clear voice, "creeping socialism."[5]

He greatly enjoyed making people laugh. At the time when Violet was involved in raising cocker spaniels, she enrolled one of them in a local dog-training academy. Several weeks later, she asked her husband to pick up the dog following a training session. When Thomas arrived at the academy, he discovered that a graduating ceremony was about to begin and the academy head asked him to give the commencement address. He happily consented, urging the assembled dog owners to continue in their "dogged" efforts in attaining their ideals, warning them against "barking up the wrong tree," and wishing them all "a doggone good life."[6]

He always appeared to be in command of himself, and although he exuded self-confidence, he did not convey a sense of arrogance.[7] His individuality set him apart from others; possessing the charisma of a leader, he looked like a leader. He had the power to impress and excite, and his self-confidence

---

1 Murray B. Seidler, *Norman Thomas: Respectable Rebel*, 2.

2 *The New York Times*, 2/16/64, BR-40.

3 Ibid.

4 Charles Gorham, *Leader at Large: The Long and Fighting Life of Norman Thomas* (Farrar, Straus & Giroux, New York, 1970), 9.

5 W. A. Swanberg, *Norman Thomas: The Last Idealist* (Charles Scribner's Sons, New York, 1976), 448.

6 Ibid., 147-148.

7 Murray B. Seidler, *Norman Thomas: Respectable Rebel*, 79-80.

compelled him to persuade his audience of the rightness of his cause. To be with him was to have the feeling of being in the presence of greatness.[1]

If these qualities led him at times to talk too much, he still was a good listener. In public debates, he was fair to his adversaries, listening closely to their positions, but once an opponent's position was presented, he was apt to demolish it with a single, powerful stroke. But he had a wholly human side also. His quick anger, for instance, was notorious. Following a cross-country flight during which he was forced to sit in a seat erroneously assigned him, he sent off an angry letter to the airline president. "I had seat # 16 which practically blocks approach to the toilets [located] behind a green curtain.... Every person, during the night, who had occasion to go behind that curtain, hit me, stepped on my feet, or waved the curtain in my face ... Only a midget could doze in relative comfort in a seat in that position. *I am not a midget.*"[2]

He loved art and music. Unlike earlier in his life when politics was all consuming, in his travels he frequented art museums, preferring those that did not emphasize the abstract. "I get all my modern art from the drawings of my grandchildren." His failure to fully develop the singing skills of his youth did not deter him from a lifelong interest in music. He loved classical and chamber music, with Bach standing among his favorites. Another of his interests was baseball. On one occasion, to the vast surprise of a group of youngsters, he correctly identified Mel Ott as the National League player hitting the most home runs the year before.[3]

Youthful listeners to a Thomas speech generally were captivated by his idealism. James Wechsler, at one time the Editor of *The New York Post*, related that as a student at Columbia University he was assigned by the student newspaper to interview Thomas during the 1932 presidential campaign. Nearly overwhelmed by the experience, he later told a friend that Thomas was the most impressive person he had ever encountered, adding that "it was evidence of the utter bankruptcy of our culture that he had no apparent chance of victory."[4] Journalist Murray Kempton, in his youth a Socialist, later in his life said that Thomas conveyed the feeling that there is something glorious about being forever engaged:

> He seemed always just back from the side of the sharecroppers or being egged by the friends of Frank Hague. In that guise, he represented the only available piece of that buried tradition of the American radical about which Dos Passos wrote. The old libertarian dream of spending one's life in lonely

---

1 Ibid., 340.
2 W. A. Swanberg, *Norman Thomas: The Last Idealist*, 366 (emphasis added).
3 Harry Fleischman, *Norman Thomas, A Biography: 1884–1968*, 304-305.
4 James A. Wechsler, *The Age of Suspicion* (Greenwood, Westport, Conn., 1953), 41.

combat against every form of enslavement... appeared to us to have no vessel but Norman Thomas.[1]

In general, college students found Thomas' idealism and unselfishness appealing, but he also won them over through his ability to speak to them as peers. When the occasion called for it, however, he did not hesitate to chide his youthful listeners, especially when they assigned blame to their parents rather than accepting responsibility for their own shortcomings.

He was sensitive to the needs and problems of other people, and often invited the humblest members of the Socialist Party into his home for lunch or dinner. He was continually searching for jobs for a desperate acquaintance or party member. He often arranged for appropriate medical treatment for those experiencing trouble in finding it themselves. It was a rare occurrence when he left a letter unanswered, even answering letters from children asking him, "What is socialism?"[2]

Thomas tried to accomplish far too much. He answered every entreaty, no matter the source. A friend once said that it was well Thomas was not a woman, because he could not say "No."[3] The burdens and difficulties of others, he made his own. The problems of so many others occupied him that friends joked that he sometimes appeared to be in two places at the same time. In one instance he wrote to a Columbia University professor for information pertinent to a book he was then writing. "I am enclosing two envelopes addressed to myself at two different places in the hope that one or the other will reach me quickly."[4]

Through it all, he possessed a respectability that the public had first denied him after he left his Harlem parish to speak on New York City street corners for the Socialist Party candidate for mayor. Most of his Princeton classmates disagreed with his political views, especially those that emanated from his socialism, but still he was a popular figure at class reunions. Over time, his political views gained a degree of begrudging acceptability, even at Princeton, and on the initiative of Thomas' classmate and former debating partner, Raymond Fosdick, the university granted Thomas an honorary Doctorate of Letters. For some of the university's graduates, this was not a popular move, as illustrated on the day he received the degree. All those to be honored gathered on the platform in academic garb. The ceremony proceeded with the Dean of the Graduate School announcing the name of each honoree and presenting him to the University President for investiture with the appropriate academic hood. Near the end of the ceremony, with only

---

1 Murray Kempton, *Part of Our Time: Some Ruins and Monuments of the Thirties* (Simon and Schuster, New York, 1955), 324.

2 Murray B. Seidler, *Norman Thomas: Respectable Rebel*, 81.

3 W. A. Swanberg, *Norman Thomas: The Last Idealist*, 160.

4 Ibid., 161.

two candidates remaining — Supreme Court Justice Cardoza and Thomas — the Dean announced: "And finally, Benjamin Nathan Cardoza." A stir occurred among the audience and a woman was heard to say in a triumphant voice, "There, I knew they'd never give that man a degree." The Dean, reminded that he had forgotten a candidate, proceeded, with some embarrassment, to present Thomas to the president for the awarding of the honorary degree. Thomas later commented that he was marked as Princeton's favorite radical, but then the competition was not that keen.[1]

Thomas gained a respectability he did not seek. Although many Princetonians remained adamantly opposed to the direction of his political thought and still others rejected his socialism and pacifism, they nevertheless felt compelled to honor him. And just as he gained the respect of his fellows at Princeton, he gained the approval of the country at large. The force of his integrity and his unselfishness in pressing for acceptance of the positions he advocated earned him the stature of a leader.

Violet's death at age 66 awakened in Thomas an old yearning for personal immortality. He wrote in his autobiography that as a youth he had passed through a phase of fearing death and questioning immortality, but that in college and immediately afterwards he gradually adjusted his views, thus managing to achieve in his own mind a degree of harmony between religion and science. In his seminary days he accepted the sort of Christianity preached by Harry Emerson Fosdick and Henry Sloane Coffin, a religion of dignity, beauty, and power, but he soon found it lacking as an intellectually satisfactory explanation of man's relationship to the universe.[2]

World War I compelled him to rethink his religious orientation. As noted in earlier chapters, he found support for the war to be irreconcilable with the basic tenets of Christianity, since war by its very nature stands as a negation of Christian ethics:

> For a Christian to support [war] cannot . . . be in accordance with the will of God, if God be at once a God of love and power. I can understand the argument . . . that although war is not Christian, it may be a judgment of God, a consequence of man's sins, and that it may become a duty to support the better cause in the conflict to which society provides no alternative method. But . . . I cannot see that the followers of Christ can ever be justified in using the devil's means of war or that a God of love can require it of them. It is, I still believe, of the essence of both Christian ethics and Christian theology that there should be a more valid, less self-defeating method of resistance to evil than war.[3]

The failure of the Church to resolve this conflict, together with man's failure to build a peaceful world following World War I — when viewed in the

---

1 Thomas autobiography, 36.
2 Ibid., 261-262.
3 Ibid., 262-263.

context of the place of man in an alien universe — led him to reject his earlier faith, based on a "far off divine event to which the whole creation moves."[1]

Following World War I, as he placed greater hope in a Socialist solution to world problems, Thomas grew increasingly critical of Christianity, and particularly of that form presented in the churches. Addressing a group of clergymen in 1926, he declared that in recent history the labor unions had accomplished far more than the churches:

> Take child labor as an instance . . . .What did Christianity . . . have to do with the abolition of child labor? Did Christianity cause its abolition? If so, it certainly took a long time, for Christianity is not new. The fact is that the labor unions brought about the clearing up of that sore. He told them directly that few improvements in society had occurred as a result of their preaching. "Christianity can do a lot more."[2]

With time, his message to the Church grew more strident. Speaking in 1932 before the Interdenominational Ministers Association, he declared the world is being crucified for "the god of profits and the Moloch of nationalism." He castigated the ministers for sitting idly by while the capitalistic system negated every Christian ideal. "The Church has never been on the side of right in a major incident."[3]

On one occasion he attended a conference that in time culminated in the formation of the National Conference of Christians and Jews. At one conference session, the topic of discussion related to why religion had made men more brotherly. Thomas took aim at the basic premise. He said it was historically untrue that religious institutions had grown more tolerant and brotherly. For example, Jews believed they were made a Chosen People by act of God. Catholics believed there was no salvation outside their church. Protestant sects believed they possessed a monopoly on the road to heaven. Thus, intolerance, not tolerance, was born of a religious creed. Wars of religion, therefore, had a certain horrible logic behind them. Thomas argued that the churches "were facing the necessity in America of teaching men . . . to be more brotherly and tolerant than the churches [themselves] had been, less cruel than the God they worshiped."[4] He was not invited to later conferences.

As the years passed, he viewed the Church as more human than divine, and as he judged it as such, his respect for it rose. He had to admit the Church met a need. Although dubiously Christian, it filled an essential place in the community. By the time he completed his autobiography in 1946, he had come to the belief that in the field of social relations, the older churches in America, Protestant and Catholic, had made substantial progress, and al-

1 Ibid., 264.
2 *The New York Times*, 6/4/26, 27.
3 *The Washington Post*, 10/11/32, 8.
4 Norman Thomas, *A Socialist's Faith* (W.W. Norton, New York, 1951), 124-125.

though they asserted significantly less influence on ethical standards than they had in his youth, he would not hesitate to advise young men to enter the clergy, provided "they [could] honestly accept whole heartedly a Christian philosophy."[1] On occasion, he even preached at a Protestant service,[2] although he remained unable to accept for himself the particulars of the Christian creed.

If he achieved a state of peace with the Church, he failed to reconcile the divergences of his own religious beliefs. Early in his adult life he realized he had lost the faith of his youth, that he no longer believed in the personal God his father had preached from the pulpit:

> For good or for evil the religion which was so much and so intimate a part of the life of my boyhood, the religion in which my father's home was founded and nourished, lives for me mostly in memory. To return to it would be an impossible and by no means lovely way of escape from life and its problems.[3]

He accepted the teaching that man was wicked, stupid and responsible for his unhappy lot, but he questioned why a God of love should not also have some responsibility for the humans he had created. His questioning led him to a belief that the universe is amoral and indifferent to man, his hopes and his fears. But then he was caught on the horns of a dilemma from which he never fully escaped. On the one hand he believed that the universe was supremely indifferent to man, while on the other he was convinced that the human heart hungered for a religious answer to man's basic questions of life. What Thomas craved was the assurance of the existence of God and of God's concern for men. As he brought his autobiography to a conclusion, he attempted to deal with that craving:

> I have said that for us as individuals and for our race there is no final fulfillment; that the end of the drama is Silence. But simply to recognize that fact and yet to be able to understand [the] universe and add to our knowledge of the mysteries of . . . life is to deliver ourselves from frustration and to achieve a triumph that death cannot take away.... Whatever we achieve in dignity and beauty of living to pass down to our children and through them to countless generations mocks frustration as the total verdict on our striving. If conscious life on this little planet is a strange interlude between two eternities of silence, it is long enough, and to spare, to give meaning to love.[4]

But he remained dissatisfied with letting the matter stand there. He finally concluded that a consideration of the question of the place of man in a majestic but an alien universe required belief in some sort of God. After dictating a history of his religious convictions, he apparently felt compelled

---

1 Thomas autobiography, 273-276.

2 *The Washington Post*, 2/1/58, C-12.

3 Norman Thomas, *As I See It* (Macmillan, New York, 1932), 154.

4 Thomas autobiography, 277-278.

to clarify one point. A handwritten notation appears in the margin of the transcript: "There is undoubtedly a Power . . . behind the universe whom . . . we may call God."[1] He ended his autobiography with the comment that he found especial value in the Christian Gospels and Christ's inspiration to the highest achievement of human fellowship. "I wish that with equal confidence, I could accept his faith in a God like him."[2]

1 Ibid., 265.
2 Ibid., 278.

Chapter 18. The Final Run for the Presidency

Following Violet's death, Thomas returned to his many battles. To enter upon those battlefields alone, without her support, was for him a battle in itself. His hopes for the future were as dark as his mood. With the arrival of the atomic age, he perceived far more doom than hope in the years to come:

> Man [has] eaten deeply of the tree of knowledge. But not of love or of wisdom. He [has] mastered the power that holds the atom and the universe together and used that power for wanton destruction. And he was at once exultant and afraid. But wisdom was not born of his fear. Nowhere [can] I find reasonable ground of assurance that we human beings, individually so weak, collectively so drunk with power, [can] escape a doom our own folly [has] decreed.. . . My fear of the future is a fear of Man for Man, not man of any particular race or nation or social creed.[1]

In the strongest of terms, Thomas denounced America's use of atomic bombs in Japan. For him, the decision to drop the bomb on Hiroshima, without a previous public demonstration over an uninhabited area of its enormous power, was "one of the blackest crimes in history." He was equally outraged by the dropping of a second bomb over Nagasaki, without waiting for the political results of the dropping of the first bomb.[2] Over the years, many Americans have condemned the use of the bombs to end the war with Japan, but at the time Thomas stood nearly alone among prominent figures who protested the bomb's use.[3] He led the way in expressing opposition to atomic warfare.

---

1 Thomas autobiography, 186-187.
2 Ibid., 216.
3 *The Washington Post*, 12/20/68, C-14.

The end of World War II found Thomas very much involved in trying to initiate and then preserve a period of peace. Now that the world's nations had survived six years of horror, how could they guarantee peace? This was an issue that would continue to occupy his thoughts for much of the remaining twenty years of his life.

In 1947, Thomas' peace efforts led to the publication of his book entitled *Appeal to the Nations*.[1] Thomas wrote most of his books out of a desire to stimulate social action to resolve the particular issue at hand, and in this work he pressed for the adoption of his program for peace. He realized that his prewar position on the entry of the United States into the war gave him little credibility in matters relating to post war foreign affairs, as many Americans would spontaneously dismiss any peace plan he advanced, remaining convinced that he had been a "prewar isolationist." He continued to insist, however, that his critics had erroneously labeled him "isolationist," that he could be considered as having assumed that role only if an isolationist were defined as a person who wanted to remain free of war. He contended that he had opposed intervention in the war and also the steps leading to it because he believed that, in the balance of good and evil, the United States could best serve its citizens, and in the long run the rest of the world, by keeping out of the war: "We did not have the wisdom and power to play God to the world by the terrible method of war."[2]

Thomas firmly believed — and expressed it in his book — that the only hope for world peace lay in general disarmament and the elimination of all forms of imperialism. To best accomplish that, the United States should request the United Nations to convoke a conference to draw plans for the complete abolition of national armies and the destruction of armaments capable of aggression. He recognized, of course, that this proposal ran counter to thousands of years of history, but in an atomic age only bold acts were likely to succeed. World leaders must substitute law for war; the nations of the world will achieve security only through a federation of peoples living as brothers in peace. That such a world could be conceived as a realistic possibility could occur only to one such as Thomas, one who had devoted his life to developing a world without cruelty, oppression, and exploitation. To many, if not most others, a world without war was an impossibility.

As the 1948 presidential election year approached, two issues predominated — world peace and racial prejudice. The common existence of racial prejudice in American society was always a matter of great concern for Thomas, and his passion for social justice made it inevitable that he would involve himself in fighting to eliminate racial bias of all sorts. His opposition

---

1 Norman Thomas, *Appeal to the Nations* (Henry Holt, New York, 1947).
2 Ibid., xi.

to World War II governmental bias against Americans of Japanese ancestry is a case in point. Much earlier in his career he had directed his attention to alleviating prejudice against African-Americans. For example, in the 1928 presidential campaign, Thomas wrote to the National Chair of the Democratic Party asking him to use his influence in the Southern states to make certain that white voter racial prejudice did not prevent black voters from casting ballots. "It is a matter of common knowledge that by force of fraud most Negroes in the South will be deprived of their votes, [and] if you have not yourself authorized this appeal to racial prejudice it would seem as if you condoned it."[1]

In the spring of 1933, he again confronted the issue. Just prior to Roosevelt's inauguration, the Socialist Party convened a meeting of more than four thousand of its members in Washington, D.C. Most of those attending from New York were scheduled to be housed in the Cairo Hotel, but when hotel management barred a black Socialist member from registering, hundreds of other members, with Thomas in the lead, marched on the hotel, canceled their reservations, and demanded refunds of moneys paid in advance. When hotel management refused all refunds, Thomas arranged with party lawyers to immediately file suit against the hotel. At that point the hotel management backed down and refunded the advance payments. But the New Yorkers then found it difficult to find rooms in other hotels, since by that time they had been blacklisted throughout the city. When Thomas discovered that a local tourist camp owned by the government and operated by the War Department had joined in discriminating against black party members, he declared war on the War Department: " How can we either protest Hitlerism with good grace or hope to escape similar ills in America when we chronically carry out a more thorough going discrimination against our colored fellow citizens than he has as yet imposed upon the Jews."[2]

The following year, Thomas wrote *Human Exploitation* in which he discussed at length the plight of African-Americans. He paid particular attention to conditions he had observed in the South, finding especially egregious the failure of the Southern states to provide adequate educational facilities for their black children. That civilized people felt justified in assigning black children to separate schools — generally far inferior to white schools — was for him incomprehensible. He was incredulous upon learning that in Nashville, Atlanta, and other major Southern cities, city officials barred Blacks from public libraries, designated for use by Whites only, while Blacks were

---

1 *The Washington Post*, 11/3/28, 4.
2 The letter is quoted in Harry Fleischman, *Norman Thomas, A Biography: 1884–1968* (W.W. Norton, New York, 1969), 141.

relegated to other facilities, separate and of far inferior quality. Jim Crowism was abhorrent and must be rejected in all of its myriad forms.[1]

During the 1936 presidential campaign, he had argued in favor of Federal anti-discrimination and anti-lynching laws, observing that the United States was the only nation ever to free a race from slavery without giving it so much as an inch of ground to call its own. He also attacked the concept of racial purity: "Whites, through generations of slavery and after slavery preached racial purity in the name of white supremacy, but forced upon the Negro the blending of blood which has made the Afro-American biologically the heir of two races, not one."[2]

In 1944 he wrote that the most monstrous abridgements of freedom had arisen out of racial prejudice. He was particularly incensed when he learned that Southern restaurant owners had expressed a willingness to feed German prisoners of war that were being transported to prison camps in this country, but were unwilling to allow the presence in their restaurants of the African-American soldiers who were traveling with the Germans as their guards. He wrote in *What is Our Destiny* that:

> I have sometimes said that in World War I our sins against liberty were like a rash; conspicuous, ugly and painful, and for that reason most susceptible to cure. In this world war they are like a hidden cancer, almost unnoticed in the body politic. Indeed, the evil is the worse because it is so often unnoticed, or even in some case justified by those who once called themselves liberals. The most serious of these abridgements of freedom arise out of our racial prejudices.[3]

World War II only made African-Americans more intensely aware of their inferior status, first in the military ranks and later in civilian life. Discrimination against African-Americans was written large in the military forces, in employment, in education, in the labor unions, in the churches, and in the Jim Crow laws across the South. Thomas proposed laws barring discrimination in employment and in housing. He admonished educational institutions, including his own alma mater, Princeton, for refusing to open their enrollment to peoples of all races. But with the end of the war, with Blacks and Whites anticipating a period of world peace, he felt that the time for direct opposition to discriminatory practices was inappropriate. Rather than engaging in acts of civil disobedience at that time, he suggested to African-Americans that they amass pressure against labor unions to require an end of racial discrimination in employment and that they place greater reliance on the ballot box to attain their goals.

---

1 Norman Thomas, *Human Exploitation in the United States* (Frederick A. Stokes, New York, 1934), 275-276.

2 *The Washington Post*, 9/21/36, X-9.

3 Norman Thomas, *What Is Our Destiny* (Doubleday, Doran, Garden City, N.Y., 1944), 156.

Thomas was moved by Richard Wright's *Black Boy*, and by Jackie Robinson's courage in accepting the role as Major League's first black baseball player. In the Fall of 1947, he wrote to Robinson:

> Now that the Dodgers have won the pennant, it is very appropriate, I think, to thank you, not only for what you did in the pennant race, but for what you have done for the colored race and for the fraternity which ought to characterize our mutual relations. You have performed a real service to your country and in general to a world which must learn to honor men for what they are and do regardless of race.[1]

Although Thomas lived among African-Americans in New York City and was prominent among those who fought against racial bias across the country, his record against Black prejudice does not stand totally without criticism. He and Violet owned a summer home in the all-white town of Cold Spring Harbor, located in the affluent Long Island north coast. The town had no black-owned property. In fact, the only African-Americans ever seen in the town were gardeners and household servants. Thomas lived in Cold Spring Harbor during many summers, but apparently accepted those conditions without raising his voice in protest.

Race played a huge role in the 1948 presidential election. Early in the year, President Truman proposed enactment of a broad-based civil rights program providing for the abolishment of the poll tax, establishment of a Fair Employment Practices Commission to eliminate discrimination in employment, and laws barring discrimination in interstate bus and train travel. Southern Democrats were appalled. Advocating the continued segregation of races, they bolted the Democratic Party and established their own political party, calling themselves "Dixiecrats." They went on to denounce Truman's proposed civil rights program as an effort to reduce Americans to the status of a mongrel and inferior race. It remained to be seen what role Thomas would play in all this, since he was not prepared to enter the 1948 presidential campaign.

Weary of defeat after defeat, Thomas promised himself in 1946 that he would never again seek public office.[2] Long before the Socialist Party national convention convened in May 1948, Thomas called for the nomination of A. Philip Randolph as the party's presidential candidate. Randolph, an African-American, a trade unionist and civil rights leader long-dedicated to justice for African-Americans, ultimately concluded that his efforts to obtain civil rights for African-Americans would remain more effective if he were not to assume the role of a political candidate. He thus rejected Thomas' prodding to accept the party's nomination. Thomas then again turned to May-

---

1 Thomas letter dated, 9/23/47, to Jackie Robinson.
2 Thomas autobiography, 257.

nard Krueger, but as in 1944, Krueger rebuffed Thomas' appeal to run.[1] By the time the convention opened, Thomas reluctantly accepted the obvious — the party had no one available but himself to stand as the party's candidate for president. With the difficulties the Socialist Party confronted in several states in getting the names of its candidates on the ballot, it was impera-tive that the party nominate one who was already well known by the public. Thus, he reluctantly reversed his decision not to accept the nomination. If nominated, he would, as in the past, resolutely continue his struggle to ad-vance the Socialist Party program.[2]

In his acceptance speech, Thomas noted the irony in that the best thing Truman had done- moving to attain civil rights for Black Americans- was that which damned him in large segments of his own party. The Republi-can Party, the followers of Abraham Lincoln, on the other hand, continued to follow the path of reaction. "No wonder," Thomas observed, "that so many thousands of good people have turned with false hope" to the Progres-sive Party and Henry Wallace, the captives of the Communist Party.[3] After breaking with the Truman administration, Wallace had agreed to run as the Progressive Party candidate for president. During the campaign, Wallace focused primarily on foreign policy issues, advocating a more conciliatory posture toward the Soviet Union.

Public response to Thomas' decision to campaign a sixth time for presi-dent was generally favorable, if not enthusiastic. *The New York Times* noted with approval that Thomas' socialism was of the "democratic variety, and it is easy to see that if he had to choose between socialism and democracy he would always choose democracy." Although the *Times* editors did not agree with many of Thomas' positions, they looked forward to his campaign: "It is good to have a left-wing splinter that is actually in the American tradition so far as its methods go. We cannot wish Mr. Thomas success in the campaign, but we are not sorry that this sort of campaign is being made by this sort of man. It won't do us any harm at all."[4]

The Washington Post was a bit more effusive in its praise, even granting its approval — of a sort — to Thomas' endeavors to subvert the country's economy:

> Nominated for the sixth time by the Socialist Party, Norman Thomas can be counted upon to bring to the campaign, as he has done in the past, caus-tic yet illuminating criticism of his major party opponents and a reasoned defense of the economic doctrines in which he believes.... [H]e has the re-spect and affection of the American people.... He would go to the root of

1 *The New York Times*, 5/8/48, 9.
2 Ibid., 5/9/48, 45.
3 Thomas' acceptance speech appears under the title "Why I am a Candidate" in Bernard K. Johnpoll, Editor, *Norman Thomas on War: An Anthology* (Garland, New York, 1974), 232-235.
4 *The New York Times*, 5/11/48, 24.

what he deems wrong with the American society and subvert the traditional American enterprise system, believing it to be neither efficient nor
free. It is reassuring that the United States still finds room for this sort of
subversion. Its impact is thoroughly healthy, prodding complacency and
fostering progress. But Mr. Thomas' attempted subversion of the country's
economic institutions is rooted in genuine Americanism — in a tested devotion to American political institutions and to the full freedom of conscience and expression which are the highest American ideals.[1]

Thomas knew the campaign would be difficult. The Socialist Party membership had shrunk dramatically over the years and, as in past campaigns, it
did not possess the financial resources required to support even a minimal
campaign effort. Thomas, therefore, had to find an innovative approach to
running for president. He recalled that William Jennings Bryan, prior to one
of his nominations by the Democratic Party to run for president, had covered
the Republican Party convention as a journalist. He asked himself why he
could not do something similar.

Earlier in the year, Palmer Hoyt, the publisher of *The Denver Post*, had invited Thomas to write a guest editorial. Thomas had declined at the time, but
as the other party conventions were about to convene, he asked his friend
and Socialist Party activist, Harry Fleischman, to approach Hoyt with a proposal that Thomas write daily columns from the Republican, Democratic,
and Progressive Party conventions. Hoyt, delighted with the idea, proceeded
to line up other newspapers to carry the columns. Besides *The Denver Post*,
Thomas would be writing for *The Los Angeles Times*, *The San Francisco Chronicle*,
The St. Louis Post–Dispatch, *The Indianapolis Star*, *The Trenton Times*, *The Phoenix Ga-
zette*, and seven other papers. Thomas then attended each of the three conventions with Fleischman at his side as legman.[2]

In his first columns written at the Republican convention, Thomas set
the tone of his reportage to follow. He noted the presence at the convention of a rubber elephant, apparently defective since it had to be periodically
inflated with hot air. He also reported the arrival of a living baby elephant,
determined to walk backwards, quite prophetic in Thomas' view. He was
appalled at the insipid platitudes flooding the convention hall, and when
Dewey was nominated with little enthusiasm from the crowd, Thomas
scoffed that it only proved that "you don't have to win friends to influence
people."[3]

The Democrats, convinced that they were about to lose the election, convened in a fog of gloom. "This convention," Thomas wrote, "is like a carnival
at a morgue lined with unburied hopes." But after the delegates adopted a
civil rights plank and the Dixiecrats marched out of the hall in loud protest,

1 *The Washington Post*, 5/13/48, 10.
2 Harry Fleischman, *Norman Thomas, A Biography: 1884–1968*, 227-228.
3 Ibid., 228-229.

the convention came to life. With spirits raised, Truman gave a fighting acceptance speech and brought the delegates roaring to their feet. Although impressed, Thomas still predicted that Truman would lose.[1] One of the better things to come out of the Democratic convention for Thomas was becoming acquainted with Hubert Humphrey. His admiration for Humphrey, primarily because of his stand on civil rights, formed the basis of a lasting friendship.

At the Progressive Party convention, the Communists were present in force. Thomas noted that the non-Communist delegates were abnormally sensitive to the color red, refusing to ride to the Philadelphia convention site on the Pennsylvania Railroad's "Red Special," and insisting upon transferring meetings scheduled in their hotel's Pink Room to its Green Room. At the outset of the convention, a reporter asked Henry Wallace whether he would debate Truman and Dewey. Wallace stated he would, but when asked whether he would debate Thomas, he responded he would not. Why not? "Well I believe in conserving my strength." Thomas noted that Wallace "showed a certain prudence" in refusing to debate him.[2]

While Thomas was subjected to the Progressives' rude remarks and dark stares, the Republicans and the Democrats cordially accepted him. They considered him a celebrity, and as a consequence he was frequently interviewed for television and radio, and by other columnists as well, thus achieving the public exposure he otherwise would not have had. Considering the moneys earned for writing the columns — all donated to the Socialist Party — Thomas deemed the entire venture a great success.

The central themes of Thomas' 1948 campaign were merely extensions of the arguments presented in his book, *Appeal to the Nations.* At times, he tried to lighten his approach to the election with humor, mostly at the expense of the other candidates. Commenting on Truman, he said, "We looked at him and we listened to him and we said to ourselves, 'It's right. Anybody can be President of the United States.'"[3] As for Dewey, who throughout the campaign spoke in generalities so as to alienate as few voters as possible, Thomas said that he woke up each morning and asked himself, "What pair of platitudes shall I put on today?"[4]

Thomas wanted to use the campaign to advance his ideas on preserving world peace, but just as the campaign was heating up, the Russians created a highly volatile international situation by halting all rail, water, and highway traffic in and out of Berlin. The United States had to confront the Russians without bringing on another world war. Thomas, sensitive to the dangers

---

1 Ibid., 230.
2 Ibid., 232.
3 *The Washington Post* 10/19/48, 12.
4 Harry Fleischman, *Norman Thomas, A Biography: 1884–1968,* 234.

the country then faced, resolved to keep questions relating to the critical relations with the Russians out of the realm of campaign politics. Before making public his own position on the Berlin crisis, he wrote to Truman: "This
letter is not written for publicity and will not be released at any time." He
proceeded to tell the president that he appreciated the firmness of the government's stand on the crisis and advised him that he advocated turning the
matter over to the United Nations.[1] Because of the seriousness of the crisis,
Thomas felt obligated to advise Truman of his position before declaring it to
the public. He was careful to follow this course throughout the campaign.

Beyond raising issues relating to world peace, Thomas made racial discrimination a central subject of debate. Speaking in Austin Texas, he offered
the Southern states his program for gaining "plenty, peace, and freedom."
His program demanded an end to all discriminatory practices, not only in
the South but across the nation, which Thomas felt was suffering from a
failure of mind and conscience. Endorsing President Truman's civil rights
program, he reminded his audiences that the Socialist Party had long advocated the adoption of civil rights guarantees and protections that would
relieve African-Americans and other minority groups from the lasting effects
of racial bias.[2]

On at least one occasion, Thomas' travels led him to cross Truman's campaign path. As Truman spoke from the rear platform of his campaign train in
Texas, Thomas stood in the crowd taking in the speech. Whether Truman
was aware of Thomas' presence is not known, but it would not have been
surprising if he had, given that Thomas' commanding height made him an
obvious figure in any crowd.

Thomas' run for the presidency was, as in previous years, an effort in education — an endeavor to inform the public concerning the basic principles
of the Socialist Party and his own principles as well. Secondarily, he sought
a good showing at the polls, as a higher vote count would redound to the
benefit of the party. Although his vote total of 140,000 was minuscule in
comparison to Truman's 24 million to 21 million vote victory over Dewey,
he had the satisfaction of nearly doubling his 1944 vote. But the end of the
road for the Socialist Party as a national political party was clearly in sight.
Thomas' role as a presidential candidate had reached its final act.

Thomas never actually ran for political office, for he never had any realistic prospect of election. He was a dissenter from a world that continuously
and systematically denied equality, freedom, and justice, from a world that
settled conflict through the force of arms. Rather than assume the role of
the typical politician, Thomas' goal was public enlightenment. If in the end

---

1 Thomas letter, dated 9/11/48, to Truman.
2 *The Washington Post*, 9/29/48, 11.

he failed to win the public's votes, he won their hearts. He was a "great de-nouncer, aroused to indignation by one injustice or another, and so skillful with words and so sharp and witty that he carried almost every audience with him, often to a standing ovation."[1] He began to be looked upon as the conscience of the American people.

1 Roger Baldwin, "Norman Thomas: A Memoir," *Saturday Review*, 4/12/69, 41.

CHAPTER 19. OPPOSING NUCLEAR TESTING, SUPPORTING DISARMAMENT

On Thomas' sixty-fifth birthday in November 1949, The New York Times paid him tribute:

> There are not many men in American public life today who command greater esteem or fewer votes than Norman Thomas. The influence which Mr. Thomas has exercised as a Socialist leader is difficult to assess; but at least he has the satisfaction of knowing that a good deal of the early Socialist program has found its way — though under other auspices — into the law of the land. And there is not much of it that would be repealed, no matter which of the two major parties was in power. Today on his sixty-fifth birthday, we extend our congratulations to this great dissenter . . . whose sincerity, eloquence, perseverance and faith have earned him an honored place in America's political annals.[1]

Thomas remained popular with the people. Their acceptance and approval of the content of the newspaper columns he wrote during the 1948 political conventions persuaded him to continue to produce them following the election. Most of his columns were commentaries on national political issues, but occasionally he ventured into other areas. When his beloved dog died in 1949, he wrote about "The Death of a Friend," leading to a plethora of sympathy letters and notes. A few columns later he quipped that he could probably garner more votes running as a dog lover than as a Socialist.

Over the following years, he used the columns to attack Republicans and Democrats alike. He criticized the Catholic Church on some issues, such as its position on birth control, but did not hesitate to weigh in against positions advanced by Protestants and Jews as well. Over time he alienated nearly everyone at one time or another, and this led to a decline in his readership

---

1 *The New York Times*, 11/20/49, E-8.

and the cancellation of his columns by some newspapers. By the late 1950s, only *The Denver Post, The Los Angeles Mirror,* and *The Trenton Times* continued to publish them.

Following World War II, Thomas participated in forming a number of organizations that addressed issues relating to world peace, civil liberties, and racial equality. A listing of the organizations in which he claimed membership in 1950-1951 gives some idea of the scope of his interests: the American Committee for Cultural Freedom, the Post War World Council, the League for Industrial Democracy, the ACLU, the Indian League of America, the Citizens' Committee for United Nations Reform, the Inter-American Association for Democracy and Freedom, the NAACP, the National Sharecroppers' Fund, the International League for the Rights of Man, the American Committee on Africa, the Newspaper Guild, the International Rescue Committee, the American Association for a Democratic Germany, and the Workers' Defense League.[1] In addition, of course, he remained active in the Socialist Party and served as a member of its National Executive Committee.

Besides his newspaper columns, Thomas used radio and television appearances to advance his causes. He frequently appeared on "Author Meets Critics," "American Forum of the Air," "Meet the Press," "Tex and Jinx," "Spotlight," "Keeping Posted," and "Town Hall Forum." The Town Hall rules limited a guest's appearance on the show to twice a year, and beginning in 1935, Thomas appeared biannually, becoming the person most in demand by the program's audience. The president of the Town Hall once commented that Thomas was one of the truly great educational forces in America, enormously respected even by those who disagreed with his positions.[2]

All of Thomas' causes did not involve the fate of thousands, as he often undertook to help individuals in trouble. Barry Miller, an Army corporal, hoping to advance through the military ranks as a radar instructor, was called to account by his superiors after it was disclosed that some years prior to enlisting in the Army he had been a member of a Trotskyite group at the University of Chicago. Without so much as a hearing, the Army reduced his rank and ordered him to be "undesirably discharged." Thomas did not know Miller, but was incensed when he heard how the Army had treated him. He protested to the Secretary of the Army, wrote to President Eisenhower, and to more than twenty of the nation's leading newspapers, and made so much of a commotion that the War Department reluctantly reviewed the case, changed Miller's "undesirable discharge" to a general discharge, and agreed to pursue fairer and more equitable procedures in the future. Thomas was only partially satisfied with this outcome, as he had called on the Army to

---

1 W. A. Swanberg, *Norman Thomas: The Last Idealist* (Charles Scribner's Sons, New York, 1976), 342.

2 Ibid., 359.

reverse the discharge order, and thus permit Miller to continue to serve.[1] In cases such as this, he was not one to stand idly by in the presence of an act of injustice.

While early in his career he had stood against United States' entry into the League of Nations, considering it little more than an alliance of impe-rialist powers acting to protect their overseas possessions, he later viewed the United Nations far more favorably. He feared, however, that the world's leaders had constructed it upon a foundation that would insure its demise. At the General Assembly's first meeting, US Secretary of State James Byrnes observed that the infant organization would have to learn to walk before it could run. Thomas noted that a more apt comparison would have been to the infant Hercules, who to save his own life had to strangle a great serpent in his cradle. "The infant United Nations must strangle the twin serpents of militarism and imperialism if it is to live at all." Even with its innate weak-nesses, Thomas believed that the United Nations provided a useful forum that enabled nations, large and small, to discuss common interests.[2] By the mid-1950s, he favored granting the U.N. greater powers, enabling it to make a more meaningful effort at enforcing the concept of the rule of law in inter-national affairs. He even pleaded for a permanent U.N. police force, sufficient in strength to intervene in and stop small wars. "In the U.N. we have an organization which, properly accepted and strengthened, can be the framer and enforcer of the law which shall supplant war."[3]

He saw no alternative to the course taken by the United Nations in op-posing Communist military aggression in Korea. Any other course would have virtually destroyed the U.N., as it would have encouraged dictators such as Stalin to believe that the world's democratic nations would always yield to military aggression. This position, which he unhesitatingly advanced, constituted still another blow to his former pacifist beliefs:

> More than ever I [become] convinced that the necessary basis for extreme pacifism is a kind of religious faith to which the fate of organized society on this planet is of comparatively little concern, or which offers the believer strong trust in God's intervention in behalf of a nation which will choose the way of suffering rather than any sort of violence. This faith I do not have.[4]

If he had not earlier abandoned his pacifist beliefs, he undoubtedly would have opposed the U.N. action in Korea. But he now firmly adopted the view that in the course of history the choice for or against war is always relative. Human tragedy is inherent in the paucity of the means of social action avail-able to humans. "War has been only the most obvious . . . illustration of the

---

1 Ibid., 372-373.
2 Norman Thomas, *Appeal to the Nations* (Henry Holt, New York, 1947), 22-34.
3 Norman Thomas, *The Prerequisites for Peace* (W.W. Norton, New York, 1959), 87.
4 Norman Thomas, *A Socialist's Faith* (W.W. Norton, New York, 1951), 320.

imperfection of the tools men in society have found themselves compelled to use."[1] War may be pursued only if any other course would culminate in a worse condition. In this spirit, he gave full support to the U.N.

Thomas opposed nuclear testing, never varying from this position from the first atomic test onward. He expressed the depth of his concern in a letter written to *The Washington Post:* "In my rather long life, nothing has ever seemed to me more important for the peace of the world and the health of mankind than an immediate moratorium on all tests involving nuclear explosions."[2]

In one of his first endeavors to persuade the nuclear nations of the world to halt testing, Thomas joined with Bertrand Russell, Linus Pauling and fifteen others in filing a lawsuit in the Washington, D.C. Federal District Court, asking the court to halt United States atomic testing. They claimed that US citizens had the right to bar government officials from engaging in the testing of nuclear weapons since fallout from the tests endangered all Americans, indeed, all the world. The competency of their legal counsel must have been questioned at the time as it would have been obvious, even to a first year law student, that the litigants were without legal standing to sue, and that the court would thus be required to terminate the suit. In fact, the court dismissed the suit soon after its filing.[3]

Realizing that his efforts at litigation had been misguided, Thomas turned to expressing his opposition to nuclear testing through an organization he helped form — the Committee for a Sane Nuclear Policy, soon to become known as SANE. Its founders, inspired by Dr. Albert Schweitzer's "Call to Conscience," were moved to develop public support for programs designed to lead mankind away from war and toward peace and justice. The organization attracted a number of well known figures including Eleanor Roosevelt, Dr. Benjamin Spock, Paul Tillich, Erich Fromm, and Roger Baldwin, as well as celebrities from around the world such as Bertrand Russell, Pablo Casals, and Dr. Albert Schweitzer.

The organization grew rapidly, and presented a voice that could not be ignored. Within three years of its formation, it filled Madison Square Garden's 18,000 seats at a rally featuring speeches by Thomas, Eleanor Roosevelt, Walter Reuther, and Alfred Landon. After the rally, five thousand of the audience marched out of the Garden, heading in the direction of the United Nations. Thomas was at the front of the marchers urging them on. Police officials, realizing matters could quickly get out of control, pleaded with Thomas to lead the marchers off the streets and onto the sidewalks. "Lead them down the sidewalks; we'll clear the way. Just lead them down the sidewalks." Thomas did just that, and the marchers moved down Broadway,

---

1 Ibid., 321.

2 *The Washington Post*, 4/22/57, A-14.

3 Norman Thomas, *The Prerequisites for Peace*, 75-76.

singing and chanting. With five thousand marchers behind him, spread out over several blocks, Thomas led the way across town to the United Nations on the east side of Manhattan. After the group assembled at the U.N. Thomas spoke briefly about barring further testing. The marchers then observed three minutes of silent prayer and — at one o'clock in the morning — departed for their homes.[1]

When Communists threatened to take control of SANE's leadership, Thomas formed still another organization — Turn Toward Peace — which aimed at coordinating existing peace, liberal, and internationalist groups under the slogan, "Peace is the personal responsibility of every American." Thomas was its first Chairman, and it soon had offices in New York, Washington D.C., Cambridge, Massachusetts and other cities, and by 1962, thirty-eight national organizations had affiliated with it.[2]

The Soviet Union's massive series of nuclear tests in 1961 and the announcement of President Kennedy's plan to resume testing in the atmosphere stirred the peace movement to renewed efforts to bar further testing. Turn Toward Peace (TTP) organized a joint national effort of peace, church, labor, and public affairs organizations to build support for alternatives to war as the central thrust of United States foreign policy. TTP quickly expanded to become one of the largest forces in the peace movement of the early 1960s.[3]

Groups advocating general disarmament closely allied themselves with the nuclear test ban movement. Thomas had been arguing for disarmament from the final days of World War II, and through the auspices of the Post War World Council, had advanced a plan that would prohibit weapons of mass destruction, terminate all peacetime military conscription, and reduce all armies to a level sufficient only to preserve internal order. He met with President Truman in August 1950, suggesting that he address the U.N., specifically appealing for world disarmament. Two months later, Truman spoke before the U.N. General Assembly and vigorously appealed for worldwide disarmament. Following Eisenhower's election to succeed Truman, Thomas turned his attention to persuading the new president to follow Truman's example in pressing for disarmament, and not long after, Eisenhower advanced his plan for world disarmament. In 1955, Thomas asserted that, "Never was I surer than now that . . . lovers of peace must concentrate on their drive for controlled disarmament."[4]

---

1 Harry Fleischman, *Norman Thomas, A Biography: 1884–1968* (W.W. Norton, New York, 1969), 262.

2 Swarthmore College Peace Collection, "Records of Turn Toward Peace, 1961-1970."

3 *The New York Times*, 4/22/62, 2.

4 Charles DeBenedetti, *An American Ordeal: The Antiwar Movement of the Vietnam Era* (Syracuse University Press, Syracuse, 1990), 15, excerpting the Post War World Council Newsletter, 2/3/55, 3.

Thomas again raised the disarmament issue in his book entitled *The Prerequisites for Peace.*[1] Thomas may have considered this slim volume, published in 1959, his most important work, since it covered issues basic to saving mankind from self-destruction. He portrayed America's efforts to preserve peace as unrealistically based on the escalating arms race between Communist and Western powers, an arms race that tended to create a "balance of terror." Instead of arming, he reasoned that Americans should work for peace through the United Nations. He was far ahead of his time in perceiving that the Cold War would ultimately give way to new realities, and that achieving an accommodation with the Russians on issues of mutual interest, such as approaches to peace, was possible.

Thomas claimed that certain Cold War positions actually worked against the cause for peace, as a number of powerful American groups had acquired vested interests in a continued arms race — the military, in living their profession; scientists, in maintaining the governmental funding provided them for research; the business community, in continuing to derive profits from its dealings with the Department of Defense; and workers, in preserving jobs dependent upon arms expenditures.[2] These groups — at least indirectly — tended to perpetuate American participation in the arms race.

Thomas would have Americans stand firmly in support of the "prerequisites for peace," which he designated as 1) disarmament, 2) military disengagement from defined geographical areas, and 3) the strengthening of the United Nations as a peace-enforcing agency. The "prerequisites," he declared, provided a viable alternative to the Cold War arms race.[3]

He did not contend that world disarmament would occur merely as a consequence of a rejection of military armaments (even if that were conceivable). Disarmament was attainable only through a plan of controlled implementation — disarmament approached gradually, in stages. Each nation must pursue the goal of reducing its military armaments to a level sufficient for police activity alone. The role of the United Nations in this plan was that of an enforcer of the international laws guiding the disarmament.[4]

In advocating disengagement, Thomas was not suggesting a return to pre-World War II isolationism. "The general growth of the interdependence of mankind, the extraordinary share of the world's wealth and power which America holds, and her role in two world wars make that impossible."[5] Nor,

---

1 Norman Thomas, *The Prerequisites for Peace* (W.W. Norton, New York, 1959).

2 Ibid., 54.

3 A summary of the proposals for peace offered by Thomas in *The Prerequisites for Peace* appear in James C. Duram, *Norman Thomas* (Twayne, New York, 1974), 133-137.These proposals are spread throughout Thomas' *The Prerequisites for Peace*: 13, 26-27, 31-47, 58, 64, 80, 158-159, 181, and 164.

4 Norman Thomas, *The Prerequisites for Peace* 87.

5 Ibid., 88.

in defining disengagement as a means of ending the struggle against dicta-torship and oppression, was he calling for a rejection of America's obligation, as the world's richest nation, to continue its role as an active and cooperative participant in the war against world poverty. Rather, he intended disengage-ment to encompass only a phased military withdrawal from defined areas that would result in militarily neutralized belts or zones. The ultimate objec-tive of disengagement was the recall of all troops, other than those serving in a U.N. police force, to positions located within each country's national boundaries.[1]

He believed his prerequisites for peace fell within the range of solutions acceptable to the nations of the world, though most of those nations were "obviously unready to accept the Sermon on the Mount as their guide in poli-tics or accept Gandhi's noble nonviolent resistance to evil as the alternative to war."[2] He considered it far more likely that Americans would agree to disarm from military strength than from weakness, and that they would de-mand that a plan of disarmament should stand as an intricate part of a mul-tilateral project for world peace. Americans were not utopians; they would never agree to lead a confused world in some outstanding idealistic act.[3] Thus, Thomas did not advance his prerequisites for peace out of some sort of "pie in the sky" idealism. He acted out of pragmatism, not idealism. He recog-nized that although men recoil with horror from the thought of nuclear war, historically war has always been an essential aspect of the life patterns of tribes, nations, and empires. Although smaller nations may renounce nuclear war, they cling to their own military forces as proof and protection of their sovereignty. Moreover, in all nations, certain groups have a stake in war or in preparation for war, finding there a source of power, prestige, and profit. Humankind, therefore, cannot rely solely on a growing fear of nuclear war to keep the peace.[4] If historical reliance on war is to be reversed, basic views of human conduct will need to be altered, and these views must include the acceptance of the concept of controlled disarmament.

Thomas used the Socialist Party as one of his many platforms for voicing his plans for disarmament. For example, in the 1950 Congressional election campaign, the party called for universal disarmament through a reduction of military arms of all nations under the control of a much strengthened Unit-ed Nations. The party further advocated that the billions of dollars saved in decreased arms expenditures be used to improve industry and agriculture throughout the world.[5]

---

1 Ibid. 89.
2 Ibid., 179.
3 Ibid.
4 Ibid., 179-180.
5 *The New York Times* , 6/5/50, 15.

While contending with the day-to-day problems associated with his efforts to halt further testing of nuclear weapons and bringing about world disarmament, Thomas was daily confronted with the virulent opposition of the Communist Party and by American super-patriots and right-wing extremists. As in the past, Communists continued to plague him, as when they tried to seize control of SANE. He pressed the Voice of America radio to refute the Communist charge that the United States was an imperialist power, a charge that had gained some currency among third-world nations at the time. He drafted a manifesto to be signed by leading American Socialists that reaffirmed their belief in democratic socialism. The manifesto, signed by Thomas, Upton Sinclair, A. Philip Randolph, James T. Farrell, Sidney Hook, Reinhold Niebuhr among others, appeared in Socialist publications around the world and was broadcast by the Voice of America.

The manifesto failed to impress the right-wing extremists, who invariably lumped socialism with communism. In July 1953, State Department security chief, Scott McLeod, announced that he would henceforth bar the hiring of Socialists for policy-making positions in the Department, and that he would see to it that any Socialist still holding such a post was removed from his or her position.[1] Thomas, perceiving that the opposition to communism expressed by the McLeods of the world also fueled the forces that would bar Socialists from serving in sensitive government positions[2] immediately protested to President Eisenhower. Summoned to the White House by the president, Thomas learned that Eisenhower had a better understanding of socialism than Thomas had been led to believe. The president assured him that he did not doubt the loyalty of Socialists and that he would not permit their exclusion from government positions.

In the early- and mid-1950s, rabid anti-Communist crusaders and super-patriots, such as Wisconsin's senator Joseph McCarthy, falsely and recklessly identified democratic socialism as another form of communism, thus deliberately confusing the public on the issue. Ironically, Thomas inadvertently contributed to the rise of McCarthyism. During the 1946 Wisconsin senatorial campaign, McCarthy's opponent, Howard J. McMurray, a liberal, non-Communist Democrat, was endorsed by the Communist Daily Worker. Thomas suggested that McMurray repudiate the Communist endorsement. McMurray ignored Thomas, but several Wisconsin newspapers reiterated Thomas' suggestion that McMurray openly reject all Communist support. When McMurray again remained silent, McCarthy assailed him for not de-

1 *The Washington Post*, 7/21/53, 1.
2 Ibid., 8/18/53, 4.

nouncing communism. This ultimately became the overriding issue of the campaign and led to McCarthy's victory.[1] The rest is history.

Thomas, endeavoring to counter McCarthyite attacks and set the record straight on democratic socialism, wrote *The Test of Freedom*.[2] Relying on years of experience battling with Communists, he detailed precisely what communism claimed to be and what it in effect actually was:

> Communism is a secular religion which seeks universal power over the bodies, minds, and souls of men. Upon this secular religion, international in scope and appeal, Lenin and Stalin, as heads of the great Soviet state, imposed a Russian imperial control.... This secular religion, its hierarchy now horribly corrupted by power, seeks the ultimate earthly salvation . . . through the achievement of its own form of economic collectivism.[3]

Although communism designates the working class as the messiah, Thomas pointed out that in reality the Communist Party fulfills that role. When it gains power the messiah becomes a despot. Since the party as a whole cannot function as an absolute totalitarian ruler, an inner circle takes over, and in that circle one man eventually becomes the semi-divine leader. Communists accept only a single commandment, laid down by Lenin himself: "Thou shalt believe what the Party tells you and do whatsoever is necessary in the judgment of the Party to advance its interests. Every change of line, every lie or deceit or act of violence thus commanded is right and holy."[4]

Thomas held it to have been a serious error for liberals in the post-war era to have minimized the Communist threat. But communism, which jeopardized the American way of life and imperiled even US existence as an independent nation, also occasioned the rise of McCarthyism, which constituted a more widespread challenge to the Jeffersonian ideal than Communism itself.[5] Thomas advocated fighting against Communism and McCarthyism on every front. But he opposed "burning down barns to catch rats," as it is generally the horses who die. He nonetheless believed "in catching rats," but noted that rats could be caught without witch-hunts.[6]

Many elements of McCarthyism antedated the Wisconsin senator's emergence to prominence. Americans in the past had suffered a kind of patriotism that identified love of country with hatred of foreigners, the rejection of non-conformity, and an exaggerated suspicion of all dissent. Thomas reminded the public that specimens of this type of patriotism were to be found in certain resolutions of the American Legion, and in even more preju-

1 Bernard K. Johnpoll, *Pacifist's Progress: Norman Thomas and the Decline of American Socialism* (Greenwood Press, Westport, Conn., 1970), 261.

2 Norman Thomas, *The Test of Freedom* (W.W. Norton, New York, 1954).

3 Ibid., 48-49.

4 Ibid., 49.

5 Ibid., 78-79.

6 Ibid., 93.

diced utterances of the Daughters of the American Revolution, years before Joe McCarthy terrorized governmental officials and many others. Thomas noted that McCarthy profited by a lie that was first propagandized by others, the lie that identified communism with democratic socialism and the welfare state.[1]

Thomas argued that McCarthyism was a form of political paranoia that perceived evil conspiracies everywhere and that America's greatest danger was internal subversion. For Thomas, however, overreaction constituted a greater danger than internal subversion. He agreed with those who viewed America's chief threat to be external, a danger emanating directly from Communist domination of the Soviet Union and China. At home, it was for Americans to prove that neither communism nor McCarthyism was the end of the American dream.[2]

Despite his intense hatred of Communists, Thomas never resorted to advocating their imprisonment, and he defended their rights to be heard and to a fair trial. On the other hand, he held that Communists had no right to hold governmental positions of responsibility and that they should be barred from teaching in public schools. In the end, his opposition to both communism and McCarthyism motivated him to adopt a pragmatic approach — a careful balancing of national security and liberty of the individual — that he firmly believed would culminate in the defeat of them both.

1 Ibid., 95.
2 Ibid., 197.

CHAPTER 20. REEVALUATING SOCIALISM

On Thomas' seventieth birthday in November 1954, his friends of many years, together with members of the Socialist Party, and those with whom he had been long associated in various peace and civil liberties groups, held a lavish birthday party at The Town Hall Club in New York City. A purse was raised for the occasion and a check for $10,000 was presented to Thomas. Clearly astonished by the amount of the gift, Thomas closely studied the check before commenting that "as an old-time Socialist campaigner, I always thought people forged signatures on $10,000 checks." He said the amount was too large to make snap judgments, but he imagined he would apply a good portion of the money to advancing the cause for controlled disarmament and the rest to further civil liberties.[1]

Despite his advancing age, he celebrated his birthday with a vigorous attack on the Democratic and Republican Parties. The chief difference between those parties, he exclaimed, was that the Democrats accepted Socialist principles cheerfully while the Republicans only reluctantly. Reminiscing that his political career might have advanced further as a Republican or a Democrat, he did not regret having remained a Socialist. He talked about Senator McCarthy as a "bad skin disease, rather than a cancer," but admitted that the "skin disease" had some excuse for breaking out. As for the future, "Our democracy is like a reluctant knight going out to engage the dragon. His armor is on awry and he drives out his horse with no flash of enthusiasm, but somehow in the end the dragon poops out and our knight wins."[2]

1 *The New York Times*, 11/22/54, 19.
2 Ibid., 11/20/54, 19.

He did not readily admit it, but he was beginning to feel his age. An arthritic knee had put him on crutches for a time and his hearing was clearly in decline. He remarked that he had a grievance against Robert Browning who, writing of old age, said, "Grow old along with me, the best is yet to be, " accusing the poet of engaging in "false advertising."[1]

While still absorbed in battles with the Communists and Senator McCarthy and his followers, Thomas decided the time was appropriate for him, and for the Socialist Party, to retire from the political arena. He called upon party members to cease expending energy on electoral campaigns that historically had produced fewer than a handful of votes. The party failed to advance the cause for Socialism when its candidates attracted fewer and fewer votes with each passing election. Socialist principles, however, would continue to gain greater acceptance with the general public if the party — rather than forcing candidates on a reluctant public — were to work through labor, farm, and other liberal groups to attain Socialist Party objectives. He saw a future for the party if it reconstituted itself as an educational body, serving a function similar to that of Great Britain's Fabian Society. The Fabians placed their faith in an evolutionary rather than a revolutionary socialism and in the furtherance of Socialist goals through education and the study and analysis of current economic and political problems.

Thomas undoubtedly was correct; a political party that was incapable of raising any more than $150,000 to finance the campaign of its presidential candidate had no place in a political world that required vast sums to defray the costs of advertising on television, the medium that was then growing increasingly dominant in the electoral process. But the party membership rejected Thomas' vision for the future and decided to field yet another candidate in the 1952 presidential election, naming Darlington Hoopes, a Pennsylvania attorney, as their candidate. Again, the party met with electoral disaster, this time receiving only slightly more than 20,000 votes. For Thomas, the 1952 presidential election was the first since 1928 that he was not the party's candidate, and the first since 1936 that he was not in control of the Socialist Party.

Although party members rejected his plans for the future, his loyalty to the party did not falter, as he continued to address its meetings from time to time. But from that point onward, he directed his main attention to the affairs of the Post War World Council and its efforts to save the world from self-destruction. But even with his attention focused elsewhere, he continued to rethink and reevaluate his Socialist positions. As revealed in his autobiography, this had been a continuing process throughout his life: "the years

---

1 Ibid.

have constrained me to change some of my judgments of Socialist theory and practice, but they strengthened my basic belief in it."[1]

The New York Times once described Thomas' brand of socialism as consisting "mainly in jumping in wherever he thinks human beings are being abused or human rights ignored, and doing something about it."[2] Although this characterization contained an element of truth, Thomas' Socialist core values were of far greater depth and complexity. He was not a Marxist, as he made clear when he joined the Socialist Party in 1918,[3] and while he accepted the concept of public ownership of basic industries and services, he rejected the Marxist premise that public ownership and basic changes to the social order could be achieved only through force and violence. He redefined Marx's "working class" to include those who used their "brains" as well as those who used "brawn" to accomplish an honest day's work on the farm or in the mine, factory, school, or office. He complained that "unfortunately, a great many workers do not recognize themselves as workers.... Even some of an owning class may be able to transcend immediate class interest for the sake of themselves and their children."[4] The very inclusiveness of Thomas' perception of the working class turned the Marxist concept of class warfare on its head.[5]

In an article written in 1930 for The World *Tomorrow*, he defined what socialism then meant for him: "In its broadest sense socialism is the doctrine that land, natural resources, and the principal means of production and distribution should be socially owned and democratically managed so that production should be for public use rather than for private profit."[6] His socialism was Marxist only in its basic assumption of the need for certain government control and regulation, and to that concept he always wedded democratic control. Contrary to Marxian dogma, Thomas envisioned the possibility of a peaceful transition from capitalism to socialism — the transition to a system that would provide for the economic security of all rather than a few — while preserving the civil liberties of all members of society. He continued throughout his career firmly believing that socialism could preserve America's basic democratic principles, but by the 1950s, he recognized that socialism in the United States confronted a major crisis.

Throughout his life Thomas felt the need to reevaluate his Socialist beliefs, and at the end of World War II he began a far more vigorous re-examination of his understanding of Socialist principles. In 1951, he wrote in

---

1 Thomas autobiography, 227.
2 *The New York Times*, 11/20/54, 16.
3 See Chapter 3.
4 *The World Tomorrow*, 8/32, 239.
5 James C. Duram, *Norman Thomas* (Twayne, New York, 1974), 66-67.
6 Norman Thomas, "Socialism Upheld," *The World Tomorrow*, 2/30, 70-73.

a work he entitled *A Socialist's Faith*,[1] that while he considered socialism as a doctrine and movement consciously concerned with the common good, he recognized that for non-Socialists, socialism was nothing more than a form of collectivism. For him, however, collectivism and social ownership were merely tools, not ends in themselves, and thus he felt free to alter his opinion regarding the extent of social ownership or collectivism necessary or desirable for the American economy.[2]

He wrote that if democratic socialism were to prevail it could not present itself as a complete philosophy. It must be experimental rather than doctrinaire, should be guided by human experience, and tested by principles of human conduct, the most significant of which included the following:[3]

• Men and women no longer acquiesce to living in poverty. What society massively produced during the war for purposes of destruction proved to the underprivileged classes what might be done to eliminate poverty and provide for abundance in times of peace. Mankind, however, has not yet learned to curb national, class, or group interests that stand in the way of the conquest of poverty and war.

• Class solidarity exists, but it is an over-simplification to portray the class conflict in terms of "the owning class" versus "the working class." Ultimately, however, we must end class divisions inherent in the acquisitive capitalist society.

• Successful revolutions are not made by the lowest and most miserable stratum of the population, but by men and women, unbroken by misery, who have experienced a taste for better things or at least a vision of them. It is nonsense, therefore, for Socialists to assume that democratic socialism will automatically follow upon a revolution of desperation. It is the business of American Socialists to develop and improve democracy and not seek salvation through crisis. Socialists must work for fundamental change with a minimum of disorder.

• "If man's great interest is necessarily in bread — and today a little cake — he does not live by bread alone." Economic satisfactions are not enough. Many schemes of social reorganization might have merit if men could be dealt with as the chess player deals with pieces on his chess board, and many things might be desirable from a purely economic standpoint but are unwelcome, or even intolerable, in terms of human values.

• Human society cannot exist without the concept of mutual aid between and among members of that society. Although cooperation must be the dominant principle in society, no society has ever existed without some sort of competition. Competition only becomes evil when humans worship the re-

---

1 Norman Thomas, *A Socialist's Faith* (W.W. Norton, New York, 1951).
2 Ibid., 3-5.
3 Ibid., 301-304.

ward rather than the deed; or when, as in an acquisitive society, the competitive element provides the victors and their children with arbitrary control over the resources and machinery by which others depend to survive.

• We owe a supreme loyalty to a basic morality, a morality greatly affected by the conditions in which we work and live, but a morality never to be reduced to a mere expression of personal, group, class, or national interests.

Thomas ended his book with the observation that two great ethical principles are increasingly well established in human experience. The first is that bad means employed for a good end corrupts the end. We can rationalize our present hatreds by nominally dedicating them to a future good, but the exercise of hatred has never produced a cooperative society bound together by love. Second, in seeking a good society, individual human beings should be treated as ends, not as means. Social order and control are necessary, but always in terms consistent with respect for personality and the essential dignity which makes of a human something other than a pawn for governments, states, or economic or political oligarchies.[1]

If it were Thomas' intent to reduce, or even eliminate, Marxism from democratic socialism as he portrayed it in *A Socialist's Faith*, it appears as if he succeeded. But he was not wholly satisfied with this reexamination of Socialist principles. Two years later, he wrote a forty-seven-page pamphlet entitled *Democratic Socialism: A New Appraisal*,[2] and again he emphasized a form of socialism that excluded most Marxist principles. At the outset of the pamphlet he stated that he was not about to engage in a repudiation of what he had previously stated and written of socialism, but rather he wanted to acknowledge the importance of new problems that had arisen in socialism and also to examine the light shed on old problems by more recent developments. "The plain truth is that here in America more measures once praised or denounced as Socialist have been adopted than once I should have thought possible short of a Socialist victory at the polls."[3] But socialism in 1953 was under sharp attack and the condition of organized socialism had never been weaker.

Thomas pointed out that the greater part of the public's misunderstanding of socialism inhered in a definition formulated by those who did not really understand it. He decided to erase public confusion by accepting, as the basic underlying ground of socialism, the definition given it in *Webster's New International Dictionary:*

---

1 Ibid., 304.

2 Norman Thomas, *Democratic Socialism: A New Appraisal* (League for Industrial Democracy, New York, 1953). The pamphlet was later reissued in a slightly different form (Post War World Council, New York, 1963).

3 Ibid., 7.

> Socialism: A political and economic theory of social reorganization, the essential feature of which is governmental control of economic activities to the end that competition shall give way to cooperation and that the opportunities of life and the rewards of labor shall be equitably apportioned.

This definition, however, had to be supplemented to specify, clearly, that 1) democratic socialism always emphasizes the necessity of democratic processes in all government controls, 2) although the dominant principle in socialism should always be cooperation, a legitimate place for some competition exists in a Socialist order, 3) government control does not necessarily mean government ownership, and 4) social ownership is a means of achieving socialism's ends rather than constituting an end in itself.[1]

He deemed it unfitting to consider socialism as a synonym for collectivism or collective ownership. Socialism has always been concerned for the good life, and it has continuously recognized the dignity of man and has desired for each individual the fullest possible opportunity for development. "Its goal has always been a society fit to be described as a fellowship of free men, who will use their resources and skills no longer for war, but for the economic conquest of bitter poverty and remedial disease."[2]

Thomas noted that Socialist insistence on state ownership had lessened since the First World War, largely because Fascist and Communistic states in Europe had sharpened the fears of the State as a master of society. At the same time, state ownership had become a less significant element of socialism in the United States because Americans had learned to impose social controls on privately owned enterprises through the development of social planning, taxation, labor legislation, and powerful labor organizations.[3]

He reminded his readers that the relationship of socialism to Marxism had always been ambiguous. In the light of modern psychology, our observations of human conduct, and our fuller knowledge of ancient cultures, it was no longer tenable to hold the rigid view of the materialistic conception of history advanced by Marx, the conception that declares the prevailing economic system determines the general character of the political and intellectual life of that era:

> Neither socialism nor any other way of life can be established or maintained in desirable form except by a conscious ethical appeal. The workers may have an especial stake in socialism . . . but socialism is for all of mankind. Fortunately for us at this time, especially in this country of potential abundance, it is broadly true that economic arrangements which are good for my neighbor are good for me.[4]

---

1 Ibid., 9-10.
2 Ibid., 10.
3 Ibid., 10-11.
4 Ibid., 13-14.

It is doubtful that Thomas anticipated the reaction that followed the publication of his pamphlet. *The Washington Post* called the pamphlet a "retreat from socialism," and accused Thomas of rejecting so much of Socialist orthodoxy that in the end there was little or nothing remaining except the name:

> Thomas has pretty well repudiated all the basic premises of the politico-economic doctrine and the party with which he has been so identified. Indeed, he has rejected so much of Socialist orthodoxy that in the end little or nothing is left of it except the name.... Thus, in . . . successive changes of opinion, Mr. Thomas seems in a way to reflect the ideological history — the early optimism, the progressive disillusionments — of the more philosophically radical members of his generation. But what distinguishes him from so many of his contemporaries is his intellectual candor and his willingness to abandon any position that he finds to be fallacious or untenable.[1]

Others also referred to the pamphlet as evidence that Thomas had abandoned his Socialist principles, a charge that he flatly denied.[2] In later years he affirmed that he had never lost faith in a socialism that pointed the way to the future.[3] He continued, however, to recognize socialism's need for renewed perspectives and new programs.

Two years later he approached the subject again. In an article written for *The New York Times*, entitled "A Socialist Reports on Socialism,"[4] Thomas tried to envision how Eugene Debs, upon the 100th anniversary of his birth, would view socialism as it existed in the United States in 1955. Thomas conjectured that if Debs were then to visit America he would find that the current form of its welfare state in considerable measure fulfilled Socialist propositions of his day — propositions that the major political parties did not even begin to consider until the Great Depression of the early 1930s. Still, he would find organized socialism very weak and the word itself in wide disrepute. Thomas pointed out, however, that the strength of American socialism always lay in its immediate demands rather than its fundamental theory. When in the 1930s the Democrats and Republicans appropriated a sufficient portion of Socialist demands to form a welfare state, popular interest shifted from Socialist principles to the choice of candidates most likely to preserve and improve the welfare state, with little regard given to fundamental Socialist theory. In short, under America's constitutional system, Roosevelt's New Deal and Truman's Fair Deal adopted Socialist proposals offered by Debs many years before and thus drew popular support away from organized socialism.[5]

---

1 *The Washington Post*, 4/26/53, B-4.

2 Bernard K. Johnpoll, *Pacifist's Progress: Norman Thomas and the Decline of American Socialism* (Greenwood Press, Westport, Conn., 1970), 269.

3 Compiled and edited by Bettina Peterson and Anastasia Toufexis, *What Are the Answers? Norman Thomas Speaks to Youth* (Ives Washburn, New York, 1970), 62-64.

4 Norman Thomas, "A Socialist Reports on Socialism," *The New York Times*, 10/30/55, SM-15.

5 Ibid.

Looking into the future, Thomas predicted — with great accuracy as it turned out — that "peace and prosperity with freedom would not be secure in a hungry, troubled, interdependent world, even if international communism should miraculously be extirpated."[1] He did not foresee the day when the need for socialism would vanish. He readily confessed that he could not write a definitive restatement of a philosophy and program of democratic socialism that would fulfill every aspect of that need, but if it were to meet the demands of the times, there were certain measures that Socialists should and should not undertake. For example, those advocating democratic socialism should insist that the good of mankind is dependent upon its steady progress toward a society fit to be described as a fellowship of free men living in nations that employ advanced technology to eradicate poverty, illiteracy, and disease. They should not, however, proclaim that such a society is easily and promptly attainable simply through application of an economic-political formula. Socialists should insist that the planning for the management of economic and social relations in an increasingly interdependent world requires the acceptance of the principle of cooperation. "In such planning, the state must play a commanding part, but as the servant of man, democratically controlled, with fostering concern for civil liberties."[2]

Freedom and social efficiency require conscious recollection that the planners are not merely building out of brick and stone, but dealing with living men and women whose cooperation in the planning is essential. Diversity of control is of great importance; over-centralization is to be avoided. The state should never be the exclusive owner of the economic apparatus. There must be room for cooperatives and — at least in the immediate future — private ownership.[3]

What the state should own is not to be settled by formula. Diminishing natural resources should in all justice be socially owned, whereas the basis for ownership of property other than that containing natural resources should be determined by occupancy and use. Where monopolies are the most efficient agents of production and distribution, they should be socially owned. "Private ownership must be made socially responsible, partly by preservation of fair competition, partly by labor legislation and collective bargaining, [and] partly by a proper system of taxation."[4]

Thomas conceded that Debs would find this program a pale version of his vision for a Socialist society. But neither would Debs find its message treasonous to socialism; he would approve of efforts to rethink the solutions to the problems raised by democratic socialism. As for Thomas, he believed the

---

1 Ibid., SM-38.
2 Ibid., SM-42.
3 Ibid.
4 Ibid., SM-47.

major parties, as in the past, would continue to adopt Socialist ideas, thus assuring a continued place in America's future for democratic socialism.

He continued to rethink the philosophic undergirding of his Socialist principles, returning again to the subject in 1963 when he wrote *Socialism Re-examined.*[1] Eight years had elapsed since *The New York Times* article and — as he approached his 80th year — he felt the time appropriate to consider how the growth of the US economy and his own development had affected his thinking about socialism. He started this new review by noting that all great concepts — democracy, Christianity, socialism — are less than self-defining. Their supporters, as well as their critics, explain them quite differently. To Democratic Socialists, socialism is the strongest and most consistent alternative to Communist repression, and yet in the United States, "socialism" is generally considered a bad word, while "capitalism" a good one. Conversely, in most of the rest of the world, "socialism" tends to be a good word and "capitalism" a bad one.[2]

In this book, Thomas again took on Marxism directly. Although he recognized that Marx stood above all others as the philosopher and apostle of socialism, he held that Marxist theory and philosophy were not synonymous with socialism. There were Socialists long before Marx, and many Socialists, active during and after his life, were not Marxists. Even professed Marxists differed sharply in their interpretation of Marxist theory and dogma. Thus, he concluded that there could have been a Socialist movement without Marx,[3] and in the end he reaffirmed his rejection of Marxist teachings:

> My appraisal of Marxism shows why I am not a Marxist. It leaves room for great appreciation for what Marx's teaching has meant for men. I have had enough training in theological casuistry, Christian and Socialist, to find my way under the general umbrella of Marxism, but not by that process do I think I can best state what the highest meaning of socialism is to me, and, I hope to others. The answer to the special problems of our times for socialism does not lie in a more extensive Marxist exegesis. This is especially true in the U.S.A.[4]

In reaffirming his belief in democratic socialism, Thomas frankly admitted that if he were asked whether it had all the answers for all of America's problems, he would have to respond negatively. American socialism had provided many valuable answers and pointed the way to others, yet it clearly was incapable of providing automatic answers to all problems. "I shall not stir multitudes, but may persuade my readers, when I say that democratic

---

1 Norman Thomas, *Socialism Re-examined* (W.W. Norton, New York, 1963; reissued Greenwood Press, Westport, Conn., 1984).
2 Ibid., 25.
3 Ibid., 35.
4 Ibid., 112.

socialism, not sure of all the answers, not promising sudden utopias, is the world's best hope."[1]

Basic to Thomas' philosophy was the belief that democracy stood on an equal footing with socialism. The pragmatic case for democracy holds that "it is better to determine issues by counting noses than breaking heads, "[2] but Thomas relied on more positive justification. Democracy "is the way of life that best conforms to what men ought to be and do; what at their best they want to be and do." In practice, democracy, even with all its imperfections, has provided better government than any other political form, and by its very nature, it permits its own improvement. Thomas firmly believed that if man cannot maintain a tolerable social order under democracy, it cannot be done at all. Under no other system can governmental power be kept from corruption or subordinated to the service of the common good.[3] It was because of his fervent belief in democracy that Thomas early in his career turned to socialism. He was convinced then and remained confident throughout his life that socialism was the only political system that could save democracy from fascism and communism.[4]

Thomas had expressed his devotion to the democratic state in a book written in 1931 — *America's Way Out: A Program for Democracy*,[5] — and he held to the positions set forth in its text for the rest of his life. He firmly held to the democratic theory that equality of opportunity must exist for all men and women and that the world we live in must be managed as a fellowship in which they have the voice of citizens rather than as subjects. Thomas observed, however, that in our democratic and economic order any citizen may vote for President of the United States, but no worker, unless he happens to own a few shares of stock, may vote for the president of the corporation in which he invests his life. "He is an insincere and shallow critic of democracy who fails to see that many of the grossest faults of our system arise not from true democracy but from the lack of it."[6]

A second essential for effective democracy is the growth of civil liberty and the conscious encouragement of the discussion of public questions based on reliable information. A third element acknowledges the need for inquiry into the efficiency of democratic machinery by social and political institutions that are current with the times. "While democracy is no mystic savior of a fallible race of men, it does express . . . the noblest political ideal

---

1 Ibid., 211.
2 Norman Thomas, *A Socialist's Faith*, 146.
3 Ibid., 146-147.
4 S. J. Woolf, "Thomas: If I were Elected President," *The New York Times*, 6/7/36, 107.
5 Norman Thomas, *America's Way Out: A Program for Democracy* (Macmillan, New York, 1931).
6 Ibid., 125.

men have yet formed. Practically in its imperfect form there is no substitute for it which offers surer hope for men."[1]

Some years later Thomas wrote:

> For the believer in the dignity of the individual, there is only one standard by which to judge a given society and that is the degree to which it approaches the ideal of a fellowship of free men. Unless one can . . . find evidence that there exists a superior . . . governing caste to which men should by nature cheerfully submit, there is no approach to a good society save by democracy. The alternative is tyranny.[2]

Murray B. Seidler, one of Thomas' biographers, stated that Thomas' advocacy of the democratic ideal was so totally unequivocal that if at any time in his life he had concluded that socialism and democracy were incompatible, he would have abandoned socialism.[3] Thomas' writings confirm Seidler's evaluation. For Thomas, the true goal of socialism was democracy.

---

1 Ibid., 129.

2 Norman Thomas, *A Socialist's Faith*, 146.

3 Murray B. Seidler, *Norman Thomas: Respectable Rebel* (Syracuse University Press, Syracuse, 1967), 292.

CHAPTER 21. CONFRONTING RACISM, THE VIETNAM WAR, AND INJUSTICE

During the final two decades of Thomas' life, disarmament and nuclear testing were issues of overriding importance for him. Still, he felt deeply about racism, the Vietnam War, and continuing acts of injustice. It is his involvement with these issues that we now turn.

Thomas' passion for justice compelled him to oppose racism and support the appeals uttered by those subjected to acts of racism. At a time when parts of the South were violently resisting the integration of the public schools following the Supreme Court's decision in *Brown v. Board of Education*[1] he wrote an open letter to President Eisenhower, beseeching him to employ the full powers of the presidency in support of the African-American struggle for civil rights. He viewed the crisis over school integration as a national moral issue requiring strong presidential leadership.

His concern for equality for African-Americans dated from his youth when his mother related to him how her childhood friends had ostracized her because her father taught African-Americans at Biddle College in Charlotte, North Carolina. Throughout his life, whenever Thomas witnessed racial discrimination, he was quick to oppose it. In 1921, as editor of *The World Tomorrow*, he ordered his staff to move to new quarters when the owners of the Manhattan building in which their offices were located demanded a lease forbidding the employment of African-Americans. He wrote at the time that the magazine's staff would have refused such a demand on principle alone,

---

1 347 U.S. 483 (1954) and 349 U.S. 294 (1955).

but in addition, one of their most faithful staff members was a black woman whom they never would have abandoned under any circumstances.[1]

Thomas was long involved in fighting for equality for African-Americans. In 1934 he had written *Human Exploitation in the United States*,[2] in which he assailed the denigration of Blacks in the South:

> By various devices, legal or illegal, the Negro is disenfranchised in many states or at least it is made peculiarly hard for him to vote. The Anglo-Saxon principle of the right of a man to a trial before a jury of his peers does not apply to him. By written or unwritten law, juries which hold issues of life and death for a Negro defendant in their hands have no member of his own race upon them. He is literally in constant danger from the mob against which he finds safety not so much by uprightness of life as by docility even when that means acquiescence to injustice. . . . Until this day, there are regions in the United States . . . where no Negro woman dare refuse a white man although it is death for a black man even to be accused of an attack upon a white woman.[3]

Thomas assisted A. Philip Randolph in organizing the Brotherhood of Sleeping Car Porters, a labor union that in subsequent years fought to advance the rights of African-American railroad workers, and he also worked with Randolph in supporting efforts to enact Federal fair employment practices laws. He joined ranks with Bayard Rustin, a chief strategist of the civil rights movement of the 1960s, and with James Farmer, one of the founders of the Congress of Racial Equality (CORE), in civil rights demonstrations and protests of segregationist policies.

Thomas participated in the "March on Washington" in 1963 and was present when Martin Luther King, Jr. give his "I Have a Dream" speech. "That was one of the happiest days of my political life," he later related. "It looked as if we were inaugurating a unique event in history — a nonviolent, revolutionary effort toward integration and brotherhood."[4]

Thomas also spoke to the vast crowd that day. King later wrote that a young black boy listening to Thomas asked of his father, "Who Is that man?" His father responded, "That's Norman Thomas. He was for us before any other white folks were."[5] For King, the story aptly illustrated Thomas' total commitment to attaining civil rights for African-Americans. Biographer and essayist Harvey Swados placed in perspective Thomas' commitment to the civil rights movement:

> No historian will be able to interpret the civil rights battle without assessing the significance of the inspiration Norman Thomas has given to such

---

1 Norman Thomas, *The Choices* (Ives Washburn, New York, 1969), 13. The story also is related by Martin Luther King, Jr. in "The Bravest Man I Ever Met," *Pageant*, 6/65, 23, 24-25.
2 Norman Thomas, *Human Exploitation in the United States* (Frederick A. Stokes, New York, 1934).
3 Ibid., 276.
4 Norman Thomas, *The Choices*, 14-15.
5 Martin Luther King, Jr., "The Bravest Man I Ever Met," 24.

striking figures as the organizers of the March on Washington, many of whom not only belong to his party but continue to look to him for intel-lectual, moral, and practical aid, both in public sessions and in behind-the-scenes activities.[1]

Although he was growing increasingly frail, Thomas continued to partic-ipate in marches, sit-ins, and other civil rights demonstrations. Two months after the March on Washington, he traveled to Mississippi to speak in sup-port of Aaron Henry, the president of the Mississippi branch of the NAACP. Henry, an African-American write-in candidate for governor, opposed the white candidates of the Republican and Democratic parties. The campaign was so absorbed by race that the candidates barely mentioned other issues, and violence was always close to the surface. When a Yale student who was assisting in the Henry campaign was arrested, Thomas noted that, "You al-most need a passport to get into Mississippi."[2] Thomas himself, while on his way to a Henry campaign event, was chased by local nightriders, and one of his close associates, Allard Lowenstein, a North Carolina State College professor, was arrested and detained in a local jail.

Early the following year, Thomas appeared before a congressional com-mittee then considering proposed legislation that would bar discrimination in employment and in the use of public facilities. He testified in favor of the legislation:

> The Socialist Party has long regarded civil rights as the nation's leading domestic problem. We have seen it as the area of American life most des-perately in need of a great act of national conscience.... We believe that the need for strong civil rights legislation is recognized by the vast majority of Americans. If such legislation is not forthcoming, if Congress permits itself to be stymied by politicians, then surely the Negro people are justified in continuing direct extra-legal action to win their rights. They are justified in taking to the streets.[3]

Happily there was no need for African-Americans to take to the streets as Congress then enacted the Civil Rights Act of 1964 and, a year later, the Voting Rights Act.

By this time in his life, Thomas had grown accustomed to meeting and conferring with US presidents and to cajoling and pressuring them to see matters as he saw them. He was sympathetic to Adlai Stevenson in the 1952 and 1956 elections but felt he could not strongly support him since the So-cialist Party was still fielding presidential candidates. In 1960, he supported neither Kennedy nor Nixon, but voted for Kennedy. Subsequently, he de-nounced the Kennedy administration for its role in the Bay of Pigs fiasco in Cuba and, long before it attracted public attention, for its Vietnam policy.

---

1 Harvey Swados, "New Reasons for an Old Cause," *Saturday Review*, 1/64, 35,36.
2 *The New York Times*, 11/1/63, 22.
3 Congressional Digest, XLIII., 3/64, 92 and 94.

In 1964, at the age of 80, he actively campaigned for Lyndon Johnson, who was opposed that year by Senator Barry Goldwater. He said all Americans had reason to be grateful to Johnson for his efforts in advancing civil rights and for his forceful fight against poverty. Thomas was even more disposed to favor Johnson since his vice-presidential running mate was Hubert Humphrey, his long-time friend. Moreover, he was frightened of Goldwater. "I am scared of his stand on foreign affairs. He shoots from the hip. He would blunder us into another war."[1]

His children and other family members tried to persuade the eighty-year-old to slow the hectic flow of his campaign activities, but he would not hear of it. Later in discussing his role in the campaign he noted that Johnson's campaign slogan had been, "All the way with L.B.J." He reminisced that "I wasn't all the way with L.B.J. — only most of the way — but I was all the way against Barry Goldwater, a dangerous man, the prophet of war. So I made speeches from Massachusetts to Hawaii."[2]

He later applauded the advances that Johnson continued to achieve in obtaining comprehensive civil rights legislation. He declared that, "No president ever spoke so forthrightly and effectively as did this Texan Democrat — a convert over whom there must have been joy in heaven."[3] However, in matters of war and peace, Thomas parted company with the president. He charged Johnson with failing to deal with the Vietnam War with the understanding and good sense he had shown in dealing with civil rights.

Thomas was among the first Americans to criticize US policy in Vietnam. From the war's outset, he condemned it. He traveled around the country, living out of an old and battered duffel bag, lecturing to campus groups and speaking at sit-ins, expressing disdain for the nation's involvement in the war. In November 1965, he helped organize a march on Washington to press the Johnson administration to halt the bombing of North Vietnam and to enter negotiations for a settlement of the conflict. Speaking to the marchers assembled around the Washington Monument, he drew a roaring ovation when he declared that the war was "cruelly immoral and politically stupid," that the United States was fighting in support of a South Vietnam government that was both corrupt and grossly inefficient.[4]

In speaking to college students about America's involvement in Vietnam, he respected their sincerity in opposing the war but was saddened by some of their tactics, such as the burning of draft cards. On those occasions he attempted to redirect their youthful energy to a more useful course. Abhorring all forms of violence, he called upon them to refrain from violent forms of

---

1 *The New York Times*, 5/30/64, 14.
2 Ibid., 12/20/68, 1.
3 Norman Thomas, "President Johnson's Great Society," *The Christian Century*, 3/9/66, 300.
4 *The Washington Post*, 11/28/65, A-1.

protest: "Just because you know what you hate . . . doesn't mean you auto-matically love the opposite. Because I oppose what America is doing to the Vietcong doesn't mean that I love the Vietcong or that I think terrorism is a virtue when used by them. I am no friend of violence on any side."[1]

Although he disliked appearing in public in a weakened and tottering condition, he refused to stop speaking against the war. Despite rapidly fail-ing eyesight, worsening hearing loss, advancing arthritis, and ever increasing other physical ailments, he persisted in following a schedule younger men in good health would find difficult to follow. As long as he had an audience, he would speak. Young college students, who rarely listened to anyone over the age of thirty, flocked to his speaking events. He directed his energy and time to ending the war, even at times making world disarmament a second-ary issue.

In the summer of 1966, it was widely rumored that the North Vietnam government would charge US pilots who had been shot down and captured during bombing runs over Hanoi as war criminals. At the time, it was feared that the North Vietnam government would order their execution as well. United States governmental officials, however, were unable to determine whether the North Vietnamese intended to go that far. Since the Johnson administrative officials had failed to determine whether the captured pilots confronted death, Thomas decided to find out for himself. He wrote directly to Ho Chi Minh, the North Vietnam leader:

> As a worker for peace and strong critic of American bombings I respect-fully report that the execution of captured American pilots would have a disastrous effect upon the American public in our efforts to win it for peace and justice in Vietnam. It would make almost certain great intensification and prolongation of war.[2]

A week later, the North Vietnam leader wired his response: "Thank you for your message. No doubt you know that the policy of the Government of the Democratic Republic of Vietnam with regard to enemies captured in war is a humanitarian policy."[3] This was the first indication that the captured pilots would not face execution. Where US government officials had failed, Thomas had succeeded.

Late in 1966, Harrison Salisbury of *The New York Times* reported from Hanoi that US bombings of military targets in North Vietnam were killing countless numbers of civilians. Salisbury's reports revealed that the Johnson administration had been engaged in a campaign of massive deception to con-ceal from the public that these killings were occurring. Incensed, Thomas

---

1 Sylvia Wright, "The Dean of Protest," *Life*, 1/14/66, 57, 60.
2 *The New York Times*, 7/20/66, 1.
3 Ibid.

immediately wrote to Johnson, and the intensity of his feelings leaps from the page:

> My eyesight is such that I now must depend on . . . friends for the news.... Harrison Salisbury's dispatches . . . have just been read to me. I have heard all this with an emotion which I devoutly hope you may come to share. Can you not see how it discredits America? Is your own heart not touched by the suffering of civilians in a war which we have not even declared? . . . Did you think of how you would regard Russian statements about bombing in situations parallel to our bombing in the Hanoi area? The Pentagon even dares to complain in an injured tone because the North Vietnamese have the effrontery to try to deal with our bombers by placing "their air defense sites , . . . radar and other military facilities in populated areas. . . ." How unsportsmanlike. I want . . . to be proud of my country. This sort of thing makes it tragically impossible. . . .[1]

To Thomas, the Vietnam War was an unmitigated evil. He spent the greater part of the final years of his life engaged in a personal campaign to pull the country out of the war. He argued repeatedly that, "The effect of the war has been totally bad — spiritually, morally, and economically."[2] He had no patience with leaders in the Johnson administration who maintained that Americans had to confront communism in Vietnam or it would spread elsewhere. "To sacrifice progress in disarmament in which our hope of peace depends in the name of checking communist interpenetration in a foreign land is sheer madness."[3] Yet he also rejected the flag burners and other extremists of the far left. "I don't like the symbolism of burning the flag of the country I love. It would be better for demonstrators to wash the flag, rather than burn it."[4]

He pressed Johnson to call for an immediate cease-fire and to agree to unconditional negotiations, aimed at attaining peace through the eventual withdrawal of American forces from Vietnam. He urged the president to apprise the Vietnamese people that Americans would then help them rebuild the devastated areas of their country.[5] In the end, he argued, the excesses of communism would be contained, not by force of arms, but by an acceptance of the ideals of democracy. Nevertheless, he agreed with Johnson on one issue. It would be contrary to America's best interests to simply order an immediate withdrawal of all of its armed forces. Withdrawal had to be achieved in stages as Americans could not abandon those Vietnamese who had joined the United States in opposing the communist forces.

---

1 Thomas letter, dated 12/27/66, to President Johnson.

2 *The New York Times,* 12/22/68, E-2.

3 Charles DeBenedetti, *An American Ordeal: The Antiwar Movement of the Vietnam Era* (Syracuse University Press, Syracuse, 1990), 90, quoting the Post War World Council Newsletter, 5/61, 3.

4 *The Washington Post,* 10/30/ 67, A-9.

5 One of Thomas' earliest pleas for withdrawal of U.S. forces from Vietnam appeared in his letter to The New York Times, 1/3/65, E-2.

For all his effort, Thomas achieved little success in altering the administration's Vietnam policies. He met with and exchanged views on the war with Secretary of State Dean Rusk, but he left that meeting discouraged. "I went. We talked, and perhaps we understand each other better now. But we made no converts."[1] Undeterred, he fought on. In a television debate with Conservative Party leader William F. Buckley, Jr., Thomas vigorously opposed Buckley's view that the United States must escalate the war to win, for to fail to win would be to lose all of Southeast Asia to communism. Thomas rejected such views as wholly unrealistic.[2]

Thomas, oppressed by the continuing Vietnam war and the arms race with the Soviet Union, feared that the United States was becoming a garrison state. An American garrison state, as he perceived it, was one whose leaders were preoccupied with a military approach to foreign policy issues. Such an approach leads to enormous military expenditures, thus diverting the nation from dealing with pressing internal problems, such as the conditions of poverty still endured by significant portions of the population. In addition, military expenditures nearly always culminate in enormous corporate profits, and thus citizens of the garrison state grow accustomed to a prosperity that is dependent upon a continuation of the arms race.

At a commencement address at Haverford College in Pennsylvania, he told the graduates that many colleges and universities, because of governmental financial support, were "profoundly, if subtly affected by the mentality of this garrison state.... Government contract becomes virtually a substitute for intellectual curiosity."[3] In his book, *Socialism Re-examined*, published in 1963, he noted that Democratic Socialists had not been sufficiently alert in making their fellow citizens aware that while the US manufactured arms in the name of national freedom, "we have been steadily and inevitably reducing the land of the Pilgrims' Pride to the status of a great garrison state."[4]

With the intensity of his involvement in national and world affairs, one would not expect Thomas either to have the time or possess the energy to devote himself to matters of individual interest. But that was not the case. Because people knew him as an easy mark, friends and strangers constantly approached him, requesting assistance in gaining relief from acts of injustice or unfairness. Unjust treatment of anyone distressed him greatly, especially in those instances where a governmental agency had mistreated the very people it was supposed to protect. He customarily rushed into action whenever the target of mistreatment was an activist seeking to improve some segment

---

1 Ibid., 11/30/65, 5.

2 Ibid., 4/10/66, 4.

3 Ibid., 6/8/63, 52.

4 Norman Thomas, *Socialism Re-examined* (Greenwood, Westport, Conn., 1963), 191-192.

of society. Even Communists did not hesitate to ask Thomas to intercede on their behalf. Junius Scales was one of them.

Scales had become entangled with the Smith Act.[1] Enacted in 1940, this piece of legislation made it a criminal offense to advocate, or to be a member of a group that advocated, the violent overthrow of the US government. Scales, a grandnephew of a former governor of North Carolina, was charged in 1954 under the Smith Act with intending, as a Communist, to overthrow the government. He was never actually charged with personally calling for violent action or with any other conduct other than that he had joined and had become an active member of the Communist Party. During the seven years that the case worked its way through the Federal court system, the Soviets suppressed the Hungarian revolt and Khrushchev disclosed Stalin's atrocities and infamies. Outraged by these revelations, Scales quit the Communist Party. The Supreme Court was not moved. It affirmed Scales' six-year sentence on the ground that he had been an active and knowing member of the Communist party. No other Communist had ever been convicted on such a charge. As voiced by one commentator, "there is something wrong with a system of justice which has an ex-Communist in jail for the crime of active and knowing membership in the [Communist Party] while 10,000 actual members, many of whom are undoubtedly as active and as knowing Communists as Scales ever was, remain free."[2]

Thomas initiated a petition to commute Scales' sentence. Signed by five hundred and fifty prominent Americans, including nine of the twelve jurors who had found him guilty, the petition was then submitted to President Kennedy. Not long afterward, Kennedy agreed to commute Scales' sentence thus releasing him from prison. Subsequently, A. H. Raskin of *The New York Times* editorial board wrote to Thomas:

> I do not delude myself that [Scales] would ever have had a commutation [of sentence] if you and the committee that took its inspiration from you had not worked so devotedly on Scales' behalf. The whole episode was a fresh indication of what your entire life has demonstrated: America will live up to its traditions of freedom if each one of us cares enough.[3]

Thomas' capacity for indignation in the presence of injustice was nearly without limit. He was always ready to leap into action to help its victims. He believed in acting immediately to gain public attention of the injustice at hand, never shunning any legitimate method available to him, however dramatic. His friend Roger Baldwin once asked him why he had written a letter to the president asking him to act concerning a matter with which he

1 The Smith Act — the Alien Registration Act of 1940.

2 *The Washington Post*, 2/15/62, A-22.

3 A.H. Raskin letter, dated 1/20/63, to Norman Thomas, quoted by Murray B. Seidler, *Norman Thomas: Respectable Rebel* (Syracuse university Press, Syracuse, 1967), 328.

was then involved. "It won't do any good, " he told Thomas. "No," Thomas responded, "I know that, but I have a duty to people who expect me to speak up."[1]

Thomas' passion for justice, fairness, and equality for those living on the lowest levels of society led him to support labor union efforts to raise the quality of life of these people. He worked on behalf of organized labor long before the public thought it respectable. In the course of years, he marched in picket lines and addressed workers' rallies throughout the United States and in the process was tear-gassed, arrested, and jailed. His efforts to attain justice, fairness and equity were prodigious. It almost appeared as if he needed to fight for a worthy cause if only to sustain himself. His life was in tune with the words of a hymn he had sung in church as a boy: "Work, for the night is coming."[2]

1 Roger Baldwin, "Norman Thomas: A Combative Life," *The New Republic*, 1/13/68, 11.
2 Murray B. Seidler, *Norman Thomas: Respectable Rebel* , 81.

Chapter 22. The Great Dissenter

In the spring of 1953, Thomas sent to each of his five children a copy of *O Rugged Land of Gold*,[1] the story of Helen Bolyan's survival of a bitterly cold winter while living alone, injured, and pregnant on a remote island off the southwestern coast of Alaska. She and her husband, the only inhabitants of the island, lived in a cabin they had constructed themselves. As winter approached, her husband left in their small boat to procure supplies for the coming months, but during the trip a sudden storm wrecked his boat and he found himself marooned on another island. No telephone communication existed between the islands. When her husband failed to return, Bolyan did not know whether he was dead or alive. She had no way of leaving the island herself and was unable to summon help. Forced to confront the Alaskan winter alone in her cabin home, Bolyan lived through serious injury and illness and gave birth to her child before she was rescued and reunited with her husband the following spring. Bolyan's courage, self-confidence, and her extraordinary achievement greatly impressed Thomas, and he wanted all his family to read her story.

What he admired in Bolyan reflected the principles that guided his own life — the refusal to surrender or capitulate to overwhelmingly difficult circumstances, to live life for the sake of others — in Bolyan's case, her unborn child — and never to abandon hope for a better future. His courage was beyond question, as proved a number of times when, while helping others, he placed his own life in jeopardy. His entire life signaled courage, self-confidence, unselfishness, and hope for a better future.

---

1 Martha Martin, *O Rugged Land of Gold* (Macmillan, New York, 1952; reissued by Vanessapress, Fairbanks, 1989).

Thomas acted on the truth as he perceived it, always according to conscience. "All my life I have craved freedom 'to know, to utter, and to argue freely, according to conscience.'"[1] But what guided his conscience? He wanted to believe in a God as Christ did, but he could not. Still, at times he felt compelled to affirm some form of belief in God. As earlier noted, he once wrote in the margin of a page in his autobiography that, "There is undoubtedly a Power . . . behind the universe whom . . . we may call God....Questions abound even if one admits — as I do — that there is a goodness in the universe not easily explained without some ultimate."[2]

Early in his life, he had rejected organized religion as a source of an ethical or moral code, and throughout his life he was greatly concerned that believers appeared constrained to force their religion on nonbelievers and those holding other faiths. Their religious creeds were rarely free of coercive intolerance. Still, his repudiation of organized religion did not lead to a rejection of Christ's teachings, at least to the extent that they inspired an ethical code — a code he described as "the highest achievement in human fellowship."[3] Yet he also placed great faith in man, who is most himself when he acts in fellowship:

> Not the fellowship of the ant hill but of individuals to whom conscious love of others is life which need not be eternal . . . to be most real in experience. Whatever we achieve in dignity and beauty of living to pass down to our children and through them to countless generations mocks frustration as the total verdict on our striving. If conscious life on this little planet is a strange interlude between two eternities of silence, it is long enough, and to spare, to give meaning to love.[4]

Ultimately, he held that if religion were defined as "a deep sense of values transcending quantitative measurement," he could accept it as necessary for human life and society.[5]

He did not deny that organized religion had greatly blessed humanity and that belief in a creed could form the basis of a personal faith, but he rejected the proposition that a moral code could not exist apart from organized religion. "What a strange Supreme Being it would be who would create men and put them on earth with no possible standard of decent conduct except as might be imparted by the conflicting revelations of rival creeds and churches!"[6] He concluded that man was far more likely to serve humanity unselfishly, while accepting the concept of universal fellowship, if his service were based on life's experience rather than on conflicting doctrines con-

1 Thomas autobiography, 248.
2 Ibid., 265.
3 Ibid., 278.
4 Ibid.
5 Norman Thomas, *A Socialist's Faith* (W.W. Norton, New York, 1951), 122.
6 Ibid.

cerning God, creation, sin and redemption.[1] This became a guiding principle of his own life.

If following his graduation from Princeton he had not been exposed to wretched urban poverty and the teachings of the Social Gospel, he might have pursued the life of a left-leaning, liberal politician. In choosing another path, he devoted more than a half century of his life to his fellow man. He felt compelled to advance his strongly held humanistic beliefs, as his father and grandfathers before him had been moved to preach the Christian Gospel to their parishioners.[2]

His perception of man was wholly realistic. "I like human beings. I'm very glad I'm one of them. But I think we're crazy. We're irrational; look at our inability to get out of war, look at the crazy things we do in our personal lives. If only we used our brains some more we might just come out very well."[3] Thomas often commented that the devil must suffer moments of profound despair whenever he observed that virtue and kindness prevailed in humankind, even in the presence of weakness and cruelty.[4]

He was the opponent of any society marked by the oppression of the human spirit, by injustice, or by the denial of equality. Frequently discouraged by the desperate state of the human race, he nevertheless persisted throughout his life to testify to his faith in humanity.

Although he had earlier abandoned faith in an absolute form of pacifism — recognizing that a stand of that nature would have been ineffective against a Hitler or a Stalin — he still accepted as a guiding principle the tenet that war was an inappropriate and an immoral means of resolving conflict. Thus he remained unable to reconcile Christianity — in the form it was preached, taught and lived — and war, either on philosophic or ethical grounds, and he persistently reminded Christians that they must never forget that humans do not build better worlds by waging war.

A passion for justice and equality also guided his life work. He noted that social justice demands that we act to enlarge the range of our freedoms. We must live and work together as a fellowship in which free men and women may assert the voices of citizens rather than as subjects. "The ideal of government of the people, by the people, and for the people, . . . rightly interpreted is our best hope of liberty and peace."[5]

It would be a mistake to add socialism to a list of Thomas' fundamental, guiding principles. Socialism was a tool, not an ultimate goal, a method, not

---

1 Ibid., 123.

2 Murray B. Seidler, *Norman Thomas: Respectable Rebel* (Syracuse University Press, Syracuse, 1967), 102-103.

3 *The New York Times*, 11/21/65, 60.

4 Thomas autobiography, 265.

5 Norman Thomas, *America's Way Out: A Program for Democracy* (Macmillan, New York, 1931), 122.

a basic life-giving principle. As a tool, he felt free to change it, to let it evolve. The good life is for all men; life should afford each individual equality of opportunity, and socialism is the means of attaining that equality of opportunity. Thomas was a humanist to whom nothing mattered more than the search for the right road to abolish war and poverty, while creating freedom and equality. "His socialism was his search for that elusive road."[1]

His written work reflected the principles that guided him throughout his life. He wrote twenty-one books and scores of pamphlets and hundreds of newspaper and magazine articles. For nearly all of his public life he wrote a column for weekly publications of the Socialist Party, first the "New Leader," then the "Socialist Call," and finally the "New America." His books, pamphlets, and articles reflect a concern for his fellow man that characterized his early career as a Social Gospel minister, and although he had abandoned his religious orthodoxy, the evangelical style of his ministry provided the basic form of his writings in later life.[2] "He never lost his passion for saving souls; only the purposes for which he saved them changed."[3]

Three major themes appear throughout his writings — attaining peace, preserving and expanding civil liberties, and eliminating poverty through democratic socialism. A world without war was the most important of his goals, and he centered his writings on the need to eliminate war as a means of resolving human conflict. His writings on civil liberties began in 1917 with his examination of the issues confronting conscientious objectors in World War I, and extended through the African-American civil rights movement of the 1960s. He never wavered from his advocacy of democratic socialism as the most effective means of creating a better society, but his books and other writings reflect the evolution of his thought concerning the particulars of the form of socialism that would achieve such a society.

His personal experiences were often an integral part of his writings, but he was unable to present them in the written word with the enthusiasm and charisma he offered as a speaker. Something was lost in the writing, and he was aware of it. He always thought of himself as a far more effective speaker than a writer, but obviously, he never allowed that to deter him from producing an enormous body of written work.

He adamantly opposed the practice of distorting the facts to support a position. Sincerity permeated his writings; his own experiences made them real. In 1919 he wrote an article for the *Nation* magazine about the silk workers' strike in New Jersey. Its opening paragraph sets a scene made vivid by Thomas' presence:

---

1 Roger Baldwin, "Norman Thomas: A Memoir," *Saturday Review* 4/12/69, 41.
2 James C. Duram, *Norman Thomas* (Twayne, New York, 1974), 48.
3 Ibid.

> "Hey You! Get a move on! You can't stand here, and you can't walk down this side of the street either. I seen you with the pickets." The speaker was a Paterson policeman, one of the small army guarding the dye works in the morning which marked the beginning of the sixth week of the strike of the dye workers in that city.
>
> "Yes," I replied, "you saw me with the pickets, but I came from New York not to picket but to find out what was happening and to write it up."
>
> "Well," said a second policeman, "You know what happens. It's always the bystander who gets it in the neck."
>
> Such was the inauspicious beginning of an illuminating conversation in which an increasing number of policemen shared.... I heard extraordinary distinctions between picketing and unlawful assemblage. One of my informants had a vague idea that a recent law forbade all picketing in New Jersey, or at least in Paterson. The striking dyers came in for little sympathy, but on the whole they and their cause were damned because the strike was foolish and they, as "any educated man" — like myself or the police — could easily tell "by looking at them," they were "ignorant foreigners."[1]

Experiences of this sort enlivened his writing on any number of occasions.

He possessed the ability to write well, and he could have written with greater stylistic merit had he made a more concerted effort at editing his work, but he rarely appeared to have sufficient time for the editing process. The typewritten copy of his dictated autobiography is particularly revealing in that regard. His handwritten comments in the margins are mostly corrections of typographical errors and, in a few instances, recordings of additional fact. But he made little effort at editing any of what he had dictated to his secretary. The rewriting and editing that one expects of any writer are wholly absent. If he had taken the time to edit his works they might have gained a wider audience — most of his books sold less than 10,000 copies — and earned him a reputation as a greater writer. But he never sought such a reputation. He wrote solely to advance his beliefs and causes. The literary merit — or lack of it — in his writings appeared to be of little interest to him.

In his writings and in his speeches, Thomas often dissented from the popular or generally accepted view. He opposed entry of the United States into World War I and supported the conscientious objectors when they refused to engage in combat. He was critical of President Roosevelt and the New Deal at a time when they were immensely popular. He denounced Soviet Union totalitarianism at a time when the United States looked upon the Russians as great allies. He condemned the dropping of the atomic bombs, though it was claimed that they shortened the war against Japan and saved American lives. He persistently attacked those who were set on denying American Communists their civil rights. Because of these non-conforming

---

1 Norman Thomas, "Organization or Violence?" *The Nation* 10/4/19, 461.

points of view, his fellow Americans thought of him as a radical and as a dissenter.

Thomas viewed himself as a dissenter. He dissented from a world that denied equality, freedom, and justice, that turned its attention away from conditions of poverty, and settled its conflicts with the use of arms. While admitting that conformity to custom was essential for the security of the human community, he argued that progress depended on those who would reach beyond conformity in search of truth. The state of the community is advanced through heresy. "Heresy has been the growing point of society. Every great religion and the whole body of science began with a challenge to accepted traditions."[1] A society that uses force to check dissent runs the risk of stagnation.

History is full of occasions where dissenters have rebelled against the established order of the church or the state and thus changed the world. But, as Thomas freely admitted, rebellion *per se* is not a virtue. The proper role of the dissenter, as he perceived it, is that of a Socratic gadfly. "Our body politic always needs its Socratic gadflies, and it forgets, disregards or suppresses its dissenters, past or present, at its peril. Of that fact . . . I am fully persuaded."[2] We live and participate in society as members of various groups — social, religious, political — to which we pledge our loyalty. The secret of a good life, Thomas wrote, is to adopt the right loyalties and then hold them in the right scale of values. The role of the dissenter is to compel us to reappraise those loyalties and values, while exercising the highest concern for the truth.[3]

Thomas first wrote about dissent, and identified himself as a dissenter, in a 1949 *New York Times* article entitled "The Dissenter's Role in a Totalitarian Age."[4] Although dissenters have often acted in grave error and have been rightly rejected, a virile society has always followed its true prophets, and obviously Thomas viewed himself as a true prophet. The prophet worth his salt never dissents for the sake of dissent. "He dissents from the established rule, custom, or theory, because, clearly or vaguely, he envisages something better which he positively desires for himself and his fellows."[5] Thomas unquestionably enjoyed his role as a dissenter: "To believe in something enough to stand on your own two feet in its behalf, to feel that you are something more than a member of the herd, is a satisfaction transcending inescapable duty. You can find in it a real joy of life. . . ."[6]

---

1 Norman Thomas, *The Test of Freedom* (W.W. Norton, New York, 1954), 42-43.
2 Norman Thomas, *Great Dissenters* (W.W. Norton, New York, 1961), 11.
3 Ibid., 13.
4 Norman Thomas, "The Dissenter's Role in a Totalitarian Age," *The New York Times*, 11/20/49, SM-13.
5 Ibid.
6 Ibid.

To be a rebel on this or that issue was never an end in itself for Thomas. He wanted to gain acceptance of a new set of ideas that he fervently believed would make democracy work as it should.[1] As he often said when people referred to him as the "defender of lost causes," "Not lost causes — causes not yet won."[2]

The pervasive conformity that infected the American public in the 1950s induced Thomas to again reexamine the role of the dissenter in society. The result was another book, *Great Dissenters*, a study of the lives of five men — Socrates, Galileo, Tom Paine, Gandhi, and Wendell Phillips — whose lives of dissent helped shaped the western world.[3]

Socrates, Galileo, Paine, and Gandhi were logical choices for Thomas' review of the world of dissent, but it appears likely that he selected Wendell Phillips, not because his views were famously known, but because he clearly identified with Phillips. His life in many respect paralleled Phillips' life. Like Thomas, Phillips devotedly loved one woman, his wife, and she, like Violet, suffered serious health problems. As in the case of Thomas' early career, Phillips sacrificed his social status and a prospective political career to support and foster an unpopular cause. As an abolitionist during the years leading to the Civil War, Phillips never altered or subordinated his outspoken positions on slavery in the name of political compromise. He was a radical pioneer, not only in advocating the abolition of slavery, but for every good cause. Like Thomas, he was a great orator. Ralph Waldo Emerson said of him that when he spoke "the whole air was full of splendors."[4] The similarity of their life experiences led Thomas to write that he could think of no dissenter with whom it would have been a greater joy to work with in close relations.[5]

Born in 1811, Phillips was the son of Boston's first mayor elected under its city charter. He attended Boston Latin School, Harvard College and Law School, and began his life as an attorney seemingly satisfied in the role of a proud leader of Boston's aristocracy. No one would have then predicted that he would become the defender of the poor and helpless, or that he would convert to an idealistic political movement advocating the abolishment of slavery in this country. But then he married Ann Green, a convinced abolitionist, and not long after he launched his career as an agitator for freedom. As an eloquent speaker, he was much in demand, speaking not only on behalf

---

1 Bettina Peterson and Anastasia Toufexis, Editors, *What are the Answers: Norman Thomas Speaks to Youth* (Ives Washburn, New York, 1970), 83.

2 W. A. Swanberg, *Norman Thomas: The Last Idealist* (Charles Scribner's Sons, New York, 1976), 279.

3 Norman Thomas, *Great Dissenters* (W.W. Norton, New York, 1961).

4 Ibid., 134.

5 Ibid., 130.

of abolition, but in support of other causes he held dear — the advancement of women's rights and the end of capital punishment.[1]

Strangely, Phillips' celebrated role in history is in part dependent upon the contrast drawn by historians between his position on the abolition of slavery and that advanced by Abraham Lincoln. Lincoln held that his paramount object was to save the Union. "If I could save the Union without freeing any slaves, I would do it; if I could save it by freeing all the slaves, I would do it; and if I could save it by freeing some and leaving the others alone, I would also do that."[2] Phillips answered: "My paramount object has always been to free the slaves and is not either to destroy or save the Union except as that may minister to my great objective."[3]

In Thomas' view, if Lincoln's greatness consisted in accepting compromise in order to accomplish what was politically possible, Phillips' greatness lay in refusing to compromise under any circumstances. The uncompromising mode that Phillips and others adopted tended to move Lincoln beyond easy compromise, beyond the politically possible, and Thomas suggested that if Lincoln had not been thus prodded, he might have been more greatly influenced by men incapable of moral indignation — by those whose primary interests and objectives were economic — and the slavery question would have been reduced to the status of one among many competing economic issues.[4]

Since Thomas evidently perceived parallels between his life and Phillips, one wonders whether he saw a parallel between Phillips' role in prodding Lincoln to emancipate the slaves and his own role in prodding Roosevelt to establish a welfare state through the adoption of Socialist principles. If he noted the parallel, that would offer another explanation why he selected Phillips as one of the world's most prominent dissenters, placing him on a pedestal equal in height to that occupied by Socrates, Galileo, Paine, and Gandhi.

Americans did not readily accept Thomas' dissenting views. On many occasions his critics labeled his positions on war and peace as "Un-American" or "traitorous." Before World War II, he was designated a "narrow isolationist" and a "friend and appeaser of Adolph Hitler." He was vilified for his radical support of the downtrodden and the oppressed. Perhaps stung by such criticism, Thomas wrote "What's Right with America," which appeared in *Harper's Magazine.*[5]

---

1 Ibid., 130-135.
2 Ibid., 148, quoting from Lincoln's letter to Horace Greeley in August 1862.
3 Ibid., 148.
4 Ibid., 155.
5 Norman Thomas, "What's Right with America," *Harper's Magazine,* 3/47, 237.

In his view what was most right about America was its reaction to the post World War II world. America emerged from the war unequaled in economic and military might, but held no desire for aggression and did not demand of its former enemies any territory or trade or special economic concessions. Even in the face of Russian aggression following the war, few Americans talked or even thought about preventive war. Nor would they tolerate it.[1]

The American experience with the preservation of civil liberties in wartime was unequaled elsewhere in the world. Except for the evacuation from the western states of people of Japanese ancestry, Americans managed to fight the war without major infringements on the rights of free speech, press, or assembly. Even in race relations, Thomas was encouraged by the progress he had witnessed over the years in the growth of plain, human decency and regard for human rights. He was also impressed with the saving quality of family life and "good-neighborly responsibility," clearly evident throughout the country:

> For all this relative freedom and fellowship in America there are various explanations in terms of the hospitality of a new, uncrowded land, its climate, its geographic position, its fertility, and its economic conditions. We are of the same blood as less fortunate Europeans. Modesty becomes us, and thankfulness for the extraordinary opportunity that has been ours. But it is not self-righteous for us to be genuinely proud of the great American tradition of liberty, which in the stormy crisis of our time, still has strength and validity.[2]

Thomas wrote that after having considered what was right about America, he would return to pointing out its failures and shortcomings, but he would do it with greater confidence, "because we have a heritage and a history which justify faith in man's capacity for freedom and fair play."[3]

---

1 Ibid.
2 Ibid., 239.
3 Ibid.

Chapter 23. Declining Health

Even as Thomas grew older, he remained receptive to new ideas and retained a willingness to scrutinize old ideas in the light of recent developments. Paradoxically, Americans appeared to consider him less radical than they had earlier in his life.

He held no government office and was wholly without political power, yet eight hundred people interrupted their daily lives to attend his 75th birthday party in 1959. Eleanor Roosevelt and Norman Cousins co-chaired a committee of sponsors that included past and present senators, governors, university presidents and scholars, journalists and editors, labor union leaders and industrialists. Murray B. Seidler, one of Thomas' biographers, was present to record Thomas' appearance as he spoke to this distinguished group:

> The guest of honor rose to address this large audience of admirers. It was hard to find a taller man in the room. His striking height; his aristocratic bearing; his long, thin, sensitive face; his lively blue eyes; his sparse, snow-white hair — every feature, every move seemed to give the correct impression that here was an elder statesman He looked the part of a leader, an overpowering personality, the center of any group. His commanding voice matched his commanding presence. Obviously, he was deeply moved, but in no sense was he flustered.... He spoke, eloquently and earnestly, indeed passionately.... He received a standing ovation.[1]

Mrs. Roosevelt commented that Thomas could always be counted on for "causes that our democracy needs,"[2] and former North Carolina senator

---

1 Murray B. Seidler, *Norman Thomas: Respectable Rebel* (Syracuse University Press, Syracuse, 1967), 1-2.

2 *The New York Times* 11/19/59, 10.

Frank P. Graham told the audience that for more than fifty years the country had been trying to "catch up" with Thomas' ideals "only to find him on some farther front wherever are the most forgotten and disinherited people."[1] Thomas took all this praise in stride, and turned to joking about his advanced age: "I'm not old, but I'm horrified at the ages of my children."[2] The next day, *The New York Times* summed it up for those who had attended the party — it was "wonderful to have Mr. Thomas around; we hope he will be here for long years to come."[3]

Though he could easily joke about his age, he greatly feared his declining health would end his ability to care for himself. Indeed, his children suspected that he was driving himself in search of death before he lapsed into invalidism. He had long suffered dreadful pain in his arthritic legs and his hearing and eyesight continued to degenerate. Each year he grew more frail. "I'm falling apart piece by piece," he grumbled.[4] His eyesight worsened to a point that at the dinner table he could barely see his food. Once he lifted a round object to his mouth and started chewing on it before his daughter could tell him it was not a cookie but a cork coaster. "My God," he said with feigned relief, "I had begun to doubt your cookery."[5] He tried to ward off further decline. He continued to abide by a rule he had observed all his life, limiting alcoholic beverages to one drink before dinner. Much to the relief of his children, he gave his car to a granddaughter and gave up driving.

Thomas never retired, remaining productive in his final years. In the first six months of 1963, at the age of 79, he spoke to audiences at thirty-one colleges. Two years later, he lectured at more than forty colleges and universities. Students at hundreds of other institutions continued to seek him out as a speaker or as a participant in debates and at teach-ins. He also found time to speak at high schools and church groups and appeared in various television discussion programs. But he did not limit his activities to speaking. Between ages 75 and 79 he wrote three books — *The Prerequisites for Peace* (1959), *Great Dissenters* (1961), and Socialism Re-examined (1963).[6]

With the passing years, his audiences appeared to look upon his physical disability more as an endearing characteristic than as a distraction. Again, biographer Seidler vividly pictures Thomas' presence at a speaking event late in his life:

1 *The Washington Post*, 11/19/59, A-2.

2 W. A. Swanberg, *Norman Thomas: The Last Idealist* (Charles Scribner's Sons, New York, 1976), 410.

3 *The New York Times*, 11/20/59, 30.

4 W. A. Swanberg, *Norman Thomas: The Last Idealist*, 460.

5 Ibid., 481.

6 Norman Thomas, *The Prerequisites for Peace* (W.W. Norton, New York, 1959); *Great Dissenters* (W.W. Norton, New York, 1961); *Socialism Re-examined* (Greenwood Westport, Conn . 1963).

> As this virtually blind, bent old man ascends the platform with great dif-
> ficulty, the audience initially wonders about the wisdom of his appearance.
> But by the time he has uttered a few sentences his listeners realize that
> they are in the presence of a mind that has triumphed over a broken body
> and a fiery eloquence that will not be extinguished. His speeches abound
> with passion, wit, and sparkling phrases. . . . He pokes fun at his physical
> maladies. "I am a tottering wreck and it's annoying," he tells his audiences.
> When asked whether he will run again [for president], he replies, "Run? I
> can hardly walk."[1]

He always tried to make light of his infirmities. He once referred to the
excellent state of health of the King of Sweden who daily played tennis at
the age of 90. "But I'm not the King of Sweden,"[2] he declared with a note of
sadness. He tried to maintain at least a modicum of his former strength by
swimming whenever he had time but was quick to admit that it was not "the
type of swimming that would help [him] rescue a drowning maiden."[3]

His 80th birthday seemed to follow too soon after his 75th. Again, friends
and associates scheduled a mammoth birthday celebration and more than
two thousand people attended the event. Martin Luther King, Jr. was among
those invited, but was scheduled to be in Oslo, Norway at the time to receive
the Nobel Peace Prize. Before departing for Oslo, King taped a message that
was read at the party:

> I can think of no man who has done more than you to inspire the vision of
> society free of injustice and exploitation. While some would adjust to the
> status quo, you urged struggle. While some would corrupt struggle with
> violence or undemocratic perversions, you have stood firmly for the integ-
> rity of ends and means. Your example has ennobled and dignified the fight
> for freedom, and all that we hear of the Great Society seems only an echo of
> your prophetic eloquence. Your pursuit of racial and economic democracy
> at home, and of sanity and peace in the world, has been awesome in scope.
> It is with deep admiration and indebtedness that I carry the inspiration of
> your life to Oslo.[4]

King's message was one among many sent to Thomas that day. Others
came from present and former supreme court justices, senators, members of
Congress, and political leaders around the country, among them Vice President Hubert H. Humphrey:

> I understand the moment of truth has arrived and you are confessing an-
> other birthday. In your instance this should be easy because you remain
> eternally young of heart and young of spirit.... Your life has been dedicated
> to the practice and ideals of democracy. It has also been a life of courage
> in the battle against all forms of totalitarianism. With equal vigor and de-
> termination you have challenged the evil forces both of fascism and com-
> munism — never flinching or retreating, always advocating the cause of

---

1 Murray B. Seidler, *Norman Thomas: Respectable Rebel*, 320.
2 *The New York Times*, 10/30/67, 1.
3 11/21/65, 60.
4 Reprinted in *Pageant*, 6/65, 23.

freedom and social justice. America is a better land because of you, your life, your works, your deeds.[1]

The nation's newspapers joined in his praise. *The Washington Post* reminded its readers that there was "hardly a cause involving compassion for the luckless or a decent respect for minority rights in which this great nonconformist has not played a part."[2] *The New York Times* described him as "this country's most valued dissenter," and that he has been called "with much justice 'the conscience of America.'"[3]

Those present at the event paid $250 to attend, and many of them endured standing in a long line to shake his hand and reminisce with him for a moment or two. He accepted a check for $17,500, commenting that it would not last long as every organization he was associated with was close to bankruptcy.[4] Thomas responded to the best wishes of his many friends with his usual low key commentary. "My future is mostly in the past."[5] "You've got to grow old. I take it as it comes. I try to get in more naps."[6]

After returning from the Nobel ceremonies in Norway, King wrote an article about Thomas for a *Pageant* magazine series entitled "The Beautiful Americans" — a series about people "who make us proud of our heritage." King entitled his article, "The Bravest Man I Ever Met."[7] He wrote that the life of Norman Thomas had been a life of "deep commitment to the betterment of humanity," and that he had "raised aloft the banner of civil liberties, civil rights, and labor's right to organize, and . . . played a significant role in so many diverse areas of activity that newspapers all over the land have termed him 'America's conscience'."[8] In referring to Thomas as the bravest man he had ever met, King cited Thomas' support for the conscientious objectors in World War I, for the sharecroppers during the Depression years, for the persecuted Japanese-Americans in World War II, and for African-Americans seeking equality and the right to vote:

> His lifelong campaign for economic and social democracy, and his unceasing drive for the maximum international cooperation for peace with justice have endeared him to millions around the globe. He has proved that there is something truly glorious in being forever engaged in the pursuit of justice and equality. He is one of the bravest men I ever met.[9]

Thomas protested to King that the mantle of the bravest man rightly belonged to King, not himself. Nonetheless, he was very pleased with King's

---

1 Ibid., 29.
2 *The Washington Post*, 12/6/64, E-6.
3 *The New York Times*, 11/21/64, 28.
4 Ibid., 12/7/64, 42.
5 Ibid., 11/21/64, 26.
6 Ibid.
7 Martin Luther King, Jr., "The Bravest Man I Ever Met," *Pageant*, 6/65, 23.
8 Ibid., 24.
9 Ibid., 25.

article, as well he should have been. In March 1966, New York's PBS Channel 13 produced a ninety-minute program entitled "Norman Thomas: Years of Protest." Hosted by a Princeton history professor, the program portrayed Thomas' life as inseparable from a chapter in the history of America's social development. A *New York Times* television critic observed that Thomas' career, beginning with his early opposition to World War I and extending to his opposition to the Vietnam War, "by way of early social work in East Harlem and being spattered with eggs in New Jersey while speaking for civil rights, makes a tremendous story."[1]

A month later, Thomas appeared as William F. Buckley's first guest in his "Firing Line" television series. Buckley welcomed Thomas as "a grand old man" while Thomas protested that Buckley was "killing him with kindness. It's an old trick to kill an opponent by kindness. After all, he's a poor old man . . . but he still has some charm, don't you know," Thomas said tapping his forehead, "but wrong up here." The show carried the title, "Vietnam, Escalate or Get Out."[2] Buckley clearly had his hands full in dealing with the "grand old man" and probably hoped that future guests would cause him less anguish.

His eyesight continued to worsen, and ultimately he depended upon others to read to him. Even at age 81 he continued to travel the country fulfilling speaking commitments, but an accident that occurred outside his Manhattan office nearly brought his speaking career to an end. As he stepped out of a taxicab, his coat caught in the door when he closed it. The cab driver pulled away from the curb. Thomas was thrown to the pavement and dragged along the street. A passerby quickly alerted the driver, and he stopped the car. He was badly bruised and remained hospitalized for several days. He told a *New York Times* reporter that he had been forced to cancel the following week's speaking engagements, but if people did not mind listening to him while peering at a badly bruised face, he hoped to meet all other scheduled commitments.[3] His children insisted after the incident that he no longer travel alone. Facing the reality that he needed someone to guide and support him, he hired a young man to accompany him on his speaking tours.

He continued speaking, but traveling from city to city became increasingly difficult. As he was approaching 83, his doctors ordered severe restrictions on his activities. In October 1967, he announced that he would retire at the end of the year. But he had another speech to deliver, and although he claimed this would be his last public appearance, no one believed him and he was not convinced of it himself.

He delivered the speech to a group of students from thirty countries. Supported by two assistants, he made his way slowly along the stage to the

---

1 *The New York Times,* 3/2/66, 83.
2 *The Washington Post,* 4/11/66, A-11.
3 *The New York Times,* 5/5/66, 27.

podium, but once he had a firm grip on it his face brightened and he went on to deliver his speech at a breathtaking pace. With his accustomed clarity, he expounded on several subjects — dissent, loyalty, transcendent human values, and the search for truth. He dissented fiercely from United States' Vietnam policy, but also condemned those who would burn the American flag in protest. He repeated his past advice. If they needed a symbol of protest, "let them wash the flag, not burn it." Setting forth guidelines for rational, humane, constructive dissent, he stated: "Loyalties are necessary; most of us live by group loyalties, but we must rise above them to the transcendent values of humanity so that we can cooperate and coexist — lest we don't exist at all."

The speech over, he waited for his two assistants to help him down from the stage. With their support he made it down, but slowly and painfully. Turning to the students, he said with a grin: "You see. That's why I say *you've* got to carry on." [1]

As nearly everyone anticipated, it was not his last speech. He said the announcement of his retirement was premature, that it had been made in error. He did not wish to cancel other speeches already scheduled. A few weeks later he was present at the University of Chicago, where he joined Senator Eugene McCarthy, Rev. Martin Luther King, Jr., and Harvard Professor John Kenneth Galbraith in addressing the National Labor Leadership for Peace. By the end of his speech he was wholly exhausted, and during his return flight to New York he felt ill. Once on the ground, he telephoned his daughter Frances, who arranged for him to be admitted to a hospital in Huntington, Long Island. He had suffered a stroke.

Up to the day of his hospitalization he was planning more speeches. When his friend Roger Baldwin chided him for such exertions at his age, Thomas responded that he had to do it in order to live. He needed an audience. He loved the excitement of the debate and the crowds. Moreover, many people looked to him to speak up on pressing issues, and he would not abandon them.[2] But he had delivered his last speech. Henceforth, he would be confined to a nursing home located not far distant from his daughter's home.

Blind, needing to resort to a hearing aid, partially paralyzed, and restricted to his bed and wheel chair by his advanced arthritic condition, even Thomas eventually accepted the fact that his public life was over. But he remained active. Unbelievably, he had another book to write. During the remaining year of his life he dictated "The Choices,"[3] a small volume of eighty-five pages in which he returned to four old themes: preventing war, achieving

---

1 Ibid., 10/30/67, 1; 10/31/67, 44.

2 Roger Baldwin, "Norman Thomas: A Memoir," *Saturday Review*, 4/12/69, 41.

3 Norman Thomas, *The Choices* (Ives Washburn, New York, 1969).

racial harmony, ending abject poverty, and preserving and expanding civil liberties.

In the book's first chapter, entitled "We Must Choose Peace," Thomas noted that many people ask, "Can we have a world without war?" If the answer is "No," we will have no world at all. In an age of thermonuclear weapons, we cannot waste time finding alternatives to war. Disarmament is the only answer. He predicted that if flying saucers ever came close enough to the United States or Russia to land, they would not do so because their commander would say, "Home, James! This madness may be catching." Disarmament, under the control of the United Nations, is the only answer to that madness.[1]

Turning to America's racial problems, he predicted that a solution will be found only after a successful war on poverty. Urban and rural slums must be eliminated; jobs and job training must be provided for all those who need them; and improved education must be granted to those living in ghettos and poverty-stricken areas of the countryside. These are the prerequisites for racial peace.[2]

In discussing the need to eliminate poverty, he did not significantly depart from positions previously advocated. Again some commentators and reviewers, and even one of his biographers,[3] accused him of having abandoned socialism. Anticipating criticism of this sort, Thomas, in the book itself, denied that he was abandoning socialism's basic principles. "I, emphatically, am still a Democratic Socialist, which means that I believe in a far more equitable distribution of the Gross National Product than we have, and an extension of social ownership to achieve that end."[4] He continued to press Americans to embrace the basic principles of democratic socialism, but he realized, considering the events of the last twenty years, their adoption would not automatically resolve all issues.[5] Rather than abandoning socialism, he further modified his understanding of it. Even in his last days, his form of socialism was still evolving.

In the area of civil liberties, he was most concerned with protecting the rights of persons who committed acts of civil disobedience while advancing the civil rights movement or in opposing the war in Vietnam. He reminded his readers that although we find guarantees for civil rights and civil liberties in the Constitution, the moral basis for those rights and liberties is derived, not from the Constitution, but from our great thinkers and moralists,

---

1 Ibid., 2.

2 Ibid., 9-24.

3 Bernard K. Johnpoll, *Pacifist's Progress: Norman Thomas and the Decline of American Socialism* (Greenwood, Westport, Conn., 1970) vii.

4 Norman Thomas, *The Choices*, 73.

5 Ibid., 73-74.

such as Henry David Thoreau, who had aptly expressed them in his "Essays on Civil Disobedience." "There comes a time in life when our conception of our duties may be determined by the conviction that we ought to obey God, rather than man."[1]

Nearing the end of his own life, he viewed humanity as fully capable of co-operating to preserve life rather than acceding to death. Even with all the mistakes made, humans can still resolve the problems they daily confront. "The question . . . is not *can we* save ourselves, but *will we* save ourselves?. . . I do have enough hope to want a return ticket in fifty years or so to see how well you have done."[2]

He celebrated his 84th birthday in his nursing home bed. In spite of his weakened condition, he remained ebullient. "The state of the country is not too good.... In fact it's quite capable of going to hell." Because the country lacked leadership and had failed to end the war in Vietnam, its morale was low: "The effect of the war has been totally bad, spiritually, morally, and economically. Think what we could have done to improve the quality of life at home with the money that's been spent in Vietnam."[3]

Harry Fleischman, whose biography of Thomas[4] has been referred to in previous chapters, was Thomas' long-time friend and Socialist Party colleague. During Thomas' last year of life, Fleischman customarily visited him in the nursing home at least once a week. Alone much of the time, Thomas was eager for discussion — of almost anything. Fleischman later referred to a sample listing of the topics of discussion that Thomas initiated from his nursing home bed — did Senator Eugene McCarthy have a realistic chance of winning the Democratic Party nomination for president? Would President Johnson reverse himself and halt the bombing of North Vietnam cities? Did Johnson have the backing of the labor leaders in the coming campaign? Was African-American anti-Semitism real? Could the Czechs realistically confront the Russians? How could socialism develop more effectively? Was the increasing involvement of organized religion in social action a reflection of its loss of a theology? Would the Princeton football team win on Saturday?[5] His interests were encyclopedic, and they were not diminished in scope or depth by approaching death.

But he grievously missed the public life. He had been active in dozens of organizations. For years, he had addressed huge audiences. His entire life involved communicating with large numbers of people. Now, living in a nursing home bedroom, all this was denied him. He did not approach death

---

1 Ibid., 55.
2 Ibid., 83-85.
3 *The New York Times*, 11/21/68, 51.
4 Harry Fleischman, *Norman Thomas, A Biography: 1884–1968* (W.W. Norton, New York, 1969).
5 Ibid., 333.

alone, since many of his friends and associates visited him, but far fewer people than he was accustomed to being with were at his side during the months preceding his death. But he retained his wit and good humor to the end. When Roger Baldwin telephoned him to ask him how he was faring, Thomas replied, "I could be worse." "How?" Baldwin asked. "I might lose my mind," he said.[1]

1 Roger Baldwin, "Norman Thomas: A Memoir," 42.

CHAPTER 24. SUMMING UP

Thomas' friend, William Sloane Coffin, a Protestant minister active in the opposition to the Vietnam War, visited Thomas in his final days. By that time, Thomas was blind and was rendered nearly immobile by arthritis. As Thomas lay in bed, they talked about God and the religious beliefs that Thomas accepted and those he had rejected. Coffin noted that, "Whether or not you believe in God is not important.... What's important is whether God believes in you. I want to say to you — you are God's faithful servant." Thomas wept silently, tears rolling down his face. "That makes me feel good, Bill."[1]

Thomas' writings give little evidence that he was especially introspective. Even his autobiography gives the impression that he was far more concerned with the state of the world than the state of his soul. If he had ever given thought to whether he believed he had lived the life of a faithful servant of God, he had revealed it to no one. As he lay in his nursing home bed, did he look back and review the events of an eighty-four-year long lifetime? Did he question whether he had always chosen correctly and whether, given the opportunity, would choose the same again?

If he looked back and questioned any aspect of his life, he probably would have first focused on his leadership of the Socialist Party. Under that leadership, the party had wasted away. Did he hold himself responsible for the demise of the party? Many historians, Socialists, and Thomas' own biographers have considered that question. Daniel Bell, Harvard Professor of Sociology, who has written extensively on socialism, Marxism, and capitalism, holds

---

1 Transcript of Bill Moyer's NOW program presented on PBS 3/5/04.

that Thomas' primary interests generally lay in personal acts of injustice, committed by individuals, and that he was always happiest when struggling with issues that were immediate and personal. By temperament, he was concerned with resolving issues, not with their political consequences. But the Socialist Party was a political movement; its goal was to change a political and economic system.

Thomas' general focus of attention did not coincide with that of his party. In centering on individual issues without regard to political ends, Thomas exhibited a basic flaw as a political party leader. Bell suggests, moreover, that Thomas suffered other significant flaws. He distrusted those of his own generation and surrounded himself with youth, who often supported him admiringly and uncritically. He also had a profound fear of being manipulated, and thus considered every attack upon his political positions as one directed against him personally.[1]

Harry Fleischman, National Secretary of the Socialist Party from 1942 to 1950 and Thomas' campaign manager in the 1944 and 1948 presidential elections, agreed in part with Bell's assessment. He conceded that Thomas tended to surround himself with younger party members but points out that a large portion of the older men and women in the party belonged to the Old Guard, "who elevated inactivity to the dignity of a theory." Many younger members, on the other hand, were far from being admiring and uncritical, but in fact were hypercritical and considered themselves more revolutionary than Thomas.[2] Fleischman observed, however, that Thomas made other mistakes in leading the party. Nearly always bored by organizational matters, he tended not to concern himself with details that, when ignored, pulled the party apart. Exciting his audiences with moving speeches, he would then forget to urge them to join the Socialist party. He was far too impatient with the Old Guard and too accepting of positions advanced by the Militants. He accepted the Trotskyites into the party, who then proceeded to undermine and destroy it.[3]

Fleishman and others, before and after him, have argued that the undoing of the Socialist Party was less the result of Thomas' faults and mistakes than the overpowering influence of Franklin D. Roosevelt. During Roosevelt's first term Socialists deserted the party, seeing an opportunity in the New Deal to attain "a half-a-loaf" rather than continuing to rely upon "pie-in-the-sky" future of the Socialist Party. Thomas saw this clearly. What completely

1 Daniel Bell, "The Problem of Ideological Rigidity," *Failure of a Dream? Essays in the History of American Socialism*, edited by John H. M. Laslett and Seymour Martin Lipset (University of California Press, Berkeley, 1974), 15.

2 Harry Fleischman, *Norman Thomas, A Biography: 1884–1968* (W.W. Norton, New York, 1969), 241.

3 Ibid., 245.

undermined the Socialist Party, he said, "was Roosevelt, in a word. You don't need anything more." Fleischman concluded that the Socialist Party confronted a decline that Thomas, no matter the course of action he undertook, could not have prevented.[1]

Michael Harrington, prominent Socialist and author of the widely read *The Other America*, was somewhat more critical in evaluating Thomas' party leadership. He held that the impact of Thomas' leadership was almost entirely personal and on that account he failed to build an effective and organized Socialist movement. When he failed to move the party into a viable relationship with American liberalism and the New Deal, the best and brightest of the party reluctantly departed for the New Deal. Harrington, unlike Fleischman, faulted Thomas for this defection; his policies, not the attraction of Roosevelt's New Deal, caused a mass desertion of the party faithful.[2]

Reinhold Niebuhr, Protestant theologian and Socialist Party member, criticized Thomas for his unwillingness to make the concessions necessary to practical politics, while Dwight Macdonald, writer and editor, adopted the opposite view, condemning Thomas as too ready to compromise with capitalism.[3] Biographer W.A. Swanberg sided with Niebuhr, contending that the art of political compromise eluded Thomas. "He was a moralist seeking to uphold morality in a profession dominated by the wily."[4] Another biographer, Murray B. Seidler, attributed Thomas' leadership failings to his receptivity to the influence of others, since Thomas often mistakenly assumed that the integrity and honesty of others were equal to his own. He placed an "overabundant faith in his fellowman."[5]

What were Thomas' thoughts on the matter? He did not ignore the deficiencies in his party leadership. In 1951, he blamed himself for the Socialist Party's failure to gain a major party status. In a letter to Socialist Party friends, he wrote that "few men had more conspicuously failed than I in the things I have tried to do in the last 35 years."[6] He had to have known of the criticism voiced by Fleischman and Niebuhr (the other criticisms came later) since each was a person he held in high esteem, and thus could not readily dismiss their views. In any event, his sense of integrity would not have permitted ready dismissal.

A good case can be made that the party would have failed even with an improvement in the quality of Thomas' leadership. The Socialist Party was

1 Ibid., 248.

2 Michael Harrington, "A Successful Failure," *The Reporter*, 11/9/61, 64.

3 W. A. Swanberg, *Norman Thomas: The Last Idealist* (Charles Scribner's Sons, New York, 1976), 287.

4 Ibid., 207.

5 Murray B. Seidler, *Norman Thomas: Respectable Rebel* (Syracuse University Press, Syracuse, 1967), 295.

6 Norman Thomas letter, dated 9/16/51, to Aaron Levenstein and Hy Fish.

in decline before he assumed a leadership role, its membership declining from 118,000 in 1919 to less than 13,000 in 1923, while the number of Socialist newspapers and periodicals fell from seventy in 1912 to seven in 1923.[1] Daniel Bell pointed out that socialism failed in the United States because, unlike countries in Europe, this country afforded open frontiers, thus providing opportunities for social ascent through individual effort. Moreover, the economy, over the long run, had steadily grown thus affording the populace with a rising standard of living. Couple these facts with the impact of succeeding waves of immigration, where sons of immigrants had heightened ambitions to escape inferior status, and the conditions necessary for the creation of a workers' class simply disappear.[2]

Harrington agrees with Bell's analysis and notes the presence of other factors that militated against the growth of American socialism. American workers were split along national lines, and nationalist tendencies militated against the development of a unified class consciousness. The American standard of living in the first three decades of the century, though far from grand, was high in comparison with the economic conditions prevailing in the European countries that immigrants to this country had left. Harrington believes that these were the factors that barred a great Socialist movement from springing to life in the United States.[3]

American workers of the early twentieth century were too well off to feel any great need to unite to supplant an economic system in which they were thriving. Rather than wanting to unite, they wanted to escape from the worker class, and they thus failed to realize a class status or even formulate a class consciousness. In addition, Roosevelt's New Deal, through its efforts to preserve capitalism by reforming it, undermined the formation of an effective socialist party movement. Each of these factors, over which Thomas had no control, blocked the Socialist Party from creating a worker movement opting for the replacement of capitalism with socialism. Thus, one can convincingly argue that though Thomas made mistakes as a party leader, even alternative courses of action would not have saved the Socialist Party from decline. The failure of the Socialist movement in the United States cannot be attributable to Thomas or any other individual. It was doomed to failure from its outset.

Thomas was not prepared to accept that fate for the Socialist Party. As he lay in the nursing home bed in 1968, he may have recalled an article he

---

1 Bernard K. Johnpoll, *Pacifist's Progress: Norman Thomas and the Decline of American Socialism* (Greenwood, Westport, Conn, 1970), 32.

2 Daniel Bell, "The Background and Development of Marxian Socialism in the United States," *Socialism and American Life*, vol. 1, edited by Donald Drew Egbert and Stow Persons (Princeton University Press, Princeton, 1952), 370.

3 Michael Harrington, *Socialism* (Saturday Review Press, New York, 1972), 250.

wrote for *The New York Times* thirteen years earlier. In tracing the history of the Socialist Party, Thomas then recognized that the many blessings and opportunities offered the workers by the American economy at the turn of the century had made it far easier for them to rise above a laborer status than for them to revolutionize the country's economy, and in the process they checked the growth of organized socialism. Consequently, by the 1930s, when Thomas came to leadership in the party, the strength of American socialism lay in its immediate demands for political change, rather than in the advancement of its fundamental theories calling for state ownership of basic industries. When Roosevelt's New Deal appropriated many of the party's demands, popular support for Socialist Party electoral candidates waned, and the party began its precipitous decline to oblivion.[1] Thomas was a realist, not one to try to conceal disaster, and thus was one of the earliest to analyze the weaknesses and causes of the failure of American socialism.

But the role of democratic socialism in the United States did not end with the New Deal. As Thomas perceived it, socialism would continue to insist that the good life depended upon steady and conscious progress toward a society fit to be described as "a fellowship of free men and nations employing our marvelous technology no longer for any war except war against poverty, illiteracy and preventable disease." Socialism would continue to insist that if all the people were to attain the good life, the planning to manage the economic and social relations of an increasingly interdependent world required acceptance of the principle of cooperation, accompanied by a reduction in the role of competition. Socialism would also insist that the state should continue to play a commanding role in such planning, but that it would function as the servant of man, acting democratically while fostering the advancement of civil liberties.[2] Little reason exists to believe that as Thomas lay dying he thought any differently about the ultimate goals of socialism.

In thinking about the American socialism he would leave behind, Thomas must have felt some vindication. Socialism had anticipated two of the most significant trends of the modern age. First, technology was making collectivism an essential aspect of modern economic, social, and political life; and second, Americans had come to believe that they could make the process of collectivism that existed in the welfare state an instrument of relief from poverty.[3] All Americans have not rejected socialism, even in its fundamental principles. There are those such as the philosopher Mortimer J. Adler who believed that "in the economic order, socialism parallels democracy, [that socialism] stands for the ideal of economic equality, as democracy stands

---

1 Norman Thomas, "A Socialist Reports on Socialism," *The New York Times*, 10/30/55, SM-15.
2 Ibid.
3 Michael Harrington, *Socialism*, 7.

for the ideal of political equality,"[1] a thought Thomas would have accepted enthusiastically.

Another area of his life that he might have reviewed from his nursing home bed was that of his role in elective politics. Since he never won an election, some historians have easily dismissed him simply as a loser. He ran six times for president, twice for New York City mayor, and on one occasion each for New York governor, New York State senator, a member of Congress and New York City alderman. As he was accustomed to saying, he ran for just about every office except that of dogcatcher, and that only because it was not an elective office in New York.

The certainty of defeat never deterred him from another run for office. He remained undeterred because he never entered a contest with any real expectation of winning. He was always convinced that running for elective office afforded him with a wonderful opportunity to educate the public in the principles of democratic socialism. In his campaign speeches he invariably stressed his devotion to Socialist principles, asking for votes as an exponent of socialism rather than as an individual appealing for political support.

His six presidential campaigns fell well short of building a Socialist movement, but Thomas was successful in each of those campaigns in popularizing immediate Socialist demands for political change. This was particularly true in the 1928 and 1932 campaigns when he forcefully argued for the adoption of programs providing for social security, a minimum wage, unemployment insurance, public housing, along with other measures, all of which the New Deal eventually fostered in one form or another. He grew in public esteem because so much of what he advocated became the law of the land.

His calls for justice, equality and freedom convinced many non-Socialists of the need for a more humane and just society. He was more successful in appealing to middle class audiences — college students and church groups — than he was in persuading blue collar workers, and his campaigns were more educational than political. Voting Socialist was more in accord with an act of conscience than a political act.[2] If he thought about this as he grew ever weaker, he would have admitted that as the world counts achievement, he had accomplished little. On the other hand, he would have held as an achievement his success in keeping Socialist ideals before an often indifferent and even hostile public.

He would have recognized, as an even greater achievement, the meaningful role he had played in advancing the cause for civil liberties and the elimination of racial injustice and inequality. Thomas used socialism as a vehicle to advance his commitment to justice and equality, and thus his life stood

---

1 Mortimer J. Adler, *Haves Without Have-Nots: Essays for the 21st Century on Democracy and Socialism* (Macmillan, New York, 1991), 20.

2 Murray B. Seidler, *Norman Thomas: Respectable Rebel*, 306.

as a dedication to the betterment of humanity. Because his instincts were primarily ethical, his position in society was that of a truly moral man, and therefore his entire public life displayed what a dedicated and moral person can accomplish. He played such a significant role in preserving and advancing civil liberties and civil rights that he was proclaimed across the country to be "America's conscience."[1]

If Thomas had looked back to Walter Rauschenbusch's teachings regarding the Social Gospel, he would have found great consolation, for Rauschenbusch held that the "highest type of goodness is that which puts freely at the service of the community all that a man is and can be."[2] This is precisely what Thomas did. He devoted himself to his fellow man.

Less than two years before his death, Thomas approached the issue of his failure: "Failure? Let me put it this way: I've never been alienated. True, I haven't done all I wanted to do in life, but I *have* tried, and I've had satisfaction in the trying.... I think the joy of life is the acceptance of challenge, and there I've known joy."[3] As a political leader who failed to build a strong political party and never won an election, Thomas was described, after his death, as a "successful failure."[4] Thomas would have found such characterization appropriate.

Some years before his entry into a nursing home, Thomas wrote a note to his children setting forth in broad outline the type of funeral he would prefer. He shunned "a nonreligious Socialist funeral with lots of speakers," and although he was not an orthodox Christian and did not believe in most of the Church's formal dogmas, Christ was still a commanding figure in his life. He therefore felt justified in asking his children to arrange a Christian burial service for him. "Keep the funeral small and private and if so desired have a memorial service later."[5]

On December 19, 1968, in the early hours of a cold winter morning, Norman Thomas died in his sleep. He was 84 years old and lucid to the end.

His death was mourned throughout the country. Leading the nation in tribute, President Lyndon Johnson stated: "With the passing of Norman Thomas, America loses one of its most eloquent speakers, finest writers and most creative thinkers.... He was a humane and courageous man who lived to see many of the causes he championed become the law of the land."[6] Vice President Hubert Humphrey said of Thomas that he was always ahead of his

1 Martin Luther King, Jr., "The Bravest Man I Ever Met," *Pageant*, 6/65, 24.

2 Rauschenbusch, Walter. *Christianizing the Social Order*. New York: Macmillan, 1919, 67.

3 Compiled and edited by Bettina Peterson and Anastasia Toufexis, *What Are the Answers? Norman Thomas Speaks to Youth* (Ives Washburn, New York, 1970), 63-64.

4 Murray B. Seidler, *Norman Thomas: Respectable Rebel*, 317.

5 W. A. Swanberg, *Norman Thomas: The Last Idealist*, 406-407.

6 *The New York Times*, 12/20/68, 1.

time, "His honesty and compassion and sense of justice left their mark on America.... We are a better people because this gentleman lived."[1]

Newspapers across the country noted his passing and most of them praised him highly. *The New York Times* described him as "the Isaiah of his times," serving as a "zealous and eloquent prophet" for a half-century warning his fellow citizens of the evils of capitalism while pointing out to them what he considered the pathways of social, economic and political justice.[2] The *Times* summed up his life achievements:

> For a half-century Norman Thomas was an eloquent and impassioned voice of his country's social conscience. In a hundred causes (or was it a thousand?) he articulated the cry for justice of those he saw deprived of it. Whether it was . . . the plight of the sharecroppers in the South, or work relief for the unemployed, or free speech in Mayor Hague's Jersey City, or the noxious conduct of Senator Joseph McCarthy, or the evil of the Vietnam War, Mr. Thomas spoke rousingly to America's moral sensibilities. His ardent views, often unpopular at the time, became a standard of decency in a remarkable number of instances. An undoctrinaire Socialist, who put freedom ahead of any dogma, he lived to see much of his social philosophy become part of the fabric of American life. . . . His is a legacy of substantial public achievement. As a social reformer he contributed mightily to shaping the present welfare state. As a matchless mover and shaker, his moral fervor for social justice has contributed to a more just America.[3]

The *Washington Post* observed that it was Thomas' misfortune to be a powerful spokesperson for a cause that had little following:

> Few men in America have contributed so much to its intellectual life and obtained so little in return as Norman Thomas. For more than half a century his voice was heard pleading for a great variety of reforms, many of which have since been absorbed into our social, economic and political systems. Yet he never was elected to public office.... Though he was widely recognized for his brilliant intellect and as a man of integrity, he seemed to have a genius for keeping out of the mainstream of American public life.... His socialism was of the old-fashioned variety which is based upon civil rights, social reforms, education and equality.... It is as a critic of our times that Mr. Thomas emerges as an especially striking figure. Though he was sometimes shortsighted, he never lost his dignity, his sincerity, his independence or his dedication to the ideals that guided him.... Without ever getting into the principal currents of political action and without ever winning acceptance for his basic ideas, he exerted a salutary influence on his generation that will not end with his passing.[4]

More than a thousand people attended a memorial service conducted at Manhattan's Community Church. Thomas was eulogized as a man who sought public office because of his passionate belief that he could help the poor and the oppressed. Dr. Donald S. Harrington, a senior minister of the

---

1 Ibid.
2 Ibid.
3 Ibid., 46.
4 *The Washington Post*, 12/20/68, A-22.

church, and the Rev. Sidney Lovett, Chaplin Emeritus of Yale University and Thomas' friend for nearly sixty years, conducted the service. Harrington praised Thomas as a genuinely virtuous man who lived everything he taught. "He was a kind of unofficial ombudsman for all America."[1] Lovett described Thomas as a "rare human being who held not the treasures of his mind and spirit dear unto himself; who shared them gladly with all who, like himself, sought justice justly, who spoke the truth with love, and who walked firmly but nonviolently in the ways of human brotherhood and peace."[2]

Throughout his life, Thomas' life perspective was less that of a radical social reformer than of one engaged in addressing injustice and inequality. This is the way the public primarily perceived him, and thus he gained the respect of the people. His biographers go a step further, pointing to other aspects of Thomas' life and character as the source of the people's respect and affection. Harry Fleischman observed that Thomas always treated people as individuals, recognizing that they were capable of rising above narrow self-interests. His innate dignity and fairness appealed to everyone. Fleischman recalled the deference that leaders of both the Democratic and Republican parties — presidents, senators, governors, and other political officials — accorded Thomas at the 1948 national conventions when he was present as a newspaper columnist. They knew Thomas would treat them fairly and they welcomed his views.[3]

Biographer, W. A. Swanberg, departing momentarily from his usual restraint and reserve, wrote that:

> To be sure, there was no one like [Thomas] in his care for all humanity.... Who else was there with such a capacity for caring? . . . But the true wonder of Thomas . . . was that he appealed to the good in mankind. His hearers knew he appealed to the good in them. It elevated them. The world seemed better when one's intelligence and nobler impulses were importuned. It made some even believe that a still better world was possible, if men everywhere would only banish hate and cultivate goodness.[4]

Swanberg referred to a letter written to Thomas by a Stanford University professor who had escorted him around the campus to his speaking appointments: "I write to you because you have assured me beyond all expectations that your commitment is a very beautiful and worthwhile thing."[5]

James C. Duram, another biographer, believed that much of Thomas' appeal was the product of a traditional evangelical style he employed throughout his life. Though early in his life he lost his faith in formal, dogmatic, Christian theology, he never freed himself from his evangelical Protestant

---

1 *The New York Times,* 12/24/68, 20.
2 Ibid.
3 Harry Fleischman, *Norman Thomas, A Biography: 1884–1968,* 301.
4 W.A. Swanberg, *Norman Thomas: The Last Idealist,* 453-454.
5 Ibid., 427. The writer was Sandra Levinson of Stanford's political science department.

background.[1] Michael Harrington recorded a similar observation: "[Thomas'] very bearing seems to incarnate a peculiarly American and Protestant sense of justice and personal integrity."[2] Roger Baldwin remembered that when Thomas' arthritis rendered it difficult for him to travel, Baldwin asked him why he persisted in punishing himself traveling all over the country making speeches, remarking that he would never dream of doing it. Thomas replied, "I know you wouldn't, but you aren't an evangelist."[3]

Biographer Bernard K. Johnpoll advanced another view. Unable to directly put his own programs into effect, Thomas could be, "in the way of Isaiah and Micah, a prophet among us to chide us when we do wrong." It was because his audiences shared his indignation at the injustices of the world that they respected and admired him. Johnpoll also agreed that in addressing his audiences Thomas performed in his chosen role of an evangelist, denouncing evil.[4]

Murray B. Seidler observed that Thomas emerged as one of the most unusual figures of American politics, and in some ways the most extraordinary. It is astonishing that in the United States — a bastion of capitalism — a Socialist leader should achieve such exceptional status. He commanded the respect even of those who vehemently rejected his Socialistic principles.[5]

An element of truth may be found in each of these analyses, but something is also missing in each. Thomas repeatedly placed himself in highly volatile situations — the silk workers strike, the sharecroppers revolt, the battles with the Ku Klux Klan, the disputes with Jersey City Mayor Hague, the protests condemning Roosevelt's war preparations before World War II, the opposition to the evacuation and internment of Japanese-Americans, the post-war civil rights demonstrations, and Vietnam peace marches. Each of these events placed him under intense public scrutiny, and in each instance his actions passed public muster. With each stand, he gained credibility and greater respect. Some may have disagreed with certain of his positions, but most Americans admired the unselfishness, honesty, and courage he exhibited in firmly standing against injustice and oppression.

Alden Whitman, the author of Thomas' obituary published in *The New York Times*, wrote on a later occasion that Thomas was far more than a Socialist leader:

> Indeed, for almost a half-century, he was uniquely the nation's conscience for social justice and social reform. He spoke to the feelings that most Americans have about themselves: that they are a fair people; that it is

---

1 James C. Duram, *Norman Thomas* (Twayne, New York, 1974), 141.
2 Michael Harrington, "A Successful Failure," 64.
3 Roger N. Baldwin, "Norman Thomas: A Combative Life," *New Republic*, 1/13/68, 11.
4 Bernard K. Johnpoll, *Pacifist's Progress: Norman Thomas and the Decline of American Socialism*, 287.
5 Murray B. Seidler, *Norman Thomas: Respectable Rebel*, 233-234.

somehow wrong for poverty to exist amid plenty; that it is a perversion of justice to be jailed for political reasons; that Constitutional rights should be respected regardless of race or creed.[1]

Those who measure Thomas' significance solely in terms of his Socialist Party leadership and his frequent runs for elective office measure him too narrowly. He was far more than a Socialist leader and perennial presidential candidate. He was rightly considered as America's conscience for social justice and social reform.[2]

Norman Thomas may not have had all the answers, but he nearly always asked the right questions, and over a lifetime his questions forced Americans to confront issues of injustice and inequality, of poverty and oppression. The basic premise of Rev. Lovett's memorial service eulogy bears repeating: Norman Thomas was a rare human being, one who "sought justice justly, who spoke truth with love, and who walked firmly . . . in the ways of human brotherhood and peace." The Great Dissenter would have been pleased with that assessment.

---

1 Alden Whitman, "Norman Thomas: The Great Reformer, Unsatisfied to the End," *The New York Times*, 12/22/68, E-2.

2 James C. Duram, *Norman Thomas*, 140.

Bibliography

Previous Biographies

Duram, James C. *Norman Thomas.* New York: Twayne, 1974.

Fleischman, Harry. *Norman Thomas, A Biography; 1884–1968.* New York: W.W. Norton, 1969.

Gorham, Charles. *Leader at Large: The Long and Fighting Life of Norman Thomas.* New York: Farrar, Straus & Giroux, 1970.

Johnpoll, Bernard K. *Pacifist's Progress: Norman Thomas and the Decline of American Socialism.* Westport, Conn.: Greenwood, 1970.

Seidler, Murray B. *Norman Thomas: Respectable Rebel.* Syracuse: Syracuse University Press, 1967.

Swanberg, W.A. *Norman Thomas: The Last Idealist.* New York: Charles Scribner's Sons, 1976.

Books

Adler, Mortimer J. *Haves Without Have-Nots: Essays for the 21st Century on Democracy and Socialism.* New York: Macmillan, 1991.

Baird, A. Craig. *Representative American Speeches: 1943-1944.* New York: H.W. Wilson, 1944.

Bernstein, Irving. *The Lean Years: A History of the American Worker, 1920-1933.* Boston: Houghton Mifflin, 1960.

Biddle, Francis. *In Brief Authority.* Garden City, N.Y.: Doubleday, 1962.

DeBenedetti, Charles. *An American Ordeal: The Antiwar Movement of the Vietnam Era.* Syracuse: Syracuse University Press, 1990.

Fosdick, Raymond B. *Chronicle of a Generation: An Autobiography.* New York: Harper, 1958.

291

Gitlow, Benjamin. *I Confess: The Truth About American Communism.* New York: E. P. Dutton, 1939.

Harrington, Michael. *Socialism.* New York: Saturday Review Press, 1972.

Hillquit, Morris. *Loose Leaves from a Busy Life.* New York: Macmillan, 1934.

Hofstadter, Richard. *The Age of Reform.* New York: Vintage, 1955.

Johnpoll, Bernard K. *Norman Thomas on War: An Anthology.* New York: Garland, 1974.

Kashima, Tetsuden. *Judgment Without Trial: Japanese-American Imprisonment During World War II.* Seattle: University of Washington Press, 2003.

Kempton, Murray. *Part of Our Time: Some Ruins and Monuments of the Thirties.* New York: Simon and Schuster, 1955.

Kennedy, David M. *Freedom from Fear: The American People in Depression and War, 1929-1945.* New York: Oxford University Press, 1999.

Kester, Howard. *Revolt Among the Sharecroppers.* Knoxville: University of Tennessee Press, 1997, first published by Covici-Freide, 1936.

Leonowens, Anna. *The English Governess at the Siamese Court.* Boston: James R. Osgood, 1873.

Mann, Arthur. *LaGuardia: A Fighter Against His Times, 1882-1933.* Philadelphia: J. B. Lippincott, 1959.

Martin, Martha. *O Rugged Land of Gold.* New York: Macmillan, 1952; reissued by Vanessapress, 1989.

McKean, Dayton David. *The Boss: The Hague Machine in Action.* New York: Russell & Russell, 1940.

Oneal, James and Werner, G.A. *American Communism: A Critical Analysis of its Origins, Development and Program.* Westport, Conn.: Greenwood, 1947.

Peterson, Bettina and Toufexis, Anastasia, Editors. *What Are the Answers? Norman Thomas Speaks to Youth.* New York: Ives Washburn, 1970.

Phillips, Harlan B. *Felix Frankfurter Reminisces: Recorded Talks.* New York: Regnal, 1960.

Pratt, Norma Fain. *Morris Hillquit: A Political History of an American Jewish Socialist,* Westport, Conn.: Greenwood, 1979.

Rauschenbusch, Walter. *Christianity and the Social Crisis.* New York: Harper, 1964. First published by Macmillan, New York, 1907; reissued by Westminster/ John Knox Press. Louisville, Kentucky, 1991. Republished under the title *Christianity and the Social Crisis in the 21st Century,* edited by Paul Raushenbush. New York: Harper, 2007.

Rauschenbusch, Walter. *Christianizing the Social Order.* New York: Macmillan, 1919.

Schlesinger, Arthur M., Jr. *The Coming of the New Deal: The Age of Roosevelt.* Boston: Houghton Mifflin, 1959.

Schlesinger, Arthur M., Jr. *The Politics of Upheaval: The Age of Roosevelt.* Boston: Houghton Mifflin, 1960.

Shannon, David A. *The Socialist Party of America: A History.* Chicago: Quadrangle, 1967; originally published by Macmillan, 1955.

Sharpe, Dores Robinson. *Walter Rauschenbusch.* New York: Macmillan, 1942.

Thomas, Hugh. *The Spanish Civil War.* New York: Harper, 1961.

Thomas, Norman. *After the New Deal, What?* New York: Macmillan, 1936.

Thomas, Norman. *America's Way Out: A Program for Democracy.* New York: Macmillan, 1931; also published by Rand School Press, 1931.

Thomas, Norman. *Appeal to the Nations.* New York: Henry Holt, 1947.

Thomas, Norman. *As I See It.* New York: Macmillan, 1932.

Thomas, Norman. *A Socialist's Faith.* New York: W.W. Norton, 1951.

Thomas, Norman. *Autobiography.* Unpublished. (Lodged at the New York City Public Library).

Thomas, Norman. *Great Dissenters.* New York: W.W. Norton, 1961.

Thomas, Norman. *Human Exploitation in the United States.* New York: Frederick A. Stokes, 1934.

Thomas, Norman. *Mr. Chairman, Ladies and Gentlemen: Reflections on Public Speaking.* New York: Hermitage House, 1955.

Thomas, Norman. *Socialism on the Defensive.* New York: Harper, 1938.

Thomas, Norman. *Socialism Re-examined.* New York, W.W. Norton, 1963, reissued by Greenwood Press, 1984.

Thomas, Norman. *The Choice Before Us: Mankind at the Crossroads.* New York: Macmillan, 1934.

Thomas, Norman. *The Choices.* New York: Ives Washburn, 1969.

Thomas, Norman. *The Conscientious Objector in America.* New York: B.W. Huebsch, 1923; later reissued under the title *Is Conscience a Crime?* New York, Vanguard, 1927.

Thomas, Norman. *The Prerequisites for Peace.* New York: W.W. Norton, 1959.

Thomas, Norman. *The Test of Freedom.* New York: W.W. Norton, 1954.

Thomas, Norman. *War: No Glory, No Profit, No Need.* New York: Frederick A Stokes, 1935.

Thomas, Norman. *We Have a Future.* Princeton: Princeton University Press, 1941.

Thomas, Norman. *What Is Our Destiny.* Garden City, N.Y.: Doubleday, Doran, 1944.

Thomas, Norman and Blanshard, Paul. *What's the Matter with New York; A National Problem.* New York: Macmillan, 1932.

Walker, Samuel. *In Defense of American Liberties: A History of the ACLU.* Carbondale, Ill.: Southern Illinois University Press, 1999.

Wechsler, James A. *The Age of Suspicion.* Westport, Conn.: Greenwood, 1953.

Weinstein, James. *The Decline of Socialism.* New York: Monthly Review, 1967.

Articles and Pamphlets

Allen, Devere. "Presidential Possibilities: Norman Thomas — Why Not?" *The Nation,* 3/30/32, 365.

Amberson, William R. "The New Deal for Share-Croppers," *The Nation,* 2/13/35, 185.

Balanoff, Elizabeth. "Norman Thomas: Socialism and the Social Gospel," *The Christian Century,* 1/30/85, 101-102.

Baldwin, Roger. "Norman Thomas: A Memoir," *Saturday Review,* 4/12/69, 41.

Baldwin, Roger N. "Norman Thomas: A Combative Life, "*The New Republic,* 1/13/68, 11.

Bell, Daniel. "The Background and Development of Marxian Socialism in the United States," *Socialism and American Life* , Vol. I, Edited by Donald Drew Egbert and Stow Persons, Princeton: Princeton University Press, 1952, 370.

Bell, Daniel. "The Problem of Ideological Rigidity," *Failure of a Dream? Essays in the History of American Socialism*, Edited by John H. M. Laslett and Seymour Martin Lipset. Berkeley: University of California Press, 1974, 15.

Douglas, Paul H. "An Idealist Masters Realities," *The World Tomorrow* , 5/32, 151.

Harrington, Michael. "A Successful Failure," *The Reporter*, 11/9/61, 64.

Herling, John. "Field Notes from Arkansas," *The Nation* 3/29/35, 419.

Kirchwey, Freda. "New Jersey Under 'The Terror,'" *The Nation*, 4/28/26, 470.

King, Martin Luther, Jr. "The Bravest Man I Ever Met," *Pageant*, 6/65, 23.

Mayer, Milton S. "Men Who Would Be President: Pretty Boy McNutt," *The Nation* 3/30/40, 415.

Mussey, Henry Raymond. "An Honest Socialist," *The Nation* 4/15/31, 418.

Swados, Harvey. "New Reasons for an Old Cause," *Saturday Review*, 1/64, 35.

Thomas, Norman. "Program for Unemployment," *The World Tomorrow* 5/30, 215.

Thomas, Norman. "A Socialist Reports on Socialism," *The New York Times*, 10/30/55, SM-15

Thomas, Norman. "Conscience and the Church," *The Nation* , 8/23/17, 198.

Thomas, Norman. "Dark Day for Liberty, *The Christian Century* 7/29/42, 929.

Thomas, Norman. "Democratic Socialism: A New Appraisal." *New York. Post War World Council*, 1963; originally issued by *The League for Industrial Democracy*, 1933.

Thomas, Norman. "Hoosier Hitlerism," *The Nation*, 9/18/35, 324.

Thomas, Norman. "If War Is to be Averted," *The World Tomorrow*, 10/26/33, 585.

Thomas, Norman. "Justice to War's Heretics," *The Nation*, 11/9/18, 547.

Thomas, Norman. "New Deal or New Day," *The World Tomorrow* 8/31/33, 488.

Thomas, Norman. "Organization or Violence?" *The Nation* 10/4/19, 461.

Thomas, Norman. "President Johnson's Great Society," *The Christian Century*, 3/9/66, 300.

Thomas, Norman. "The Dissenter's Role in a Totalitarian Age," *The New York Times*, 11/20/49, SM-13.

Thomas, Norman. "The Pacifist's Dilemma," *The Nation* 1/16/37, 66.

Thomas, Norman. *The Plight of the Share-Cropper*. League for Industrial Democracy, 1934.

Thomas, Norman. "Socialism Upheld," *The World Tomorrow*, 2/30, 70.

Thomas, Norman. "What Happened at Detroit," *The World Tomorrow*, 6/28/34, 320.

Thomas, Norman. "What's Right with America," *Harper's Magazine*, 3/47, 237.

Thomas, Norman. "Where the Socialists Stand," *The New York Times*, 9/29/29, XXI.

Wallace, Henry, A. "Wallace Points to Dangers of Tenancy," *The New York Times*, 3/31/35, SM-4.

Whitman, Alden. "Norman Thomas: The Great Reformer, Unsatisfied to the End," *The New York Times*, 12/22/68, E-2.

Woolf, S.J. "Thomas: If I Were Elected President," *The New York Times*, 6/7/36, 107.

Wright, Sylvia. "The Dean of Protest," *Life*, 1/14/66, 57.

NEWSPAPERS AND JOURNALS

The Call

The Christian Century

Commonweal

Memphis Press-Scimitar

The Nation

The New Republic

The New York Times

Pageant

The Reporter

Saturday Review

Socialist Call

The Washington Post

The World Tomorrow

INDEX